Ethics and Dialogue

in the Works of
Levinas, Bakhtin, Mandel'shtam, and Celan

MICHAEL ESKIN

OXFORD
UNIVERSITY PRESS

OXFORD
UNIVERSITY PRESS

Great Clarendon Street, Oxford OX2 6DP

Oxford University Press is a department of the University of Oxford.
It furthers the University's aim of excellence in research, scholarship,
and education by publishing worldwide in

Oxford New York

Athens Auckland Bangkok Bogotá Bombay Buenos Aires Calcutta
Cape Town Chennai Dar es Salaam Delhi Florence Hong Kong Istanbul
Karachi Kuala Lumpur Madrid Melbourne Mexico City Mumbai
Nairobi Paris São Paulo Shanghai Singapore Taipei Tokyo Toronto Warsaw

with associated companies in Berlin Ibadan

Oxford is a registered trade mark of Oxford University Press
in the UK and certain other countries

Published in the United States
by Oxford University Press Inc., New York

© Michael Eskin 2000

The moral rights of the author have been asserted
Database right Oxford University Press (maker)

First published 2000

British Library Cataloguing in Publication Data

Data available

Library of Congress Cataloging in Publication Data
Eskin, Michael.
Ethics and dialogue: in the works of Levinas, Bakhtin, Mandelshtam, and Celan /
Michael Eskin.
p. cm.
Includes bibliographical references and index.
1. Poetry 2. Ethics in literature. 3. Lâvinas, Emmanuel.
4. Bakhtin, M. M. (Mikhail Mikhaælovich), 1895–1975. 5. Mandel§'htam, Osip,
1891–1938—Criticism and interpretation. 6. Celan, Paul—Criticism and
interpretation. I. Title.
PN1077.E86 2000 809.1—dc21 00-044595

ISBN 0-19-815992-7

1 3 5 7 9 10 8 6 4 2

Typeset in Sabon
by Joshua Associates Ltd., Oxford
Printed in Great Britain
on acid-free paper by
Biddles Ltd., Guildford & King's Lynn

For Lisa

Acknowledgements

It is a pleasure to be able to express my gratitude to those who in one way or another participated in the writing of this book, which I began as a doctoral dissertation in comparative literature at Rutgers University: M. Josephine Diamond, for supporting me and my projects both materially and intellectually throughout the years, for being a wonderful graduate chair and friend, and for giving my wife and me the opportunity to spend most of the writing process in lower Manhattan; Gerald Pirog, for introducing me to the study of Bakhtin, for taking me on as his advisee, for his encouragement, relentless support, mentorship, and friendship, and for never failing to sustain the necessary sense of irony; Derek Attridge, for introducing me to Levinas, for generously agreeing to be my co-advisor, for being an acutely attentive and critical interlocutor, and for his continuous support far beyond the scope of doctoral study; Frederick A. Lubich, for agreeing to be one of my readers, for his critique and support, and for his good humour; Michael Holquist, for kindly agreeing to be an outside reader and for his general help and advice in connection with the publication of this book; Ed Cohen, whose generosity, guidance, advice, pedagogical skills, intellectual acuity, and sense of humour greatly contributed to making my sojourn at Rutgers one of the most rewarding periods in my life; Michael McKeon, for his advice and support; Harvey Waterman and the Graduate School-New Brunswick for their generous support; the Master, Fellows, and staff of Sidney Sussex College, Cambridge University, for sustaining me throughout the completion of this book and for providing a friendly and engaging academic environment; my students at Rutgers and Cambridge, whose diverse responses to poetry inform this book; all the poets, authors, and scholars whose engagement with questions of ethics and poetry has been the constant dialogizing background for my own attempt at tackling some of the problems involved.

I should also like to thank the following institutions and their respective staff for allowing me access to and helping me to obtain indispensable research materials: Rutgers University and its various libraries, and, in particular, the staff of Archibald Stevens Alexander Library; the Deutsches Literaturarchiv (Marbach a. N.), and, in particular, Jochen Meyer and Nicolai Riedel, for kindly granting me access to Celan's library and autographs; the various departmental libraries at the University of Munich; the New York Public Library; Firestone Library of Princeton University; Raymond Fogelman Library of the New School University; the Elmer Holmes Bobst Library of New York University; and Cambridge University Library.

In particular connection with the publication of this book, I should like to thank my editor, Sophie Goldsworthy, for her faith in this project; the various readers for Oxford University Press, whose rigorous comments and critique greatly contributed to the improvement and final shape of this book; Frances Whistler and Jeff New for seeing it through publication and for meticulous copy-editing; Oxford University Press for agreeing to publish it; Jochen Meyer, Jane Grayson, and Clarence Brown for their advice regarding copyright issues; Pavel Nerler and the Mandel'shtam Society for kindly granting permission to quote Mandel'shtam's works from the superb four-volume Mandel'shtam Society edition; Suhrkamp Verlag and S. Fischer Verlag for kindly granting permission to quote Celan's texts.

On a more personal note, I should like to thank my mother and my friends, without whose presence in my life nothing would be possible. I am grateful, in particular, to Joshua Fausty and Edvige Giunta for their friendship, advice, support, and generosity throughout the years and beyond. My dear friend and fellow phenomenologist Kathrin Stengel has, as always, provided emotional support and the necessary intellectual rigour at the right moment. Stephan Grotz, whose friendship, intelligence, and personal involvement in my projects throughout the years have been a constant source of encouragement and inspiration, has yet again critically accompanied the development and formulation of a complex argument. Finally, Gregor Elbel, who has been a reference point in my life since our high-school days in Munich, never failed to be present throughout the good and the more difficult times. Thanks to all of you.

To you, Lisa, I owe more than I can even begin to articulate here.

M. E.

Cambridge
January, 2000

Contents

PART II. POETHICS

Prefatory Note

Levinas, Bakhtin, Mandel'shtam, and Celan share a funda-
mental concern with the transcendental significance of dialogue.
Like few other authors, they call for the interpretation of their
writings in conjunction with others' writings. Since I provide a
conceptual explication for my concomitant engagement of these
four authors in the main body of my study, I restrict myself to a
few clarifying methodological, structural, and formal remarks at
this point.

Throughout this book, I adopt—following Levinas and
Bakhtin—the method of detailed phenomenological descrip-
tion. Notwithstanding the unity of my overall argument, every
chapter (with the exception of the transitional fourth chapter)
can be approached—more or less meaningfully in direct
proportion to the progression of my inquiry—as the discrete
elaboration, description, and analysis of a particular set of
problems. In other words, although an adequate assessment of
the viability of my argument presupposes a comprehensive
grasp of the book in its entirety, a productive reading of
individual chapters—depending on the reader's particular
interests—does not necessarily depend on the prior or sub-
sequent perusal of other chapters.

For the convenience of readers who do not read Russian, all
Russian texts—with the exception of Mandel'shtam's poetry
and few other instances—are transliterated. Aside from such
orthographically established proper names as 'Dostoevsky', all
transliterations from Russian (including names and titles) follow
J. T. Shaw's second system: *The Transliteration of Modern
Russian* (Madison: University of Wisconsin Press, 1967; New
York: MLA, 1979). Throughout the text I use an abbreviated
form of citation, providing—in parentheses—either the author's
name and the page number(s) of the cited work if only one work
by an author is listed in the Bibliography, or, if more than one
work by the same author appears in the Bibliography, the
author's name followed by an abbreviated version of the cited

work's title and the page number(s). Consecutive quotations from the same work by the same author are followed by page number(s) only. Unless otherwise indicated, all translations are my own.

Abbreviations

For full details of the works listed here, see the Bibliography.

AQE   Levinas, *Autrement qu'être ou au-delà de l'essence*

AST   Bakhtin, *Estetika slovesnogo tvorchestva*

AT   Levinas, *Altérité et transcendance*

AV   Levinas, *L'Au-delà du verset: Lectures et discours talmudiques*

BSS   Bakhtin, *Sobranie sochinenii*, vol. v

DD   Levinas, *De dieu qui vient à l'idée*

DEHH   Levinas, *En découvrant l'existence avec Husserl et Heidegger*

DL   Levinas, *Difficile liberté: Essais sur le judaïsme*

DLDA   Voloshinov, 'Discourse in Life and Discourse in Art'

DP   Buber, *Das dialogische Prinzip*

DwL   Levinas (and Richard Kearney), 'Dialogue with Emmanuel Levinas'

ED   Derrida, *L'Écriture et la différence*

EE   Levinas, *De l'existence à l'existant*

EI   Levinas, *Éthique et infini: Dialogues avec Philippe Nemo*

EN   Levinas, *Entre nous: Essais sur le penser-à-l'autre*

GW   Celan, *Gesammelte Werke*, vols. i–v

LKS   Bakhtin, *Literaturno-kriticheskie stat'i*

LU   Husserl, *Logische Untersuchungen*

MB   Clark and Holquist, *Mikhail Bakhtin*

MPL   Voloshinov, *Marxism and the Philosophy of Language*

MSS   Mandel'shtam, *Sobranie sochinenii*, vols. i–iv (Mandel'shtam Society edition)

NE   Aristotle, *The Nicomachean Ethics*

NP   Levinas, *Noms propres*

PPD   Bakhtin, *Problemy poetiki-tvorchestva Dostoevskogo*

R   Bakhtin, *Raboty 1920-x godov*

SuZ   Heidegger, *Sein und Zeit*

SW   Jakobson, *Selected Writings*, vol. ii

TI   Levinas, *Totalité et infini: Essai sur l'extériorité*

VLA   Bakhtin, *Voprosy literatury i estetiki: issledovaniia raznykh let*

A word, undeniable, from a language before language . . . I must reach out to you in words . . . these words that either you read *now* or else will never read. Will they reach you? Have they reached you? Two ways of asking the same question, a question to which I will never know the answer, never. To me this letter will forever be my words committed to the waves: a message in a bottle with . . . your name.

(J. M. Coetzee)

Thank you for writing to me . . . You offer me a glimpse of yourself in the only way you can. As soon as I receive a letter from you, you are with me. If the images of absent friends please us . . . how much more pleasing is a letter, which brings real traces . . . of an absent friend! For the imprint of a friend's hand on a letter provides that sense of his person which is our greatest pleasure when we meet face to face.

(Seneca)

When we . . . receive a poem, all we know about the poet is what we learn through the poem . . . the I who approaches us is the subject of this single poem. But when we read other poems by the same poet . . . their subjects combine . . . to form the unitary polyphonic existence of the person.

(Martin Buber)

Introduction:
Dialogue, Ethics, Poetry

Dialogue and Ethics—two terms rife with diverging, if not, at times, contradictory meanings; two terms capturing those aspects of human reality which have called for the depiction of human beings as political beings.[1] One need only think of the differences between Aristotle's eudaimonistic and Kant's deontological conceptions of ethics, or Herder's mentalistic and Benveniste's pragmatic approaches to dialogue.[2] Coming into consciousness in and through (speech) interaction with others and, thus, always already social, the human being may aptly be called the dialogic and, by extension, ethical being.[3] For the ethical, while subtending and pervading the social, is in turn informed by it and inextricably interwoven with its dialogic fabric: insofar as the dialogic character of the social is—as Martin Buber points out—fundamentally predicated on human beings' 'comportment toward each other', that is, on their axiological 'orientation toward each other' (DP 149), which may but need not manifest itself in and through externalized verbal communication, it is always already ethical. Given the dialogic character of the social *and* the social constitution of the ethical, the study of dialogue as a 'universal phenomenon permeating all human speech and all relations and manifestations of human [existence]' (PPD 248)[4] falls into the domain of ethics (notwithstanding its diverse conceptualizations). Among the verbal manifestations of dialogue, poetry stands out as one of its most self-reflexive modes: poems do not only emerge 'in response to other poems' (Bloom, 49), but tend—especially poems written in the twentieth century—to foreground their

---

[1] I use 'human reality' in Voloshinov's sense as referring to the realm of human activity and sociality in general (MPL 94–5).

[2] See NE 1095a; Kant, *Kritik der praktischen Vernunft*, 212; Herder, 43; Benveniste, *Problèmes*, ii. 85.

[3] I use 'other' throughout as signifying the 'other human being'.

[4] See also PPD 294; Iakubinskii, 34; Malinowski, 313–15; Gadamer, 350; MB 175; Morson and Emerson, 49; Fassbind, 15–18.

dialogic constitution both materially and thematically.[5] Poetry thus provides a particularly unobstructed view of the complex enmeshment of the dialogic and the ethical. How and in what way poetry articulates (with) the dialogic and the ethical, how and in what way the dialogic and the ethical condition and inform poetry, I explore in the following pages by examining the texts of four authors who underscore, throughout their works, the inseverability of dialogue, ethics, and poetry.

Devoted to dialogue as a fundamental, constitutive, and multi-layered moment in the make-up of human reality, and, more specifically, to its enactment in and through poetry, the present study begins from the supposition that the texts of Emmanuel Levinas, Mikhail Bakhtin, Osip Mandel'shtam, and Paul Celan depict, theorize, and enact different, yet interdependent, levels of dialogue, understood as the discursive relation(s) between human beings.[6] Dialogue is predicated on five constituents: a human being's orientation toward the other(s); the interlocutors' respective situations;[7] mediated or unmediated (in a broad sense) modes of contact; (one or more) communicative media (e.g. voice, body, paper); and the dynamics of signs.[8] Consequently, it can—like any (exchange of) utterance(s)—be investigated on various levels, which, as Bakhtin points out, exceed the purely linguistic analysis of speech: 'Dialogic relations between utterances [and, hence, speaking human beings] . . . fall into the realm of metalinguistics. They radically differ

---

[5] I henceforth use 'poetry' and its cognate forms, following Levinas ('La réalité et son ombre', 785) and Bakhtin (*VLA* 82), with reference to literature in general and to poetry in the narrow sense. Regarding the responsive character of modern poetry in particular, see Kristeva, 196.

[6] I do not deal with 'dialogue' as a literary genre in particular. Voloshinov notes two contextually pertinent senses of 'dialogue': 'Dialogue, in the narrow sense of the word, is . . . one of the forms . . . of verbal interaction. But dialogue can also be understood in a broader sense, meaning not only direct face-to-face vocalized verbal communication between persons, but also verbal communication of any type whatsoever' (*MPL* 95). For further discussions of 'dialogue' see: Fassbind, 15–18; Holquist, *Dialogism*, 57–63; *MB* 175; Stierle and Warning, 49–63, 297–334.

[7] See Austin, 115, 138–9; *BSS* 186–7, 308.

[8] The mode of signification varies depending on the interlocutors' respective situational contexts and the chosen medium of communication. Iakubinskii emphasizes the diversity of semiotic modes and media other than 'language' in the narrow sense of the word, such as visual, gesticulatory, etc. (27). I use 'sign', following Voloshinov and Umberto Eco, as opposed to 'signal'. While the functioning of a 'signal' elicits a reaction, the functioning of a 'sign' depends on semiosis as (a certain form of) interpretation or understanding (see *MPL* 68; Eco, 28–67).

from . . . linguistic relations between elements, both in the language system and in the discrete utterance' (*BSS* 321).

In contrast to influential post-structuralist conceptions of textuality, which undermine the (ontological) significance of the speaking or writing human being by valorizing the text's subject-constituting productivity,[9] the metalinguistic concept of text as utterance inevitably links each utterance to its author's active position in the 'chain of speech communication': 'The literary work, like the response in dialogue . . . is a link in the chain of speech communication . . . the literary work is, in its entirety, a real and unitary utterance having a real author and real addressees' (*BSS* 177, 204).[10] Bakhtin's emphasis on the author's (and addressee's) inseverability from his or her utterance(s) does not imply a return to Romantic notions of the author's textually deposited personality or intentions; rather, it points to a fundamental conceptual distinction, which informs his writings on literature and language as a whole, namely, the already-mentioned differentiation between the linguistic and metalinguistic perspectives on text. The sentence or text in general,[11] Bakhtin suggests, is a unit of language and is to be distinguished from the utterance as a unit of speech communication. A relatively complete thought, the sentence is directly related to a single speaker's other thoughts within the entirety of an utterance and is embedded in a single speaker's discourse. It relates to extra-verbal reality, to the given speech situation—including the utterances of others—through its entire surrounding context, through the utterance as a whole. When the sentence is not surrounded by the discursive context of a single speaker, that is, when it forms a complete utterance, a

---

[9] In line with her general replacement of intersubjectivity by intertextuality, Kristeva, for instance, emphasizes the subject's production by the geno-text, the 'generation of this "I" which assumes the position of representing its signifying activity' (219). See also Barthes, 'The Death', 168.

[10] The distinction between 'work' and 'text' is irrelevant in the present context. I use 'textuality' and 'text' in Bakhtin's 'broad sense', as signifying 'any coherent complex of signs' (*BSS* 306), 'printed, written, or oral' (*AST* 369). Since the category of 'utterance' is the pragmatic (in Morris's and Carnap's sense) equivalent to 'text' as a purely linguistic or semiotic construct or process, every utterance is necessarily textual (see below). Bakhtin undermines any essentialist attempt at distinguishing between written and oral discourse. See Emerson, 'Editor's Preface', pp. xxxiv.

[11] For my subsequent exposition of Bakhtin's discussion of the sentence/utterance dichotomy, see *BSS* 174–7.

rejoinder in dialogue, it faces the given extra-verbal speech situation and others' utterances without mediation. Incapable of determining an interlocutor's response or responsive position, the sentence acquires this capacity in and through the utterance as a whole. The sentence is not delimited on either side by a change of speakers; it is a grammatical category and acquires stylistic features when it is considered as part of a whole utterance. Bakhtin stresses that only utterances which consist of words and sentences, not sentences or words themselves, can be exchanged. While the change of speakers comes to the fore with extreme clarity in living dialogue (the basic mode of speech interaction), the character of the boundaries of utterances is the same in other domains of communication. Thus, notwithstanding their differences from rejoinders in living dialogue and notwithstanding their structural complexity, scientific and artistic works must equally be regarded as units of speech interaction—as utterances. They, too, are delimited by the alternation of speakers, whereby these dialogic boundaries acquire a specific internal character insofar as the speaker—in this case, the author of the work—evinces his or her individuality in a particular style. This individual, stylistic imprint marks the work and distinguishes it from other works. The work, Bakhtin emphasizes, like the rejoinder in living dialogue, is oriented toward the other's response.

Depending on the frame of reference, a text may be studied as a text, that is (in Bakhtin's terminology), linguistically, or as an utterance, that is, dialogically or metalinguistically.[12] Like Barthes, Bakhtin concedes—from within the linguistic attitude—the author's structural absence from his or her text; however, he refrains from universalizing the linguistic attitude as the only valid perspective on textuality.[13] Only from within the

[12] Regarding Bakhtin's distinction between sentence and utterance, the so-called 'scissors of Bakhtin' (Gogotishvily and Gourevitch, 176), see: Holquist, 'Answering', 310–12; Morson and Emerson, 125–7. This distinction parallels a similar distinction in analytical language philosophy (see e.g. Austin, 139; Strawson, 7).

[13] See Barthes, 'The Death', 169. Bakhtin writes: 'Similarly to the word, the sentence, as a unit of language, has no author . . . only by functioning as a whole utterance does it become an expression of the position of a singular speaker in a concrete situation in speech communication' (*BSS* 187). Given Bakhtin's explicit alignment with Husserlian phenomenology (*R* 14, 35, 130), his critical method can be interpreted as informed by the phenomenological notion of changing 'attitudes', which allow different views of the same object (see Averintsev's note on Husserl and

metalinguistic attitude does a text-turned-utterance point to its author (and addressee(s)) in his or her extraverbal *dialogic* situation, whereby the author's personal imprints[14] manifest themselves within the utterance as a certain style. Concomitantly, since dialogue is a 'universal phenomenon, permeating all human speech and all relations and manifestations of human life' insofar as they have 'sense and meaning' (*PPD* 248), it is only by way of its diverse manifestations (actual or recorded) that dialogue—as a *phenomenon*—can be witnessed at all.[15] Every actual or recorded dialogue, as the exchange of utterances or their objectivation, is informed and punctured by its dialogic conditions, which it in turn formally indicates.[16] Bakhtin does not posit an ideological or intentional continuity between author and text— to be subsequently uncovered by the reader—but, rather, the textual manifestation of an utterance's dialogic-existential conditions, its embeddedness in 'speech communication', which is constituted by speech acts executed from particular positions in the 'real and singular event of being' (*R* 15).[17] It is crucial not to mistake Bakhtin's textual approach for 'ideological' criticism of

Bakhtin in *R* 323). Thus, from within the linguistic attitude a text is perceived as a linguistic construct; from within the dialogic or metalinguistic attitude it is perceived as an utterance. See Husserl, *Die phänomenologische Methode*, 32–7, 131–224 (esp. 196); Todorov, *Mikhail Bakhtin*, 24.

[14] Although Bakhtin, to my knowledge, never explicitly defines his broad concept of the author, which encompasses the concrete speaker of a concrete utterance, the living (present or absent) or dead author of a materially recorded text, as well as the other as the 'author of my life' (*R* 211), it radically differs from such concepts as Wayne C. Booth's 'implied author' (Booth, 74–5) and Michel Foucault's 'author function' ('What is an Author?', 124), insofar as both are fundamentally upshots of the linguistic attitude. In contrast to Booth and Foucault, Bakhtin's 'author' signifies the 'real man' (Booth, 75) himself and not his 'ideal version' (74) or functional analogue. However, Bakhtin's author must not be reduced to a biographical or intentional entity (see below).

[15] By correlating the universality of dialogue with everything that has 'sense and meaning', Bakhtin implicitly limits the universality of dialogue to the existential realm of social interaction (see *MPL* 14–15, 26, 34, 37, 68; *BSS* 159, 189, 337).

[16] I borrow the term 'objectivation' from Dilthey, who refers to the 'objectivations of spirit' (*Die Philosophie*, 63). It must be distinguished from 'objectification' or 'objectivization'. It simply signifies the textually congealed state of an originally enacted utterance. 'Formal indication' signifies—in line with Heidegger (*SuZ* 28–9, 116)—the indicatory relation between a phenomenon and its conditions.

[17] Bakhtin emphasizes the existential roots of human activity (including utterances) and argues for its fully responsible assumption by each individual (*R* 44; see also 52). He defines Being itself as dialogue: 'To be means *to communicate*' (*PPD* 187). In this sense I refer to Bakhtin's writings as dialogic-existential (without aligning him with Heidegger or Sartre). 'Dialogic-existential' signifies Bakhtin's view

any kind; rather, it can be described as a pragmatic stylistics explicitly narrowed down to the study of the manifestations of dialogue in literary texts (as one of the numerous modes of utterance, which Bakhtin also calls 'speech genres'): 'only . . . as a principle of concrete literary construction . . . is [dialogue] essential for the literary critic' (*PPD* 213).[18]

While acknowledging any text's inevitable relation to its real author/speaker and his or her directedness toward interlocutors, Bakhtin focuses—from within the metalinguistic attitude—on the dialogic traces permeating and organizing texts/utterances internally and within the 'chain of speech communication', that is, intra- and intertextually: 'Dialogic relations [exist] among texts and within the text' (*BSS* 308). While the second feature marks the text internally—it is pervaded from within by these dialogic relations—it 'discloses itself only in a chain of texts' (312). Style, as the author's textual imprint, must consequently be understood less as a linguistic or rhetorical category than as the manifestation of the author's particular perspective on or position within the heterogeneity and multiplicity of dialogic exchanges constituting his or her particular speech or writing situation; the particular orchestration of dialogue in each text points to its author's particular point of view in a particular situation within the never-silent dialogue of social intercourse (*VLA* 113). Bakhtin's specific non-linguistic concept of style as the 'juxtaposition... of different [voices,] languages, and styles . . . within the higher unity of the work' (76)—predicated on the interplay between an author's individual grip on the surrounding dialogue and the dialogic forces permeating his or her utterances—inaugurates a form of textual criticism not based on traditional stylistics, rhetoric, or linguistics but on the study of the dialogic relations between voices and languages within a text, without reducing the

of utterances as manifestations of human existence—see also Holquist's stratifica-
tion of Bakhtin's dialogue beginning with the level of 'existence' (*Dialogism*, 2–39)
and the designation of Bakhtin's philosophy of language as '[e]xistentialist philol-
ogy' (*MB* 9). In order to indicate the significant differences between Levinas's ethics
and Bakhtin's dialogism, I use 'ethics' in reference to Levinas's writings only.

[18] While Bakhtin explicitly disavows pragmatism in the Jamesian tradition (*R* 19,
25), his overall critical stance can justly be called pragmatic in Morris's and
Carnap's sense. Morris defines 'pragmatics' as the study of 'the relation of signs
to interpreters' (Morris, 6), that is, interlocutors; Carnap, following Morris, defines
it as 'the field of all those investigations which take into consideration [the] action,
state, and environment of a man who speaks or hears' (Carnap, 4).

text either to an author's monologic expression or to a mere impersonal 'mosaic of citations' (Kristeva, 85).[19]

While Bakhtin elaborates an internal and external approach to utterances insofar as they are permeated by traces of intersubjectivity *and*, simultaneously, constitute and inform it, Levinas investigates dialogue on a pre-existential, pre-ontological level, that is, in Levinas's terms, on the ethical level: 'Ethics is before ontology' (*AT* 109).[20] According to Levinas, 'dialogue [in the ethical sense], or more precisely . . . the ethics of dialogue' (*DD* 230), precedes and conditions dialogue as an exchange of rejoinders in the chain of speech communication.[21] The distinction between the ethical and communicative levels of dialogue is central to Levinas's understanding of ethics as pre-communicative and pre-verbal discourse directed toward the other (*TI* 104; *AQE* 78), as a *'language before words, the original language'* (*TI* p. iii).[22] It is clear that both Levinas and Bakhtin endeavour to give a cogent account of the same complex, unitary phenomenon, namely, human sociality, insofar as it is fundamentally dialogic. And it is precisely because they approach this phenomenon from two distinct, yet complementary phenomenological perspectives that only a synoptic reading of their analyses yields an integral

[19] Bakhtin discusses 'style' and its correlation to 'speech genres' in *BSS* 159–206 and in *VLA* 72–88; see also *MPL* 45–63. He strictly opposes *Stilanalyse* (Vossler, Spitzer) as the investigation of the reflection of the author's 'soul' in his or her linguistic expression, that is, as the investigation of speech in light of its subservience to an autonomous speaker (see esp. Spitzer, 1–17, 498–536).

[20] This formula appears with insignificant variations throughout Levinas's oeuvre (see e.g. *EE* 12; *TI* 133; *AQE* 180). As Levinas points out, his ethics of dialogue radically 'departs from tradition, which drew the ethical . . . from knowledge and Reason as the faculty of the universal' (*DD* 228). I use 'ethics' and 'ethical' in Levinas's sense. Ponzio emphasizes that the 'problem of . . . dialogue is at the center of Bakhtin's and Levinas's thought' ('Bachtin e Lévinas', 119).

[21] See *TI* 104, 193, 228; *AQE* 176, 224, 226, 234. Although Levinas reiterates the non-linguistic, non-systematic character of what he calls ethical discourse throughout his writings, it must not be forgotten that, aside from the instances in which ethics is explicitly described as dialogue (*EE* 160–1; *TI* 313; *DD* 230; *AT* 108), it *is*, according to Levinas, a certain *Saying* and always informed by the structure of interlocution (*TI* 62–3, 70–1, 93, 97–8, 166, 198–9, 220, 242, 313; *AQE* 264).

[22] In line with his double notion of dialogue, Levinas distinguishes between two kinds of communication, one ethical—'pure communication' (*DEHH* 228)—the other based on the ethical and corresponding more or less to the common meaning of the term as through language, exchange of information, etc. (*TI* 70; *AQE* 188).

picture of that social domain which undergoes a theoretical split in their writings.

Levinas conceives ethical dialogue—in contradistinction to dialogue as reciprocal speech communication—as a non-reciprocal, asymmetrical dynamic, in which I respond to and am responsible to and for the other, in which my dialogic orientation toward the other is neither analogous to nor contemporaneous with the other's orientation toward me.[23] He specifies the pre-verbal ethical dynamic as a mode of signification which transpires in the other's 'proximity' and establishes 'contact' between interlocutors:

[T]he hypothesis that the relationship with an interlocutor would still be a knowing reduces speech to [an] exercise . . . of thought, whereas [it] is, in addition, a *proximity* between me and the interlocutor, and not our participation in a transparent universality. Whatever the message transmitted by speech, speaking is contact [parler est contact]. One must then admit that there is in speech a relationship with a singularity located outside the theme of speech, a singularity who is not thematized by speech but is approached. Speech and its logical work would then unfold not in the knowledge of the interlocutor, but in his proximity . . . Proximity is *by itself* signification . . . This is the original language, the foundation of the other one, the precise point at which this mutation of the intentional into the ethical occurs, and occurs continually, at which the approach *pierces* consciousness, is the . . . human face. Contact is responsibility . . . This relationship of proximity . . . in which every transmission of messages . . . is already established, is the original language, a language without words or propositions, pure communication. (Levinas, 'Language', 115–19)[24]

Levinas emphasizes the signifying character of ethics, in which the interlocutor becomes 'all sign, signifying himself'

[23] Levinas's insistence on the non-reciprocity of ethical dialogue (based on his concept of diachrony) separates him from other philosophers of dialogue, such as Buber (and Bakhtin). Dialogue in the formal sense is 'reversible and can be read from right to left as well as from left to right. In ethics, in which the other is both higher and poorer than I, the I is distinct from the you' (*NP* 40). Ethical non-reciprocity culminates in Levinas's concept of ethical substitution (see Ch. 1).

[24] Derrida's claim that 'in ethics, in the sense given to it by Levinas, the principal, central prohibition is that of contact' (*ED* 95) is largely based on *TI* (published 1961). 'Langage et proximité' (*DEHH* 217–36) was published in 1967 and could not have possibly been taken into account in Derrida's 1964 essay. Derrida's interpretation is certainly valid if 'contact' is understood in the restricted sense (engaged by Derrida) of 'intuitive contact'. In *AQE* (1974) Levinas reiterates that ethics transpires as contact, as 'Saying-contact' (dire-contact) (*AQE* 249).

(*AQE* 31). Ethics, the language of proximity, is also called 'Saying', as opposed to 'Said': 'Saying [Dire] thus understood, is giving a sign . . . by turning oneself into a sign', and not the 'communication of a Said [Dit] which would immediately cover up and extinguish or absorb the Saying' (223). The 'condition of all communication' (82), Saying is '[p]roximity [and] contact . . . before language, but without which language as the transmission of messages would not be possible' (32). It is, in consistency with ethical non-reciprocity, a 'response preceding all questions' (47), '*signified*—like an order—in the [other's] face' (*EN* 161). This semioticization of ethics is consistent both with its definition as language, discourse, or Saying and with Levinas's insistence that ethics can be witnessed only by way of the Said, that is, through the semiosis of actual language and its products (in the quotidian sense), that is, by way of the Said, which is coextensive with ethics: '[I]s it necessary . . . that Saying . . . manifests itself, that it enters into a proposition and into a book? It is necessary . . . [that it] . . . states itself . . . by an abuse of language, owing to which, in the indiscretion of the *Said*, everything shows itself' (*AQE* 75, 243).[25]

Levinas singles out two particular modes of speaking—the philosophical and the poetic—which, more than other modes, bring to light ethical Saying. Philosophy is 'called upon [phenomenologically] to reduce . . . the Said to Saying' (*AQE* 243, 278), insofar as Saying 'can only be attained by way of the Said, which shows itself' (76). Philosophy, being 'consigned to the *Said* . . . says that of which it is but the servant, which it, however, masters by saying it, in order to reduce, in a new *said*, its own pretensions' (200). Poetry, on the other hand, as 'the first of languages', is itself 'a modality' (*NP* 50) of ethical signification.[26] This qualification

---

[25] See also *AQE* 48, 79, 221, 237; Greisch and Rolland, 401; Ziarek, 87. Although the semioticization of ethics already informs *TI* (90–100, 198–9), it is fully elaborated, with modifications and important shifts, in *AQE* (published 1974). I use 'semiosis', 'semiotic' and further derivations in the Peircean sense, in reference to 'the action of almost any kind of sign . . .' (Peirce, *Philosophical Writings*, 282). By 'Said' Levinas means language as a system, the process of speaking (communication), and texts/works within language (*AQE* 17, 223; see also Wiemer, 401; Taylor, 196). The interdependence between Saying and Said is suggested in *TI* (97–8), insofar as the witnessability of ethics depends on verbal interaction. Levinas distinguishes between the Said in general and the 'pure Said', which explicitly signifies written discourse (*AQE* 264).

[26] Although Levinas literally says, '[d]oesn't [Paul Celan] suggest poetry itself as

of poetry corroborates Levinas's declaration that 'proximity [i.e. ethics] . . . is poetry' (*DEHH* 228).

The poem, defined as 'the fact of speaking to the other', precedes 'all thematization' (*NP* 53). In contrast to philosophical discourse, which must perpetually undo its own theme in order to bring to light that which it is 'about', Levinas suggests that (a certain kind of) poetry *is* the textual manifestation, the objectivation of ethics as a fundamentally semiotic dynamic *and*, simultaneously, this dynamic itself.[27] While 'philosophical speaking . . . betrays in its said the proximity which it translates before us' (*AQE* 261), ethics 'bares itself in the poetic *said* and the infinite interpretation it calls for' (263). Levinas implies an internal dichotomization of poetry as (a mode of) ethical, pre-linguistic semiosis *and* as a speech genre. As ethical semiosis poetry *ethically* precedes the philosopher's discourse on ethics; as a speech genre it stages ethics on all of its textual levels.[28] By short-circuiting Saying and Said as inseverably depending on each other *and* by highlighting specific modes of speaking (Said), which more favorably than others allow glimpses of Saying, Levinas moves the question of genre into the centre of ethics. Since, as Bakhtin notes, we only speak in 'definite speech genres' (*BSS* 180), that is, in 'typical form[s] of utterance' (191), Levinas's emphasis on (two specific) speech genres—poetry and philosophy—reveals itself as existentially motivated (in addition to its ethical motivation). If ethics is witnessable only by way of interpersonal discourse, speech genres are necessarily involved. Given that Levinas's rapprochement of ethics and poetry *must be*

an unheard of modality of *otherwise than being*' (*NP* 50), his overall depiction of poetry in the same terms as ethics points to his agreement with Celan's imputed suggestion (see Ch. 1).

[27] Levinas concurs with Bakhtin, who insists that any text, written or oral, *is* an utterance. Levinas's definition of poetry is highly ambiguous, since it implies its ethical status while simultaneously rephrasing Celan's dialogic conception of poetry as a mode of verbal communication (see Ch. 1). Insofar as the ethical contact with the other involves my 'turning myself into a sign' signifying the 'donation of the sign', that is, the donation of myself, Levinas implies both that I *am* a poem (in the ethical sense) and that the poem is I, when he depicts poetry in ethical terms as 'Saying without said . . . a sign of this donation of the sign' (*NP* 49).

[28] While philosophy always remains a discourse *on* a subject, poetry *does* what philosophy is 'about'. Derrida's observation that Levinas's discourse, in the final analysis, remains 'an ethics of ethics' (*ED* 164), a metadiscourse, underscores philosophy's incapacity to attain a pre-linguistic, pre-logical, ethical level of signification, which, Levinas suggests, is the prerogative of poetry (*NP* 50).

the thematic, philosophical corollary of a reading of the Said, that is, of actual poetry, the question arises: what kind of poetry does Levinas have in mind? He clearly points out that it is Paul Celan's poetry in particular which *does* what he philosophizes. The ethical significance of Celan's poetry for Levinas comes to the fore not only in his essay on Celan, 'Paul Celan: De l'être à l'autre' (*NP* 49–56), but also in the fact that Levinas selected a verse by Celan, 'I am you, when I am I', from the poem 'In Praise of Remoteness' (*GW* i. 33), as a motto to the central chapter—on substitution—of *Autrement qu'être*. Thus, Levinas's exposition of ethical substitution can effectively be read as the philosophical elaboration of Celan's poetic insight.[29]

Celan's dialogic conception and practice of poetry, I suggest, palpably address and stage Levinas's and Bakhtin's philosophical claims and, thereby, testify to their actual viability. While Celan's highly intertextual writings acquire unprecedented significance in the light of Bakhtin's metalinguistics, his poetic and poetological engagement with ethical concerns reveals its full scope in the light of Levinas's ethics. [30] Insofar as Levinas's and Bakhtin's philosophical observations imply propositional validity, they must be verifiable, as it were, in the Said, in actual speech communication, which, as Bakhtin points out, necessarily clothes itself in speech genres. Given the enmeshment of ethics, dialogue, and speech genre, the relationship I wish to establish between Levinas, Bakhtin, and Celan can be outlined as follows: whereas Levinas gropes for the underpinnings of existence and human interaction and Bakhtin studies dialogue as the supreme enactment of existence, Celan thematizes and performs a particular speech genre, poetry, in such a way that his texts can plausibly be read as poetologically complementing and poetically staging and illuminating both Levinas's correlation of

---

[29] Levinas depicts ethics as my response to the other; this response is a responsibility for the other, a responsibility which leads to the substitution of myself for the other (*AQE* 156–205).

[30] 'Polyphonic' and 'intertextual' are not synonyms. While the former, in Bakhtin's sense, implies the personal aspect of voice in a text, the latter, in Kristeva's sense, signifies the constitution of texts. For discussions of intertextuality in Celan's poetry see e.g. Lehmann, Goltschnigg, Menninghaus, and Ivanovic. Thematic affinities between Celan and Levinas have been noted by such critics as Pöggeler, Fassbind, Lesch, Wiemer, and Ziarek.

Saying and Said and Bakhtin's claim that dialogic-existential relations 'pervade utterances from within' (*BSS* 312). In analogy with Bakhtin's metalinguistics, which bridges the conceptual 'hiatus without elision' (*AQE* 113) in Levinas's correlation of Saying and Said, of the ethical and communicative realms, Celan's writings thematically complement and instantiate Levinas's ethics and Bakhtin's metalinguistics.[31] It is important to keep in mind that while ethics, according to Levinas, originarily transpires in the unmediated, pre-linguistic, yet discursive contact with the other, all other forms of written or oral discourse, which are necessarily mediated, may only point to or indicate this fundamental dynamic in various degrees—depending on the speech genre.[32] Similarly to Bakhtin's notion of the authorial dialogic imprint, Levinas conceives a person's ethical trace in his or her utterance in terms of style:

[E]very sign is [a] trace. In addition to what the sign signifies, it is the passage of the one who delivered the sign. The significance of the trace doubles the signification of the sign in communication. The sign holds itself in the trace. In the case of a letter, for example, its significance would lie in the writing and the style of the letter, in everything that brings it about that during the very emission of the message, which we capture on the basis of the letter's language . . . someone passes . . . This trace can in turn be taken as a sign. (*DEHH* 200)

I interpret Celan's texts as such mediated forms of utterance, with particular attention to traces of the dialogic-existential and ethical which can be found in them.

Celan's texts, however, cannot be studied in isolation. Given

---

[31] My thematic rapprochement between Celan, Levinas, and Bakhtin is justified precisely in the context of a synoptic reading of Levinas's and Bakhtin's works. (Dostoevsky's writings, for instance, could be adduced as much closer test-cases for Bakhtin's insights, were the latter to be discussed in isolation.) I deal with this and related issues—such as Bakhtin's attitude toward poetry—in Chs. 2 and 3.

[32] In his writings up to *TI* Levinas stresses the ethicity of direct, unmediated, discursive contact with the other, which leads him to favour oral discourse as indicative of ethics: 'oral discourse is discourse in its plenitude' (*TI* 98). With the publication in 1963 of 'La trace de l'autre' (*DEHH* 187–202), and, most conspicuously, in *AQE* (published 1974), Levinas shifts his attention from the mere (conjectured) depiction of ethical Saying to its inevitable manifestation in the Said, which is permeated by traces of its ethical condition. The semiotic universality of the Said does not allow for an essentialist distinction between oral and written discourse (*AQE* 262), which differ only with regard to their respective material carriers (phonic versus graphic). For an alternative view of this problematic, see Robbins, *Altered Reading*, 17, 61.

their avowedly dialogic constitution they must be read as part of a dialogue. Since Celan developed his poetics with explicit reference to Mandel'shtam's works, and since both Mandel'shtam's life and writings had a profound impact on Celan's poetry following the publication of *Sprachgitter* (*Speech Grille*, 1959), and, most significantly, on his poetic cycle *Die Niemandsrose* (*The No One's Rose*, 1963), which is dedicated to the 'memory of Osip Mandel'shtam' (*GW* i. 207), close attention to Mandel'shtam's writings is the necessary condition for an adequate critical engagement with Celan. Furthermore, Mandel'shtam's contention that poetry necessarily constitutes itself in and through (poetic) dialogue with a 'secret interlocutor' (*MSS* i. 275) in 'posterity' (184) implicitly calls for the consideration of his own poetry as not merely oriented toward, but, moreover, as received, understood, and retroactively constituted by (an) interlocutor(s), whose 'responsive understanding' (*BSS* 168–70, 318) may in turn manifest and objectivate itself in (equally) poetic utterances.[33]

Celan, who believed to have found Mandel'shtam's 'message in a bottle' (*GW* iii. 186),[34] is not merely one of the potentially unlimited number of the Russian poet's interlocutors. Celan's particular significance as Mandel'shtam's interlocutor is underscored by the intensity of his reception of Mandel'shtam's writings—an intensity which manifests itself poetologically, in translations and in original poetry, and which is best captured in Celan's confession: 'Mandelstamm: rarely have I had the feeling, as with his poetry, of walking . . . alongside the Irrefutable and the True, and *thanks to him*' (cited in Terras and Weimar 363). The force of these words, in which Celan voices his spellbinding impression of Mandel'shtam's writings, is poetologically consummated in his reported admission that translating Mandel'shtam's poetry into German was as important a task for him as writing his own poetry.[35]

Insofar as the meaning of a linguistic sign or complex of signs is, as Jakobson writes, 'its translation into some further, alternative sign [or complex of signs]' (*SW* 261), and insofar as translation is, as Gadamer stresses, the verbal manifestation or objectivation of

---

[33] See Attridge, 'Trusting', 66; id., 'Literary Form', 245; Gadamer, 365.
[34] Celan's translation of Mandel'shtam's famous metaphor for poetry 'letter in a bottle' (*MSS* i. 183–4) as 'Flaschenpost'.
[35] See Terras and Weimar, 365, 367; Ivanovic, 230.

a person's understanding of an utterance (Gadamer, 362–6), translation reveals itself as the necessary first step in the reception of any utterance. Consequently, Celan's translations of Mandel'shtam's poetry can be interpreted as the objectivations of a primary understanding whose full responsiveness culminates in Celan's original poetry devoted to Mandel'shtam—as the continuation and elaboration of this primary understanding. Celan's dialogue with Mandel'shtam, which we intuit on the basis of his Mandel'shtam-translations and their original counterparts in *Die Niemandsrose*, vindicates the Russian poet's insistence on the dialogic constitution of his own poetry and provides an exemplary instance for investigating the poetic enactment of ethics (Levinas) and existential dialogue (Bakhtin).

In what follows I explore the ethical and dialogic dimension of the poetic encounter between Mandel'shtam and Celan with particular attention to its manifestation in Celan's translations of Mandel'shtam's poetry and *Die Niemandsrose*, which present two aspects of a unitary poetic utterance in response to Mandel'shtam's interpellation. My inquiry thus ultimately pursues a triple objective: the investigation of Celan's and Mandel'shtam's poetry in the light of its poetological presuppositions; the interpretation of these presuppositions and their poetic enactment in the light of their ethical-dialogic conditions; and, finally, the clarification of these conditions in the light of their poetic and poetological enactment. The apparent circularity underlying the argumentative structure of my inquiry is based on its decidedly hermeneutic methodology: the anticipatory grasp of the whole necessarily precedes the interpretation of the parts, which in turn modifies the view of the whole. I propose to interpret the dialogue between Mandel'shtam and Celan as complementing and thus inter- and intratextually continuing Levinas's ethics and Bakhtin's metalinguistics of dialogue, which in turn, as I have suggested, bridges Levinas's unaccounted-for gap between the ethical (Saying) and communicative realms (Said). While Mandel'shtam's and Celan's poetics can be read as meta-discursively complementing Levinas's and Bakhtin's philosophies on a yet higher level of dialogic specificity[36]—capturing a discrete, but not

[36] I refer to the progression from ethics (Levinas) through metalinguistics (Bakhtin) to poetics (Mandel'shtam and Celan). See below.

isolated, slice of human reality, as it were—Celan's poetic response to Mandel'shtam's address can be read as exemplarily staging and indicating ethics and dialogue as they condition and trace human interaction. Celan's texts thus offer the unique opportunity of witnessing the very processes of ethical and dialogic tracing in the Said.

My critical penchant toward Celan's poetry is motivated less by structural and pragmatic limitations than by the fact that Celan's two-step response to Mandel'shtam—by way of translation *and* original poetry—conspicuously instantiates the theoretical problematic at the heart of this study. The asymmetry of Celan's dialogue with Mandel'shtam replicates Levinas's characterization of ethics as a non-reciprocal, asymmetric dynamic. In addition to the fact that it was Celan who responded to Mandel'shtam's non-specified poetic missive (and not vice versa), his response transpired by way of translation, that is, by way of (linguistic) substitution, which I read as continuous with ethical substitution. Furthermore, since, as Bakhtin emphasizes, dialogic relations pervade an utterance from within, the inter- and intratextual investigation of the dialogic constitution of one person's utterance(s) in relation to another person's utterance(s) presents itself as the (logical) first step of a metalinguistics of dialogue. Finally, because Celan's dialogue with Mandel'shtam transpires as a 'hermeneutic dialogue', it is only through Celan's texts that Mandel'shtam 'gets to speak at all'.[37]

Although Celan's writings have been and are being widely and vigorously discussed in a variety of critical contexts, their ethical and metalinguistic significance, as it emerges in the poet's dialogue with Mandel'shtam in particular, has, to the best of my knowledge, not been addressed.[38] Similarly, Mandel'shtam's

[37] It is important to keep in mind that Celan (1920–70) and Mandel'shtam (1891–1938) never met and that Mandel'shtam did not know Celan or his work. Gadamer distinguishes between 'live' or 'real dialogue' and 'hermeneutic dialogue': '[T]he hermeneutic situation when one is confronted with a text is [not] identical with the hermeneutic situation between live interlocutors. Texts are "permanently recorded expressions of life" and want to be understood; this means that only through one of the interlocutors, the interpreter, the other interlocutor in hermeneutic dialogue, the text, gets to speak at all' (Gadamer, 365).

[38] For a survey of the burgeoning critical literature on Celan, see the continuing bibliography published in the *Celan-Jahrbücher*. Critical studies on Celan's relation to Mandel'shtam can be divided into studies which deal with Mandel'shtam-oriented intertextuality in Celan's poetry based on his reception of Mandel'shtam's poetics

poetics and poetry, while increasingly gaining critical attention, have hardly been studied in the light of their reception by Celan.[39] Levinas's writings, in turn, have only marginally been discussed with specific attention to their intrinsic dependence on poetic precedents, and their concomitant potential for an ethical interpretation of poetry which would exceed (purely) thematic or ideological considerations.[40] There is no study which deals with Levinas's significance in the particular context of Celan's dialogue with Mandel′shtam. Finally, although Bakhtin's terminology has been widely used, the import of metalinguistics as productively complementing Levinas's ethics in its relation to poetry, and, particularly, to the poetic dialogue between Celan and Mandel′shtam, has yet to be elaborated. My inquiry is divided into two parts. In Part I I elaborate Levinas's ethics, Bakhtin's metalinguistics, and Mandel′shtam's and Celan's poetics of dialogue in the light of their mutual interdependence. Part II is devoted to a close examination of Celan's translations of Mandel′shtam's poetry and the poems of *Die Niemandsrose* against the backdrop of their ethical and dialogic underpinnings.

(e.g. Terras and Weimar, Parry, Broda, Böschenstein, Lehmann, and Olschner) and studies which deal with Celan's Mandel′shtam-translations as indicative of the two poets' momentous 'encounter' (e.g. Parry, Rexheuser, Olschner, and Lehmann). Some studies deal with the translations and with Celan's original poetry as informed by the translations (e.g. Parry, Olschner, Lehmann, and Lönker). More recently, Celan's poetry has been interpreted as thematically close to Levinas's ethics (e.g. by Pöggeler, Lesch, Fassbind, Wiemer, and Ziarek). However, the question of the textual manifestation of ethics as concretely organizing Celan's texts has been addressed only marginally and in fairly general terms.

[39] Critical studies of Mandel′shtam's writings evince the tendency to focus on the disclosure of subtexts, on the intratextual analysis of devices, and on historical and philological issues (e.g. Taranovsky, Broyde, Ronen, and Uspensky). The recent collection of critical essays on Mandel′shtam edited by Aizlewood and Myers, for instance, does not include anything on Mandel′shtam's reception by Celan. Critical studies which deal with both poets (e.g. Parry, Lehmann, Olschner, Böschenstein, and Felstiner) tend not to address questions of ethics.

[40] Following the Russian formalists (esp. Iakubinskii and Shklovskii), I use 'poetry' and 'poetic' as opposed to 'prosaic' or 'practical' language. Thus, 'poetry' signifies both literature in general and poetry in the narrow sense. For discussions of Levinas's writings in connection with poetry, see e.g. Eaglestone, Robbins, Ziarek, and Lesch. By 'poetic precedents' I mean specifically the writings of those authors whom Levinas mentions throughout his oeuvre (e.g. Pushkin, Dostoevsky, and Grossman).

PART I

Dialogues

While sharing in its general conception, Levinas's, Bakhtin's, Mandel'shtam's, and Celan's notions of and approaches to dialogue evince important differences, which can be roughly formulated as follows: for Levinas, dialogue is both an originary, pre-existential mode of ethical communication, which constitutes the dialogically summoned 'I' *and* the linguistic, or properly 'discursive' interaction between human beings; Bakhtin conceives dialogue as a universal phenomenon informing human existence *and* as the relation between utterances as manifestations of this existence; Mandel'shtam and Celan problematize 'dialogue' on the level of utterance, as constitutive of poetry and, by extension, of the poet as the author of his or her poetic utterances. A chiasmic relationship between these conceptions of dialogue emerges: while Levinas depicts the ethical underpinnings of dialogue, thence proceeding upward to its properly discursive enactment (from Saying to Said), and Mandel'shtam and Celan, inversely, trace dialogue from its poetic manifestations downward to its ethico-existential implications, Bakhtin's metalinguistics of dialogue provides the pivotal relay between ethics and poetics (as one among many generic metadiscourses). In other words, Bakhtin's metalinguistics of dialogue offers a viable answer to the question: how do we get from Saying, from the level of the ethical, to the level of the Said, or, to put it differently, how does the ethical connect to the diverse modes, or genres of speech?

In the three following chapters I outline Levinas's, Bakhtin's, Mandel'shtam's, and Celan's theoretical positions, with specific attention to their interdependences. Focusing on their respective approaches to and elaborations of dialogue, I delineate a viable framework for an ethical-dialogic engagement with and reading of Celan's encounter with Mandel'shtam.

CHAPTER ONE

Emmanuel Levinas:
The Ethics of Dialogue

> When I speak of a first philosophy, I refer to a philosophy
> of dialogue which cannot not be an ethics.
>
> (*AT* 109)

SITUATING LEVINAS

Before embarking upon a detailed analysis of Levinas's ethical
philosophy, I would like to situate it in the context of 'Western'
ethics, thereby setting the stage for the elucidation of its
specificities and idiosyncrasies. Insofar as ethics, according to
Levinas, is not based on 'reason as the faculty of the universal'
(*DD* 228) it is neither normative (material) nor formal.[1] In
contrast to such post-Kantian endeavours as Husserl's attempt
at a scientific foundation of a 'formal axiology as an a priori
formal discipline of values and value contents' (*Vorlesungen*, 3–
4) or Scheler's project of 'a strictly scientific and positive
foundation for philosophical ethics' (*Formalism*, p. xvii) under-
stood as a systematized, general hierarchy of values, Levinas
advances an ethics of singular responsibility, in which the
unique ethical subject—as the condition of its universal epi-
stemological correlate—is dialogically constituted: 'Ethics as . . .
responsibility toward the other . . . far from dissolving you
within generality, singularizes you, posits you as . . . a [unique]
I' (*NP* 90).[2]

Levinas's notion of ethics equally departs from eudaimonistic,
Stoic, and pragmatic conceptions of ethics, which are informed

---

[1] Regarding the distinction between formal and material ethics, see *R* 27–32;
regarding Levinas's relation to Kant, see Greisch and Rolland, 82–90.

[2] See *ED* 146; Bernasconi and Critchley, 107; Wiemer, 227. In *TI* Levinas writes:
'universal norms silence unicity . . . singularity cannot find a place in a totality' (272–
3; see also *AQE* 29, 83, 113, 188, 228).

by Aristotle's emphasis on praxis as the path to happiness.[3] However, Aristotle's insistence on the principally non-cognitive character of the ethical (*NE* 1103a14–15), which only 'occurs' between concrete human beings in concrete situations (1142a24–30, 1143a25–b6), already points to one of Levinas's central claims, namely, that ethics transpires in the 'concreteness of the encounter' (*EN* 200–2) with the uniquely other.[4] Levinas's indebtedness to Aristotle is most visible in his adoption *and* displacement of Aristotle's term for ontology, 'first philosophy':

> The intellectual, and even spiritual life, of the West . . . demonstrates its fidelity to the first philosophy of Aristotle, whether one interprets the latter according to the ontology of book G of the *Metaphysics* or according to the theology or onto-theology of book L where the ultimate explanation of intelligibility in terms of the primary causality of God is a reference to a God defined by being qua being . . . It is in the laying down [of this preoccupation with being], that we find ethics [as] first philosophy. ('Ethics', 76, 85)[5]

Levinas's insistence on the non-ontological character of ethics is directed against contemporary ontology and existential phenomenology—in particular, against Heidegger and Sartre.[6] Levinas's opposition to contemporary ontology is philosophically

---

[3] In *TI* Levinas notes that 'the traditional distinction between theory and practice will be obliterated' (15).

[4] Following Buber, Levinas characterizes his ethics as an 'ethics of encounter' (*EN* 239; *DEHH* 202; *DP* 15–16, 29, 35–7, 43, 56, 61–2, 78). Regarding Aristotle's ethical emphasis on situational singularity, see Nussbaum 27, 37–8, 54–105.

[5] See Aristotle, *Metaphysics* 982b9, 1026a16, and 1051b1–2. Ontology is, in Levinas's terms, 'theory as the cognition of beings . . . which reduces the Other to the Same' (*TI* 33). By 'West' Levinas presumably refers to the 'philosophical tradition inherited from Parmenides' (Peperzak, *To the Other*, 13) and constituted—if one is to believe Levinas's own writings—by such select authors as 'Plato, Aristotle . . . and Plotinus . . . on the one hand, and the philosophers of the last four centuries (from Hobbes and Descartes to the present) on the other hand' (ibid.). Peperzak rightfully criticizes such sweeping generalizations—characteristic of Heidegger's, Levinas's, and Derrida's writings in particular—and points to their historical and philosophical 'myopia': 'The period between Plotinus and Descartes (a period of thirteen hundred years) [is] simply ignored' (ibid.). Of course, this 'ignorance' must be understood in strategic terms.

[6] This should not gloss over the fact that in 1948 Levinas situates his own philosophy in the realm of ontology (see *Le Temps* 17). Levinas's consistent opposition to the primacy of ontology is characteristic of his writings beginning with 'L'Ontologie est-elle fondamentale?' (1951). For a discussion of Levinas's relation to Heidegger's ontology in particular, see Greisch and Rolland, 15–45.

and politically motivated: 'A philosophy of power,' Levinas notes, 'ontology, as first philosophy, which does not question the Same, is a philosophy of injustice. Heideggerian ontology, which subordinates the relation to the other human being [Autrui] to the relation to Being in general . . . persists in the obedience to the anonymous and leads, fatally, to another power, to imperialist domination, to tyranny' (*TI* 38).[7] Levinas's subversion of existential ontology is most pointedly articulated in such phrases as: 'responsibility precedes Essence' (*AQE* 180) and 'signification [i.e. ethics] precedes essence' (29).[8] These parodic reformulations of Heidegger's stipulation of the precedence of existence over essence (*SuZ* 43) and its restatement by Sartre (*L'Être*, 23, 318), culminate in the programmatic claim that 'ethics is before ontology' (*AT* 109). Aside from its overall anti-ontological purport, Levinas's critique is specifically geared toward Sartre's concept of commitment [engagement] as an originary mode of existence: 'It is in a responsibility which does not justify itself by any prior commitment [engagement], in the responsibility for the other, in an ethical situation, that the meta-ontological and meta-logical structure of [ethics] emerges . . . of a responsibility anterior to commitment [engagement]' (*AQE* 162–3).[9] It is hardly surprising that Levinas crowns his

[7] Levinas's critique aims at Heidegger's view that 'Being-in-the-world' with others (*Prolegomena*, 326–35) must be interpreted in the light of 'Dasein's Being' (*SuZ* 12, 121). In 'Liberté de parole', Levinas makes a similar comment: 'Political totalitarianism rests on ontological totalitarianism' (*DL* 289). Inveighing against Heidegger's 'Bodenständigkeit' [rootedness (in the native soil)], Levinas writes: 'It is not certain that National Socialism stems from the mechanistic reification of people rather than from the rustic rootedness and feudal adoration of people subject to their commanding superiors and masters' ('La philosophie et l'idée de l'infini', 246). However, as Derrida points out, even a presumably non-violent philosophy such as Levinas's cannot completely dispense with violence: '[A]ny philosophy of non-violence can only opt, *within history*—but could it be meaningful elsewhere?—for the lesser violence within an *economy of violence*' (*ED* 136, n. 1).

[8] 'Essence' does not mean 'substance' but, as Levinas explains, translates the German 'Sein' [Being] and, more specifically, its grammatical meaning as a gerund (*AQE* 9). 'Essence' should be understood as a nominalized present active participle. It underscores the processual character of Being.

[9] See also *AQE* 191; DwL 25. Levinas displaces Sartre's and Heidegger's concepts of the existential situation (*SuZ* 299–300; Sartre, *L'Être*, 538–615) in favour of an anterior 'ethical situation' (*EE* 171). Levinas's repudiation of 'engagement' is also a critique of his own early texts, in which he (nominally) accepts the philosopheme that human beings are engaged in existence prior to their ethical relation(s) to (the) other(s) ('De l'évasion' (1934/5) 388; *EE* 152, 157). Regarding Levinas's relation to Sartre, see: Strasser, 307; Wiemer, 52–9.

polemic against Sartre by undermining the latter's proverbial dictum that 'we are condemned to freedom' (*L'Être*, 541): 'This [ethical] mode of responding without anterior commitment [engagement] is . . . anterior to freedom' (*AQE* 184).[10] Finally, Levinas's ethics must be distinguished from Habermas's and K.-O. Apel's 'discourse ethics' as well as from Foucault's discourse analysis. Although Levinas frequently designates ethics as 'discours', the term implies neither Habermas's and Apel's formal concept of discourse as a practical, intersubjective, consensus-oriented 'procedure' based on universalizability and informed by an universal or transcendental pragmatics, nor the complex semantic cluster of Foucault's 'discours'.[11]

THE MEANINGS OF 'ETHICS' IN THE WRITINGS OF LEVINAS

What does 'ethics' mean in Levinas's writings? Any critical response to this question has to acknowledge *and* suspend Derrida's injunction that 'Levinas's writing . . . forbids this [i.e., first and foremost, Derrida's own] prosaic disincarnation into the conceptual schema, which is the first violence of all commentary' (*ED* 124 n.). After all, the bare fact of Derrida's own philosophical commentary demonstrates that the imputed interdiction is ineffective. In a later text in response to Levinas, Derrida suggests that in order to engage Levinas's text at all there 'would have to be a writing that performs . . . a performative heretofore never described' ('At This Very Moment', 34–5). While Derrida obviously attempts to enact such a performance, he can neither dispense with Levinas's conceptuality nor with his own conceptual grasp of Levinas's discourse, which underlies and conditions the performance. The commentator's de-

---

[10] Insofar as Sartre's dictum is informed by Heidegger's concepts of 'facticity' and 'thrownness' (Geworfenheit), Levinas's critique of Sartre equally applies to Heidegger. Elsewhere Levinas writes: 'Existence is not condemned to freedom but invested and judged as freedom' ('La Philosophie', 251). For further polemical, explicit and implicit, references to Sartre in Levinas's writings, see *Le Temps et l'autre*, 44, 68; *DEHH* 198; *AQE* 122, 128, 163, 184, 217; DwL 16–17. Levinas's explicit and implicit references to Heidegger are too numerous to be listed.

[11] See *TI* 29; see also 30, 38, 45–80, 222, 271; *DL* 21, 290; Habermas, 75–6, 104, 113; Apel, *Sprachpragmatik*, 8, 44. Foucault's most concise definition of 'discours' is: 'complex of utterances which depend on the same formative system' (*L'Archéologie*, 141; see also *L'Ordre*; *La Volonté*, 133).

pendence and reliance on 'the conceptual schema' is (at least partially) due to the fact that Levinas's writing is avowedly philosophical (*AQE* 262) and as such—notwithstanding its stylistic idiosyncrasies—characterized by 'specifically philosophical [modes of] problematization or thematization' (Bernasconi and Critchley, 77).[12] Levinas himself explicitly states that *Totalité et infini* '*opens a philosophical discourse*' (*TI* p. i); he characterizes his writings in such scientific-philosophical terms as '*analyses*' (p. ii, 41) and '*investigation*' (p. iii), and stresses that his philosophical writings are completely indebted to the phenomenological method (*TI* 14). Indeed, Levinas's repetitive, reiterative, and multi-perspectival approach to the ethical methodically stages Husserl's eidetic reduction as a means of grasping the essential structure of a phenomenon by intuiting its diverse appearances or aspects.[13] Furthermore, Levinas's exposition to the *universal* primacy of ethics is overtly apophantic; both of these aspects—apophansis and universality—are characteristic of scientific and philosophical speech genres.[14]

---

[12] In a famous footnote, Derrida observes that 'the thematic development of *Totality and Infinity* is neither purely descriptive nor purely deductive. It proceeds with the incessant insistence of waves pounding onto the shore: return and repetition, always the same wave against the same shore, whereby, however, each return of the wave brings about infinite renewal and enrichment' (*ED* 124 n.). This leads Derrida to the conclusion that *TI* 'is a work of art and not a treatise' (ibid.).

[13] See Husserl, *Die phänomenologische Methode*, 204. Levinas explicitly qualifies his philosophical discourse as '*eidétique*' (*TI* i) and points to his interest in the structure of ethics (*AQE* 162).

[14] Regarding the concept of apophansis, see: Aristotle, 'On Interpretation', 17a1–5, 17a25 (cited in *The Organon*). According to Aristotle, poetry, for instance, does not fall into the realm of apophantic discourse (ibid.) since it does not make ontological assertions, or, as Philip Sidney (following Boccaccio) puts it: 'the poet, he nothing affirms, and therefore never lieth' (123). It is precisely this philosophical apophansis which Levinas attempts *phenomenologically* to reduce in the very process of its enactment (*AQE* 67–74; see also Bernasconi and Critchley, 100). I should stress that I do not posit an essentialist distinction between scientific-philosophical and other types of discourse. In my functional delimitation of speech genres I follow Frege, Russell, Austin, Searle, and Genette. In line with Aristotle, Frege and Russell distinguish between merely formal/logical as opposed to ontological apophansis (Frege, 'Über Sinn und Bedeutung', 32; *Kleine Schriften*, 347; Russell, *Logic*, 46, 54). Both allow for the meaningfulness of assertive discourse without extratextual, ontological reference by way of 'parity of form' (Russell, *Introduction*, 168; *Logic*, 46; Frege, *Kleine Schriften*, 347), as is the case in fictional and poetic discourse. Austin underwrites the validity of Frege's and Russell's distinction by admitting sentences that 'have . . . the look—or at least the grammatical make-up—of "statements"' without being '*utterances* which could be "true" or "false"' (12). Searle's 'pretended reference' (330) and Genette's 'pseudoreference' (*Fiction*, 25)

What, then, to resume the question, does 'ethics' mean in Levinas's writings? Above all, it is important to note its contextual polysemy. At least three of its multiple meanings are engaged by Levinas: (1) ethics as a traditional philosophical discipline, and (2) ethics as his own philosophical discourse on (3) ethics as my originary relation to the other. Although Levinas clearly situates his intellectual enterprise within the philosophical tradition of the 'West' by referring to it in terms of *ethics* and *philosophy*,[15] he endeavours to work against and beyond ethics as an established philosophical discipline, aiming at a dialogic 'concept of ethics . . . which departs from tradition' (*DD* 228). The enmeshment of the first two senses of ethics raises the question of the possibility of breaking away from tradition within traditional discourse at all, insofar as in the very attempt at its dislocation or, to use Levinas's term, 'interruption' (*AQE* 262), philosophical tradition is being reaffirmed from within the sub-narrative of its presumed dislocation, of its 'unsaying' [*dédire*] (*TI* 16). Philosophical tradition, Levinas notes, 'is capable of saying all its ruptures' (ibid.).[16] The inescapability of philosophical tradition has at least one crucial corollary for an ethically adequate assessment of Levinas's own philosophical discourse: as philosophical discourse it perforce remains within the confines of discursive reason, within the 'order of philosophical demonstration . . . and thematization' (Bernasconi and Critchley, 75). It is precisely this insight which lies at the root of Levinas's careful distinction between philosophical and poetic language and their respective significance with regard to ethics (in the third sense). Philosophical discourse, even in its specifically Levinasian variant, may very well operate against a philosophical order and (attempt to) unsay its constitutive generic and semantic frameworks; it nevertheless remains caught within them—in Levinas's case admittedly so: ethics (as the philosophical discourse on ethics) assumes the role

reconfirm this distinction. In announcing his text as a philosophical inquiry Levinas establishes a pragmatic non-fiction contract (Genette, *Paratexts*, 94–103; Searle, 322–4) with the reader, who is thus invited to approach the text apophantically, that is, as ontologically assertive.

[15] See Levinas, 'La Philosophie', 247; *TI* 79; *DEHH* 189–90; DwL 25. According to Diogenes Laertius, Socrates introduced ethics as a philosophical discipline (i. 327).

[16] Elsewhere, Levinas writes that 'we have no option but to employ the language and concepts of Greek philosophy, even in our attempts to go beyond them' (DwL 28).

of first *philosophy*. For its interruption it depends on another discourse: poetry.[17]

The plausibility of Levinas's insistence on the philosophical primacy of ethics over ontology is based on the precedence of my relation to the other over my Being, understood as my intentional and intelligible correlate, that is, as my existence.[18] It is in this sense only that, according to Levinas, ethics (in the third sense) interrupts and precedes essence/Being (*AQE* 75–6): insofar as Being transpires as the human being's intentional correlate, that is, in Heidegger's terms, as the always already comprehended ground of Dasein's existential concern, and as such figures as the 'object' of ontology, it is, according to Levinas, always already preceded and anticipated by my accusative 'interpellation' (*TI* 65) by the other, that is, by ethics (in the third sense).[19] Levinas subverts Heideggerian ontology in a double sense: by situating ontology as the (human) *logos* on Being within ethics (in the first and second senses) and by grounding existence as Dasein's (intentional) relation to Being in the pre-ontological structure of ethics in the third sense (*AQE* 162).[20]

'. . . l'éthique en l'humain . . .'[21]

By positing the precedence of ethics over ontology as an explicit reversal of Heidegger's (and Sartre's) existentialism, Levinas underscores the interhuman significance of ethics as 'an irreducible structure on which depend all other structures' (*TI* 77), including the 'structure of Dasein's Being' (*SuZ* 130), that is, existence. Ethics,[22] Levinas reiterates, is an interhuman

---

[17] As I argue below, Levinas's multiple references to poetry as 'examples' of ethics (in the third sense) serve more than a seemingly hermeneutic purpose: more importantly, they interrupt Levinas's own philosophical discourse.

[18] 'Intentional' in Husserl's sense, as correlative of consciousness (*Die phänomenologische Methode*, 198); 'intelligible' in Heidegger's sense, as always already 'understood' (*SuZ* 183, 207). Levinas notes: '*Being and Time* . . . advances perhaps only one thesis: Being is inseparable from the intelligibility of Being' ('La Philosophie', 245).

[19] Heidegger defines Dasein's Being, that is, existence, as 'care', which signifies Dasein's concern for its own Being (*Prolegomena*, 406–20; *SuZ* 121, 180–200).

[20] Levinas's double subversion corresponds to Heidegger's double concept of ontology as 'the explicit interrogation of the Being of beings' (*SuZ* 12) and as Dasein's originary 'comprehension of Being' (ibid.).

[21] '. . . ethics in the human . . .' (*EN* 182).

[22] When using 'ethics', I now refer to ethics in the third sense only.

dynamic, which transpires in my concrete encounter(s) with the other(s), in which I bear witness to and for the other (*AQE* 223–39). 'I analyse', Levinas writes, 'the interhuman relation as if in the proximity with the other . . . the other . . . were *ordering* me to serve him' (*EI* 94). In this relation, the other 'calls on my response' (*TI* 271) and 'on my responsibility' (229). Ethics is a fundamentally asymmetrical and non-reciprocal dynamic: in contrast to Buber's formal concept of dialogic 'reciprocity' (*DP* 149), and in line with Husserl's asymmetrical conception of pre-linguistic communication based on indication, ethics transpires asymmetrically and non-reciprocally—my obligation to the other is gratuitous, a 'radical generosity'.[23] Levinas's ethical subversion of ontology must not be mistaken for any kind of 'mystical' or quasi-'mystical' endeavour: insofar as Levinas contends that ontology—in Heidegger's double sense as the theoretical interrogation of Being and Dasein's onto-logical constitution—is posterior to my relation to the other, ethics, in which I am constituted as a response-able person,[24] necessarily precedes ontology. In other words, my comprehen-sion of my own Being and, consequently, my theoretical inter-rogation of my own existence always already occur against the backdrop of and within my relation to the other.[25] In contrast to Heidegger's Dasein, which is originarily responsible to and for itself, that is, liable to assume an authentic existence, Levinas posits the primacy of my ethical response-ability to and for the other. This is precisely what Levinas means when he defines

---

[23] See *DEHH* 191–2; *EN* 172; *TI* 46, 249–50; *AQE* 75, 134, 140, 188; *NP* 36–43. I discuss Levinas's relation to Husserl's semiotics below.

[24] I henceforth use 'response-able' and 'response-ability' in reference to ethical dialogue only. My particular hyphenated spelling captures the foundational char-acter of ethics. Concomitantly, I will use 'answerable' and 'answerability' in reference to Bakhtin's conception of existential dialogue only (see Ch. 2). The term 'responsibility' refers to the existential or socio-political realm in general. At times Levinas uses 'responsabilité' in reference to the ethical and the socio-political. It is the interpreter's task to decide which 'responsabilité' is intended in a given passage.

[25] Adriaan Peperzak comments: 'My responsibility for the others has begun before I become aware of my own being . . . Responsibility can be described as a pre-phenomenal and pre-ontological inspiration, but this should not lead us to the idea of an ethereal something, a soul or ghost that hides behind the skin of a human body. Against all forms of anthropological dualism Levinas's analyses show that human subjectivity exists as a sensible, affective, working, speaking, and suffering body' ('From Intentionality to Responsibility', 17–18; see also Greisch and Rolland, 19).

ethics as (inter)human: the 'human begins when the vitality [of my existence], innocent in appearance but potentially murderous, is curbed [by and for the sake of the other]' (*AV* 131).

The primacy of ethics, however, is (at least) doubly motivated: the systematic subversion of ontology is complemented by Levinas's philosophical reappropriation of another tradition, which, although 'at least as old' as the philosophical tradition of the 'West', 'does not reduce every other to the same' ('La Philosophie', 247). Levinas has the biblical, Judaic tradition in mind: 'The interhuman relationship . . . can . . . be construed as part of [existence]. But it can also be considered from another perspective—the ethical or biblical perspective that transcends the . . . language of intelligibility' (DwL 20).[26]

What does Levinas mean by the formulaic 'reduction of the other to the same'? The combination of the terms 'Other' [Autre] and 'Same' [Même] in Levinas's texts *philosophically formalizes* the intuited concrete ethical dynamic between 'the other (human being)' [Autrui] and 'Me' [Moi].[27] The reductive

---

[26] Regarding the dichotomy of 'Hebraism and Hellenism' in Levinas's writings, see *ED*; Robbins, *Prodigal Son*, 100–32; Taylor, 185–217.

[27] Levinas emphasizes the formulaic character of the terms 'Same' (Même) and 'Other' (Autre) (see, 'La Philosophie', 244; *TI* 33, *EE* 13; *AV* 138, n 11). The French terms 'l'autre', 'les autres', and 'autrui', which Levinas employs throughout his writings—using both upper-case *and* lower-case spelling (inconsistently, as far as I can tell)—evince subtle but crucial differences. While 'autrui', a *singulare tantum*, only refers to human beings, 'l'autre' and 'les autres' can refer to anything. If 'l'autre' contextually refers to a human being, it is more specific—referring to only one human being—than 'autrui', which can signify one or many human beings. However, 'l'autre' (sing.) can also be more general than 'autrui', as when it refers to the general 'other' (for instance, 'god'). 'Autrui' is always more specific than 'les autres' (pl.). (Littré specifies: ' "les autres" is more general than "autrui" . . . "autrui" means *this* specific other' (i. 749)). In formulaic discourse, 'l'autre' is general while 'autrui' would not be used, since it always refers to (a specific) human being(s). Thus, in 'l'un/le même et l'autre', 'l'autre' is the general other, and not 'another (human being)' and, hence, not as specific as 'autrui'. However, in 'moi et l'autre', 'l'autre' is a contextually defined singular person and, hence, more specific than 'autrui'. In view of Levinas's correlation of 'l'un/le même' with 'l'autre' and of 'moi' with 'autrui', the latter seems to be used in a more specific mode than the potentially more specific 'l'autre'. Similarly, in the formula 'le même et l'autre', 'l'autre' is used on a general level. However, sometimes Levinas uses 'l'autre' in reference to a singular person. The alternating use of 'autre' and 'autrui', which corresponds to the alternating use of 'même' and 'moi' must be viewed as part of Levinas's endeavour to unsay his own apophantic discourse, which 'betrays' [trahit] the unthematizable, that is, ethics, in thematizing it (*AQE* 113, 239–42; Peperzak, 'From Intentionality to Responsibility', 20). Only the formalization of ethics justifies Levinas's emphasis on the 'structure of ethics' (*AQE* 162).

relationship between other and same, or 'totality', as Levinas also calls it by way of a polemic response to Hegel, refers to any structure or dynamic in which one of the constituents is subjected to inclusion, subsumption, or sublation, and is thereby deprived of its singularity.[28] From within this Greek tradition of the primacy of the 'same' in its various manifestations,[29] Levinas reverts to the biblical, Judaic 'perspective that transcends the Greek language of intelligibility' (DwL 20) and emphasizes heteronomy and heterology (27; *DL* 25). Levinas's ethical revaluation of Judaism is socio-politically motivated: only if I do not reduce the other, if I realize that 'my freedom is anteced by an obligation to the other' (ibid.), can a 'fascist or totalitarian' (30) politics be prevented. In view of the socio-political disaster of National Socialism, which (for both Levinas and Celan) exacerbates the 'philosophy of the same' in all its facets by literally converting the philosophical 'reduction of the other to the same' into the factual annihilation of the other, that is, into the 'Holocaust of millions of victims under Hitler' (*DL* 186), Levinas relentlessly expounds the rights of the other: only if my subjectivity is always already dependent upon the other, if my subjectivity is constituted in response to the other's demand, if *my* autonomy is heteronomous, can socio-political 'reduction', that is, domination and, ultimately, annihilation be counteracted (DwL 26–7); only if the other 'orders me to serve' will I question my 'autonomy' (ibid.) and 'feed [him]' (28), will I let the other be. 'If the moral-political order', Levinas summarizes, 'totally relinquishes its ethical foundation, it must accept all forms of society, including the fascist or totalitarian, for it can no longer evaluate or discriminate between them . . . This is why ethical philosophy must remain the first philosophy' (30).

Levinas's concept of ethical substitution has to be understood against this socio-political backdrop. What does Levinas mean by 'substitution'? Through the other's interpellation I become

---

[28] See Levinas, 'La Signification', 129; Hegel *Wissenschaft*, ii. 35–6, 52, 122–6; *Phänomenologie*, 72–5.

[29] 'Greek' acquires eponymic significance in Levinas's writings. Aside from its linguistic meaning, it signifies a 'certain, specifically Greek way of thinking and speaking' (DwL 18, 28) involving such terms and concepts as '*morphe* (form), *ousia* (substance), *nous* (reason), *logos* (thought) or *telos* (goal), etc.—that constitute a specifically Greek lexicon of intelligibility' (ibid.).

response-able; the other forces me to assume responsibility for 'the other's misery and failure and even the responsibility which the other may have for me' (*AQE* 185). My response-ability and, consequently, my factual responsibility to and for the other are always greater than the other's responsibility for me: 'being oneself . . . always means to be more response-able [than the other(s)], to be responsible for the responsibility of the other' (185–6). Levinas calls this insurmountable surplus of response-ability 'substitution'. Ethically, I substitute myself for, that is, I am always more response-able than the other(s), while remaining infinitely separated from the other(s).[30] Philosophically, 'substitution' is rooted in Levinas's relentless polemic against Heidegger. 'Substitution' translates and displaces Heidegger's concept of 'Vertretbarkeit' [substitutability] as one of the characteristics of Dasein's 'everydayness'.[31] 'Dasein's substitut-ability by another belongs to the possibilities of Being-with. In everydayness . . . substitution is not only possible in general, but it constitutes Being-with' (*SuZ* 239). However, Heidegger dis-avows the possibility of substitution with regard to existence, which singularizes each person. Levinas, conversely, locates the ethical principle of principles precisely in my ethical substitution for the other.

In Genesis Levinas finds the paradigmatic ethical foundation for a viable socio-politics (DwL 30). Without 'theologizing' the philosophical description of ethics, Levinas valorizes the ethical and socio-political implications of the Torah.[32] The concept of creation implies the subject's dependence on the other for the gift of Being and, simultaneously, the irreducible separation between creator and creature. For Levinas, the biblical accounts of human creation (Genesis 1: 27; 2: 7) present the blueprint for

---

[30] Ethical substitution is highly problematic, since it leads, according to Levinas, who implicitly refers to the Third Reich, to the passage from the 'pain endured to the responsibility for the persecutor, and thus from suffering to expiating for the other' (*AQE* 176). Here Levinas is very close to Sartre's depiction of the collusion between torturer and tortured (*Qu'est-ce que la littérature?*, 218).

[31] See Levinas, 'La Philosophie', 245; *EN* 238–9.

[32] Levinas notes: 'I always make a clear distinction, in what I write, between philosophical and confessional texts. I do not deny that they ultimately have a common source of inspiration. I simply state that it is necessary to draw a line of demarcation between them as distinct methods of exegesis, as separate languages. I would never, for example, introduce a Talmudic or biblical verse into one of my philosophical texts, to try to prove or justify a phenomenological argument' (DwL 18).

a factually plausible subversion of any (philosophical) attempt
to perceive the relation to the other as ontologically secondary:
'The wonder of creation does not solely consist in being a
creation *ex nihilo* . . . but in the creation of a being capable
of . . . learning that it is created and of questioning itself. The
miracle of creation consists in creating a moral being [être
moral]' (*TI* 88–9).[33] Existence, Levinas suggests, is preceded
by the bare fact of being created, that is, of being always already
related to and dependent on the other(s). Transposing the
paradigmatic structure of biblical creation onto the interhuman
plain, Levinas underscores the primacy of filiation (and parent-
hood) as the paradigmatic relation to the other(s): birth (con-
ception) precedes existence (in Heidegger's and Sartre's senses),
the gift of life/Being precedes my condemnation to freedom.[34] I
am always already ethical insofar as I am related, obligated, and
thus response-able to and for (an)other human being(s). Levinas
is factually justified in writing that the 'ethical relation does not
graft itself onto an anteceding relation . . . It is foundation and
not superstructure' ('La Philosophie', 249). Parenthood and
filiation, furthermore, enact *the* originary form of ethical sub-
stitution. 'The father', Levinas notes, 'does not simply cause the
son. *To be* one's son means to be in one's son, substantially,
without, however, being identical with him . . . The son assumes
the father's unicity while remaining exterior to him' (*TI* 311).
By foregrounding filiation, the originary relation to the other,
or, what he calls 'creatureliness' [créaturialité] (*AQE* 147),
Levinas subtly emphasizes the literal inhumanity of Heidegger's
concept of 'thrownness' [Geworfenheit], thereby, subtextually,
continuing his critique of ontology on socio-political grounds:
humans are (ethically) created, born—humans are not
'thrown'.[35] It is also important to note that, in the light of

---

[33] Although Levinas uses 'éthique' far more frequently than 'moral(e)', he does
not seem to make a semantic distinction between the two terms throughout *TI*.

[34] See *TI* 234–5, 310–13, 325–7; DwL 29. Although Levinas speaks of 'paternité'
in particular, I refer to 'parenthood' in general, eschewing the question of gender and
the feminine in Levinas's writings.

[35] 'Throwness . . . is the mode of Being of a being which *is* its own possibilities'
(*SuZ* 181); it means being 'at the mercy of the world' (199). The noun 'Geworfen-
heit' is the substantivized form of the past participle 'geworfen' of the verb 'werfen'
(to throw), which, within the isotopy of procreation, is only applied to animals in
German. Thus, dogs 'throw' puppies, while human beings 'give birth' [gebären]. As
'geworfen' Dasein is idiomatically stripped of its humanity by Heidegger. Levinas is

Genesis 2: 7, Levinas depicts ethics as 'deep breathing' (277), as 'my inspiration by the other' (ibid.).[36]

Levinas's concept of 'creatureliness' can, furthermore, be interpreted as a dislocation of Rudolf Otto's religious philosophy. While Otto conceives the human being as a 'creature' facing the 'holy', or 'numinous', which is 'beyond all creatures',[37] Levinas contends that 'ethics [is] without any trace of the "numinous"' (*TI* 213). That Levinas does in fact polemicize against Otto is corroborated—aside from the quotational use of 'numinous'—by Levinas's observation that the 'ethical relation defines itself in opposition to the relation to the holy' (*TI* 77–8). Levinas's most significant polemical response to Otto, however, consists in his appropriation and simultaneous displacement of Otto's influential concept of 'the wholly other' (das ganz Andere) (Otto, 30), 'the absolutely other' (l'absolument autre).[38] In contrast to Otto, who introduced 'the wholly other' to capture an aspect of the experience of the numinous, thus automatically emptying it of the ethical in favour of the 'religiously mysterious' (6, 27), Levinas reinvests 'the wholly [or absolutely] other' with and reinscribes it within the ethical by situating it on the interhuman plain in reference to the other human being: 'The absolutely Other is the other human being' (*TI* 28).[39]

indebted to Franz Rosenzweig, whose *Der Stern der Erlösung* is 'too frequently present in [*TI*] to be cited' (*TI* 14), for his ethical notion of 'creature' (see Rosenzweig, *Der Mensch*, ii. 255).

[36] Genesis 2: 7 reads: 'And the Lord God formed man *of* the dust of the ground, and breathed into his nostrils the breath of life' (King James's version). Levinas sees his philosophical task precisely in reducing the 'Said to respiration, which opens itself to the other and signifies to the other its signifiance itself' (*AQE* 278). The topos of breathing is equally central to Mandel'shtam and Celan (see Ch. 3). Regarding Levinas's use of 'signifiance', which I preserve in its French spelling, see below.

[37] See Otto, 5–10. In his groundbreaking study *Das Heilige* (1917), Otto introduced the neologism 'das Numinose' to characterize 'the holy *minus* its ethical moment' (6). The experience of the numinous manifests itself as the human being's 'feeling of the other's absolute superiority' (22). Buber's critique of Otto's valorization of the numinous (*DP* 82, 98, 104) informs Levinas's opposition to Otto.

[38] Although Levinas borrows the term 'absolument autre' from Vladimir Jankélévitch, he points to the fact that Jankélévitch himself borrowed it from Otto ('La Philosophie', 241; *Sur Maurice Blanchot*, 13–14).

[39] Since the numinous, in Otto's sense, is the 'holy *minus* its ethical moment' (Otto, 6), the 'wholly other', as one aspect of the numinous is a fortiori non-ethical. Depending on the context, Levinas uses the term 'absolument autre' in reference to

ETHICS AS LANGUAGE

My relation to the other, Levinas observes, 'originally transpires as discourse' (*TI* 29), which 'accomplishes a relation in such a way that . . . the Other [Autre] remains transcendent to the Same [Même]' (28–9). This '[o]*riginal language . . . of the unheard [of]* . . . *of the non-said*' (p. iii) is a 'movement of transcendence' (29) toward the other human being, which maintains

a profound distance . . . irreducible to the . . . synthesizing activity of understanding . . . between me [moi] and the Other [Autrui], a radical separation which prevents the reconstitution of totality . . . An interrogation of the Same [Même] is brought about by the Other [Autre]. This interrogation of my spontaneity by . . . the Other [Autrui] is called ethics . . . Transcendence, the reception of the Other [l'Autre] by the Same [Même], of the Other [Autrui] by Me [Moi] concretely transpires as the interrogation of the Same [Même] by the Other [Autre], that is, as ethics. (29–33)

This passage documents Levinas's alternating use of formulaic and phenomenologically descriptive discourse: the formulaic 'reception of the Other [Autre] by the Same [Même]' concretely occurs as the reception 'of the Other [Autrui] by Me [Moi]', which is immediately reformalized as 'the interrogation of the Same [Même] by the Other [Autre]'. My relation to the other 'is essentially interpellation, the vocative' (65). Ethical discourse 'is anterior to the negative or affirmative proposition, it inaugurates language [as system], in which neither the "no" nor the "yes" is the first word' (32).[40] Ethical discourse conditions and informs conceptual and linguistic universality. It involves 'interlocutors, a plurality' (70), whose originary 'commerce does not consist in mutual representation' (ibid.) or in the 'participation

god (see e.g. DwL 23) and in reference to the other human being (see e.g. DL 33; TI 15). In view of his insistence on the accessibility of god through the ethical relation to the other human being, the absolute alterity of god is predicated on the absolute alterity of the other human being (*TI* 76–7). As I illustrate below, 'god' has a very specific meaning in Levinas's texts. The ethical conception of the 'absolutely other' must also be understood as an oblique polemic against Hegel's concept of the 'absolute' and Heidegger's use of the term in reference to Being (*Wegmarken*, 306). Both 'creatureliness' and 'wholly other', occupy an equally central place in Celan's poetics and poetry (see Ch. 3).

[40] See also *DD* 125; Greisch and Rolland, 82. Levinas implicitly refers to Rosenzweig's stipulation of a pre-apophantic discourse (*Der Mensch*, ii. 255–6; see also Llewelyn, *Emmanuel Levinas*, 153–4).

. . . in the common domain of language [as system]' (ibid.). Their originary 'commerce' is precisely ethics: 'transcendence, radical separation, the interlocutors' mutual strangeness' (ibid.). Insofar as ethical dialogue conditions the realm of the general and universal, it necessarily also conditions the manifestations of language (as system) in human speech.

In order to account for the specific mode of the other's ethical address, Levinas introduces one of his ethical master concepts, the 'visage', defining it as the 'manner in which the Other presents himself surpassing my idea of the Other' (*TI* 61):

The visage speaks. The manifestation of the visage is already discourse. The one who manifests himself continuously undoes the form which he presents. This way of undoing the form adequate to the Same in order to present oneself as Other [Autre] is to signify, to have a sense, or direction. To present oneself as signifying/as signifier [en signifiant] is to speak [ibid.]. The visage, expression par excellence, formulates the first word: the signifier emerging at the tip of his sign. (193)

My originary interpellation by the other as visage 'is the production of sense' (ibid.). The exceptional character of this manner of signifying 'consists in ordering me toward the other's visage' (*AQE* 26). This order constitutes me as a response-able being, solicits from me a response to 'a non thematizable provocation . . . prior to all understanding . . . prior to consciousness' (ibid.). The language of the visage is an 'assigna-tion which identifies me as the unique' (83) infinitely response-able human being: 'The other's visage signifies a response-ability to me which is irrecusable and precedes my free consent, any pact or contract' (141). 'Visage', Levinas clarifies, does not designate the human face 'in the narrow sense' (*EN* 244) but the 'the expressive in the other (and the entire human body is . . . visage in this sense)' (*EI* 94).[41] In the light of the concept of visage as the other's mode of interpellation, Levinas defines ethics as a ' "vision" without image, devoid of the objectifying, synoptic, and totalizing virtues of vision' (*TI* 8).

---

[41] See also Robbins, *Altered Reading*, 55–72. By using 'visage'—one of the common French terms for 'face' or 'countenance'—Levinas continues his critique of Heidegger's 'animalization' of Dasein as 'thrown': 'The visage . . . differs from the animal face [face animale] . . . in its brutish stupidity' ('La Philosophie', 248). I further discuss the concept of 'visage' in the context of Husserlian semiotics below. For an in-depth discussion of 'expression' in this context, see: Hand, 115–18; Greisch and Rolland, 390.

While in *Totalité* Levinas depicts ethics as the pre-systematic, original language 'before words' (p. iii) in general, and concentrates on the other's mode of ethical signification, in *Autrement*, he devotes particular attention to the specific mode of signification characterizing my response to the other's visage.[42] It is to this appeal or call of the other as visage (*EN* 239) that I respond in what Levinas calls 'Saying'[43] before using any language whatsoever. In Saying, I do not say anything, I signify my response-ability in response to the other's assignation, in a 'passivity more passive than any passivity' (*AQE* 170) notwithstanding its apparent activity' (239).[44] Whereas a language of the non-said, a 'communication . . . as the condition of all

---

[42] Levinas emphasizes the continuity of his thought. In the preface to the second edition of *De l'existence*, he points out that notwithstanding 'shifts in terminology, formulae, concepts, and certain . . . theses' (*EE* 13) his ethical philosophy has, throughout, 'remained faithful to its goals' (ibid.). Some of the terminological and conceptual shifts alluded to by Levinas are: the abandonment of 'ontological language' (*TI* p. i; *DL* 412), which, according to Levinas, still informs such texts as *EE* (1947), *Le Temps* (1948), and *TI*; the specification of the distinction between ethical discourse and language as speech (parole) and system (langue) in terms of Saying (Dire) and Said (Dit), respectively, most overtly in *AQE*; the abandonment of the category of experience, which informs such texts as 'La Philosophie' (1957) and *TI*; the introduction of the concept of ethical substitution, especially in *AQE*; the emphatic use of the concept of the trace beginning with 'La Trace de l'Autre' (1963; in *DEHH*), and, especially, in 'La Signification' (1964), and *AQE*; the revaluation of the significance of poetry—repudiated in 'La Réalité' (1948) and *TI*—as a modality of ethics in such texts as 'Langage et Proximité' (1967; in *DEHH*), 'Paul Celan' (1972; in *NP*), and *AQE*; the increasing semioticization and dialogization of ethics, most obviously in 'La Trace', *AQE*, and 'La Proximité de l'Autre' (1986; in *AT*); the displacement and extension of the signification of the concept of justice from my relation to the other—informing such texts as 'La Philosophie' and *TI*—to the inclusion of the 'third' in *AQE* and subsequent texts.

[43] Levinas uses 'Saying' (Dire) throughout *AQE* and subsequent works. Saying designates ethics and my response in particular (see esp. *AQE* 17, 48, 75).

[44] See also *TI* 225; *AQE* 147, 150, 159, 161, 167, 173, 186, 223, 226. An adequate critical elucidation of Levinas's complex notion of ethical 'passivity' cannot be undertaken within the limited scope of the present chapter. Suffice it to point out that it involves Christian images of suffering and self-sacrifice (*AQE* 232) and, to a certain extent, the behaviour of some characters in Dostoevsky's texts, which are central to the development of Levinas's ethics (especially Liza in *Notes from Underground* and Zosima in *The Brothers Karamazov*; Levinas explicitly intertwines 'passivité', 'patience', and 'passion' (*DEHH* 191; *AQE* 89, 91–3, 173) against the implicit backdrop of their common Latin root, 'pati' (to suffer, to endure), thus underscoring the pertinence of the Christian context). Equally, if not more, important is Levinas's constant awareness of the Holocaust: he depicts Jewish suffering during the Third Reich as 'a suffering at the limit of all suffering, which suffers all sufferings' (*DL* 185). Questions of passivity and activity and their paradoxical enmeshment are also central to Dostoevsky's ethics, Buber's dialogism, and Sartre's poetics, all of which inform Levinas's philosophy.

communication' (82) can be philosophically explicated in terms of Husserlian semiotics (see below), it is not philosophically obvious why Levinas conceives pre-linguistic dialogue between singularities in such ethical terms as response-ability, absolute ethical asymmetry, and responsiveness 'preceding all questions . . . to the other's proximity' (47). Here again recourse to the Judaic tradition illuminates Levinas's thought. Continuing his philosophical reappropriation of Judaism, Levinas again turns to the Torah for the elaboration of his idiosyncratically 'visual' conception of ethical language:

And the angel of the Lord appeared unto [Moses] in a flame of fire out of the midst of a bush: and he looked, and, behold, the bush burned with fire, and the bush was not consumed. And Moses said, I will now turn aside, and see [*'ere'e*] this great sight [*mare'e*], why the bush is not burnt. And when the Lord saw that he turned aside to see, God called unto him out of the midst of the bush, and said, Moses, Moses. And he said, Here *am* I [*hinneni*]. (Exodus 3: 2–4)[45]

Since, as Dante remarks, 'God [cannot] have used what we call speech' (*Literature*, 18), Moses responds to a non-linguistic call, which addresses him singularly by his proper name, and, thereby, constitutes him as an unique *ethical subject* consigned to a non-transferable socio-political responsibility. The 'Here *am* I' in response to the call of the absolutely other, the 'paradigmatic response of responsibility' (Robbins, *Altered Reading*, 32), precedes the self-empowerment of the subject in speculative, transcendental, or existential terms. I am I thanks to my relation with and interpellation by the other. The apparent, purely apophantic function of the copula[46] disguises its ethical foundation in the other's call. Furthermore, Moses's exteriorized response, a response already translated into a language system, succeeds a non-linguistic response, a 'vision'—mark the emphasis on vision in the quoted passage—which, in line with the Judaic proscription of images (Exodus 20: 4), lacks the image of the (divine) interlocutor and is thus a ' "vision" without image'.[47]

---

[45] See also Genesis 22: 1, 7, 11. Levinas cites the biblical formula 'Here I am' or 'Here am I' (me voici), throughout his oeuvre as the supreme instance of ethical assignation (see e.g. *AQE* 262, 283).

[46] Although no explicit copula is used in the original Hebrew text, 'hinneni' meaning literally, 'Here I', implies ontological predication.

[47] See also Exodus 33: 20–3. Levinas emphasizes: 'The proscription of images is indeed the supreme commandment of monotheism' ('La Réalité', 786).

Similarly, the ethical relation to the other human being tran-
spires 'beyond the [finalizing] image that I have of the other
human being' (*TI* 77). It is this non- or pre-linguistic, hence pre-
systematic communication with the other which Levinas calls
ethical discourse or language.

In contrast to Heidegger's emphasis on Dasein's vigilance to
the call of his or her conscience, which enables Dasein to assume
an authentic existence (*SuZ* 271–89), Levinas points out that I
must be 'vigilant [to the] call of the other' (DwL 29). It is the
other who constitutes me 'as a subjectivity, as a singular person'
(26), as an irreducibly responsible 'I'.[48] Before being able to
obey the 'call of [my] conscience' (Heidegger) I must have
already been ethically constituted as an 'I' through the 'call of
the other', which awakens my unique 'ethical conscience' (*TI*
293)—in analogy with Abraham's and Moses's interpellations
by god. My ethical obligation to the other implies, as I
mentioned earlier, a fundamental asymmetry between us, an
asymmetry grounded in the paradigmatic asymmetry between
creator and creature. In ethics responsibilities are not
exchanged: I am always already more responsible to and for
the other than the other is to and for me, precisely because my
ability to respond is absolutely singular in its scope and signific-
ance.[49]

While the discursivization of ethics conceptually reverses
ontology against the backdrop of the biblical paradigm, the
ethicization of language is predicated on the observation that
speech is always already transcended by the interhuman (*AV*
133–9). 'Transcendence', however, must neither be equated, as
Peperzak implies, with the existential realm nor with (the
movement toward) the 'beyond' or 'otherworldly'.[50] Such an
understanding of 'transcendence' is ruled out by Levinas's strict
distinction between ethics and the realm of the numinous. Even
in those instances in which Levinas describes ethical transcen-
dence as a transcendence toward 'god', it happens between
human beings. Since the notion of transcendence informs the
claim that Saying underlies and conditions the Said, Levinas's

[48] See also *AQE* 83, 113, 188 n.
[49] See *TI* 249–50; *AQE* 134, 140, 188. Levinas calls this asymmetry 'dyssemétrie
morale' (*TI* 331).
[50] See Peperzak, 'From Intentionality', 17; Greisch and Rolland, 80.

complex notion of god as the supreme mode of transcendence has to be elucidated. The 'God of ethics' (DwL 31) radically differs from the 'God of traditional ontology' (ibid.), understood as 'ontological presence' (ibid.). Levinas conceives god as the ethical dynamic itself (*AV* 133) and defines 'god' as 'the civilizing force' [la force civilisatrice] (*DL* 25), whereby 'civilizing' idio-syncratically signifies the suspension of the other's reduction to the same and my vigilance to his or her call (*AV* 133). God does not 'exist', god 'passes (*se passe*)' (DwL 31)[51] as my infinite ethical relation to the infinitely other human being (ibid.): 'The infinite is the radically, the absolutely other human being' (Levinas, 'La Philosophie', 247). Levinas converts infinity—the specification of the *summum ens*—into the other's infinite otherness and into my infinite ability to respond to and for the other: 'The positivity of Infinity is the conversion into response-ability' (*AQE* 27).[52] 'God' reveals itself as a *chiffre* for the ethical in Levinas's philosophy. The conversion of ontological infinity into ethical infinity disseminates the meaning of infinity. It signifies my infinite ability to respond to and for the other; my infinite separation from the other as well as the other's infinite separation from me, that is, his or her absolute otherness notwithstanding the proximity between us;[53] the fact that the other infinitely surpasses my idea (thought) of the other; and, finally, the unique other [autrui] him- or herself (*TI* 227). Levinas's distinction between ethics and religion is informed by oscillating perspectives on the interhuman rather than by an ontological dichotomy between two realms of intelligibility: while ethics refers to the concrete 'interrogation of my spon-taneity by ... the Other [Autrui]' (*TI* 33), religion—defined as 'the tie that establishes itself between the Same and the Other [Autre] without forming a totality' (30)—formally captures the infinity of ethical transcendence. Levinas calls this the 'double structure of the infinite' (232), which means that the 'relation with the infinite' (ibid.) transpires both ethically and religiously. Concomitantly, Levinas implies a double notion of transcendence: my ethical

---

[51] 'Se passer' means 'to be going on', 'to happen', 'to transpire'.

[52] See also *EN* 163.

[53] 'Absolute', as Levinas points out, in the literal sense of 'absolvere' (Lat. to separate, to sever) (*AV* 147–8). He depicts the passing of the infinite as 's'absoudre' (to absolve oneself) (*DEHH* 200). See, also, Levinas, 'La Philosophie'; *TI* 42; *DEHH* 200; *AQE* 26–7.

transcendence toward the other and the transcendence of the formal structure of ethics with regard to the concretely ethical.[54]

If religion, the formal structure of ethics, that is, a post facto formal extrapolation retroactively informs and motivates that which it is grounded in, then ethics must proleptically always already transpire within the formal structure of the infinite. The infinite will have always already traced ethics.[55] Ethics, the enactment of religion, although logically posterior, is 'factually' anterior to its own formalization. Ethics, Levinas stresses, 'is not the simple corollary of the religious; it is, in itself, the element in which religious transcendence receives its original sense' (*AV* 133). This metalepsis echoes Levinas's equally metaleptic dislocation of the primacy of ontology.[56] Insofar as ethics, the interhuman relation par excellence, will have always already been traced by the infinite, Levinas is justified in saying that the other's visage appears 'in the trace' (*DEHH* 202) of the infinite. The infinite will have always already informed my interpellation by the other, who calls on me from within its trace, that is, from within the trace of the formal structure of ethics. This fundamentally temporal structure of ethics and, by extension, of the dialogic constitution of subjectivity radically contrasts with Augustine's monologic conception of time as originating *within* rather than *between* human beings, which in turn informs Husserl's and Heidegger's concepts of temporality.[57] Time, considered from within the ethical attitude, originates as my relation to the other. 'How could time possibly emerge in a single subject?', Levinas asks (*EE* 159), given that the 'absolute alterity

[54] In 'La Trace' Levinas suggests a distinction between a 'transcendence . . . to the second degree' (*DEHH* 189) and, implicitly, a presupposed transcendence 'to the first degree', which would be my concrete relation to the other. In the preface to *TI*, Levinas explicitly defines 'l'infini' in general and formal terms as 'transcendence with regard to totality' (7) and specifies that the infinite is the 'concept of this transcendence . . . rigorously developed' (ibid.). Regarding Levinas's diverse uses of 'transcendence', see also: *TI* 28–9, 66, 74–7, 85, 89, 91–2, 190; *AQE* 114, 188, 220, 263–4, 279; *DD* 223; DwL 26.

[55] Levinas calls this the 'absolute past', the 'trace', or 'illeity' (*DEHH* 199–202). Wiemer notes that 'the (inter)human signifies as the trace of the relation with the infinite, with God' (Greisch and Rolland, 397).

[56] See Robbins, *Prodigal Son*, 120. Metalepsis, the figure of the reversal of the early and the late, underlies Levinas's claim that ethics precedes ontology.

[57] See Augustine, 281–4; Husserl, *Phänomenologie*, 80, 95–102, 117; Heidegger, *Wegmarken*, 190–1; *SuZ* 329, 376.

of the other instant . . . cannot be found in the subject' (ibid.).
'This alterity', Levinas continues, 'comes to me from the other . . .
time is constituted in my relation with the other human being . . .
that is, [in and through] dialogue' (160). My response-ability to
and for the other human being 'is time' (*EN* 180).[58] My ethical
relation to the other is predicated on my 'passage to the time of
the Other' (*DEHH* 192), or, to speak with Celan, to 'that which
is most . . . the other's own: his time' (*GW* iii. 199). Levinas's
emphasis on diachrony must be understood along the lines of his
overall opposition to totality, which would inevitably obtain in
the synchronic identification of my relation to the other in terms
of reciprocity by a third party's thetic consciousness: 'Diachrony
is . . . the non-totalizable, and, in this precise sense, the Infinite'
(*AQE* 26).[59] Ethics is diachronic on account of its proleptic
relation to the infinite *and* on account of its discursivity. Dis-
course cannot but transpire as a certain kind of semiosis; semiosis
in turn—the action of signs—is necessarily diachronic.[60]

SEMETHICS

For reasons of clarity in argument and rhetorical economy, I
henceforth use the neologism 'semethics' in reference to ethics as
the object of Levinas's ethical philosophy. 'Semethics' morpho-
logically fuses 'semiotics', 'semantics', and 'ethics', thus lexically
capturing Levinas's semiotic conception of my relation to the
other. Notwithstanding Ockham's razor, 'semethics' is a pro-
ductive heuristic tool: it takes account of the semiotic aspects of
the interhuman and, thereby, constantly reminds the critic that
Levinas's phenomenological descriptions must be interpreted
against a semiotic backdrop.[61]

[58] See also *TI* 249.

[59] Due to ethical diachrony, my socio-political 'responsibility toward the other is
also a responsibility toward the *future*, since it involves the struggle to create
openings within which the other can appear beyond any programmes and predic-
tions, can come to transform what we know or think we know' (Attridge,
'Introduction', 5 (in: Derrida, *Acts of Literature*); see also Attridge, 'Trusting', 70).

[60] Peirce defines 'semiosis' as 'the action of . . . any kind of sign' (*Philosophical
Writings*, 282). Regarding the problem of synchrony and diachrony in language,
and, more specifically, the inevitably 'diachronic density within any synchronic
state', see Attridge, *Peculiar Language*, 125.

[61] I first used 'semethics' in my 'Introduction' (245, 247, n. 12); I equally discuss
semethics in 'A Language' and 'Translating'.

The seeming circularity of Levinas's characterization of ethics as discourse and the subsequent stipulation of its diachronicity on the basis of its discursivity reveals itself as a phenomenologically cogent description of the proleptic and metaleptic oscillation between ethics and the infinite. How does this oscillation 'happen'? How does the infinite manifest itself as and within ethics? How does the conversion of the infinite into semethics occur?—By way of translation, Levinas suggests: semethics 'translates [traduit] the Infinite' (*AQE* 26); the infinite 'translates . . . itself [se . . . traduit] into . . . Saying' (30).[62] My response to the other's interpellation, which issues forth 'in the trace' of the infinite, is inherently semiotic and thus indeed justifies the depiction of my relation to the other in discursive terms. The dynamic of interpellation and Saying is the very *meaning* of infinity if, as Jakobson argues (following Peirce), meaning constitutes itself in and through translation (*SW* 261).[63] While the originary translational character of my relation to the other sufficiently warrants its interpretation in semiotic terms, such an interpretation is all the more plausible in view of Levinas's emphatic semioticization of its minutest details: 'The one who announces himself in and through the [linguistic] sign as signifying the sign', Levinas notes, 'is not the sign's signified, but . . . gives it' (*TI* 93). 'The sign', Levinas continues, 'does not signify the signifier as it signifies the signified. The signified is never complete presence; always in turn a sign, it never comes straightforwardly. The signifier, the one who emits the sign, is *facing* [me directly] despite the mediation of the sign' (97–8). The sign signifies both its signified and its signifier. While the signified—in a Peircean twist to an otherwise Saussurean depiction of signification—is always already caught up in the process of semiotic mediation becoming in turn a sign, the signifier is *announced* by the sign and addresses the interlocutor without mediation.[64] The signifier,

---

[62] 'Traduire' can also mean 'to express', which only corroborates the semioticity of my relation to the other. My emphasis on 'translation' rather than 'expression' is motivated by Levinas's frequent allusions to the well-known formula 'traduttore, traditore' (see *AQE* 113, 237, 261), which foregrounds the translational aspect of 'traduire'.

[63] See Peirce, ii. 228. I cite Peirce's papers according to the volume/paper numeration in the *Collected Works*.

[64] Peirce defines the sign as '[a]nything which determines something else (its

that is, the human being manifests him- or herself in his or her words. The word 'is a sign which interprets itself already, which carries its own key. The presence of the interpreting key in the sign . . . is precisely the presence of the Other' (ibid.).

Communication, Levinas explains, cannot be reduced to the exchange of messages which signify thoughts by way of linguistic signs (*AQE* 82).[65] The exchange of messages already implies 'my prior exposition [i.e. transcendence] to the other human being' (ibid.), who obligates me to respond: 'Expression does not so much manifest the presence of a being by moving from the sign to the signified as it presents the signifier itself. The [linguistic] sign can emerge as a sign only against the backdrop of the prior sociality of signifiers. The signifier must present himself prior to any [linguistic] sign . . . must present a visage' (*TI* 198).

It is not the mediation of the sign which expedites signification, but it is signification (the originary event of which is the face-to-face) which makes the function of the sign possible . . . The other's visage is sense, and any recourse to words situates itself within the originary face-to-face of language. Any recourse to words presupposes the comprehension of the first signification, a comprehension which, before letting itself be interpreted as 'consciousness of', is sociality and obligation. Signification is the Infinite . . . the Other . . . The essence of language is

interpretant) to refer to an object to which itself refers (its *object*) in the same way, the interpretant becoming in turn a sign, and so on *ad infinitum*' (ii. 303); the 'interpretant' is 'ordinarily called the *meaning* of the sign' (iv. 536), or what Saussure calls the 'signifié' (Jakobson, *Language*, 442–3). Although it would be convenient if it were established that Levinas had indeed been directly familiar with Peirce's and Saussure's writings, the verifiability of such first-hand knowledge on Levinas's part is irrelevant to the contextual pertinence of Saussure's and Peirce's texts. As early as 1934, that is, long before Derrida's and Kristeva's popularization of Peirce's concepts (see Derrida, *Of Grammatology* (1967), 47–50; Kristeva (1968), 9–28), Levinas could have plausibly come across Peirce's writings: In an issue of *Revue philosophique de la France et de l'etranger* (118 (1934), 284–5), in which Levinas published an article on phenomenology ('Phénoménologie'), he could have read a review of the first two volumes of Peirce's *Collected Papers* (the second volume contains most of Peirce's seminal texts on semiotics). While Levinas could have possessed first-hand knowledge of Saussure's *Cours*, he definitely encountered his concepts and terminology in Merleau-Ponty's *Signes* (1960) and Derrida's *La voix* (1967) and *De la grammatologie* (1967). Both authors deal with Saussure in connection with *LU*. Regarding Levinas's familiarity with Merleau-Ponty's and Derrida's writings, see 'La Signification', 129–33; *NP* 65–72.

[65] 'Message' in Jakobson's sense, as the sign itself (*Language*, 69). Levinas equates the visage's signification with 'being present in one's own *message*' (*TI* 68).

the relation with the Other . . . the ethical event of sociality even underlies inner speech. (226)

In apostrophizing me the other signifies him- or herself as the very message of his or her interpellation, soliciting my semethical response, my infinite obligation to become response-able. In responding to the other, in Saying, Levinas specifies, the interpellated in turn 'does not give a sign [in the communicative sense], he makes himself a sign' (*AQE* 83). Semethically, I am the sign of my obligation, I signify myself as the sign of my response-ability. In response to the other's visage I *am* 'all sign, signifying [my]self' (31), 'giving the sign of this giving of the sign' (ibid.). In order clearly to distinguish semethical signification from signification in the systematic sense, Levinas (re)introduces the term 'signifiance' in reference to my relation to the other, while using 'signification' in reference to linguistic semiosis proper.[66] Signifiance is 'a signification to be distinguished from that signification which characterizes words in the Said' (*AQE* 78); it is '[s]ignification to the other in proximity' (ibid.), my originary constitution in 'brotherhood' (132) with regard to the other, the originary mode in which my 'relation with the visage' (*TI* 313) transpires: '[T]he signifiance of Saying . . . is signification par excellence. In a system, signification is predicated on the mutual definition of terms within the synchrony of totality . . . To have a signification in the Said means that an element refers to other elements' (*AQE* 112).[67] Aside

[66] I use 'signifiance' throughout in its original French spelling. In English translations of Levinas's works, it is usually rendered as 'signifyingness'. While the term's use by Levinas may be interpreted as participating in its post-structuralist revival, it is philosophically and biographically more plausible to attribute its ethical functionalization to Levinas's engagement with Husserl's and Heidegger's texts, who distinguish between 'Bedeutung' (signification) and 'Bedeutsamkeit' (signifi(c)ance) (see *LU* 37, 71; *SuZ* 82). The term 'signifiance' replaced (*c.*1155) 'senefiance' (*c.*1080) and 'signefiance' (*c.*1119) and had been employed as synonymous with 'signification' and with 'indice' as the mark by which something shows itself (*c.*1165–70). The term was subsequently obliterated and only recently rediscovered in the context of contemporary linguistics and semiotics (Benveniste and the authors around *Tel quel*, such as Sollers, Kristeva, and Barthes), most likely by way of its English relative 'significance' (Wiemer, 195–200), which had been used by such contextually pertinent thinkers as Peirce (for instance, ii. 92). The phenomenological motivation of Levinas's use of 'signifiance' is all the more plausible in view of the fact that he had been using the term long before Kristeva or Barthes (see e.g. *TI* (1961) 293).

[67] Levinas's concept of systematic language is informed by Saussure's notion of 'langue' (*Cours*, 23–35).

from characterizing my originary dialogue with the other, signifiance also refers to the relation between the trace and semethics, as the phrase, 'signifiance of the trace' (*DEHH* 196) indicates.

Levinas by no means attempts to reduce reality and the external world to the status of text in a superficially post-structuralist manner. Rather, in attending to the indelible semioticity of my relation to the other he provides philosophically cogent parameters for the theory that language is principally dialogic and for the related socio-linguistic claim that mind and consciousness are socially constituted. Thus, Bakhtin's and Voloshinov's insistence on the dialogic formation of the human mind presupposes an originary, mutually responsive addressivity between human beings.[68] For these and other thinkers (Iakubinskii, Vygotskii, Halliday, *et al.*), Michael Holquist suggests, 'language . . . enable[s] . . . society which in turn permit[s] the existence of individuals' (*Dialogism*, 56). The uniqueness of Bakhtin's contribution in this context, Holquist continues, is to have probed the specificity of language which allows it to serve 'as the threshold between selves and others' (57). By positing language's 'capacity to model addressivity and dialogue' (ibid.), Bakhtin, according to Holquist, 'takes the implications of dialogue to their radical extreme and assumes that at no level where communication is possible is the subject ever isolated' (57). Indeed, in reference to metalinguistics Bakhtin uncovers the irreducibility of dialogue. However, is the level of metalinguistics the most basic level of dialogue? Doesn't Bakhtin leave the very universality of dialogue unexplained? Levinas goes one step further than Bakhtin by interrogating the ethical underpinnings of dialogue (in Bakhtin's metalinguistic sense). Why, one may ask with Levinas, do humans constantly engage in dialogue? Why is it that the minutest and most fundamental moments in existence may be rationalized in dialogic terms?[69] It is because I am always already obligated to respond to and for my interlocutor(s) that dialogue in the existential sense can become Bakhtin's principle

---

[68] See *VLA* 158; *MPL* 12–15, 25, 34.

[69] See esp. Holquist, *Dialogism*, 50. Even what Holquist calls the 'lowest level of dialogue', that is, 'the organism's physiology' (ibid.), is still part of the existential realm in terms of its theoretical conceptualization.

of principles; it is only because I am semethically 'without excuse . . . and without an alibi' (*AQE* 223) that I am existentially without an alibi, that I am, in Bakhtin's famous formulation, 'without an alibi in existence' (*R* 43, 46–7); it is only because I am semethically engaged by the other that language is dialogic. Levinas subverts the implicit hierarchy in Bakhtin's articulation of the 'basic moments' of existence as 'I-for-myself, the other-for-me, and I-for-the-other' (KFP 52); for Levinas, the order is unambiguously 'the other (for me) . . . I-for-the-other, I-for-myself', whereby the 'I-for-myself' already exceeds my originary relation to the other.

My Saying responds to the other's visage. The visage 'signifies an irrecusable response-ability to me' (*AQE* 141). This moment is, according to Levinas, 'the originary semantic situation, in which the human being receives a sense, an orientation' (*EN* 199). The visage literally *means* me in the 'accusative case' (*AQE* 222), as Moses's paradigmatic response to god's interpellation, 'me voici' (lit. 'me here'), indicates. Replicating the translational dynamic between ethics and infinity, my response to the other's 'commandment' (ibid.) transpires as its meaning or sense, that is, *translates* it semethically into my orientation toward the other.[70]

Having provided the reader with a preliminary understanding of semethics, I should now like to interrogate its semiotic underpinnings with the aim of elaborating a conceptual framework for its explication. For the semiotic character of my relation to the other—regardless of its biblical backdrop—must be philosophically grounded in order to acquire the argumentative force and rigour implied in Levinas's claim that his writings are 'completely indebted to the phenomenological method' (*TI* 14). While critics have noted Levinas's attention to semiotics, the actual semiotic viability of his ethical philosophy has—to the best of my knowledge—not been sufficiently probed.[71] Thus, a careful examination of Levinas's ethical

[70] I use 'meaning' and 'sense' in a loosely synonymous fashion at this point, in analogy with Husserl's anti-Fregean equation of 'Bedeutung' and 'Sinn' in *LU*. In addition, 'sense' implies orientation and directedness. Regarding Levinas's use of 'sens' as 'orientation', see e.g. 'La Signification', 139–40. Rosenzweig's claim that 'revelation is orientation' (*Der Mensch*, iii. 125) and Heidegger's existential concept of semiotic orientation (*SuZ* 79) certainly inform Levinas's text.

[71] See e.g. Peperzak, 'From Intentionality'; Ponzio, 'Semiotics', 25–6; *Man*, 233–50; Wiemer, 154–229; Funk, 251–358; Llewelyn, 'Approaches'; Eaglestone; Robbins, *Altered Reading*, 23–6, 57–63.

functionalization of semiotics with regard to its theoretical and factual plausibility must, perforce, precede any further philosophical and a fortiori socio-political engagement of his philosophy. In other words, if Levinas's ethics is to be interpreted and assessed not merely metaphorically but as philosophically cogent, it must, first and foremost, be shown to make sense semiotically. Only if semethics can be semiotically vindicated can it be stipulated as foundational and, simultaneously, dependent on the Said for its accessibility. Which sign concept informs Levinas's notion of a non-intentional, passively constituted human sign or signifying human being, who signifies his or her own signifiance singularly and without mediation— without recourse to a system of references, without requiring conceptual understanding? Which sign concept informs Levinas's notion of a human being who signifies infinitely and substitutes him- or herself for the other, who is the condition of and key to any language system?

THE SEMIOTIC UNDERPINNINGS OF SEMETHICS

Levinas's ethical functionalization of semiosis exposes itself to two crucial objections: if, as Benveniste (following Saussure) claims, 'there cannot be a trans-systematic sign' (ii. 53), how can there be semiotic singularity and immediacy, which is not tacitly informed by a 'system of references' (*DL* 408), a code or 'langue', in relation to which it will have always been already an individuality (in Hegel's sense), rather than a singularity?[72] Concomitantly, if, as Derrida suggests, a sign is necessarily recursive, that is, by definition *not* an 'irreplaceable and irreversible unicity' (*La Voix*, 55), how can it function semethically?

Benveniste's and Derrida's claims only seemingly preclude the validity of semethics as a pre-systematic dynamic. While Benveniste and Derrida are certainly right in the light of Saussure's concept of the linguistic sign as a differential entity informed by a system (*Cours*, 25), their claims cannot possibly be sustained in the light of other, more complex, concepts of semiosis.

---

[72] Levinas emphasizes the non-referentiality of semethics throughout his writings. In Hegelian logic, individuality relates to universality by way of particularity (*Wissenschaft*, ii. 35).

Husserl's and Peirce's semiotics, in particular, provide a viable framework for a productive elucidation of semethics. Husserl's distinction between two basic categories of signs, 'index' and 'expression', offers a point of entry into Levinasian semiotics. While 'every sign is a sign for something' (*LU* 30),[73] all signs do not signify in the same manner: expressions are actively intended linguistic signs or complexes of linguistic signs and are grounded in 'indication', whereas indices proper are non-linguistic (in the functional, systematic sense) and always non-intentional.[74] Husserl specifies the 'index':

Something may be called an index [Anzeichen] only if it serves a [human] being as an indication [Anzeige] of something . . . Such expressions [Äußerungen] are not expressions [Ausdrücke] in terms of communicative speech. Unlike the latter, they are not identical in the consciousness of the one expressing himself with the expressed experiences; in [indices], the one does not communicate anything to the other; [indices] lack intentionality [and] have no meanings in the sense of linguistic signs. (31, 37, 38)

In contrast to expressions, indices are not intended as signs; their semioticity is constituted by and depends on the contiguous addressivity of human beings. As the quoted passage suggests, Husserl also distinguishes between two modes of expression, 'Ausdrück' and 'Äußerung', which refer to the active mode of linguistic expression and the 'passive' mode of indication respectively. Having outlined the basic modes of signification, Husserl turns to the concomitant modes of reference:

Sign and object can be related directly or indirectly, by way of mediation through other signs . . . In the case of indirect signs it is necessary to distinguish between that which the sign signifies/means [bedeutet] and that which it refers to [bezeichnet]. In the case of direct signs, meaning and referent are identical . . . In the case of indirect signs, conversely, the relation between sign and object is mediated; the sign refers to the object precisely by way of these mediations, and it is for this reason that these mediations constitute the sign's meaning. (*Philosophie der Arithmetik*, 343; see also *LU* 33, 37, 42, 54)

[73] Husserl calls this the 'substitutive function of signs' (*LU* 73). Peirce, too, stresses that every 'sign . . . stands . . . for something' (ii. 228). See also Derrida, *La Voix*, 24; Benveniste, ii. 51.

[74] Every expression primarily indicates that it is an expression; this indexical function underlies every linguistic sign (*LU* 37–8, 39, 40; see also Derrida, *La Voix* 20–1, 40).

The distinction between direct or unmediated and indirect or mediated semiosis involves the distinction between semiosis predicated on a certain non-logical awareness and semiosis grounded in conceptual or logical comprehension: while indices indicate directly, that is, contiguously, without having recourse to an 'ideal system of [conceptual] references' (*LU* 33), without signifying by way of signifieds or concepts, expressions necessarily involve the latter and, consequently, 'rational comprehension' [Einsichtigkeit] (ibid.) partially independent of immediate contexts and speech situations and based on an 'ideal systematicity' (ibid.). In contrast to expressions, indices are 'non-comprehensible' [uneinsichtig] (34), always depend on the singular here and now of their occurrence for their functioning, and are constituted by what Husserl calls 'Vermeinen' [envisaging] (41).[75] Vermeinen is a particular mode of pre-thetic, pre-thematizing intentionality—an 'intentionality of a completely different kind' (*TI* 8)—which transpires singularly in a given speech situation or any other situation in which someone envisages a datum as an index. Expressions 'mean' [bedeuten], indices 'indicate' [anzeigen] in response to the other's contiguous envisaging; expressions refer to states of affairs or objects by way of their meanings, while indices indicate their objects directly or contiguously, whereby meaning and referent coincide; indices always refer to facts, states of affairs, or existents, while expressions do not have to refer to facts or existents (*LU* 32–3, 77). Husserl summarizes:

What makes communication possible is the verbally mediated correlation of the interlocutors' physical and material experiences. Speaking and listening, manifesting [Kundgabe] and . . . apprehending [Kundnahme] are correlated . . . All expressions [Ausdrücke] in communication [also function] as indices [Anzeichen] . . . They serve the listener as signs of the speaker's 'thoughts' . . . Understanding manifestation [Kundgabe] is not a mode of conceptual knowledge or a kind of apophantic judgement; it consists in . . . the perception of the speaker by the listener . . . as a person . . . If the essential character of perception [Wahrnehmung] is an intuitive envisaging [Vermeinen] . . . and such

---

[75] My translation of the gerund 'Vermeinen' is contextually motivated. Husserl's terminology explicitly departs from 'normal speech' (*LU* 37). Conventionally, 'vermeinen' (lit. to allege, to think, to assume, to presume) is hardly ever used in the verbal sense; most frequently it can be encountered in its adjectival form 'vermeintlich' (lit. alleged).

envisaging is possible and, in fact, takes place in most cases without any conceptual [mediation], then apprehension [Kundnahme] is merely the perception of manifestation [Kundgabe]. (39–41)[76]

Speech is always already embedded in and transcended by the interlocutors' *personal* addressivity. Every enacted linguistic sign signifies according to a code *and* indicates its speaker to the other as a person oriented toward his or her interlocutor, whereby, according to Husserl, the speaking person and his or her speech form a unity: the unity of the signifying human being *as* speaker. Husserl suggests that the interlocutor is constituted through 'Vermeinen' as an integral part of his or her responsive self-indication as interlocutor. Consequently, my interlocutor non-intentionally indicates him- or herself as interlocutor, 'bears witness' (37) of him- or herself as interlocutor *and* of me as his or her addressee. Whereas expressions are actively enunciated and require understanding based on conceptual mediation, indices (including, Husserl suggests, persons) *manifest themselves* and are *envisaged* rather than understood.

Husserlian semiotics is particularly pertinent with regard to Levinas's master concept of the visage. Why does the other present him- or herself as visage? Levinas's phenomenological use of 'visage', the nominal form of the verb 'viser' (lit.: to envisage, to intend), derives directly from Husserl's Vermeinen. Both Levinas and Hubert Elie, the French translator of *Logische Untersuchungen*, render Vermeinen as 'visée'.[77] 'Visage' then replicates the nominal character of the gerund Vermeinen and absorbs its semantic specificities as a human being's pre-systematic, pre-conceptual relation to a datum, which it thereby constitutes as an index. Insofar as 'visage' derives from Vermeinen, semethics is—notwithstanding its thematic groundedness in Exodus 3: 2–4—indeed a ' "vision" without image, devoid of the objectifying synoptic and totalizing virtues of vision' (*TI* 8), or, simply, to use Husserl's term, 'uneinsichtig'.[78] The visage phenomenologically 'envisages' (ver-

---

[76] I translate 'Kundgabe' and 'Kundnahme' following the French translations of Husserl's text (see Derrida, *La Voix*, 43; Husserl, *Recherches*, 40–1).

[77] See DwL 14 ('intentional rapport' (visée)); Husserl, *Recherches*, 31, 48.

[78] 'Einsichtig' and 'uneinsichtig' literally mean 'capable of being *looked* into' and 'incapable of being *looked* into', respectively, and derive from the German noun 'Sicht' (vision, sight).

meint) (*LU* 32) its addressee and thereby constitutes it as a sign, and, more specifically, as an index, the semiotic correlate of Vermeinen, which underlies linguistic signification, that is, the indelibly index-based expression. If I am semethically constituted by the other's visage in the phenomenological sense, then I must respond *as* an index in the phenomenological sense: contiguously, singularly, and without systemic mediation. It is in this phenomenological-semiotic sense that Levinas posits semethics as an unmediated dynamic, as contact: 'The immediate is the interpellation . . . the imperative of language . . . The immediate is the face to face' (*TI* 44), 'the exposition of the self to the other . . . in the contact of saying' (*AQE* 134). Phenomenologically, indexical contiguity informs Levinas's emphasis on semethical proximity, contiguity, and the overall testimonial character of semethics (223–39), in which, to use Husserl's terms, 'the one witnesses for and to the other' (*LU* 37).[79] Levinas's depiction of semethics in terms of encountering reveals itself—in addition to its overtly Buberian backdrop—as semiotically motivated:[80] the other encounters me as a sign, as an index, indicating my responseability to the other's envisaging. Moreover, Levinas's biblically motivated emphasis on the other as 'neighbour' (*AQE* 141; *EN* 239) is phenomenologically grounded in semiotic contiguity.

The plausibility of interpreting semethics in light of Husserlian semiotics is further corroborated by Levinas's use of the terms 'manifestation' and 'expression': the visage is 'expression' and interpellates as 'manifestation' (*TI* 61, 98, 198). On the pre-systematic, non-totalizing level of semethical dialogue, these terms translate the Husserlian non-linguistic (in the systematic sense) modes of expression, namely, 'Äußerung' and 'Kundgabe', respectively:[81] both modes of expression are characteristic of pre-linguistic dialogue and underlie speech communication; concomitantly, Levinas's insistence on the *personal* character of semethics ('to express oneself, that is . . . to present oneself as a person' (*TI* 293)), is informed by Husserl's depiction of the other's indexical constitution as a dynamic

[79] Levinas writes: 'Proximity receives sense . . . in . . . contiguity' (*AQE* 245; see also 121).

[80] The central concept of Buber's dialogism is the interhuman 'encounter' (*DP* 15–16, 29, 35–7, 43, 56, 61–2, 78).

[81] See Husserl, *Recherches*, 40–2. Levinas, however, displaces Husserl's terms by having them refer to the other rather than myself, as Husserl has it.

between 'persons'.[82] Against the backdrop of Husserlian semiotics, Levinas is phenomenologically justified in describing me as a sign functioning as an index constituted by the other's interpellation as visage, and thus signifying singularly, passively, and without mediation, that is, contiguously. However, Husserlian semiotics fails to provide a semiotic explanation for two central constituents of semethics: substitution and infinite response-ability.[83]

Levinas's metaphor of the semiotic 'key', which captures the other's interpretative function with regard to his or her interpellation,[84] calls for a Peircean (re)reading of semethics and its Husserlian underpinnings. The semiotic 'key' pragmatically displaces Peirce's concept of the 'interpretant'.[85] Designating what is 'ordinarily called the *meaning* of the sign' (Peirce, iv. 536) and thus functioning as 'the key which the receiver uses to understand the message he receives' (Jakobson, *Language*, 443), the 'interpretant'—'in turn a sign' (Peirce, ii. 203) 'created in the mind of a person' (ii. 228)—undergoes a transformation in Levinas's text, which foregrounds the dormant *personal* grammatical meaning of 'interpretant' as a present active participle, that is, 'the one who interprets':[86] rather than referring to the semantic level of signification, it designates the person, who, as a (Husserlian) index, semiotically legitimates his or her functionalization as the semiotic key, the interpretant, to his or her message. As an interpretant, the other, according to Peirce, necessarily *creates* another sign *in* the interlocutor, which Levinas expands—by way an inverted synecdoche[87]—to comprise the interlocutor's entire

[82] Certainly, Buber's attention to the inter*personal* character of dialogue is equally relevant here (*DP* 45–6, 65–6, 71).

[83] While positing the substitutive character of any sign with regard to its referent, Husserl does not theorize the substitutive relation between the envisaging human being and the thus constituted index.

[84] 'Th[e] presence of the interpreting *key* in the sign to be interpreted is precisely the Other's presence in the sign' (*TI* 98; my emphasis).

[85] See Peirce's two complementary definitions of the 'sign' as: 1. 'Anything which determines something else (its *interpretant*) to refer to an object to which itself refers (its *object*) in the same way, the interpretant becoming in turn a sign, and so on *ad infinitum*' (ii. 303); 2. 'something which stands to somebody for something . . . It addresses somebody, that is, creates in the mind of that person an equivalent sign, or perhaps a more developed sign. That sign which it creates I call the interpretant of the first sign' (ii. 228; for further clarification, see ii. 92, 242).

[86] Interestingly, as Jakobson notes, Peirce's readers have frequently 'misinterpreted' the 'interpretant' precisely along these lines (*Language*, 442–3).

[87] Any sign, Peirce notes, 'stands to somebody' (ii. 228).

person; the interlocutor emerges as the other's interpretant, that is, *personally* translates the other's *meaning*.[88] Reinterpreting Levinas's semiotic conception of my relation to the other in Peircean terms corroborates the validity of Husserl's notion of Vermeinen for Levinas's ethical philosophy, insofar as Vermeinen implies meaning in the performative sense,[89] highlighting the translational and, hence, semiotic character of semethics. Furthermore, my translational relation to the other semiotically elucidates Levinas's concept of ethical substitution. In translating the other, I indeed semiotically substitute myself, that is, *stand for* the other insofar as, according to Husserl and Peirce, a 'sign [by definition] . . . stands for' something or somebody; semiotically, Saying cannot but transpire as substitution.[90]

Peirce's conceptualization of semiosis as creation provides a semiotic framework for the thematic roots of Levinas's ethical philosophy in Genesis 1: 27 and 2: 7. The other's semethical status as an interpretant diachronically presupposes his or her prior creation by another interpretant. Only after having been constituted by yet another human being can my interlocutor interpellate and create me as an 'equivalent, or perhaps more developed sign', while translating him- or herself into an irreducible other.[91] It is precisely this translational relation between signs which allows for the semiotic explication of Levinas's attention to parenthood (creation) and filiation as paradigms of semethics: every sign is 'itself and another' (Derrida, *Of Grammatology*, 49).

Among Peirce's diverse types and classes of signs[92] only one

[88] An interpretant, according to Peirce, necessarily translates itself into another 'equivalent . . . or . . . more developed sign' (ii. 228), thus creating meaning.

[89] 'Vermeinen' consists of the performative prefix 'ver-' and the verb 'meinen' (lit. to think, to believe, to have an opinion, to mean). Thus, to envisage someone or something implies to mean someone or something. In Husserlian terms, a sentence like 'ich vermeine dich' should be translated as 'I mean you'.

[90] Peirce, ii. 228; *LU* 30. Substitution does not imply the other's reduction; substitution must be understood diachronically and not in terms of replacement. Insofar as, according to Peirce, every sign—in addition to 'stand[ing] for' the other— also signifies 'to somebody' (ii. 228), my substitutive response is necessarily always already addressed to the other, for whom I semethically substitute myself.

[91] I should stress that Levinas does not deal with the other's implied dependence on yet another other for his or her ability to interpellate me. It is understood that I cannot possibly be aware of this as a semethical subject. See also Derrida, *Adieu*, 60–3.

[92] Peirce distinguishes between three types and ten classes of signs, a comprehensive discussion of which exceeds the present framework (see ii. 247, 254–64).

sign *always* functions contiguously, non-conceptually, and potentially pre-systematically, namely, the index: 'the action of indices depends on association by contiguity, and not association by resemblance or upon intellectual operations' (Peirce, ii. 306). In contrast to other signs, the 'immediate Interpretant of an Index must be an Index' (ii. 294) in turn. Thus, every indexical interpretant must have been created by another index. Furthermore, since 'the condition that a Sign must be other than its Object is . . . arbitrary' (ii. 230), the immediate object, that is, referent, of an index can be the index itself. Finally, the index, in its extreme form as 'sinsign', occurs singularly and is not recursive.[93] Peirce's index thus ideally complements Levinas's appropriation of Husserlian semiotics, according to which the index is the non-intentional object of *Vermeinen*. Created as an index by the other, who must in turn have been pre-created as an index by yet another, I signify, or, rather, indicate myself as an index in contiguity with the other and with myself as my own referent.[94] The actual performance of this formal depiction of indication transpires, according to Peirce—and this fully explains my rapprochement between Peirce and Levinas—as a simple and singular 'here': 'The index asserts nothing; it only says' (iii. 361): 'here' (ii. 305), or, to use Levinas's biblically motivated terms: 'me voici', 'here I am'.

Both Husserl and Peirce underscore the non-apophantic character of indication,[95] which also characterizes semethics: semethics, Levinas writes, transpires 'prior to the negative or affirmative proposition, it inaugurates language, in which neither the "no" nor the "yes" is the first word' (*TI* 32); apophansis, Levinas stresses, is only a 'modality of Saying' (*AQE* 79). Levinas's stipulation of the foundational character of semethics acquires semiotic cogency in the light of Husserl's and Peirce's insistence on the semiotic primacy of indication: whereas Husserl explicitly posits the dependence of systematic language and speech on indication, Peirce implicitly underlays any linguistic element with originary (self-)indication in pointing out that 'every sign . . . signifies primarily that it is a sign' (*Selected Writings*, 71),

---

[93] 'A *Sinsign* (where the syllable *sin* is taken as meaning "being only once" . . .) is an actual existent thing or event which is a sign' (Peirce, ii. 245).

[94] Self-referentiality is the extreme case of contiguity.

[95] See Peirce, iii. 361; *LU* 39–41.

while nonetheless *creating* an interpretant in another person and thus remaining inherently dialogic. Furthermore, insofar as the interpretant—an 'equivalent or . . . more developed sign' created in the human mind—is constitutive of signification, semiosis is essentially human; the human being in turn is essentially semiotic, and, by way of an inverted synecdoche, the ultimate interpretant, hence, the ultimate sign, which signifies him- or herself as the key to any potential linguistic signification (in Levinas's terms: the interpreting human being is present 'in the sign' (*TI* 98)).[96] Peirce rightly notes that 'we . . . ultimately reach a Sign of itself, containing its own explanation and those of all . . . significant parts' (ii. 230), namely: 'man'.[97] Peirce's dictum that 'man is a sign', and, more specifically, originarily a sinsign, provides a plausible theoretical framework for semethics, and, in particular, for semethical self-referentiality. The semioticity of the human being, which necessarily implies originary human diachronicity, semiotically undergirds Levinas's claim that my relation to the other is originarily diachronic.

Levinas's attention to the semiotic character of the human being and the human essence of semiosis is thematically pre-dicated on midrash (lit. 'solicitation of meaning')—the para-digm of signification for Levinas. In midrash, Levinas contends, meaning is not simply deposited in a text but arises in the process of the reader's or interlocutor's solicitation: 'The rela-tion between signifier and signified', Levinas notes, 'is not the only mode of signification. The signification of the signifier . . . only responds to the mind which solicits it. The mind is also part of the process of signification. Interpretation is essentially this solicitation . . . which emanates from persons . . . who would thus belong to the process of signification' (*AV* 136).

As I have noted earlier, the other must have always already been pre-created by yet another other in order to be able semethically to create me. An interpretant—and every sign is

---

[96] See also Bakhtin's similar observation that the human being 'puts himself entirely into the word' (*PPD* 193).

[97] Peirce's famous dictum that 'man is a sign' (*Selected Writings*, 71) must be interpreted as an inverted synecdoche. Obviously, Peirce does not deny physical being; rather, he 'humanizes' semiotics. Saussure, too, views the human being as constitutive of and inherently involved in semiosis (27–8). Similarly, Voloshinov conceives the human psyche in semiotic terms (*MPL* 26; see also Pirog, 'The Bakhtin Circle's Freud', 596).

the interpretant of another sign—is caught up in infinite semiosis, in a dynamic of infinite translatability, ultimately grounded in the infinite self-referentiality of the human sinsign. This means that semethics will have always been already a polylogue, or, at least, traced by the interpellation of 'the third'.[98] Levinas's observation that my relation to the other always already involves the third is thus semiotically justified. I do not only translate the other, but, indirectly, potentially *all* others, whose voices resonate in my interlocutor's interpellation. Consequently, I am indeed semethically *infinitely* response-able. My response to the other is always already polyphonic. Singular and unique in its responsiveness and response-ability, it nonetheless translates and is traced by a multiplicity of inter-pellations and responses and is thus formally infinite. Semioti-cally, Saying is indeed 'more passive than any passivity' (*AQE* 170), in that I, as a passive sinsign (index), respond to and for a potential infinity of others. Peirce's notion of infinite semiosis, in which an interpretant translates itself into another interpretant 'and so on *ad infinitum*', corroborates Levinas's insistence on infinite response-ability: the other is indeed in the trace of the infinite third, or 'illeity', which semiotically traces the other's visage as something that has 'properly speaking . . . never *been* there' (*DEHH* 201; my emphasis) in the ontological sense.

ETHICS AND POETRY

Among Levinas's many pronouncements on poetry and art in general,[99] his 1972 essay on Celan stands out as a sustained attempt to capture the relation between poetry and the ethical. Although disguised as a commentary on three poetological texts by Celan—a letter to Hans Bender (18 May 1960), Celan's Büchner Prize Speech, 'Der Meridian', and 'Conversation in the Mountains'—'Paul Celan: De l'être à l'autre' (Paul Celan: From Being to the Other) (*NP* 49–56) is an eloquent testimony to

[98] Throughout his oeuvre, Levinas emphasizes the 'reference of any dialogue to the third [le tiers]' (*TI* 313; see also 281, 334; *AQE* 33, 108, 130–1, 146, 144, 188, 202, 204, 234, 245–9, 251; *EN* 172, 201; *AT* 112). By 'le tiers' Levinas means any numerically singular or plural third party exceeding semethical dialogue as well as 'illeity', or god (i.e. the infinite) (*DEHH* 199–202).

[99] See e.g. 'La Réalité'; *TI* 149, 222; *AQE* 70–1, 122, 235, 263, 280; (*DL* 181–8); DwL 29; *DEHH* 228; *EN* 202; *Sur Maurice Blanchot*.

Levinas's own understanding of the ethical significance of poetry (and the poetic significance of ethics), as it constitutes itself in his dialogue with Celan's texts.[100] This essay not only problematizes and displaces Levinas's earlier negative view that the 'disinterestedness' to which poetry—as one among the arts—invites is not one 'of contemplation but of irresponsibility' ('La Réalité' (1948), 787);[101] more importantly, it testifies to the extent to which ethics and poetry inform each other.

Although Levinas had already suggested a rapprochement between ethics and poetry in 'Langage et proximité' 1967 (*DEHH* 217–36), it is in 'Paul Celan' that he—presumably reporting Celan's views[102]—explicitly qualifies poetry in such ethical terms as 'gratuitous' (*NP* 55), 'signification older than ontology and the thought of being' (ibid.), and 'saying without said' (52).[103] Poetry is the enactment of the 'significance of signification itself' (56; see also *AQE* 17). Like semethics, the poem—defined as 'the fact of speaking to the other' (*NP* 53)—precedes 'all thematization' (ibid.) and 'makes language possible' (*DL* 188). Poetry 'situates itself precisely on the pre-syntactical and pre-logical level' (*NP* 50). It is the 'language of proximity . . . the first of languages, response preceding the question' (ibid.).[104] As an 'unheard of modality of *otherwise than being*' (55),[105] poetry, which Levinas—like Celan—distinguishes from art, ruptures the 'immanence to which [systematic] language is

[100] The subtitle, 'De l'être à l'autre', which, in its original publication, was the essay's full title, indicates the tendentiousness of Levinas's interpretation. Although differing in terms, it formally and thematically converges with the title and, hence, theme, of Levinas's early philosophical text, *De l'existence à l'existant*. Thus, Levinas's Celan essay can plausibly be considered part of Levinas's overall philosophical project.

[101] A similar view is still presented in *TI* (222).

[102] Several of Levinas's characterizations of poetry in 'Paul Celan' are preceded by such introductory phrases as: 'We find Celan telling us' (*NP* 50), 'It turns out that for Celan' (ibid.), 'In Celan's words' (52), 'For Celan' (55), 'Doesn't he suggest' (ibid.)

[103] 'Saying without Said' ('Le Dire sans Dit') is the title of a subsection in *AQE* (78–81). See also *DEHH* 191–2; *EN* 172.

[104] See also *DEHH* 217–36; AQE 47; *EN* 200.

[105] The entire sentence reads: 'Doesn't he suggest poetry as an unheard of modality of *otherwise than being*' (*NP* 55–6). Given Levinas's overall characterization of poetry in ethical terms, the oblique suggestion that Celan himself conceives 'poetry as an unheard of modality of *otherwise than being*' underscores Levinas's implicit agreement with Celan's alleged viewpoint. The lexematic contamination of Celan's imputed stance with such ethical vocabulary as '*otherwise than being*' and 'unheard of' (Levinas qualifies semethics as a '*Language . . . of the unheard of*' (*TI* p. iii)) blurs the boundaries between Levinas's and Celan's discourses.

condemned' (*Sur Maurice Blanchot*, 79 n.) and enacts my transcendence toward the other (*NP* 52–3).[106] In contrast to art, which, according to Levinas, is the ultimate exposition of Being in that it exhibits itself as *being* art,[107] poetry—understood in terms of Celan's 'Dichtung'—does not 'do' or 'produce' anything; rather, it is a '[s]ign given to the other' (54) 'by way of a poem' (57), in which I 'dedicat[e] [myself] to the other' ('le moi se dédie à l'autre') (54).[108] Interestingly, the verb 'to dedicate' (dédier)—which Levinas borrows from André du Bouchet's very liberal translation of Celan's line, 'Wer es schreibt [i.e. das Gedicht], bleibt ihm mitgegeben' ('The one who writes [the poem] remains given to it') (*GW* iii. 198), as '*Qui le trace se révèle à lui dédié*' ('The one who traces it reveals himself as dedicated to it') (Celan, *Strette*, 191)—fuses ethics and poetics: 'dédier' paronomastically conjoins Celan's 'mitgegeben' and its referential displacement by Levinas with philosophical 'dédire' (unsaying); in dedicating itself (to the other), poetry unsays philosophy.[109]

Levinas's identification of semethics and poetry, which dislocates any received notions of poetry as an art form and textual genre, presupposes a fundamental distinction between 'poetic saying' (dire poétique) (*NP* 53) and 'poetic *said*' (*dit* poétique) (*AQE* 263), that is, poetry as a speech genre, whereby only the latter participates in the term's received array of meanings.[110] As

---

[106] Regarding the distinction between art and poetry, Levinas writes: 'But, after all, the word "poetry" does not name a species of which the word "art" would be the genre' (*Sur Maurice Blanchot*, 79n.). Hand notes: 'poetry is exempt from Levinas's negative view of art' (86–7 n. 2).

[107] Art, Levinas writes, is 'ostension par excellence—the Said reduced to a pure theme . . . the Said reduced to the Beautiful, the vehicle of . . . ontology' (*AQE* 70).

[108] Like French, English lacks a second term for 'poetry', which translates both the German 'Dichtung' and 'Poesie'. Celan makes a clear distinction between *Kunst* (art), which includes poetry as *poiein*, and *Dichtung*, which testifies to the 'presence of the human' (*GW*, iii. 177, 189–90). See Pöggeler, '—Ach, die Kunst!'; Lesch; Gellhaus, 'Die Polarisierung'.

[109] Throughout his essay, Levinas relies on André du Bouchet's translation of 'Der Meridian' (Celan, *Strette*, 179–97). After quoting this line in du Bouchet's translation (*NP* 52) Levinas displaces the object of dedication by identifying it with the poem's addressee rather than—as Celan has it—with the poem.

[110] By 'Said', it will be remembered, Levinas means language as a system, a code, the process of speaking (communication), and texts/works within language (*AQE* 17, 223). Levinas distinguishes between the Said in general and the 'pure Said', which explicitly designates written discourse: 'In writing saying makes itself pure Said' (*AQE* 264).

poetic said—that is, precisely because it evinces similar discursive traits as its semethical ground, on which, in fact, these traits depend—poetry is best equipped to stage semethics on the existential and generic levels of dialogic *activity*. As I illustrate below, Levinas's rapprochement between semethics and poetry as a speech genre is predicated on the discursive explosion of totality: whereas semethics effectuates the most fundamental 'interruption of Being' (*AQE* 75), poetry is the most outstanding discursive possibility of subverting totalization and violence on the socio-political level. Echoing his Celan essay, Levinas observes that while 'man can repress saying, and this ability to keep silent, to withhold oneself, is the ability to be political' (DwL 29), he can also 'give himself in saying to the point of poetry . . . to the other' (ibid.). This point needs further clarification.

Levinas's dichotomization of politics and poetry is based on the Heraclitean notion that the political is an 'expression of our ontological nature' (ibid.) insofar as it is inherently partisan and interested, that is, grounded in war, the most obvious 'face of Being' (*TI* 5–6); war reduces human beings to 'bearers of forces which command them' (ibid.).[111] While it is the task of ethics constantly to point to the necessity of assuming and pragmatically realizing the semethical underpinnings of the political and thus perpetually to interrupt and critique the political in the name of the other human being (DwL 29–30), poetry 'goes one step further' (*NP* 53) in that it indeed—by dispensing with apophansis (see below)—disrupts violence (totality), even the violence ethics necessarily commits: due to its apophantic character ethics, although an indispensable condition and corrective of the political, is necessarily totalizing, hence violent.[112]

---

[111] Aside from its literal meaning, 'war' in this context implies the reduction of the other to the same in any form. Guided by interest, calculation, and partisan objectives, politics is necessarily totalizing and thus belligerent in the ethical sense (DwL 29–30). Levinas's broad notion of war and its repudiation, is *ex negativo* informed both by Heraclitus's dictum 'War is the father of all things, of all things king' (fr. 53, in: Diels and Kranz, i. 162) and by Hobbes's 'war of every man against every man' (*Leviathan*, 106–8), which in turn can only be terminated by an act of power, that is, of war.

[112] Attridge notes that 'it is the political that is to be corrected by the ethical, and not vice versa' ('Trusting', 70). Levinas's emphasis on the interdependence between ethics and politics goes back to Aristotle, who considers ethics—despite its methodological priority—as part of the 'mastercraft . . . of politics' (*NE* 1094a29; *Politics* 1323a14–16). Levinas reverses Aristotle's hierarchy.

Levinas's endeavour to unsay his own philosophical discourse is motivated precisely by this insight and manifests itself in a particular style which constantly displaces its own eidetic procedures, without, however, being able to escape apophansis. Given Levinas's emphasis on the philosophical continuity of his oeuvre, which avowedly employs the method of phenomenological reduction, violence will have always been the point of departure and the telos of ethical philosophy. Philosophy cannot possibly unsay or interrupt itself without simultaneously 'weaving together the interruptions themselves' (Derrida, 'At this Very Moment', 18): philosophical discourse, Levinas points out, 'is capable of saying all its ruptures' (*AQE* 262).

For its unsaying, philosophical discourse, that is—in this instance—ethics, depends on other modes of discourse.[113] Derrida suggests that such 'nonviolent language . . . would be a language of pure invocation, pure adoration, proffering only proper nouns/names [noms propres] in order to appeal to the other' (*ED* 218), since 'it would be a language without the verb *to be*, that is, without predication' (ibid.).[114] However, Derrida does not mention that kind of 'nonviolent language', which, although it may use the verb 'to be', does it 'not seriously' (Austin, 22) in the ontologically referential sense, does not assert or predicate ontologically (apophansis) but rather by 'parity of form' (Russell, *Logic*, 46) only. Such language has traditionally been considered characteristic of poetry, which, by 'potentially confirming or unsettling philosophical presuppositions without [itself] offering philosophical arguments', exemplarily enacts the 'undoing of

---

[113] The fact that the 'the reference to the interlocutor continuously pierces through the philosophical text' (*AQE* 264) does not invalidate the philosophical impossibility of subverting apophansis apophantically. Derrida's claim that owing to its dialogic character Levinas's ethical philosophy succeeds in interrupting itself '*at the very moment* when . . . the philosophical *récit* . . . pretends to reappropriate for itself the tear within the continuum of its texture' ('At this Very Moment', 21) is epistemologically unproductive, as it equally applies to non-philosophical modes of discourse, insofar as they are constitutively dialogic.

[114] Derrida explains: 'Predication is the first violence . . . Both the verb "to be" and the act of predication inform every verb and every common noun' (*ED* 218). Praying, for instance, is a mode of non-predicating speech, a language of pure invocation, since it consists in 'dis-interest-ing oneself, setting oneself free from the unconditional attachment to Being' (Levinas, 'De la prière', 192, cited in Greisch and Rolland, 270). Incidentally, Celan notes—citing Malebranche—that poetry's dialogicity and attentiveness to the other is 'the natural *prayer* of the soul' (*GW* iii. 198; my emphasis).

philosophy'.[115] Since any apophantic discourse is potentially interruptible by non-apophantic, hence 'nonviolent', discourse, poetry is a potential 'moment or structural possibility in every text, whatever its public genre' (Attridge, 'Singularities', 114). Insofar as 'poetry' is considered the most general term for non-violent discourse, Derrida's 'language of pure invocation' would always already be poetic. As the interruption of ethics, poetry replicates ethics as the interruption of politics, and semethics as the interruption of Being, which in turn informs both ethics and politics; poetry—being socio-politically interruptive par excel-lence—exemplarily accomplishes the critical task of ethics and thereby, ironically, reveals its deeply political significance. Poetry exceeds the 'limits of what may be thought by [merely] suggesting, by letting be understood without ever rendering understand-able—by implying meanings which differ from meanings acquired by signs through the simultaneity of a system or through the logical definition of concepts' (*AQE* 263). Poetry textually stages the other's semethical excess with respect to the '*idea of the Other in me*' (*TI* 43), that is, semethical untotalizability and infinity, which traces 'the poetic *said* and the infinite interpreta-tion it solicits' (*AQE* 263). By pragmatically suspending onto-logical referentiality, poetry—like semethics—explodes Hegelian logic, in which the individual synthesizes the universal and the particular. Poetry, Kristeva notes,

takes the most concrete signifieds, concretizes them to the utmost degree, and, simultaneously, raises them to a level of generality which

---

[115] Attridge, 'Introduction', 2, 17 (in: Derrida, *Acts*; see also Attridge, 'Closing Statement', 25). I specifically refer to the Aristotelian strain of poetics, which in one way or another adheres to Aristotle's anti-Platonic conception of poetry as ontologically non-referential, hence non-apophantic ('On Interpretation', 17a1–8, cited in *The Organon*). One need only think of Boccaccio's dictum that even if poets 'do say in their works that there are gods . . . they neither believe nor *assert* it as a fact, but only as a myth or fiction' (Boccaccio, 65), and Sidney's famous paraphrase of this dictum (Sidney, 123). More recently, such authors as Frege, Austin, Searle, Kristeva, and Genette have underwritten poetry's non-referential status in the ontologically assertive sense. This does not mean that poetry relinquishes the referential function of language (which, according to Jakobson, it could not possibly do); rather, it refers to the world of the text itself. I should remind the reader that I use 'poetry' both in reference to literature in general and in reference to poetry in the narrow sense. Levinas himself suggests such a rapprochement by referring to both as 'poésie' ('La Réalité', 785). I should also stress that I am not attempting objectively to define 'poetry', being solely interested in elaborating a productive framework for Levinas's specific understanding of poetry.

surpasses that of conceptual discourse. [Poetry] creates a universe of signification in which the signifieds are more concrete and more general, more tangible and more abstract than in ordinary [and philosophical] discourse. Poetry seems to be able to *represent* a concrete object . . . while . . . enacting such a high degree of generalization that all individualization vanishes. The poetic signified . . . is simultaneously concrete and general. In a non-synthetic application, it short-circuits the concrete and the general, and, thereby, rejects individualization . . . (Kristeva, 191)

Similarly, Derek Attridge argues that 'a text in which . . . the relation between singularity and generality [is] staged with haunting power' (cited in: Derrida, *Acts*, 16) testifies to the poetic.

In Levinas's writings, the interruption of ethics by poetry takes place in the shape of frequent quotations from poetic texts, which literally halt the flow of philosophical description and, without arguing anything themselves, contaminate and significantly determine the argument.[116] Levinas's repeated invocation of Dostoevsky's statement, 'We are all responsible for everyone and everyone before everyone, and I most of all' (*EI* 98), is a case in point.[117] Not only does it poetically corroborate and inform Levinas's stress on infinite response-ability and substitution (97–8), but, most importantly, it cuts through Levinas's phenomenological descriptions. Similarly, the repeated invocation and permutation of Vasily Grossmann's lines, 'the generosity of an old woman, who has given a piece of bread to a prisoner . . . the generosity of a singular person toward a singular person' (278), not only poetically supports Levinas's emphasis on semethical generosity in terms of 'taking the bread from one's mouth, satisfying the other's hunger' (*AQE* 84, 126), but, more importantly, interrupts phenomenological reduction.

One of the most significant disruptions of Levinas's ethical philosophy is no doubt effectuated by Celan's poetry. Thus, Levinas's central concept of ethical substitution is—in addition

---

[116] Levinas's quotations from poetry include passages from the Torah—Levinas explicitly qualifies biblical language as poetry (*DL* 182)—and the works of Dostoevsky, Rimbaud, Baudelaire, Grossmann, Pushkin, Valéry, and Celan (see 'La Réalité', 10; *EI* 95, 97–8; 'La Signification', 127–8, 142–3; *DEHH* 193; *AT* 116–17; *AQE* 156, 176, 228). For a general discussion of Levinas's philosophy and its relation to literature, see Robbins, *Altered Reading*.

[117] See also *EI* 95–6; *AQE* 228; Dostoevsky, *Brat'ia Karamazovy*, ii. 325–6.

to its phenomenological-semiotic underpinnings—explicitly linked to Celan's poem 'In Praise of Remoteness' ('Lob der Ferne'), a verse from which, 'I am you, when I am I', precedes as a motto the central chapter, 'La Substitution', of *Autrement qu'être* (156), where the concept of substitution is elaborated.[118] If, as Hendrik Birus points out, it is one of the central functions of the motto to continue and reinforce a tradition (Birus, 386) and to articulate in a nutshell the problematic of the text it precedes (390), then Levinas's Celan motto is a perfect specimen. Aside from embedding ethics within a specifically poetic framework, it also focalizes its major theme: Celan's verse non-apophantically performs *and* displaces the apophantic, totalizing formula par excellence—the law of identity: 'I am I' ($A = A$)—in favor of my substitution for the other, while preserving an irreducible separation between me and the other.[119] In the light of its Celan motto, *Autrement qu'être* as a whole, insofar as it is a refutation of the primacy of onto*logy*, can be interpreted as a response to and philosophical demonstration of Celan's poetic intimation.[120] In fact, Celan's poetry and poetology have already traced and thus disconcerted the philosophical discourse of *Autrement qu'être* long before the reference to 'Lob der Ferne'. When discussing the ontological character of art, Levinas uses the example of the cello, whose being transpires and comes to the fore in its resounding: 'The *Being* of the cello . . . temporalizes . . . itself in the work of art' (*AQE* 71) before it—in this instance: music—'reverts into notes—identities which arrange themselves according to scales . . . from the acute to the grave' (ibid.). In view of Levinas's citation of the last three verses of Celan's poem 'Cello Entry' ('Cello-Einsatz') (*GW* ii. 76)[121] as a motto to his 1972 Celan essay, the use of the cello example in the later work in conjunction with the terms 'acute'

---

[118] Levinas notes: 'This chapter was the germ of the present work' (*AQE* 156). Interestingly, Levinas did not use Celan's verse as an epigraph to the original essay, 'La Substitution' (1968), which subsequently became the central chapter of *AQE*. One may speculate about Celan's potential influence on Levinas, who could have encountered 'In Praise of Remoteness' (in Denise Naville's translation) in the 1965–6 Dec.–Jan. issue of *Les Lettres nouvelles*, that is, at least a year before he publicly elaborated his concept of ethical substitution in 'La Substitution'.

[119] See *DEHH* 187; *AQE* 67–72.

[120] See also Robbins, *Altered Reading*, 131.

[121] This poem is included in French translation ('Irruption du violoncelle') in the volume *Strette*, which Levinas uses throughout his Celan essay.

and 'grave', which play a central role in Celan's Büchner Prize Speech (see Ch. 3), reveals itself as motivated by Celan's text. Similarly, the ethical concept of the 'desire for the absolutely Other' who 'does not fulfill it but hollows it out' (*TI* 22–3) is avowedly derived from Valéry's verse 'desire without default' from the poem 'Praise of Columns' ('Cantique des Colonnes') (Valéry, 120) and is thus indeed structurally disrupted by the poetic.[122] Levinas's master concept of the visage is yet another case in point: in addition to its philosophical and semiotic underpinnings, it is a fortiori motivated by Dostoevsky's emphasis on the ethical significance of the human face in *The Brothers Karamazov* and thus functions as a constant disruption of its own philosophical rigour.[123]

How does Levinas's metaphorically stipulated continuity between semethics and poetry in the common sense make sense semiotically? That is, how are Saying and Said, and, more specifically, the poetic Said, semiotically articulated? For—it will be remembered—just as any Said depends on Saying for its possibility, Saying depends on the Said for its witnessability and, according to Levinas, necessarily 'manifests itself . . . by an abuse of language' (*AQE* 75). Language, Levinas stresses, is both pre-ontological *and* a code (74). The interrogation of the semiotic continuity between Saying and Said involves the more general question of the continuity between pre-systematic and systematic semiosis. How does Levinas semiotically bridge the gap between the pre-systematic, infinite semiosis of human sinsigns and the codified, systematic semiosis of linguistic signs?

In analogy with his 'humanization' of the Peircean interpretant, Levinas 'humanizes' Saussure's concept of the 'signifier' (signifiant), whose linguistic character is dislocated in favour of its personalized grammatical meaning as a present active participle, that is, 'the one who signifies': 'The one who announces himself in and through the [linguistic] sign as signifying the sign is . . . [t]he signifier, the one who emits the sign' (*TI* 97–8). By *personally* fusing 'signifiant' and 'interpretant' in the human sinsign, Levinas semiotically conjoins semethical infinity *and* its inseverable relation to the Said,

---

[122] See Levinas, 'La signification', 143.
[123] See e.g. Dostoevsky, *Brat'ia Karamazovy*, i. 321–2, 342.

since 'signifier'—as one of the constituents of the linguistic sign
as conceived by Saussure—by definition implies the stipulated
totality (Saussure, 30) of a linguistic system, while 'interpretant'
by definition implies infinite semiosis regardless of semiotic
boundaries. The human being signifies both semethically and
systematically. The 'humanization' of a linguistic category puts
emphasis on Saussure's observation that the linguistic sign is an
'entirely *psychic* phenomenon' (28): both the 'acoustic image'
and the 'concept'—subsequently renamed 'signifier' and 'sig-
nified', respectively—are primarily 'facts of consciousness'
(ibid.). Instead of adopting Saussure's course of abstraction
from the individual speaking human being in favour of the
investigation of an all-encompassing language system, Levinas
foregrounds the fact that any element in a language system is
also a fact of human consciousness, that is, literally, human.
Replicating his rhetorical move with regard to Peircean semio-
tics, Levinas again employs the device of the inverted synec-
doche to conceptualize the human being as signifier.

Insofar as the Saussurean signifier is always already textual in
Bakhtin's sense, the human being must also be originarily
textual, without being any less human for that matter.[124] This,
of course, semiotically vindicates, while being itself thematically
vindicated by, Levinas's midrashic conception of interpretation,
according to which the human interpretant is always already
caught up in semiosis: 'The [person] is part of the process of
signification' (*AV* 136). The indelible textuality of semethics as
the ground of all textuality is further underscored by Levinas's
attention to the paradigmatic character of the Hebrew Bible.
After all, the paradigmatic instance of semethical interpellation,
god's interpellation of Moses, happens in a text: it is a dynamic
'whose reality, in fact, could, in the final analysis, only be
attested to by a text which is itself already part of the utterance
of [that] truth which it should be able to establish' (135).
Furthermore, Levinas's specification of the biblical text as
'biblical poetry' (*DL* 182)—in line with the common designation
of the individual units of the biblical text as verses (Fr.: verset)—
underscores the emphatically poetic character of semethics.

---

[124] In its scope, Bakhtin's broad notion of text as any 'coherent complex of signs'
resembles Derrida's broad notion of text as pertaining to 'all possible referents'
(*Acts*, 16).

As I have mentioned earlier, semethics always already involves the diachronic contamination of my response to the other's interpellation by the third, even though I cannot possibly be aware of it in my semethical response, since awareness presupposes a conscious subject, whose existence depends on its prior semethical constitution. The fact that semethics, as the most fundamental dialogic dynamic, involves the third, explains Levinas's insistence on the necessary 'reference of every dialogue to the third' (*TI* 313). However, while it is the originary semethicity of the human sinsign as always already diachronically traced by the third which conditions existential sociality, it is the factual impossibility of my ever being alone with the other[125] which justifies Levinas's additional conceptualization of the semethical interlocutor as signifier: the signifier by definition depends on a system of references, in which 'all terms are [synchronically] related' (Saussure, 159) 'to *all* others' (*TI* 313).

On the existential level, the entrance of the third means comparability, thematization, and the possibility of justice—in a general sense—as the 'union of a singular occurrence and a general law'.[126] Because I am semethically constituted from within a social totality my response to the other's interpellation is thematizable, comparable, generalizable, and subject to judgement on the part of the third. Levinas implies as much by using the term 'signifier', which complies both with Benveniste's repudiation of semiotic trans-systematicity and with Derrida's insistence on the necessary recursivity of signs, which are never 'irreplaceable and irreversible' unicities (from the point of view of the third). Due to its capacity to create existential universalizability, semethics can indeed become the foundation of a 'moral-political order' (DwL 30). Concomitantly, while ethics as the specific philosophical investigation into semethics 'must', according to Levinas, 'remain the first philosophy' (30), poetry, as the discursive correlate of semethics must assume its role as the corrective of both ethics and politics.

---

[125] As Heidegger puts it: 'Being-with [others] is an *originary* trait of Dasein's existence in the world' (*Prolegomena*, 328). It should be remembered that semethics is not historically prior to existence but logically.

[126] See Derrida, *Acts*, 18. Regarding the third in connection with justice, see *TI* 67, 69, 89, 281, 313, 334; *AQE* 33, 108, 115, 130–1, 144, 146, 188, 202, 204, 234, 245–6, 251; *AT* 112; *EN* 202.

The transition from semethics to active speech in its generic manifestations must take the route of the singular human being, or, in Kierkegaard's terms, the 'straits' of the singularity (*Die Schriften*, 112). The singular human being existentially emerges as the author of his or her utterances, which—by virtue of being continuous with Saying—are necessarily polyphonic, that is, traced by the voices of others. Just as I, the author, am traced by others' interpellations, so my utterance—as the manifestation and performance of my heteronomous constitution as a re-sponse-able subject—is traced by others' voices, to whom I actively respond, and, in addition, by myself as signifier, as an integral part of my utterance, as its interpretant. In this sense, Celan can claim that the author (of a poem) 'remains given to it' (*GW* iii. 198): not as its intentional origin in the romantic sense but as the indelible link between the semethic condition of language and its most ethical manifestation: poetry. In the case of written utterances, Levinas argues, the author's traces show themselves in his or her 'writing and style . . . in all that brings it about that during the emission of the message, which we capture by way of the [utterance's] language . . . someone passes purely and simply' (*DEHH* 200). Every utterance—and at this point Levinas's ethical analyses call for their metalinguis-tic continuation—is traced by its author's indelible existential situation and orientation toward the other: 'But even the ultimate discourse, in which all other discourses are stated—I interrupt it by saying it to the one who listens to it and who is situated outside the discourse's Said . . . This reference to the interlocutor permanently pierces the text' (*AQE* 264).

CHAPTER TWO

Mikhail Bakhtin:
The Metalinguistics of Dialogue

SITUATING BAKHTIN

Reading Bakhtin's and Levinas's works side by side is not only philosophically plausible given both thinkers' overall preoccupation with dialogue and otherness, but, more importantly, foregrounds their complementarity within an overall dialogic framework. As I have mentioned in my Introduction, because Levinas and Bakhtin investigate the same unitary phenomenon—dialogic reality—from two distinct phenomenological perspectives, only a synoptic reading of their works yields an integral picture of that social domain which undergoes a theoretical split in their writings. Rather than reducing Bakhtin's and Levinas's writings to a common denominator, however, by focusing on their abounding thematic resemblances—the mere tabulation of which only compounds the difficulties presented by each author—I point to some of their crucial differences, which in turn help to throw into relief their affinities. In other words, Levinas's and Bakhtin's writings can be engaged in a productive and mutually illuminating dialogue precisely because their numerous thematic points of intersection are predicated on fundamental conceptual differences. Even a cursory survey of Bakhtin's writings reveals his continuous interest in such issues—equally central in Levinasian ethics—as human interaction, responsibility, alterity, and the social significance of language, to name only a few.[1] Notwithstanding apparent shifts in topics and specific areas of interest, Bakhtin's works evince an indisputable continuity when 'his overriding goal . . . is seen as a philosophical [inquiry]' (*MB* 4) into the modes and manifestations of dialogue, which concep-

---

[1] For an extensive discussion of thematic resemblances between Bakhtin and Levinas, see Ponzio's texts on the subject, and Nealon, 33–48.

tually embodies 'the interconnected set of concerns that dominate Bakhtin's thinking' (Holquist, *Dialogism*, 5).[2] It must be emphasized, however, that the stipulation of intellectual continuity does not imply closure. Bakhtin himself notes the dialogic relation in his thinking between the fundamental '[u]nity of a becoming (developing) idea' (*LKS* 531) and his penchant for a '[m]ultiplicity of perspectives', his 'love for variations and a multiplicity of terms for one phenomenon'. This partially explains the 'incomplete state' (ibid.)—both in terms of expression and exposition—of many of his texts.[3] Clark and Holquist's insight that the continuity of Bakhtin's thought consists more in the questions asked 'rather than in the bewildering variety of answers he proposed at different points in his . . . life' ('A Continuing Dialogue', 101) implicitly points to Bakhtin's intellectual and methodological proximity to Levinas, who also presents a variety of responses to a fundamental set of philosophical (ethical) concerns. The two authors' methodological affinity is hardly surprising given their explicit adoption of the phenomenological method: like Levinas, Bakhtin emphasizes that his inquiries are phenomenologically descriptive, that is, informed by the investigator's

[2] See also Adlam, 45–53. I do not specifically deal with the hotly debated question of the authorship of the Bakhtin circle's disputed texts (for a list of these texts, see: Titunik, 'Bakhtin', 536–7; *MB* 353–7), taking for granted—on the grounds of internal and biographical evidence—that Bakhtin did—if not himself write—at least greatly participate in the development of themes presented in such texts as *MPL* and DLDA (the only two disputed texts relevant in the present context). I should stress that in the context of my enquiry the question of the authorship of the Bakhtin circle's disputed texts is marginal at best, as I do not focus on those issues on which Bakhtin seems to disagree with Voloshinov, the signatory of *MPL* and DLDA. Thus, Voloshinov's/Bakhtin's argument in DLDA concerning the groundedness of any utterance in an existential context recurs in *VLA* (72–233) and *BSS* (159–206, 306–28)—all texts signed by Bakhtin—which implies that Bakhtin either adopted some of Voloshinov's views (if the latter could be established as the text's sole author) or was already responsible for their initial articulation in DLDA. Similarly, the semiotic conception of consciousness presented in *MPL* is upheld in *VLA* (72–233) and *BSS* (306–28), which again implies that Bakhtin either adopted Voloshinov's views or already co-articulated them in *MPL*. Regarding the critical debate about Bakhtin's disputed texts, see e.g. Bocharov; Morson and Emerson, 63–4, 101–19; Holquist, *Dialogism*, 8; *MB* 146–70; Clark and Holquist, 'A Continuing Dialogue', 98–9; Titunik, 'The Baxtin Problem', 93–4.

[3] Bakhtin is careful not to 'turn a shortcoming into a virtue' (*LKS* 531), and admits that many of his texts are simply not finished externally. However, sometimes 'it is hard to separate external from internal incompleteness' (ibid.).

varying approaches to and perspectives on the object(s) of critical scrutiny.[4]

Bakhtin began his career as a philosopher, heavily influenced by German idealism, Neo-Kantianism, and phenomenology.[5] As Clark and Holquist rightly emphasize, it is crucial to keep in mind—without thereby disavowing intellectual development and growth ('A Continuing Dialogue', 101)—Bakhtin's 'philosophical base' as implicitly informing his subsequent writings. In contrast to what he calls 'theoretism' (*R* 18–19, 21, 31)—which subsumes the Neo-Kantian project of reinstating philosophy as the foundational science on transcendental axiological grounds, Husserl's attempt at inaugurating a scientifically rigorous transcendental epistemology and 'formal praxis' (*Vorlesungen*, 126–59), as well as such, more 'practically' oriented, endeavours as pragmatism and the philosophy of life—Bakhtin was from the start concerned with concrete human life as it is actually lived and experienced by singular human beings in concrete contexts and situations, and repudiated philosophical abstraction (as an end in itself).[6] Notwithstanding his opposition to theoretism,

[4] Insofar as Bakhtin attempts to capture the 'basic concrete moments' (*R* 52) of dialogic reality, that is, its invariable structure, he—like Levinas—performs Husserl's eidetic reduction (see also Holquist and Clark, 306; Pirog, 'Bakhtin', 406).

[5] See *R* 14, 35, 323–5; *MB* 4, 7–9; Holquist, *Dialogism* 3–5, 17–18; Perlina 13; Shein.

[6] I should stress that throughout my enquiry 'situation' and 'context' do not necessarily imply limitations in time or space. A person's concrete and singular situation may 'stretch' into the past (memory) and the future (expectation) insofar as certain singular moments in time and space acquire concrete and singular situational significance for the person in question. Bakhtin's opposition to 'theoretism' underscores his philosophical affinity with Levinas. Windelband defines philosophy as 'the critical science of universal values' (Windelband, i. 29). Husserl views philosophy as the 'the science which is motivated by the idea . . . of absolute knowledge' and depicts its task as 'scientifically to form, define, and elucidate this initially unexplained and blurred idea, to develop its principles and principal disciplines, and to apply these principles as ideal norms to particular instances of cognition' (*Vorlesungen*, 164). (On Bakhtin's relation to such Neo-Kantians as Windelband and Rickert, see *R* 13, 36–7; on Bakhtin's particular interest in Hermann Cohen, see *MB* 57–62; Perlina 13.) Bakhtin's opposition to pragmatism 'in all its varieties' (*R* 19) is mostly based on the fact that pragmatism, in its broadest definition, purports to be 'a genetic *theory* of what is meant by truth' (James, 515; my emphasis), that is, yet another mode of 'theoretism'. Bakhtin's critique of pragmatism also targets its implicit dichotomization of mind and action/'life', most obvious in Peirce's contention that pragmatism is the 'theory that a *conception*, that is, the rational purport of a word or other expression, lies exclusively in its . . . bearing upon the conduct of life' (*Selected Writings*, 183), whereby ('the conduct of') life and thought remain

however, Bakhtin's appeal to my singular Being and its enactment by me as bridging the presumed dichotomy between intellectualist and vitalist approaches to dialogic reality is very much indebted to both pragmatism and vitalism. Thus, Bakhtin's 'attempts to overcome the dualism of cognition and life, thought and singular concrete reality' (*R* 15) by unmasking its abstract-fictional character in view of the inseparable unity of singular life as 'an answerable, risky, and continuous act' (17)[7] perpetually confronted with challenges and demands, is highly reminiscent both of William James's synthetic conception of pragmatism and Dilthey's view of human life as a constantly challenged process; in addition, it invokes Blondel's philosophy of action, in which 'action' 'arbitrat[es] the contention between intellectualism and pragmatism' (Blondel, p. xxii).[8] Insofar as Bakhtin's 'philosophical base' underlies and informs his subsequent inquiries into language and poetry, an adequate reception of the latter largely depends on a clear grasp of the former.

THE PHILOSOPHY OF THE ACT

Similarly to Levinas, Bakhtin elaborates a first philosophy while displacing its traditional conceptualization as either ontology or epistemology (*R* 16, 25, 31, 34). Unlike Levinas, however—and

implicitly separated. Bakhtin's opposition to the philosophy of life is informed by his repudiation of Dilthey's conceptual dichotomization of the human (life-oriented) and the natural (concept-oriented) sciences (see *AST* 349; Dilthey, *Die Philosophie*, 69–70); it is equally informed by his disavowal of Bergson's abstract-theoretical notions of 'durée' and 'élan vital' (see *R* 20–1, 26).

[7] Following Vadim Liapunov's translations of Bakhtin's texts, I use the terms 'answerable' and 'answerability' in reference to Bakhtin's depictions of dialogic reality in particular.

[8] Pragmatism, according to James, is a 'philosophy that will not only exercise your powers of intellectual abstraction, but that will make some positive connexion with this actual world of finite human lives' (James, 494–5). James denounces the escapist character of 'all our theories' (501), thus—paradoxically—avowing pragmatism's socio-political significance notwithstanding its theoretical status. Clark and Holquist's oxymoronic designation of Bakhtin's thought as a 'pragmatic axiology' (*MB* 63) must be understood in precisely this sense: as being embedded in actual human life and relating to actual acting human beings. All in all, Bakhtin's 'pragmatism' is closer to Morris's and Carnap's deictic notion of pragmatics than to Peirce's and James's pragmatisms (see Morris, 6; Carnap, 4). Bakhtin's attention to the concreteness and singularity of human life and action equally participates in a Russian counter-tradition which opposes utopianism and emphasizes the concreteness of everyday life and responsibility (see Mandelker, 33–78).

this fundamental difference informs all further similarities and dissimilarities between the two thinkers—Bakhtin does not posit my pre-ontological, pre-epistemological relation to the other, which would warrant an ethics (in Levinas's philosophical sense) as first philosophy. On the contrary, Bakhtin attempts to develop a first philosophy that accounts for my active 'place in Being' in its ontological, epistemological, and social concreteness. Whereas Levinas philosophizes my passive semethical constitution as the condition of any kind of agency, Bakhtin's first philosophy sets in precisely at the moment when 'I have found myself in Being (passivity)' (*R* 42) and necessarily become an '*active* participant in it' (ibid.; my emphasis). At the risk of repeating myself, I should stress that the phenomenological transition from the levels of dialogic reality depicted by Levinas and Bakhtin, respectively, does not imply a 'mystically' pre- or non-physical level of 'Being' followed by Being proper. As Judith Butler points out, language 'sustains the body not by bringing it into being or feeding it in a literal way; rather, it is by being interpellated . . . that a certain social existence of the body first becomes possible' (Butler, 5); the other's semethical 'address animates the subject into existence' (25). Thus, the 'one who acts . . . acts precisely to the extent that he or she [has been first] constituted as an actor' (16).

The human act, Bakhtin suggests, is the relay conjoining the distinct realms of life. The presumed split between the 'world of culture' (*R* 11)—which would be constituted by the objectivations of our activity, that is, by domains of meaning, such as the sciences, arts, and history—and the 'world of life' (ibid.), in which we would actually 'create, know, contemplate, liv[e], and die' (ibid.), that is, the world in which our activity transpires, is an abstraction from the only true reality of the integral human act: 'Truly real and participating in the unique event of Being is this act in *its entirety*; only this act is completely alive . . . *is* inescapably—comes to be, and is accomplished; it is a real living participant in the event of Being' (ibid.).[9] Hence, a 'philosophy

[9] Bakhtin terminologically alternates between the 'event of Being' (sobytie bytiia) (*R* 15, 20), 'Being as event' (bytie kak sobytie) (24), and 'Being-event' (bytie-sobytie) (34). All three terms are functionally equivalent in Bakhtin's texts. His specific use of 'event' in connection with Being is overtly Neo-Kantian. As early as 1907 Windelband distinguished between 'Being' (Sein) and 'event' (Geschehen), which he substituted for 'becoming' (werden). 'Geschehen', according to Windelband, 'con-

of the act' (filosofiia postupka) (32) must assume the task of first philosophy: 'Only from within the actual act, singular and unitary in its answerability, can unitary and singular Being in its concrete actuality be accessed; first philosophy can orient itself only with respect to such an actual act' (ibid.). It is crucial to note at this point that Bakhtin's conceptualization of Being as event—following Windelband's distinction between Being as mere (stipulated) physical givenness and Being as it is irreducibly experienced by human beings—underscores the phenomenological character of the philosophy of the act: '[T]he *event* of Being is a phenomenological concept, since to living consciousness Being reveals itself as an event in which living consciousness actively orients itself and lives' (R 238). Thus, when Bakhtin refers to Being as event or to the event of Being, he always already implies Being as onto*logical*, that is, as an intentional correlate (in Husserl's sense)—not as putatively 'objective' physical Being—and, consequently, as fundamentally constituted through human activity.

In addition to its phenomenological significance, Bakhtin's ontological valorization of the term 'event' (sobytie) mobilizes its inherent morphological potential, namely, the semantically significant concatenation of the prefix/preposition 'so-' and the noun 'bytie'. In Russian, 'so' literally means 'with',[10] 'bytie' literally means 'Being'; thus 'so-bytie' literally means 'Being with'. Clark and Holquist point to Bakhtin's 'obsessive word play, especially with the prefix *so-*, indicating simultaneity in its aspect of sharing, which is roughly equivalent in English usage to *co-*, as in *co-author*' (MB 74). Being for Bakhtin is thus always already 'Being with', or, '*co*-being' (Holquist, *Dialogism*, 25).[11]

cerns the human being . . . takes place with him, in him, or at least for him' (ii. 19). Furthermore, Windelband distinguishes between 'nomothetic sciences' (Gesetzeswissenschaften) and 'sciences of event' (Ereigniswissenschaften), which are rooted in and focus on the 'singularity and incomparability' of actual events (Ollig, 57; Bambach, 75). Bakhtin displaces Windelband's opposition between Being and event by conceiving Being *as* event.

[10] Although 'so' functions as a prefix in 'sobytie', in itself it is a preposition. If the word following the preposition starts with a vowel, the 'o' is dropped; if it starts with a consonant, the 'o' is preserved (exception: words starting with an 's', which require the preservation of the 'o' for the sake of easier pronunciation). 'So' or 's' can also mean 'beginning with', as in: 's tekh vremen' (from those times on) or 's tekh por'/'s togo vremeni' (from that time on).

[11] See also Emerson, 'Editor's Preface', p. xl; Averintsev's and Bocharov's commentary in AST 385. Clark and Holquist point to Bakhtin's emphasis on the

In contrast to Heidegger's concept of 'Being with' (Mitsein), which is supervenient upon Dasein's originary concern with itself as 'thrown', Bakhtin's notion of Being as 'Being with' signifies the factual priority of 'Being with' over existence in Heidegger's sense. 'The Being of the human being . . . (both internal and external)', Bakhtin notes, 'is, fundamentally, interaction. To be—means *to interact* . . . To be means to be for the other and through the other—for oneself' (*PPD* 187). *In view of the intentional character of Being as event and in view of its originary interhuman constitution I henceforth refer to it—by way of displacing Heidegger's term along Bakhtinian lines—as 'co-existence'*. Emotions, desires, thoughts, words, utterances, cognition, understanding, and valuation—for Bakhtin, these are all acts in which singular lives manifest themselves; life itself, understood as a continuous train of experiences, emerges as a multi-layered and complex web of acts (of experiencing).[12] In analogy with his intentional view of Being as co-existence, Bakhtin's actological conception of life excludes purely biochemical or physiological processes, that is, not actively intended processes, which sustain life or Being in a general sense. In fact, the Russian term 'postupok', which is here rendered as 'act' presupposes intentionality and implies answerability.[13]

While Bakhtin does not deny Being as mere 'givenness' (dannost'), that is, Being as mere physical 'being there', he emphasizes that for the human being co-existence is never merely given but always a 'task' (zadannost'). In view of the perpetual task of co-existing, it is impossible for the human being to assume a neutral stance. Bakhtin points out—employing an overtly Kantian and vitalist terminology—that the 'world-as-event is not the world . . . as givenness; no object, no relation is

originary sociality of existence: 'Existence is defined [in Bakhtin's philosophy] as the sharing of experience with others' (*MB* 165).

[12] See *R* 12, 14, 20–2, 28, 31, 38, 50, 54, 66, 82, 143, 166, 229, 231.

[13] 'Postupok' (lit. the step taken) is only used in reference to human beings. Insofar as Bakhtin's philosophy of the act underlies 'the dialogism to come' (Emerson, 'Bakhtin at 100', 111), an ontological universalization of Bakhtin's master concept of dialogue as applying to all levels of life is only permissible in a figurative sense: Clark and Holquist rightly emphasize that the 'body's relation to its physical environment provide[s] a powerful conceptual metaphor for modeling the relation of individual persons to their social environment' (*MB* 175), without, however, being identical with the latter. Bakhtin sometimes uses the term 'akt' in the sense of 'postupok'.

given as something simply given, as simply being there; every-
thing is always given as a task' (R 35). Pure givenness cannot
possibly be experienced: 'Insofar as I really experience an
object . . . the object becomes a changing moment in the
ongoing event of my experiencing-thinking, that is, acquires the
status of something which is a task for me, and, more precisely,
is given to me in a certain unity of co-existence, in which
givenness and task, Being and "ought", Being and value are
inseparable' (ibid.).[14] In contrast to Kantian and post-Kantian
transcendentalisms, Bakhtin foregrounds the continuity
between mind and world (of which my body is presumably a
part), self and other, without, thereby, conflating the two. Any
stipulated theoretical a priori is always already the manifesta-
tion of singular co-existential activity, which implies and
presupposes my relation to the other.[15] Epistemological inqui-
ries into the Being of things in themselves or the possibility of
cognition (Kant, Husserl) are already predicated on the enact-
ment of singular co-existences; interaction, Bakhtin suggests,
underlies all modes of human engagement, mental or physical.
In paying particular attention to 'value' and 'ought', further-
more, Bakhtin underscores the irreducible link between episte-
mology and ethics.[16] However, Bakhtin, like Levinas, subverts
any transcendental attempt at establishing an a priori set of
formal 'oughts' or a 'formal discipline of values' (Husserl,
Vorlesungen, 4). Values, according to Bakhtin, are created by

[14] Hermann Cohen, who was a strong influence on Bakhtin, insists that the world
is not merely 'given' (gegeben) but 'given as a task' (aufgegeben) (Cohen, 142–5,
170–1). Regarding the philosophical significance of the terms 'given' and 'given as a
task' , see also: Kant, *Kritik der reinen Vernunft*, i. 15, 25, 66, 82, 91–92, 98;
Husserl, *Ideen*, 42, 156–7, 337–8; Rickert, 144, 371–83. In order to preclude a
tacitly Heideggerian and Sartrean retroactive interpretation of Bakhtin's writings, I
use the term 'task' rather than 'project' to translate 'zadannost'' and its cognate
forms. Bakhtin's use of the category of 'experience' throughout his early writings
emphasizes his partial proximity to the philosophy of life and his dislocation of
Kant's transcendental inquiry into the conditions of possibility of experience in
favour of its concreteness.

[15] Judith Butler suggests as much when she writes that the 'act, an enigmatic and
problematic production of the . . . *body*, destroys from its inception the metaphysical
dichotomy between the domain of the "mental" and the domain of the "physical"'
(11).

[16] Bakhtin's 'ought' translates Kant's 'Sollen': 'All imperatives are expressed by an
Ought and thus indicate the relation of an objective law of reason to volition' (*Kritik
der praktischen Vernunft*, 227). In contrast to Kant, Bakhtin abandons the term's
formally universal implications.

humans and are, consequently, inseparable from their concrete enactment, their continuous reaffirmation or displacement by human beings in concrete situations. My singular 'ought' is inevitably predicated on the concrete situation which I actively engage in at a given moment.

What are the claims and strategies of the philosophy of the act—Bakhtin's first philosophy? What is its philosophical task? First philosophy, Bakhtin writes, must describe the concrete, fundamental moments of the 'architectonic of the actual world of the . . . unitary and singular act' (*R* 52). These moments are: 'I-for-myself, the other-for-me, and I-for-the other' (ibid.). All spatio-temporal relations, sense positions, and values (scientific, aesthetic, social, ethical, political, and religious), Bakhtin observes, organize themselves around and are informed by these architectonic reference points, by 'these central emotional-volitional moments' (ibid.). In these lines, Bakhtin *in nuce* stakes out his projected enterprise while clearly delimiting it in relation to his intellectual sources.

Bakhtin's most important move is to displace Kant's transcendental edifice of pure philosophy. Adopting Descartes's discourse of building,[17] Kant purports to construct a 'system of pure philosophy' (*Kritik der Urteilskraft*, 17), or 'transcendental philosophy' (*Kritik der reinen Vernunft*, i. 64), whose cornerstones are supplied by his three *Critiques*. It is the first *Critique*'s task to provide—'architectonically, that is, based on principles [a priori]' (ibid.)—the construction plan for the entire philosophical edifice. Not surprisingly, the first *Critique* culminates in 'the architectonics of pure reason' (ii. 695–709). By 'architectonics' Kant means specifically the 'art of systems' or the 'science of scientificity in our cognition' ('die Lehre des Szientifischen in unserer Erkenntnis') (695); 'system' in turn implies the 'unitary subsumption of manifold cognitions under one idea' (696). Taking into account Kant's claim that the ultimate objective of such an art of systems is an ethical one—'universal happiness' (709)—Bakhtin turns Kant against himself by foregrounding his implicit Aristotelianism. This in turn justifies the displacement of Kant's abstract architectonics

---

[17] See Descartes, *Discours*, 28–9, 36, 45.

onto the concrete interhuman, ethical plain: After all, Aristotle, arguing that happiness is the supreme, most valuable good (*NE* 1095a), assigns its study to the *architektonikê téchnê* of ethics (1094a14–15, 28–9, 1094b13), to the architectonic, that is, leading art of ethics. It is important to keep in mind that Bakhtin reads Kant within an Aristotelian ethical framework, whose significance for Bakhtin is evidenced in his appropriation of Aristotle's term 'first philosophy' and his emphasis on action rather than (a priori) knowledge.[18] Specifying his overall emphasis on the act as the subject of first philosophy—this in itself identifies the latter as an ethics[19]—Bakhtin observes that the philosophy of the act 'can only be moral philosophy' (*R* 53). Notwithstanding its debt to Kant's emphasis on the primacy of practical reason over conceptual understanding and to the Neo-Kantian's axiological valorization of ethics over other branches of philosophy, however, Bakhtin's philosophy of the act radically departs from traditional notions of ethics, both material and formal. Insofar as it deals with the architectonic of co-existence, that is, that level of human sociality which underlies and informs the sphere of values and norms, the philosophy of the act can be described as a *co-existential ethics* prior to ethics in any traditional sense. My concrete, active relatedness to acting others makes the creation and enactment of values and norms possible in the first place. Any doctrine, science, or cultural objectivation is always already grounded in the concrete acts of concrete human beings, which condition the emergence of culture in its very diversity.

Given that the philosophy of the act purports to be the first philosophy by virtue of attending to interhuman activity as the most immediate manifestation of co-existence, it must not proceed in the same theoretist manner which is characteristic, according to Bakhtin, of existing forms of ethics; it must not abscond itself into the realm of philosophical abstraction.

---

[18] The end of ethics, Aristotle writes, is not 'knowledge' (gnôsis) but 'action' (praxis) (*NE* 1095a5–7). Despite the fact that he devotes separate treatises to the topics of ethics and politics, Aristotle does not conceptually distinguish between the two, characterizing *NE* as the 'study of politics' (*NE* 1094b13): their only difference consists in their immediate validity for singular human beings and states, respectively. Consequently, when he calls politics the *architektonikê technê* this designation equally applies to ethics.

[19] Ethics has traditionally been concerned with human activity.

Although Bakhtin never resolves the implicit contradiction informing his philosophical opposition to theoretism—the *philosophy* of the act is itself necessarily a form of theoretism—he suggests a way out by emphasizing that the specific philosophical description which he performs is the most immediate manifestation of his own, that is, Bakhtin's co-existence as a human being actively engaged in *doing* philosophy. 'Answerable consciousness', Bakhtin points out, 'is not based on a founding principle but on one's actual acknowledgment of one's participation in unitary co-existence, which cannot be . . . expressed in theoretical terms but only described and experienced' (*R* 41). Having theoretically established the contextual inadequacy of theoretical discourse, Bakhtin radically personalizes his speech: 'I, too, co-exist . . . I occupy a singular, unrepeatable . . . place which cannot be occupied by anyone else . . . The uniqueness of my co-existence compels and obligates me. Rather than knowing or cognizing . . . my *non-alibi in co-existence*, which conditions the most concrete and singular ought of any of my acts, I acknowledge and confirm it' (ibid.; see also *LKS* 512). Both Bakhtin's 'I' and its accompanying deictic markers testify to the performance of his 'truly real' act of writing in a singular co-existential situation. In the immediate context of the quoted passage, Bakhtin's first-person discourse reveals itself as anything but an exemplifying, philosophical *façon de parler*.[20] Rather—and notwithstanding the author's indelible structural absence from his or her text—it turns Bakhtin's outwardly theoretical treatise into a highly personal and almost confessional utterance, thus anticipating and announcing his subsequent metalinguistic inquiries into the functioning of utterances and their groundedness in the dialogic relations between singular human beings, which in turn permeate utterances from within. Bakhtin is very close to Levinas in that both emphasize that any discourse, regardless of its level of abstraction, is always told to someone by someone in a unique situation (see *AQE* 264). Bakhtin implicitly valorizes the semantic ambiguity of the genitive case in 'the philosophy of the act': it can be understood both as a philosophy *about* the act, that is, as yet another theoretism, *and* as a singular utterance in

---

[20] Derrida observes that the 'name of a philosophical subject, when he or she says "I," is always, in a certain sense, a pseudonym' (*ED* 163).

a particular speech genre (the philosophical), that is, as the manifestation of a generically specified discursive performance of its author's, that is, Bakhtin's, co-existence. It is only in the latter sense that Bakhtin can plausibly claim to obviate theoretism, which severs itself from its 'ontological roots' (*R* 44). Thus, a more accurate, yet slightly tendentious translation of Bakhtin's 'filosofiia postupka' could read: 'the philosophy of my act'.

Of course, the Bakhtin whose existential trace the reader finds in his text is a different Bakhtin from the real Bakhtin, who was born and died, to whom the reader has by definition no access. It is a Bakhtin who is reborn in every new reading, who is, consequently, never identical with his limitless singular selves, but who will have nonetheless always already passed as a truly existing human being and who will have always already informed the reader about this by personalizing his account. The philosophy of Bakhtin's act is not merely one among other philosophical approaches to dialogic reality. It is, due to its personalized thematization of the most immediate manifestation of co-existence, indeed the first possible philosophy, if, as Bakhtin argues, the category of the act is considered the basic co-existential category. The philosophical primacy of Bakhtin's philosophy of the act consists precisely in the discursive enactment of its very theme: The act of reflection transpires as the reflection of the act.

THE ARCHITECTONIC OF CO-EXISTENCE

Although Bakhtin's philosophy of the act reveals itself, within the overall framework of my inquiry, as posterior to Levinas's ethics—as a 'second' philosophy—given that the constitution of an agent must necessarily precede his or her agency, it is, from an existential point of view, indeed the first philosophy in that it purports to capture the originary enactment of co-existence and, thereby, lay the foundation for further knowledge.

The conceptual shift characterizing the move within dialogic reality from semethics to co-existence is most clearly visible in Levinas's and Bakhtin's respective schematizations of sociality. While Levinas reiterates the priority of the other, who interpellates *me* (in the accusative case), thus enabling me to become an agent, an 'I' (in the nominative case), Bakhtin takes the 'I' as the most fundamental moment in co-existence for granted. Whereas semethics could be formalized as 'the other—me—I', the architectonic of co-existence is constituted by the moments 'I-for-myself, the other-for-me, and I-for-the other'.[21] Although Bakhtin underscores my co-existential dependence on the other and vice versa, he clearly states that 'I-for-myself [am] the central source of my acts and active affirmation . . . of any value whatsoever, for the I-for-myself is the only point in which I am answerably grounded in my singular co-existence' (R 56).[22] In other words, Bakhtin does not problematize the initial emergence of the active 'I' by way of the other; although any active agent, any self 'needs . . . an other' (Emerson, 'Bakhtin at 100', 111), although it is 'a function of the other . . . without which it could not be' (*MB* 189), the self is always already an *actively experiencing* self. Bakhtin does not resolve the apparent contradiction between the stipulation of a fundamentally active 'I' and the simultaneous claim that 'I exist [only] with the help of the other' (*LKS* 515)—which suggests my (partial) originary passivity. A Levinasian interpretation of this apparent contradiction, however, uncovers an implicit supposition on Bakhtin's part of two levels of dialogic reality: the semethical and the co-existential. Semethically, I indeed owe my existence to an interlocutor; co-existentially, I am always already an actively experiencing agent, who needs the other not in order to be 'animated into existence' (Butler, 25), but, rather, as Bakhtin subsequently explains, to perform a central formative, aesthetic function (see below). Insofar as semethics traces every interhuman dynamic, co-existence can indeed be said to be heteronomous and fundamentally active at the same time.

The co-existential architectonic of human reality involves its participants in an interactive dynamic. In contrast architectural building blocks, 'I' and 'other'[23] are not static and do not congeal into an unshakeable structure but constantly reshape their relations in altering their spatio-temporal co-ordinates, in perpetually displacing senses and values. The co-existential

---

[21] Bakhtin's rhetorical valorization of 'I' is complemented by the fact that although both 'I' and 'other' appear twice in the formula, only the first-person pronoun is in the nominative case both times.

[22] See *LKS* 515; Emerson, 'Bakhtin at 100', 111; *MB* 189.

[23] The 'I-for-the other' is not a separate constituent but captures my awareness of myself as the function of the other.

architectonic of 'I' and 'other', furthermore, inevitably involves the 'third': not only the witness, for whom this architectonic manifests itself and who 'cannot [possibly] occupy a neutral position with regard to *I and the other*' (R 191) and thus necessarily participates and co-constitutes the co-existential architectonic, but also any potential third, who will have always already informed my relation to the singular other at a singular moment in a singular place, and who is implied in the term 'drugoi' (other), which Bakhtin uses to designate the other.[24] Similarly to Levinas, who points to the semethical significance of the third as informing my interpellation by the other (as both 'autre' and 'autrui') and explicitly denies the possibility of ever encountering the other without at the same time encountering the third, Bakhtin points to the co-existential, significance of the third in underscoring the 'fundamental difference . . . between the concrete experience of one's self and the experience of . . . all *others*' (R 66–7). While there is always a singular other facing me, the other always refers to the third. (The stipulation of the co-existential presence of the third in my relation to the other underlies Bakhtin's subsequent emphasis on the constitutive metalinguistic role of the third in dialogue, who either proleptically informs the constitution of dialogue as an interlocutor in the future, a 'superaddressee', or literally axiologically inflects the words exchanged between two persons.)

How do I actually relate to the other? How does the other relate to me? In analogy with Levinas's claim that semethical interpellation 'is not real but ethical' (*DL* 23), Bakhtin insists that my co-existentially active relation to the other is 'more than rational' (R 33): it is '*answerable*' (ibid.). I am always already answerable to and before the other from within my singular time and place, in which, Bakhtin writes, I have no 'alibi'. Bakhtin's insistence on my 'non-alibi in co-existence'[25] parallels Levinas's emphasis on the semethical impossibility of evading the other's interpellation and the obligatory response (Saying)

---

[24] Like the French 'autrui', the grammatically singular 'drugoi' implies a potential plurality of others. See also *BSS* 483, 493, 496; Holquist, *Dialogism*, 21; Gogotishvily and Gourevitch, 235.

[25] *R* 41–4, 46–8, 50, 53. Bakhtin's concept of my 'non-alibi in co-existence' directly informs his subsequent rapprochement between answerability and linguistic response (see Gogotishvily and Gourevitch, 179).

solicited by it. Levinas even uses the same criminological meta-
phor as Bakhtin when he depicts my response to the other as
'Saying . . . without excuse, without evasion or alibi' (*AQE*
223).[26] In co-existence, I indeed do not have an alibi, I am
always answerable—even for the (impossible) act of divesting
myself of my answerability.[27] My irreducible answerability,
however, presupposes my ability to respond, my response-
ability in Levinas's sense: because I am capable of responding,
I can become answerable.

Insofar as we are always already aware of co-existence, that
is, insofar as it is intentional, it transpires, Bakhtin suggests,
between consciousnesses. Consciousness, Bakhtin stresses, 'is
essentially identical with the *person*' (*PPD* 192). In contra-
distinction to Husserl's view of consciousness as the impersonal
stream (Bewußtseinsstrom) and *repository* of all our experi-
ences, Bakhtin conceives consciousness as the originary mode of
experiencing, as the very mode and performance of co-exist-
ing.[28] Architectonically speaking, the acting human being co-
exists as embodied consciousness (*R* 66), whereby the somatic
continuity between mind and body is guaranteed by the semiotic
make-up of consciousness and experience (see below).

In addition to answerability, the architectonic of co-existence
is predicated on three further moments: 'outsidedness' (vnena-
khodimost'), 'surplus of vision' (izbytok videniia), and the
oscillation between 'completeness' (zavershennost') and 'incom-
pleteness' (nezavershennost').[29] All of these moments parallel

---

[26] 'The unicity of the I', Levinas writes, 'is the fact that no one can answer in my
place' (*DEHH* 196).

[27] Insofar as Bakhtin conceives life itself as a continuous 'life-act' (*R* 51),
answerability is ultimately coextensive with a person's life.

[28] See *VLA* 90; Husserl, *Die phänomenologische Methode*, 44; *Phänomenologie*,
24; Pirog, 'Bakhtin', 406.

[29] See e.g. *R* 17, 21–2, 74, 91, 96–7, 139, 164, 173, 196, 222–3; *PPD* 199; *LKS*
507. Todorov translates 'vnenakhodimost'' as 'exotopie' ('Bakhtine', 506); Clark
and Holquist render the term as 'extralocality' (*MB* 79). I opt for Liapunov's
translation of the term as 'outsidedness' (see Bakhtin, *Art*, 204, 235). I translate
'izbytok' as 'surplus' in order to emphasize Bakhtin's terminological proximity to
Levinas. Although at least two other translations of 'zavershennost'' and 'nezaver-
shennost'' are available in English (Morson and Emerson render both terms as
'finalization' and 'unfinalizability', respectively; Liapunov uses 'to consummate' and
its derivations (Bakhtin, *Art*, 25)), I choose 'completeness' and 'incompleteness'
because these terms literally correspond to their Russian counterparts, replicating
the connotation of stasis invoked by the suffix '-nost''.

semethical separation, semethical surplus of response-ability, which involves a fundamental asymmetry between me and the other, and, finally, the infinite character of semethics. Outsidedness simply means that I and the other cannot possibly coincide in our respective spatio-temporal positionings. Consequently, co-existence involves my irreducible separation from the other. This in turn implies mutual perception—as is suggested by the formulae 'I-*for-the-other*' and 'the *other-for-me*' (my emphases)—and, thus, the indelibly aesthetic character of co-existence.[30] Given the irreplaceability of my place in co-existence, my apprehension of the other cannot possibly be homologous or identical with the other's apprehension of me. My relation to the other is 'radically asymmetrical' (Todorov, 'Bakhtine', 504), even if it may appear symmetrical to a bystander. No one but me can experience my very own co-existential non-alibi and the answerability it entails.

Outsidedness implies my surplus of vision with regard to the other's surplus of vision with regard to me. Bakhtin writes: 'A human being cannot actually see or make sense of his own exteriority . . . only others can really see and understand his genuine exteriority owing to their outsidedness and to the fact that they are others' (*LKS* 507).[31] My surplus of vision underscores my aesthetic, formative significance for the other and implies—insofar as it is based on outsidedness, which, as I have noted, is a crucial feature of my active place co-existence—my surplus of answerability as well. The other depends on me, and I, conversely, need and depend on the other as on someone who is solely capable of bestowing a distinct shape on my life, of gathering me into a whole by supplying those moments which are by definition inaccessible to me from within my singular

[30] See e.g. *R* 17, 81–3, 91, 96–7, 107, 173, 190. I foreground the Greek sense of 'aesthetic' (aisthanestai: to perceive, apprehend, understand). See Clark and Holquist, 'A Continuing Dialogue', 100; Emerson, 'Editor's Preface', p. xxxix; Averintsev's and Bocharov's commentary in *AST* 385.

[31] Similarly, Levinas stresses 'the moral . . . impossibility of seeing oneself from the outside' (*TI* 46). Both Levinas's concept of my semethical surplus and Bakhtin's concept of my surplus of vision are informed by Husserl's concept of 'surplus of meaning' (Überschuß an Sinngehalt). Consciousness, according to Husserl, constitutes horizons against the backdrop of which objects appear and are 'appresented' (appräsentiert); through appresentation—the fact of knowing more about an object than is actually perceived—the object necessarily retains a 'surplus of meaning' (*Phänomenologie*, 17).

place and time, such as 'exteriority, fullness of external appear-
ance, [and] background' (*R* 98). Without the other, Bakhtin
emphasizes, I would be 'dissipated and dispersed in the world-as-
task . . . and in the open event of ethical activity' (ibid.). I depend
on the other's confirmation and aesthetic completion. The
other's aesthetic productivity is predicated on his or her 'spatial,
temporal, axiological, and semantic [smyslovoi] outsidedness'
with regard to me. The other becomes the 'author of my life', I
become his or her 'hero' (211), and vice versa.[32] The author gives
birth to the hero 'on a new plain of co-existence—something
which the hero could not possibly accomplish' (14) on his or her
own. Pertinently, Clark and Holquist emphasize the fact that
although 'the self/other distinction is a recurring preoccupation
of many systems of thought . . . Bakhtin is the only major figure
to frame the problem in terms of authorship' (*MB* 80). It is
through the other's aesthetic productivity that I receive a body
localizable and discernible in the time and space of a social,
communal world; it is through the other's aesthetic productivity
that my singular 'field of vision' (krugozor) is complemented by a
communal 'environment' (okruzhenie), in which I acquire ethi-
cal, axiological significance and which exceeds the pure ethicity
of my singularly experienced ought. Owing to the other's
aesthetic and axiological engagement, my inner life and direct-
edness are correlated with the external orientation and value of
my body. The other creates me as a 'unitary and singular human
being' (*R* 154). In this sense, Bakhtin reiterates, 'it is permissible
to speak of the human being's *absolute* aesthetic need for the
other, for the other's seeing, remembering, completing, and
unifying activity, which alone can create an externally completed
person' (116; my emphasis).

However, rather than congealing me into a fixed form and,
thereby, depriving me of the possibility of 'open activity'—this

---

[32] Throughout *Avtor i geroi* (*R* 69–255) Bakhtin oscillates between the depiction
of the possible relations between authors and heroes in literature and the depiction
of the possible relations between human beings in terms of authorship. In 'real' life
the other human being is both my hero and the author of my life (*R* 177, 211–12,
222). Bakhtin views the modes in which 'people create other people in literary
authorship as a paradigm for thinking at all levels of creating' (*MB* 80). Given
Bakhtin's 'law of placement' (*MB* 70), according to which '[y]ou can see things
behind my back . . . that are closed to my vision' (71) authoring, although mutual,
can never be symmetrical. For my subsequent exposition of Bakhtin's treatment of
authorship, see esp. *R* 97–8.

would undermine Bakhtin's contention that only the act is truly real—the other's aesthetic activity incites its own transgression on my part, enjoins me to assume answerability: 'Those moments in the other's consciousness, which could complete us, are anticipated by our own consciousness; they lose their force of completion, and lead our own consciousness to expand its orientation' (*R* 99). Co-existence enacts itself by way of an oscillation between my aesthetic completion through the other and my simultaneous transgression of this ever displaced completion. On the one hand, I must be 'incomplete, open to myself in order to live' (97), I must 'be axiologically ahead of myself and not coincide with my mere being there' (ibid.); on the other hand, only the other can impose a *perceptible* form on me, that is, precisely create me as an answerable agent.[33] Since there is always more than one other, who aesthetically creates me, I am always already the hero of more than one author. Similarly, I as the other's author have more than one hero in my life (177, 222). (This will subsequently reveal itself as crucial in the context of metalinguistics. It is precisely because co-existence is originarily aesthetic that Bakhtin chooses to investigate its architectonic through the prism of such an aesthetically saturated activity as art, and, more specifically, poetry.)

How does the oscillation between my aesthetic creation by the other and my incessant transgression of the aesthetic bounds imposed on me actually transpire? By way of empathy, Bakhtin suggests: 'Empathy, the perception of the contemplated individual from within this individual, is the essential . . . moment in aesthetic contemplation' (21). However, empathy alone is not enough for aesthetic productivity to occur, since it would abolish the distance necessary for perception and aesthetization. Consequently, Bakhtin adds: 'The act of empathy is always followed by an act of objectivation, that is, by the positioning of the empathetically comprehended individual outside oneself . . . by the return of the empathizing consciousness to itself; only then, from its own position, does consciousness aesthetically

---

[33] Bakhtin's caveat that my aesthetic completion through the other ostensibly 'removes [me] from the open, unitary and unique event of co-existence [and] places [me] beyond . . . mutual liability and answerability' (*R* 98; see also 230) does not contradict his simultaneous insistence on my irreducible answerability. Rather, it points to the complex enmeshment of co-existence and its aesthetization.

form the unique, empathetically apprehended individuality' (ibid.). 'Upon looking at myself through the other's eyes', Bakhtin concludes, 'I always . . . return to myself' (99). Empathy and objectivation, Bakhtin stresses, are not activities which I may or may not engage in depending on my mood or inclination; they are ineluctable constituents of the architectonic of co-existence and as such an ever renewed task: 'I *must* aesthetically experience and complete [the other]' (107; my emphasis). Co-existence transpires as a continuous empathetic and objectivating exchange, between me and the other. I author and confirm the other as a 'determining axiological force with regard to my own life' (211), thereby making him or her the 'internally comprehended author of my own life' (ibid.); similarly (although I cannot possibly experience this from my place in co-existence), the other authors me as an axiologically determining force with regard to his or her life. Bakhtin makes clear that empathy goes both ways—from me to the other and from the other to me—without being axiologically symmetrical. Phenomenologically capturing my response to the other's aesthetic productivity, Bakhtin observes that 'those moments which I recognize and anticipate through the other become immanent to my consciousness, translate themselves, as it were, into its language, without consolidating themselves . . . without disrupting my life's unity, which—being always ahead of itself—never coincides with its given state' (99). Even if I were able to grasp my own consciousness in the very moment of its completion by the other, I *for myself* could not possibly be completed. I will have always already taken into account the other's aesthetic activity and surpassed it. I, not the other, will have 'the last word' (ibid.); and I will never say the completing word to myself.

Similarly to Levinas, Bakhtin introduces the topos of the 'visage' phenomenologically to specify my relation to the other: 'Before the hero's visage [lik] forms into a stable . . . whole, the hero puts on many a . . . mask [lichin] . . . How many layers must first be removed even from the visage/person [litsa] of the one closest to us if we are to see the person's true and integral visage [lik]' (91). The conceptualization of author and hero in terms of 'visage' or 'person' is not only thematically justified in view of Bakhtin's prior insistence on my co-existential

surplus of vision. More importantly, it continues and corrobo-
rates the theme of personal answerability, which Bakhtin sets up
as the fundamental 'ought' in his very first published text, 'Art
and Answerability' (1919): 'The person [lichnost'] must become
answerable through and through' (*R* 7). It is important to keep in
mind that the Russian terms 'lik' (lit. facial contours, face,
countenance), 'litso' (lit. face, visage, person), 'lichina' (lit.
larva, mask), 'lichnost'' (lit. person, personality) are semantically
and morphologically closely related allowing Bakhtin to move
from one term to the other without breaking the thus established
isotopy. Bakhtin opposes the person—a concept which is equally
central to Mandel'shtam—to the reified, objectified 'human
being'. The person, Bakhtin suggests, is a co-existential, ethical
category; it designates the concrete, singular, answerable agent
(*PPD* 191–5). Dialogic relations are only possible between
persons (ibid.).[34] Bakhtin's attention to the other's visage/
person (litso/lichnost') is crucial for his subsequent transposition
of these categories onto the specifically linguistic aspects of
dialogic interaction (see below). In contrast to Levinas, however,
Bakhtin's use of the visage/person isotopy is not so much
indebted to Husserl as to Dostoevsky and Scheler. Dostoevsky's
implementation of the same terms in such texts as *Winter Notes
on Summer Impressions* (1863) and *The Brothers Karamazov*
(1880) provides a particularly illuminating foil for the inter-
pretation of Bakhtin's writings.[35]

Suffice it to adduce only a few relevant passages from
Dostoevsky's works to illustrate their influence on Bakhtin.
Confronted with the materialism of the Parisian bourgeoisie of
the Second Empire as it belied the fraternal ideals of the French
Revolution (*Zimnie zapiski*, 105), with the 'soullessness and
heartlessness of Western life [and] its . . . unashamed contempt
for anything other than the pursuit of worldly gain' (Frank, 238)
in the name of 'individual isolation . . . self-preservation [and]

[34] N. K. Bonnetskaia pertinently notes: 'For Bakhtin . . . Being is emphatically the
Being of the person. Bakhtin's purely existential notion of dialogue originates here'
(*Bakhtinologiia*, 40).

[35] In *Winter Notes* Dostoevsky presents his reflections on impressions gathered
during two and a half months of travelling through Europe in the summer of 1862.
For the pivotal role of *Winter Notes* in Dostoevsky's oeuvre, see Holquist,
Dostoevsky, 48; Frank, 233. Regarding Bakhtin's familiarity with Scheler's works
and, in particular, with *Formalism* and *Wesen*, see *LKS* 135 and *PPD* 62.

self-determination' (*Zimnie zapiski*, 106), Dostoevsky advances his own ethical vision: '[O]ne must . . . become a person . . . voluntary self-sacrifice . . . imposed by no one . . . is a sign of the greatest development of the person . . . the greatest freedom' (107).[36] Availing himself of the morphological and semantic possibilities of Russian, Dostoevsky foregrounds the enmeshment of 'visage' and 'person' by observing that a person's/visage's (litsa) true security does not consist in personal [lichnom] isolated endeavours but in the 'communal wholeness of humanity' (*Brat'ia Karamozovy*, i. 342). This observation is preceded by the following contextually significant passage, in which the dying monk Zosima talks about Dmitrii Karamazov, addressing a small group of people including Aleksei Karamazov: 'Only once or twice in my entire life have I seen such a facial expression [vyrozhenie litsa]—delineating a human being's entire fate . . . I sent you to him, Aleksei, because I thought, your fraternal face/visage [lik] might help him . . . As for you, Aleksei, I have many times blessed you for your face/visage [lik]' (i. 321–2). Dostoevsky's ethical valorization of the connection between 'visage' and 'person' does not only already inform Bakhtin's earliest texts (long before he devoted himself to the explicit literary study of Dostoevsky's works in the second half of the 1920s), but also provides an additional horizon for the interpretation of Levinas's idiosyncratic phenomenological transformation of Husserlian Vermeinen.

Scheler's philosophical significance for Bakhtin's conception of the acting person comes to the fore when the former's distinction between the philosophically abstract 'ego' and the concrete existentially grounded experiencing-acting person is taken into account:

[T]he person [in opposition to the ego] *is the concrete and essential unity of being of acts* . . . The person is not an empty 'point of departure' of acts; he is, rather, a concrete being . . . Therefore, a concrete act can never be fully and adequately comprehended without the . . . intending of the . . . person . . . the person *is* and experiences himself only as a being that executes acts . . . the *whole person is*

---

[36] Liza enacts just such a self-sacrifice in Dostoevsky's *Notes from Underground* (1864). The ethical purport of Dostoevsky's text is evidenced by his emphasis on the question of freedom and will, which has traditionally been assigned to the domain of ethics. Dostoevsky advances similar ethical views in *Stat'i*, 63–4.

contained in *every* fully concrete act, and the whole person '*varies*' in and through every concrete act . . . the person himself, living in each of his acts . . . permeates every act . . . the *person* who lives in the execution of acts can a fortiori never be an object. The only and exclusive kind of givenness of the person is his *execution of acts* (including the execution of acts of reflecting on acts). It is through this execution of acts that the person experiences himself at the same time . . . It *belongs to the essence of the person* to exist and to live solely in the execution of intentional acts. (Scheler, *Formalism*, 383–90)

Scheler's text provides yet another supporting backdrop for my earlier interpretation of Bakhtin's concept of co-existence as intentional. Co-existence reveals itself as emphatically intentional insofar as it is enacted by persons, who, Scheler suggests, cannot possibly not intend the acts in and through which they exist. Scheler, furthermore, theorizes the relation between consciousness and person in terms which are hermeneutically conducive to an adequate interpretation of Bakhtin's view that the architectonic of co-existence transpires between acting consciousnesses; Bakhtin's claim that 'consciousness is, essentially, identical with the *person*' (PPD 192) echoes Scheler's contention that he 'who uses the term *consciousness* . . . as intentionally directed acts filled with meaning . . . may also call the person the concrete "consciousness-of"' (*Formalism*, 392). The person, Scheler notes, 'is the single and necessary existential form of [consciousness] insofar as we are concerned with concrete [consciousness]' (389).[37] Equally important for an understanding of Bakhtin's concept of the 'world-as-event', that is, 'world-as-co-existence', is Scheler's insight that a person—unlike objects—can never be 'part' of a world', but, rather, always acts in and enacts a specific world (393).

Bakhtin's valorization of authorship as the paradigmatic mode of co-existence does not only contextually mobilize one of its classical meanings ('creator'), thus underscoring my creative relationship to the other and vice versa, but it also reflects his conception of consciousness, and, concomitantly, of experience as fundamentally semiotic:[38] '*consciousness . . . can*

[37] In *Wesen*, Scheler writes that 'the Ego finds its ultimate individuation in its experienceable groundedness in the unitary *person*' (237).

[38] In what follows I do not claim to present a valid theory of consciousness but, rather, the Bakhtin circle's particular view of consciousness.

arise and become a viable fact only in the material embodiment of signs' (*MPL* 11); it 'cannot be given as an object . . . but only in the expression of signs' (*BSS* 309); 'there is no . . . experience outside of [the] embodiment in signs' (*MPL* 85).[39] If signs in turn 'emerge . . . only in the process of interaction between one . . . consciousness and another . . . [c]onsciousness becomes consciousness . . . only in the process of social interaction' (11). The semiotic development of consciousness (in a very broad sense as some sort of initial self-awareness), furthermore, which begins with any 'organic activity or process'—since '*anything and everything occurring within the organism can become the [semiotic] material of experience*, since everything can acquire semiotic significance' (29)—culminates in the phenomenon of the 'inner sign' (34), and, more specifically, in '*inner speech*' (29), the most 'subtle and pliable semiotic material' (ibid.). In short, consciousness is conceived as '*verbally constituted*' (15), as 'the *inner word*' (14). Co-existence, Bakhtin suggests, always already transpires as dialogue between consciousnesses; consequently, Bakhtin posits the '*dialogic nature*' (*PPD* 198) of co-existence *tout court*.

CO-EXISTENCE AS DIALOGUE

Bakhtin highlights the interhuman constitution of consciousness as marking the permeable '*borderline* separating' the 'organism and the outside world' (*MPL* 26) by depicting the development of consciousness[40] as a perpetual 'struggle for hegemony within us of diverse [razlichnykh] verbal ideological points of view' (*VLA* 158), which are capable of infiltrating us precisely because language—the core constituent of consciousness—does not allow for impermeable boundaries between persons. In contrast to Levinas, who conceives my relation to the other as an anti-Heraclitean dynamic of peace, Bakhtin stipulates the fundamental struggle between me and the other (*PPD* 238; *AST* 348). By using the term 'razlichnykh' (lit.

[39] See also *VLA* 158–9; *MB* 182, 206, 228–9; Bakhtin obviously adopts a Humboldtian approach to language and consciousness.

[40] Although at this point the text literally reads 'our ideological becoming' (*VLA* 158), it is clear that 'ideological' a fortiori implies 'consciousness', insofar as the '*word is the ideological phenomenon par excellence*' (*MPL* 13) and consciousness is essentially verbal, according to Bakhtin.

diverse, different) instead of, for instance, 'raznykh' (lit. different, diverse), Bakhtin, furthermore, subtly underscores the originary heteronomy of singular consciousness: 'raz*lich*-nykh' morphologically and semantically continues his earlier emphasis on the personal character of co-existence; it contains the morpheme 'lich-', which also constitutes the term *'lich*nost'' (lit. person, personality). Thus, when Bakhtin stipulates the constitution of my consciousness—and this means my constitution as a person—through the agon of diverse points of view in me, he posits the co-existential authoring activity of the 'other in me' (*R* 211). If co-existence transpires as the fundamentally active give and take between consciousnesses, that is, between persons, and if persons are discursively, that is, dialogically constituted, a person's most fundamental co-existential activity reveals itself indeed as an act of authoring, whereby authoring simply signifies dialogic activity.

Bakhtin's dialogic conception of consciousness and, hence, co-existence, enables him to operate with a notion of empathy which does not depend on such emotionalistic or psychologistic conceptions as 'co-experiencing' (Nachfühlen) or 'co-living' (Nachleben).[41] Thus, when Bakhtin writes that he simply acknowledges 'the indisputable fact that . . . empathy is possible' (*R* 107), without dealing with the 'psychological problem of empathy' (ibid.), he does not beg the question of empathy by relying on phenomenological evidence but tacitly valorizes a non-psychological theory of empathy based on language. It is precisely because persons are verbally constituted, because they are originarily dialogic that they can consciously, that is, dialogically, substitute themselves for each other—without, thereby, obliterating their singular and irreplaceable loci in co-existence. I can empathize with the other because we share the same verbal make up: just as interlingual translation is indisputably possible (*BSS* 309–10), so is interpersonal empathy, insofar as it is predicated on dialogue. Justifiably, Bakhtin writes that 'those moments which I recognize and anticipate through the other . . . translate themselves . . . into [my own]

---

[41] See Scheler, *Wesen*, 19. I use the term 'empathy' to translate Bakhtin's 'vzhivanie' in order to indicate his debt to a particular discursive tradition (including romanticism and vitalism). For alternative translations, see Morson and Emerson, 54.

language' (*R* 99). Empathy reveals itself as the exemplary mode of interpersonal translation, of the translation of one consciousness into another, whereby, as is always the case with translation, the 'original' is not obliterated.

Given that consciousness as a fundamentally active, co-existentially singular and, hence, answerable entity is essentially verbal, that is, dialogic, Bakhtin is indeed right in contending that 'I become conscious of myself, become myself only by opening myself to and for the other, through the other and thanks to the other' (*PPD* 186). Without giving up his place in co-existence the other is always already in me by virtue of the sociality, the dialogicity of language. As Michael Holquist notes: 'In dialogism, the very capacity to have consciousness is based on *otherness*. This otherness is not merely a dialectical alienation on its way to a sublation that will endow it with a unifying identity in higher consciousness. On the contrary: in dialogism consciousness *is* otherness' (*Dialogism*, 18). Language reveals itself not only as the person's constitutive feature, but, more importantly, the means by which persons are indelibly bound to each other.

Language is the communal constitutive medium which enables persons to interact, through which they infiltrate and create each other, in which they encounter each other. Because consciousness is essentially semiotic and because the sign is the social phenomenon par excellence, consciousness is essentially a borderline phenomenon, a threshold (*PPD* 186), existing solely on the interpersonal borderline. Persons enter into contact with one another through language; consciousness emerges precisely through the contact with another consciousness. Similarly to Levinas and Celan, Bakhtin conceives dialogue as an encounter, as the 'dialogic encounter of two consciousnesses' (*BSS* 333). Consciousness, Bakhtin stresses, 'consists precisely in [my] encounter with the other. This is the *highest level of sociality*' (*PPD* 186). By way of language persons 'travel' back and forth between each other, performing co-existence as dialogue. My translational relation to the other, furthermore, linguistically rationalizes Bakhtin's conception of co-existence as a substitutive, empathetic dynamic and retroactively vindicates, as it were, Levinas's insistence on semethical substitution. The dialogicity of co-existence also clarifies Bakhtin's emphasis on answerability: being constitutively dialogic—the 'word' (and, hence, consciousness), Bakhtin observes, 'is born [as a] living response' (93) to other words—I am originarily capable of responding to the other's address. My answerability is indeed based on my ability to answer, that is, on my dialogic make up, which in turn is grounded in my semethical response-ability.[42]

The fundamentally dialogic and translational character of co-existence always already implies understanding, since, according to Bakhtin, neither verbal response nor verbal translation are possible without understanding, which is itself brought about in the process of translation: 'The other's word posits the . . . particular task of being understood' (*AST* 348).[43] Understanding reveals itself as yet another central moment co-constituting the architectonic of co-existence as task. Understanding—the hermeneutic mode of a person's relation to a verbal sign and, consequently, to the other person as verbal consciousness—must underlie my dialogic reception of and response to the other person.[44] Co-existential understanding, that is, understanding 'in the proper sense of the word' (*MPL* 69), is, above all, 'orientation in the . . . given context and . . . situation' (ibid.). It underlies response as the basic constituent of verbal interaction. To understand another person's utterance is 'to orient oneself with respect to it ' (102). Insofar as the other's word or utterance always already posits the task of being understood, I must always already actively relate to it, that is, I must always be already actively engaged in understanding: 'In the actual life of speech any concrete understanding is active' (*VLA* 95). Moreover, understanding is already response insofar as I translate each significative element of an utterance addressed to me into an 'active and responsive context' (*MPL* 102): '*Any true understanding is dialogic in nature*' (ibid.).

Underwriting L. P. Iakubinskii's insights into the significance of the 'apperceptive moment' (Iakubinskii, 38) in dialogue,

[42] M. K. Riklin pertinently notes: 'Therefore, answerability is responsiveness: the openness of real speech' (Gogotishvily and Gourevitch, 179).

[43] Caryl Emerson notes that 'translation . . . was for [Bakhtin] the essence of all human communication . . . To understand another person at any given moment . . . is to . . . translate' ('Editor's Preface', p. xxxii).

[44] See *MPL* 68. Bakhtin underscores the co-existential role of understanding when he notes that 'the act is a potential text and can [consequently] be understood' (*BSS* 311).

Bakhtin notes that understanding the other's word involves its appropriation and assimilation within my own 'field of vision' (*VLA* 95), that is, within the 'context of [my] inner speech', which 'is the locale in which another's utterance is received, comprehended and evaluated [and] where [my] active orientation takes place' (*MPL* 118). Concrete understanding, Bakhtin continues, is 'inseverably linked to response as to an active principle: it is response which originarily creates the conditions for understanding, the active preparation for it' (*VLA* 95); the active reception of another's utterance consists in framing it within 'a context of factual commentary' (ibid.) in my own consciousness, and, simultaneously, in preparing a response to it. Thus, understanding is not only active, but, moreover, 'actively responsive' (*BSS* 173). Of course, this has been implied all along in Bakhtin's supposition that the other's word solicits understanding, which is, thereby, necessarily constituted as a response to the other's address. This means that I—as a dialogically constituted person—emerge in and through actively responding to the other. The architectonic of co-existence reveals itself as fundamentally hermeneutic. In fact, active responsive understanding turns out to be the originary mode of encountering the other, the very mode in which dialogue unfolds. Bakhtin's insistence on my non-alibi implies my non-alibi in understanding, which of course has a wide-ranging socio-political significance. The hermeneutic character of co-existence indeed implies an inescapable answerability on my part, insofar as I am permanently engaged in interpreting *and* evaluating the world I live in.[45]

Bakhtin's specific notion of understanding as one of the constitutive moments of the architectonic co-existence entails a distinction between 'meaning' (znachenie) and 'sense' (smysl) (*VLA* 94; *BSS* 189, 336–7): whereas meaning is the abstract-semantic correlate of a dictionary word, which is itself, according to Bakhtin, only an artificial abstraction from the word's originary dialogic character, sense transpires between dialogically *oriented* singularities in and through co-existential dialogue: 'Senses are shared among different [persons]' (*BSS* 321). Given that meaning is grounded in sense—that language is

---

[45] Bakhtin notes: 'You cannot separate understanding from valuation' (*AST* 346).

grounded in speech, in concrete dialogue—sense must, however imperceptibly, always already inform meaning. Bakhtin insists that ultimately 'there cannot be words which belong to no one' (335), that 'in each word voices resound—albeit, at times, infinitely distant . . . almost impersonal voices' (ibid.). In contrast to meaning, sense is constituted in response to an address and is thus intimately linked to understanding.[46] Moreover, since understanding is intrinsically axiological, sense and value are originarily enacted and perpetually displaced in co-existential dialogue. Unlike meaning, sense emerges 'between speakers . . . in the process of active, responsive understanding' (*MPL* 102) and is 'potentially infinite' (*AST* 350). Sense only emerges and transpires in and through dialogic encounters between persons or between the objectivations of mediated or unmediated dialogic encounters between persons: 'Dialogic relations are [also] relations of sense between utterances in speech communication' (*BSS* 325). Bakhtin's valorization of the co-existential significance of sense parallels Levinas's valorization of the semethical significance of sense as originary orientation and anticipates Celan's insistence on the constitution of poetic sense in and through dialogue.

The fact that co-existence transpires dialogically necessarily implies that it also transpires diachronically, insofar as speech is diachronic. This also means that two persons cannot possibly 'have' the 'same' time. In analogy with Levinas and Celan, Bakhtin posits—complementing his earlier emphasis on spatial co-existential singularity—a fundamental distinction between 'my time and the time of the other' (*R* 185).[47] In fact, even the stipulation of 'my time', which implies a certain stasis, a certain fixed temporality on my part, becomes problematic in that I—as a verbally constituted entity—must necessarily be fundamentally diachronic. In this sense Bakhtin—like Levinas—argues that my very co-existence, being fundamentally diachronic, is always ahead of itself, never coincides with itself (97–9).

Finally, Bakhtin suggests—thereby replicating Levinas's ethical

---

[46] Bakhtin defines sense as response (*AST* 350).

[47] See also *LKS* 523, where Bakhtin reiterates the co-existential distinction between my space and time and the space and time of the other. Clark and Holquist point to Bakhtin's indebtedness to Einstein for his specific view of time and space (*MB* 69–71; see also Holquist, *Dialogism* 19–21, 156–7).

attention to the third in 'every dialogue' (*TI* 313)—that co-existence inevitably involves the third.[48] In view of the facticity of the plurality of others any dialogic encounter will have always been informed by the immediate or mediated presence of a third (in a broad, non-numerical sense), who either—in the most immediate of cases—testifies to and thus inflects dialogue as a present participant or witness, or—in the case of his or her physical absence—informs dialogue by virtue of the fact that any word or utterance will have always been already permeated and traced from within by the co-existentially determined words, voices, intonations, valuations, and accents of at times infinitely distant past or anticipated others (*VLA* 89–90). Insofar as every word is continuously 'born in dialogue as [a] living response . . . to what has already been uttered' (93), and insofar as every word is 'immediately . . . directed toward a future responding word' (ibid.), which it provokes and antici-pates and by which it is in turn proleptically constituted, every word, every utterance, and every consciousness are constitu-tively triadic. The word's/utterance's 'internal dialogicity' (ibid.) indicates its diachronic character, which in turn conditions the inevitably diachronic character of dialogue. The irreducible diachronicity of dialogue will have always already placed its actors within a triadic nexus, in which past, present and future consciousnesses encounter each other. (The triadic character of dialogue complements and conceptually continues the facticity of the third in co-existence.)

Interestingly, Bakhtin's responsive conception of language, according to which a word is not primarily conceived as a referring sign consisting of material carrier and meaning (in all its historical varieties), but as a responding organism, whose ever renewed birth occurs in its perpetual re-enactment in dialogue, is implicitly informed by Husserl's notion of internal time consciousness. Bakhtin's consistent anthropomorphization of the word-utterance, its conception as a diachronic living being,[49] traced by other('s) words, to which it responds and which it anticipates, can be interpreted as a dialogic displace-

---

[48] See e.g. *R* 66–7, 117, 191, 195; *PPD* 183, 259; *BSS* 321–2, 335; *LKS* 527.

[49] Bakhtin refers to the word in such terms as birth, life, and behaviour (*VLA* 88–90, 93, 97), ascribes a visage/face/countenance (litso/lik/oblik) to it (85–6, 90–1, 110–11) to it, and endows it with the ability to 'glance' (*PPD* 415).

ment of Husserl's diachronic conception of human consciousness: the word itself becomes that living, dynamic time-space in which retentions and protentions join to produce consciousness as a dynamically extended continuum.[50]

It is crucial to note that the third in dialogue is not merely the 'superaddressee' (*BSS* 337), whom Bakhtin stipulates as a 'constitutive moment in [any] utterance' (ibid.), who represents 'absolutely just responsive understanding' (ibid.), who structurally informs every dialogue as a metaphysically or historically distant participant, and who 'in various epochs, depending on the reigning worldview, [takes on] different concrete ideological expressive forms, such as "god," "absolute truth" . . . the "people" . . . "science," etc.' (ibid.).[51] By devoting particular attention to the third, Bakhtin takes account, as I have suggested, of the facticity of others, of the fact that, being verbally constituted, dialoguing persons will have always been already traced by the voices and words of concrete—at times almost imperceptible or distant—thirds.

METALINGUISTICS

Given that co-existence is dialogic, it is exemplarily staged and indicated in and through verbal interaction and its objectivations (texts); it is precisely because consciousness is essentially semiotic that the most sophisticated semiotic medium—human language[52]—most visibly stages and testifies to co-existence as a dialogue between consciousnesses. Dialogue, it will be remembered, is a 'universal phenomenon, which permeates all human speech and all relationships and manifestations of human life, in short, everything that has sense and meaning' (*PPD* 248). Consequently, the study of the diverse modes of dialogue and its manifestations moves to the centre of the critic's attention.

[50] See Husserl, *Phänomenologie*, 100–21. A word's de facto spatio-temporal extension only underscores its phenomenological significance. Bakhtin's word concept anticipates Derrida's Husserl-based concept of 'différance' (*Marges*, 8). The reception of Bakhtin's writings in the context of post-structuralism focuses—among other things—on this particular aspect.

[51] I do not deal with the religious/theological aspects of Bakhtin's writings in the present context. For an in-depth treatment of the theological dimension of Bakhtin oeuvre, see: Coates; Gogotishvily and Gourevitch, 221–52; Adlam, 45–53.

[52] See Benveniste, ii. 60.

Not surprisingly, Bakhtin turns—following his philosophical and aesthetic inquiries into co-existence and authorship—to the study of language and, more specifically, to poetry as its most complex manifestation. This shift is thematically motivated. If co-existence is dialogic then it is only through actually transpiring or already transpired dialogue(s) that co-existence can be witnessed at all. This in turn implies that the stipulation of the dialogic character of co-existence already presupposes my actual experience of and participation in dialogic interaction. Notwithstanding its ontological posteriority, lived dialogue ontically precedes co-existence as a 'phenomenological concept' (*R* 238). From a purely phenomenal point of view, Bakhtin's initial attention to co-existence reveals itself as posterior to his subsequent attention to the manifestations of dialogue. Bakhtin thus performs his critique of theoretism in the very progression of his own writings—in successively moving away from what is still a rather theoretist and idealist position to a more concretely descriptive attitude.

Co-existence manifests itself originally in and is in turn informed by concrete utterances exchanged between concrete persons in concrete situations: '*The immediate social situation and the broader social milieu . . . determine . . . from within . . . the structure of an utterance*' (*MPL* 86); these 'extralinguistic (dialogic) moments permeate an utterance . . . from within' (*BSS* 312). Consequently, Bakhtin focuses on the study of utterances, which may consist of a sentence or a single word and are characterized by their co-existential link to singular speakers. (The change of speakers, it will be remembered, determines the boundaries of an utterance.) One of the immediate indications in an utterance of its groundedness in co-existence consists in its singular intonation—which most palpably evinces a person's singular valuation and accent: 'Intonation establishes a firm link between verbal discourse and the [stipulated] extraverbal context . . . living intonation moves verbal discourse beyond the border of the [linguistic]' (*DLDA* 102).

Since linguistics, according to Bakhtin, does not provide the necessary tools for the study of dialogue, being solely concerned with 'relations among elements both in the language system and in the individual utterance' (*BSS* 321) without taking into account the extratextual co-existential aspects of verbal interaction, the investigation of the latter requires its own methodology. The methodology which Bakhtin advocates is aptly called 'metalinguistics', whereby the 'meta-' does not imply that linguistics is the object of this new 'science of utterance', but, rather, that it addresses problems exceeding the scope of linguistics (*PPD* 395).[53] Of course metalinguistic investigations cannot 'ignore linguistics and must make use of the latter's results' (ibid.). Linguistics and metalinguistics, Bakhtin continues, 'study the same concrete, extremely complex and multi-faceted phenomenon, namely, the word; however, they study it from different sides and different angles' (ibid.). While the study of texts as linguistic constructs (including the study of the relations between texts as linguistic constructs) falls into the realm of linguistics, the study of the dialogic relations between texts as utterances falls into the realm of metalinguistics (*BSS* 321). Whereas linguistics deals with units of language, metalinguistics deals with the relations between units of speech communication as manifestations and enactments of co-existence. Thus, metalinguistics pertains to the same phenomenon as the philosophy of the act, namely, the architectonic of co-existence; however, rather than eidetically reducing co-existence to its skeletal structure, to its fundamental moments ('I-for-myself, the other-for-me, and I-for-the other'), it approaches it as an emphatically dialogic reality, that is, from the perspective of its discursive performance. Metalinguistics does not deal with just any type of utterance, but with such utterances which exemplarily enact and indicate the above mentioned aspects of co-existence. Thus, insofar as co-existence is fundamentally aesthetic, insofar as it is a dynamic of authoring, utterances which exemplarily stage and problematize authorship and aesthetization must be the prime object of metalinguistics. Such utterances are of course best represented by poetic texts: 'verbal art ... most keenly [stages] all the permutations of sociolingual interorientation' (*MPL* 122). The metalinguistic study of poetic or literary texts is thus called upon to facilitate and pursue—by way of a switch of attitude—what started out as a philosophical/aesthetic inquiry into co-existence.

Bakhtin develops metalinguistics in close connection with his

[53] Presumably, Bakhtin's term 'metalinguistics' derives from Benjamin L. Whorf's *Collected Papers on Metalinguistics* (1952) (see *BSS* 641–2).

analyses of Dostoevsky's writings, which for Bakhtin represent much more than a test case for his assumptions about language, dialogue, and consciousness.[54] Not only does Bakhtin develop central themes of his earlier, philosophical texts— such as the question of consciousness and the 'person'—in his Dostoevsky book, but, more importantly, he constructs an image of Dostoevsky in the light of his own philosophical presuppositions, which, as I have suggested, are themselves rooted in Dostoevsky's writings. Consequently, in the process of interpreting Dostoevsky's novels Bakhtin reveals as much about his own dialogic agenda as about his purported subject of inquiry; this clearly comes to the fore in Bakhtin's claim that Dostoevsky's poetics can only be comprehended 'in the light of Dostoevsky's fundamental artistic task, as it is *formulated by us*' (PPD 210; my emphasis). A brief glance at Bakhtin's reading of Dostoevsky's texts reveals itself as indispensable for an interpretation of Bakhtin's own position. What is it about Dostoevsky and his writings that makes both central to Bakhtin? What is Dostoevsky's 'fundamental artistic task'?

In view of the fact that, as I have mentioned earlier, Bakhtin's attention to personal answerability is directly indebted to Dostoevsky, the consideration of Dostoevsky's 'ethico-religious . . . worldview' (PPD 213), which Bakhtin summarizes as 'to confirm the other's "I" not as an object but as an other subject' (212), is in itself crucial for an adequate reception of Bakhtin's oeuvre. But—and this distinguishes Dostoevsky, according to Bakhtin, from other authors—in addition to simply possessing

---

[54] It is important to keep in mind that *MPL*, which—in the form of a theory of utterance—presents the Bakhtin circle's earliest extensive account of what later came to be called metalinguistics, was published in the same year (1929) as Bakhtin's book on Dostoevsky, which in turn enacts metalinguistic analysis. The thematic proximity between both texts is underscored by the fact that *MPL*, too, relies on Dostoevsky's prose for its argument (see e.g. 103–4). As far as I can tell, Bakhtin introduced the term 'metalinguistics' in his own idiosyncratic use during the period in which he was reworking his book on Dostoevsky, whose second edition appeared in 1963, in 'The Problem of the Text' ('Problema Teksta'), a collection of notes made between 1959 and 1961. Bakhtin uses 'metalinguistics' repeatedly in the second edition of his Dostoevsky book (see e.g. *PPD* 395–6). Insofar as the latter is not so much a revision than a more focused elaboration of problems discussed in the first edition, Bakhtin's explicitly metalinguistic approach to questions earlier discussed without explicit recourse to this term and, consequently, to the conceptual framework it invokes, retroactively points to the 'metalinguistic' character of the earlier text.

an 'ethico-religious worldview', Dostoevsky raises this world-
view to the principle of aesthetic creation, to a 'fundamental
creative task'; thus, he not only prefigures Bakhtin's ethical
philosophy, but, more importantly, paradigmatically stages the
architectonic of co-existence in the poetic mode. Dostoevsky's
achievement, Bakhtin notes, consists precisely in the successful
presentation of the person in 'aesthetic-objective terms as an
other person' (215), without reifying or 'merging his own voice
with the other person' (ibid.). While Dostoevsky was certainly
not the first to valorize of the person, he was, according to
Bakhtin, the first fully to realize 'the artistic image of the other
person . . . of multiple other persons . . . in the unity of a . . .
spiritual event [sobytie]' (ibid.), that is, in the unity of his
novels (ibid.).[55] Bakhtin's subtle emphasis on the thematic
affinity between his interpretation of Dostoevsky's novels and
his earlier philosophical text and, consequently, on the irredu-
cible link between metalinguistics and co-existential ethics—
unambiguously established by the implementation of the term
'spiritual event' to depict the constitution of Dostoevsky's
novels—is corroborated by his explicit concern throughout
Problems of Dostoevsky's Poetics with the artistic presentation
of 'the co-existential [sobytiinom] juxtaposition of integral
persons' (222). Faithful to his claim that co-existence determines
and permeates utterances from within, Bakhtin underscores the
necessarily co-existential, or, rather, metalinguistic character of
Dostoevsky's texts as utterances. Only their metalinguistic
character, that is, their concrete transformation and realization
through artistic means of co-existence interests Bakhtin from
within the metalinguistic attitude: 'Dostoevsky's worldview
becomes the principle of an *artistic* vision of the world and of
the artistic construction of a *verbal* whole—the novel. Only as
such, as the concrete principle of poetic construction and not as

---

[55] The 'tendentious' character of Bakhtin's reading of Dostoevsky's writings has
been emphasized by René Wellek and Joseph Frank, both of whom take exception to
Bakhtin's claim that Dostoevsky 'invented a wholly new kind of "polyphonic
novel"' (Frank 346). As Clark and Holquist note, Bakhtin himself 'came to
regard the Dostoevskian novel not as an absolutely unprecedented event in the
history of the genre so much as the purest expression of what had always been
implicitly present in it' (*MB* 276). I should stress that I am not presenting a
putatively 'objective' view of Dostoevsky's aesthetics but Bakhtin's interpretation
of it.

the ethico-religious principle of an abstract worldview is it essential for the literary critic' (213).

How does the stipulated transformation of worldview into poetic construction concretely manifest itself? In Dostoevsky's novels, Bakhtin argues—employing more or less the same vocabulary that is characteristic of his philosophy of the act— 'the author's word is juxtaposed to the fully valid . . . word of the hero . . . It is oriented toward the hero as toward the word [of another subject] and thus dialogically addresses the hero. The author does not speak *about* but *with* the hero' (*PPD* 262, 270). The author's 'external point of view [on the hero] . . . is deprived of the completing word' (258). 'Dostoevsky's hero', conversely, 'strives to break the completing . . . and enframing force of *alien* words about him' (265). Dostoevsky 'is interested in the hero as a singular point of view on the world and on himself, as a sense-creating and valuating human being' (252). In Dostoevsky's novels 'the human being never coincides with himself' (266)—this would imply the hero's completion through the author—since the 'person is only accessible *dialogically*' (ibid.). Insofar as true dialogue is only possible between independent persons or consciousnesses, 'the hero's consciousness is given as an other, *alien* consciousness, without being objectified or completed, without becoming the object of the author's consciousness' (ibid.). In Dostoevsky's novels the 'hero's every experience, every thought is internally dialogic, polemically coloured, full of antagonism . . . a *response* in unfinalized dialogue' (238). Concomitantly, the author's artistic stance toward the hero is, Bakhtin reiterates, 'a *completely realized dialogic position*' (270), which engages the hero as an incomplete, independent, fully valid (polnotsennoe) interlocutor. In Dostoevsky's novels, the 'hero is the subject of a profoundly serious and *actual*—as opposed to a rhetorically *pretended* or *conventionally* literary—dialogic address' (ibid.). One cannot fail to observe that Bakhtin's depiction of Dostoevsky's texts terminologically and conceptually corresponds to his prior depiction of the architectonic of co-existence. Hence, it is crucial never to lose sight of the co-existential presuppositions informing the elaboration of metalinguistics. It is not the singular co-existential situation of a presumably 'real' person 'behind' an utterance which is the prime object of metalinguistics, but, rather, the specific modes of the discursive enactment and indication of the intimated—presumed or actual—dialogic architectonic underlying and permeating utterances.

As I have mentioned earlier, Bakhtin posits not so much a putative ideological or intentional continuity between speaker and utterance, between author and text, but, rather, the textual manifestation of the relation between an utterance and its groundedness in co-existence, which reveals itself from within the metalinguistic attitude as the 'chain of speech commun- ication' (*VLA* 93–4; *BSS* 177). Bakhtin's metalinguistic approach to the nexus between the architectonic of co-existence and its textual enactment is highly reminiscent of Scheler's claim that 'in order to know about the existence of a [person], we do not need to know anything about his or her body. Even in those instances in which we are given a *sign* or a *trace* of a [person's] spiritual activity, such as a work of art or the experienceable unity of a willing force, we clearly perceive an acting [person]' (Scheler, *Wesen*, 236). Dostoevsky's novels, Bakhtin suggests, exemplarily stage, without merely representing, the architec- tonic of co-existence on the discursive level, thereby exposing it to metalinguistic analysis. It is important to note, however, that although Bakhtin develops and elaborates metalinguistics on the basis of Dostoevsky's novels, the insights gained in connection with Dostoevsky are by no means restricted to the latter's oeuvre or to poetry in general, and acquire self-standing methodological significance in Bakhtin's writings following the first edition of his Dostoevsky book (1929).

CENTRAL CONCEPTS OF METALINGUISTICS

In contrast to linguistics, metalinguistics studies the 'word neither as part of the system of language nor as a "text" excised from dialogic interaction, but precisely in the sphere of dialogic interaction, that is, in the originary sphere of the word's life' (*PPD* 418). Metalinguistics thus studies utterances, the most overt manifestations and objectivations of the architectonic of co-existence. Given that it deals with dialogue from a perspect- ive that is neither co-existential in the strict sense nor linguistic, metalinguistics must provide its own conceptual inventory so as not to subject itself to the conceptual strictures of discourses characteristic of other approaches to dialogic reality. More importantly, since metalinguistics is methodologically based on co-existential ethics, its conceptuality must be correlative to such co-existential master concepts as the 'architectonic of co-existence', 'answerability', 'outsidedness', 'surplus of vision', and 'completeness/incompleteness'. In fact, given the metaleptic relation between the discursive objectivations of the architectonic of co-existence and the eidetically reduced architectonic of co-existence, the former—as indicative of the latter—must necessarily evince the same features as those which have been established as characteristic of the architectonic of co-existence: answerability, outsidedness, surplus of vision, and completeness/incompleteness; in short, the architectonic of co-existence must always already be witnessable in its discursive objectivations. It is, therefore, important to keep in mind that the concepts of metalinguistics capture processes which inform the architectonic of co-existence.

In connection with his analyses of Dostoevsky's novels, Bakhtin develops his metalinguistic master concept of 'polyphony',[56] which metalinguistically corresponds to and informs the ethical concept of the architectonic of co-existence with all of its concomitant features and signifies the entire range of aspects characteristic of interpersonal dialogue as it is uncovered by Bakhtin in Dostoevsky's novels. Bakhtin summarizes Dostoevsky's ultimate artistic task as the 'construction of the polyphonic novel' (214). Bakhtin introduces polyphony not as a universally referential concept designating any multiplicity of voices, but as a specifically metalinguistic concept for the description of the discursive objectivations of co-existence in poetry. The concept's explicit valorization of 'voice' underscores its architectonic significance, since 'voice' necessarily implies the presence of a speaking person. Polyphony can thus be meta-linguistically defined as the instantiation of co-existential dialogue between independent persons, between a 'multiplicity of fully valid voices within the limits of one poetic work [proizve-deniia]' (240). Polyphonic analysis, consequently, aims at the

---

[56] See e.g. *PPD* 26, 31, 122, 184, 220, 226, 238–42. Although Morson and Emerson claim that 'Bakhtin clearly states that Dostoevsky invented polyphony' (Morson and Emerson, 231), as far as I can tell, Bakhtin only states that Dostoevsky is the 'creator of the *polyphonic novel*' (*PPD* 209).

depiction of the discursive encounters between singular, co-existential sense positions as they constitute a poetic work and not as they might have transpired outside the text. Polyphonic analysis deals with utterances within a poetic utterance, whereby the latter itself is conceived as a response in the ongoing dialogue of co-existence.

Polyphony takes into account and is informed by the facticity of the 'diversity of speech' (raznorechie), the 'diversity of languages' (raznoiazychie), and the 'diversity of voices' (raznogolositsa),[57] and may be artistically achieved—depending on the respective utterance's speech genre—by way of hybridization, the dialogized juxtaposition of languages, or the presentation of genuine dialogues.[58] Whereas polyphony is an analytical concept, which captures and interprets the artistic manifestations and objectivations of co-existential constellations, 'raznorechie', 'raznoiazychie', and 'raznogolositsa' are purely descriptive concepts designating factual processes, namely, that at any given moment more than one person addresses more than one person in more than one idiolect, in more than one sociolect, and in more than one language. Thus, 'raznorechie', 'raznoiazychie', and 'raznogolositsa' indicate and inform the architectonic of co-existence as a dynamic of concrete, 'actual measurements and ratios . . . and the endless variety that these may assume in specific' (*MB* 8) situations and contexts. While any utterance[59] always already presupposes singular persons, the diversity of utterances in turn always already enacts, informs, and indicates the architectonic of co-existence. Such eidetically constructed co-existential categories as outsidedness, completeness/incompleteness, surplus of vision, and answerability must functionally

[57] Emerson and Holquist translate 'raznorechie' as 'diversity of speech types' or 'heteroglossia' (Bakhtin, *The Dialogic Imagination*, 262–3, 428, 430); 'raznoiazychie' as the 'diversity of languages', 'heteroglossia', or 'polyglossia' (262, 284, 430); 'raznogolositsa' as the 'diversity of individual voices' (262).

[58] By 'hybridization' Bakhtin means 'the mixture of two social languages within the confines of one utterance, the encounter within the arena of this utterance of two distinct, periodically and/or socially separated consciousnesses' (*VLA* 170; see also 118). By the 'dialogized juxtaposition of languages' Bakhtin means such metalinguistic modes as stylization, variation, and parody (172–6). In all three cases, 'there is no direct mixture of two languages within the confines of one utterance—only one language is actualized in the utterance, but this language is presented in the light of another language, which is not actualized and remains outside the utterance' (174).

[59] In the remainder of this section I use 'utterance' in reference to speech, voice, and language.

determine and organize the dialogic interplay within and between utterances as the only possible, phenomenologically immediate, access to dialogic reality. Utterances are by definition spatio-temporally never identical and, consequently, 'outside' each other; at the same time, they complete—without thereby reducing—each other, by being spoken in response to and in anticipation of each other, by bestowing sense and orientation upon each other, by semantically and pragmatically complementing each other in a potentially infinite chain of responses (based on the inexhaustibility of the semantic potential of language). Any utterance, furthermore, needs other utterances as the necessary dialogizing background for its ever-contested self-definition, for the gift of its ever-displaced singularity. By being outside each other, utterances do not merely exceed each other but, moreover, acquire a certain 'situational dialogic surplus' in that each utterance is internally determined by a singular constellation of traces of utterances responded to and anticipated; this entails a singular dialogic— not a quantitative—surplus on the part of each utterance with regard to all other utterances. Finally, utterances principally imply answerability, insofar as they are spoken in response to and in anticipation of other utterances.

Utterances, however, do not emerge in a vacuum and are always, Bakhtin stresses, subject to the discursive constraints of 'typical forms of utterance' or 'speech genres' (*BSS* 180), whose use is determined by the situation in which a person finds him- or herself at a given moment, by a person's interlocutor(s), by a person's speech objective, and so forth.[60] Hence, the speech genre of an utterance—in addition to its intonation—is the most immediate and obvious manifestation and indication of an utterance's extraverbal context; it is the most obvious trace of the extraverbal situation determining an utterance, the most visible trace in the utterance of its position within the social diversity of speech and language (*VLA* 106, 111). Insofar as the 'various domains of human activity' (428) are discursively mediated (*BSS* 159–60), the latter's generic objectivations manifest and indicate the concrete performance of the former.

Bakhtin distinguishes between two types of speech genres,

---

[60] The question of speech genres, which Bakhtin extensively deals with in 'The Problem of Speech Genres' (1952–3), is already addressed in *MPL* (1929) (20–1).

primary (including all verbal forms of everyday interaction, such as letter, order, request, official document, etc.) and secondary (including all kinds of artistic and scientific—predominantly written—forms). Secondary, or complex speech genres absorb and transform primary speech genres and 'emerge in conditions of . . . relatively advanced and organized cultural intercourse' (161). Upon being incorporated into secondary speech genres, primary speech genres 'obliterate their unmediated relation to (extraverbal) reality and to others' utterances' (ibid.), retaining their significance and dialogic orientation solely within the whole of the work into which they have been sublated and which, in turn, functions as an utterance—albeit a complex one—in everyday dialogue. In contrast to primary speech genres, which are 'closely dependent on all the factors of the [immediate] extraverbal context' (DLDA 106) of their production for their adequate reception—whereby every utterance is a '"password" known only to those who belong to the same social purview' (101)—secondary speech genres evince 'relative independence . . . from the immediate contexts in which they [emerge]' (MB 209).[61] The absorption and transformation of primary speech genres into secondary speech genres implies that secondary speech genres are structurally metageneric, that is, utterances about utterances, and may thus intratextually enact encounters between utterances as they transpire, may transpire, or (might) have transpired in everyday life. Consequently, secondary speech genres are particularly capable of revealing the actual and potential manifestations of the architectonic of co-existence in its limitless constellations. Among the secondary speech genres, those are most conducive to an illumination and indication of the intricacies of co-existential dialogue, which, as I have mentioned earlier, explicitly enact and thematize polyphony: poetic forms of utterance.

It is important to keep in mind that the distinction between primary and secondary speech genres—although informed by an utterance's relative dependence on the extraverbal context of its production—does not imply that utterances belonging to

---

[61] I should repeat that 'extraverbal context' or 'co-existential situation' does not necessarily imply narrow spatio-temporal delimitations. Two persons, located at a relatively great distance in time and/or space from each other, frequently engage in primary generic dialogue, such as letter-writing, telephone conversations, etc.

secondary speech genres are any less situated, any less singular, less co-existentially contextualized. As utterances—and any poetic work, according to Bakhtin, written or oral, is itself an utterance responding to other utterances in the chain of speech communication—utterances falling into the realm of secondary speech genres are by definition equally grounded in singular situations, in singular co-existential constellations as utterances falling into the realm of primary speech genres. If any utterance by definition enacts singular co-existence in its dialogic responsiveness and addressivity, that is, as a nexus of interpellations and responses, and insofar as it clothes itself in a more or less typical form, poetic utterances—secondary speech genres in general—reveal themselves as only thematically and constructionally distinct from utterances belonging to the realm of primary speech genres. Consequently, a poetic utterance's relative independence from the immediate context of its production does not so much imply that its ties to the singular co-existential nexus of its production are loosened or severed than its ability to function despite the potential lack of information regarding the co-existential situation of its production on the part of its recipients. In contradistinction to primary speech genres proper, which *always entirely* depend on and are informed by the diachronic concatenation of their more or less immediate pragmatic contexts, secondary speech genres acquire additional dialogic significance by being able to create secondary contexts, into and within which their own and other 'real' or virtual primary contexts are absorbed and transformed, that is, in which virtual or purportedly 'real' personal encounters are (re)enacted and displaced in any shape or form on a variety of discursive levels. In the world of secondary contexts, which graft themselves onto the singular co-existential contexts of utterances, '[t]wo [or more] utterances, which may be distant from each other in time and space, which may not know anything about each other' (*BSS* 335), may be engaged in dialogue within the singular utterance in which they find themselves. Rather than aiming at ideological criticism, that is, at a facile ascription of a poetic text's features to its material (social, historical, biographical) conditions or at the tabulation of intertextual traces,[62] the study of polyphony (as

---

[62] In view of the philosophical presuppositions of Bakhtin's enquiries into language and literature, Kristeva's proclamation of the replacement of intersubjec-

part of metalinguistics) purports to depict the specific modes in which a person's indelible enactment of his or her dialogic position in co-existence organizes—morphologically, structurally, thematically, and so forth—his or her poetic utterances.

An apparently irreducible contradiction emerges between Bakhtin's stipulation of absolute answerability in co-existence, of my absolute non-alibi, and the concomitant postulate that I 'always speak in certain speech genres' (*BSS* 180): if I am always already answerable, that is, if my co-existential responses to the other are always unique and singular, how can they simultaneously transpire in typical, universal forms of utterance? In fact, this apparent contradiction informs Bakhtin's entire notion of co-existential singularity as based on the verbal constitution of consciousness: if I am verbally constituted and if words will have always been already spoken by others, from whom I receive them, how can I possibly be singular or unique?

While this important objection points to an ostensible conceptual dilemma at the heart of metalinguistics, it is in fact based on a premiss that does not apply to Bakhtin's argument. It assumes that singularity and, consequently, answerability consist in originality, which of course excludes the fundamental 'citationality of discourse' (Butler, 27).[63] If, however, singularity and answerability are conceived in terms of use and constellation, Bakhtin's insistence on the linguistically and generically heterologous character of speech does not invalidate his simultaneous insistence on personal singularity and answerability. On the contrary, the fundamental citationality of discourse works to 'enhance and intensify our sense of responsibility' (ibid.), insofar as every singular speaker becomes and must become answerable not only for his own utterances, that is, the enactments of his or her co-existence, but also for infinite others' utterances, whose resonances originarily constitute the person. What the speaker is answerable for is not the original creation of the utterance's linguistic material, but for each act of uttering itself: 'The responsibility of the speaker does not consist of remaking language *ex nihilo*, but rather of negotiating the legacies of usage that constrain and enable that speaker's

tivity by intertextuality on the basis of Bakhtin's writings (Kristeva, 85) reveals itself as a misinterpretation.

[63] See also Derrida, *Marges*, 388–90.

[utterance]' (ibid.). In contrast to the citationality of discourse, which is a linguistic axiom, Bakhtin underscores the non-citationality of utterance: 'An utterance . . . is always . . . something, which had hitherto not existed, something absolutely new' (*BSS* 330).[64]

Since any utterance is born in dialogue, since it 'cannot fail to touch upon thousands of living dialogic threads [and] become an active participant in social dialogue' (*VLA* 154), since it will have always already responded to and anticipated others' utterances, it will have always been already burdened with the task of assuming a singular take on the surrounding multiplicity of utterances, voices, and so on. While I cannot possibly become answerable for language (in the linguistic sense) or for my discursive make-up, I must become answerable for the singular twist that I put on the universe of utterances through my own utterances. This singular twist is the style of an utterance; in the style of an utterance, the speaker's dialogic singularity manifests itself most visibly (*BSS* 162–3). Bakhtin devises his metalinguistic notion of style in opposition to received—poetically, rhetorically, and/or linguistically defined—concepts of style and, in particular, in opposition to such stylisticians as Karl Vossler and Leo Spitzer who, contemporaneously with Bakhtin, investigated style as the reflection of an author's 'soul' in his or her utterance.[65] All of these conceptions of style, according to Bakhtin, suggest the possibility of a facile, monologic realization of my putatively unmediated relation to my own speech (*VLA* 83). Style—from the metalinguistic point of view—refers neither to 'the basic division of [utterances] into "high" and "low"' (*DLDA* 108), to an utterance's figural constitution, nor to a simplistically conceived reflection of an author's individuality in his or her utterances. In the most general terms, style, according to Bakhtin, consists 'in the [singular] juxtaposition and combination' (*VLA* 76) of (a limitless variety of actual or fictitious) utterances 'within the . . . unity [of one utterance]' (ibid.): the work. Above all, the metalinguistic concept of style implies that

---

[64] For Bakhtin, Caryl Emerson notes, 'two utterances can never be, and must never be, equivalent . . . His entire understanding of the word, and of the specificity of the utterance, invalidates the very concept of repetition' ('Editor's Preface', pp. xxx, xxxv).

[65] See *DLDA* 108, 109–10; *MPL* 50–6; *PPD* 394–5; *VLA* 77, 85, 87, 89; *BSS* 431–2; *AST* 339; Spitzer, 4.

'style is a social [rather than an individual or rhetorico-poetic] phenomenon' (DLDA 109) and that it, consequently, involves the utterances or texts of at least two people and, implicitly or explicitly, of an additional third. Insofar as co-existence enacts itself in and through speech, and insofar as speech clothes itself in speech genres, 'style is inseverably bound . . . to speech genres' (*BSS* 162–3). The selection of a speech genre is the originary manifestation of style, which in turn indicates the speaker's singular dialogic orientation in co-existence at the moment of utterance: 'Where linguistic analysis sees only words and the interrelations of their abstract factors . . . there, for . . . concrete [metalinguistic] analysis, relations among *people* stand revealed, relations [enacted] and fixed in verbal material' (DLDA 109). For this reason I suggested, in my Introduction, thinking about metalinguistics in terms of a pragmatic stylistics.

Bakhtin's metalinguistic concept of style defies any attempt at interpreting his insistence on the inseverable connection between utterance and co-existence in simplistic terms. Although any utterance, any text 'is always . . . the revelation of a person' (*BSS* 310), the mode of this 'revelation' is neither unproblematic and simple nor undistorted and unmediated. Just as a person perpetually (re)constitutes him- or herself in a complex process of dialogic penetration, so a person's verbal performances produce texts, whose degree of complexity and 'individuality' depends on their function and generic status. Thus, 'primary speech genres, which require a standard form' (163) are least conducive to the manifestation of a person's dialogic singularity; complex speech genres in general, and poetic genres in particular, conversely, are extremely conducive to the stylistic manifestation of a person's co-existential unicity. Far from implying a facile romantic-vitalistic supposition of self-expression, this signifies the emergence in the utterance of what Bakhtin calls—thereby yet again underscoring the intricate conceptual connection between the philosophy of the act and metalinguistics—an author's or utterance's 'stylistic visage' (stilisticheskii oblik) or 'linguistic visage' (iazykovoi oblik, iazykovoe litso).[66] A person's/utterance's stylistic visage is every bit as complex as a person's very personality. Conse-

---

[66] See *VLA* 85–6, 90–1, 96, 110–11. Caryl Emerson pertinently notes that Bakhtin '*visualizes* voices, he senses their proximity and interaction as bodies. A

quently, it reveals itself in degrees of complexity depending on the speech context, the interlocutors, and the speech genre: while primary speech genres tend to manifest 'only the most superficial . . . aspects of a person' (163), secondary speech genres—poetry in particular—allow for the contouration of stylistic visages in their respective complexity. In general terms, an utterance's stylistic visage comprises all aspects of the utterance which make it singular and unique—including, of course, linguistic (phonological, morphological, lexematic, syntactic, grammatical, semantic), rhetorical, generic, topical, and other aspects—which indicate the utterance's groundedness in a singular sense nexus in the chain of speech communication and which corroborate pertinent metalinguistic assumptions. Insofar as metalinguistics deals with written or oral utterances from within the metalinguistic and not, say, the historical-referential attitude, it creates and delineates the dialogically constituted author of the utterance under scrutiny, that is, it 'necessarily posit[s] an author' (Morson and Emerson, 133), who, if metalinguistic analysis is carefully and convincingly conducted, may plausibly 'approximate' the dialogically constituted sense position of the utterance's 'real' author. While the 'author'—who can only be experienced, according to Bakhtin, in and through his or her discursive performances—will, ontologically speaking, always remain a more or less adequately devised metalinguistic stipulation, his or her stylistic visage will indeed be indicative of a specific singularity's dialogic position in co-existence.

A poetic utterance's stylistic visage—as it emerges in the course of metalinguistic analysis—manifests its singular polyphonic make-up and constitutes the ultimate objective of metalinguistic analysis. An utterance's stylistic visage is thus neither 'mystically' continuous with its purportedly 'real' bearer, that is, with the utterance's 'real' author, nor equatable with its 'implied author': if 'stylistic visage' were interpreted as capturing an author's intentional continuity with his or her

voice . . . is one [person] orienting itself among other [persons]' ('Editor's Preface', p. xxxvi). Bakhtin's concept of the stylistic visage continues and underscores his anthropomorphization of language (see above). By fusing 'style' and 'visage' Bakhtin subtly polemicizes against Viacheslav Ivanov's claim that 'in order to find style . . . it is indispensable to relinquish . . . one's visage' (169). (Regarding Bakhtin's awareness of Ivanov's writings, see *AST* 374–83.)

utterance—in line with a simplistic reading of Buffon's 'le style est l'homme même'[67]—then the fundamental dialogic impossibility of uniform and unmediated intentionality would be disavowed; if, on the other hand, an utterance's stylistic visage were interpreted as another name for what Wayne C. Booth calls the 'implied author', then its groundedness in co-existence, in actual dialogue and answerability, would not be taken account of, insofar as the 'implied author' is the result of purely immanent textual analysis.[68] In fact, as Booth himself points out, the stipulation and construction of the implied author, who, as the 'sum of his own [conscious or unconscious narrative] choices' (ibid.) would monologically guarantee the 'unity of the work',[69] cannot possibly be maintained within the framework of metalinguistics, which uncovers the fundamental independence of voices and consciousnesses within poetic utterances.

An utterance's stylistic visage is thus more than its 'implied author' and less than the unproblematized expression of its author's 'individuality'. Insofar as any utterance is fundamentally dialogic and, concomitantly, insofar as style is fundamentally social, an utterance's stylistic visage always already involves a multiplicity of singular utterances and can thus never be the product or result of immanent textual analysis. Consequently, metalinguistic analysis approaches an utterance only in relation to other utterances—never as an isolated entity—in and through the dialogue within which it constitutes itself; in short, it studies 'polyphony' (in a conceptually expanded sense). Depending on the speech genre in question, metalinguistic analysis may focus— in the case of primary speech genres—on an utterance's relation to co-existentially distinct utterances, or it may, but does not have to, focus—in the case of a poetic utterance in particular— on an utterance's relation to other utterances within an utterance (polyphonic analysis in the strict sense). Furthermore, since any utterance presupposes a co-existential singularity, metalinguistic

---

[67] Cited in Wilpert, 739.

[68] 'It is only by distinguishing between the [real] author and his implied image that we can avoid pointless and unverifiable talk about such qualities as "sincerity" or "seriousness" . . . we have only the work as evidence for the only kind of sincerity that concerns us: Is the implied author in harmony with himself . . .?' (Booth, 75).

[69] See Booth's introduction to Caryl Emerson's translation of *PPD* (Bakhtin, *Problems*, p. xxiii).

analysis cannot possibly content itself with the mere disclosure of intertextuality. Whether it focuses on the dialogic relations between persons and utterances within one utterance or between co-existentially distinct utterances, metalinguistic analysis always aims at the disclosure of an utterance's stylistic visage and is, consequently, avowedly 'personal', insofar as the stylistic visage in one way or another indicates and informs a singular, dialogically constituted person. This means that the results of metalinguistic analysis are not formalizable or universalizable a priori. It also means that metalinguistics is a pliable method, (re)forging and (re)adapting its conceptual tools with every new reading—in dialogue with the text(s) at hand. In contradistinction to structuralist analysis, which, Bakhtin argues, turns fundamentally dialogic relations 'into [logically rather than dialogically connected] concepts (of various degrees of abstraction)' (*LKS* 530), metalinguistic analysis takes account of singular 'voices and dialogic relations' (ibid.) in their specific enactment(s). Consequently, nothing is principally alien to metalinguistic analysis (as long as it facilitates the delineation of an utterance's stylistic visage), including extratextual 'data'—historical, biographical, ideological, and so on—which constitute the utterance's co-existential context. As long as extratextual references are not used to boost attempts at reducing an utterance to the simplistic ideological expression of its author's dialogic position in co-existence, recourse to an author's overall, more or less immediate and relevant, co-existential enmeshment is not only metalinguistically permissible but indispensable, insofar as these extratextual relations inform and resonate within and are in turn indicated and informed by the utterance as participating in the performance of its author's co-existence. While such extratextual recourse is absolutely required for the functioning of primary speech genres, it acquires various degrees of necessity in the case of secondary speech genres, depending on the utterance in question and on the scope of the particular analysis: thus, in the case of occasional poetry (Gelegenheitsdichtung), for instance, such recourse is implied in its very conception.

CHAPTER THREE

Osip Mandel'shtam and Paul Celan: The Poetics of Dialogue

It is in poetry that, according to Levinas and Bakhtin, semethics and the architectonic of co-existence most overtly enact and manifest themselves.[1] From the ethical point of view, poetry's exemplary role is due to the fact that it discursively replicates and thus indicates the semethical subversion of totality by dispensing with apophansis and its semantico-referential corollaries. From the metalinguistic point of view, poetry most visibly stages and informs co-existence because it is most capable of discursively (re)enacting the limitless intricacies of co-existential dialogue by (re)creating—on various levels of discourse (thematically, semantically, rhetorically, syntactically, lexically)—a potentially limitless number of (secondary) co-existential contexts; in short, poetry's metalinguistically exemplary role is due to its capacity to be polyphonic, that is, to engage consciousnesses and utterances in a potentially limitless variety of dialogic encounters. Consequently, just as poetry necessarily complements and throws into relief semethics and the architectonic of co-existence within the multilayered dialogue of human reality, so the poetics of dialogue metadiscursively complements the ethics and meta-linguistics of dialogue in explicitly focusing on the dialogically most significant speech genre.

While Levinas's inclusive notion of poetry[2] presents no conceptual or generic difficulties regarding its significance as the discursive crest of dialogue and is easily adoptable and instrumentalizable within the framework of a poetics of dialogue, Bakhtin's heterogeneous and notoriously discriminatory view of poetry in the narrow sense does not allow for its equally smooth functionalization within such a framework. Bakhtin's comments on poetry and its metalinguistic significance are far from uniform

---

[1] See 'Introduction', n. 5. [2] See Ch. 1, n. 116.

or unambiguous, and are in need of critical scrutiny. Thus, before embarking upon my discussion of Mandel'shtam's and Celan's texts in the light of ethics and metalinguistics I would like to address the vexed question of Bakhtin's relation to poetry, and to Mandel'shtam in particular.

THE METALINGUISTICS OF POETRY

Highlighting Bakhtin's devaluation of poetry in the narrow sense[3] accompanied by the simultaneous valorization of novelistic discourse has become a commonplace in Bakhtin criticism.[4] In contrast to novelistic discourse, which Bakhtin suggests, (ideally) artistically enacts the word's 'originary dialogicity' (iskonnaia dialogichnost') (*VLA* 88)[5]—due to its presumed ability to stage the social diversity of speech and languages by juxtaposing consciousnesses, points of view, utterances, languages, and styles without subjecting them to the author's unifying and authoritative discourse—poetry 'does not artistically put to use the word's natural dialogicity' (98), being informed by a 'single (i.e. author's) language and verbal consciousness' (99). Poetry, Bakhtin argues, is predicated on the 'idea of a unitary and singular language and a unitary and monologically sealed-off utterance' (109). The '[u]nitaryness and singularity of [poetic] language constitute the indispensable

---

[3] See e.g. *VLA* 98, 144. Bakhtin distinguishes between poetry in general, which also includes the 'novelistic word' (*VLA* 82), and poetry in the narrow sense, which presumably comprises such poetic modes as the lyric, the encomial ode, and so forth, that is, personalized and/or highly organized modes of poetic speech, whose language blatantly differs from the languages spoken in the co-existential contexts of their production (see esp. *R* 82–4, 222–7; *PPD* 415; *VLA* 82, 91; *BSS* 480; *LKS* 528). Regarding the conception of lyric poetry as private, personal, and emotionalized, in short, as the more or less unmediated expression of its author's states of mind, which was prevalent in Russia at the beginning of the twentieth century, see Zhirmunskii, 123, 131–2. Since Bakhtin never defines his concept of poetry in the narrow sense, it can only remain an elusive backdrop for his discussion of novelistic discourse. I henceforth use 'poetry' and 'poetic' in reference to poetry in the narrow sense, in particular.

[4] See e.g. Lehmann, 'Ambivalenz und Dialogizität', 373; Lachmann, *Dialogizität*, 51, 55; Stierle and Warning, 489–515; Todorov, *Mikhail Bakhtin*, 64–5; Morson and Emerson 319–25.

[5] Bakhtin also speaks of the word's 'natural dialogicity' (*VLA* 98), 'internal dialogicity' (93, 95–6, 140, 143), and external 'dialogic orientation' (92). I translate 'dialogichnost'' as 'dialogicity' and not as 'dialogism' in order to mark Bakhtin's own distinction between 'dialogizm' (*PPD* 185, 190–1, 220) and 'dialogichnost''.

condition for the unmediated realization of intentional . . .
individuality . . . and its monologic continuity' (ibid.). One of
the primary means to achieve such monologic closure consists in
the imposition of unitary rhythmic form on the poetic utterance:

By allowing for the unmediated participation of every aspect [within
the poetic utterance] in the intonational system of the whole . . .
rhythm mortifies in their very conception those social-verbal universes
and visages/persons, which are potentially ingrained in every word: in
any case, rhythm imposes definite boundaries upon them and does not
allow them to unfold or materialize. Rhythm strengthens and tightens
even further the unity and self-enclosedness of . . . poetic style and of
the unitary language stipulated by this style. (110–11)[6]

It is important to note that in Bakhtin's writings 'rhythm'
signifies not only—and not so much—the interplay between
an utterance's metrical arrangement and a language's accentual
system, but, more importantly, 'schema' and 'form' (in line with
its Greek array of meanings).[7] Thus, the degree of a poetic
utterance's rhythmic consistency metalinguistically corresponds
to and indicates the degree of a person's aesthetic completion by
the other in co-existence, whose temporal aspect Bakhtin depicts
in terms of rhythmic completion (*R* 178–84).

In contrast to novelistic discourse, which artistically stages
any word's originary heterologous character and refraction by
and through other(s') words and consciousnesses on its way to
its object,[8] poetry suggests both words' unmediated availability
to their author(s) and their unmediated link to their objects—as
if they were 'severed from any interaction with alien words'
(*VLA* 98). In poetry, the author 'fully realizes himself . . .
utilizing each form, each word, each expression according to
their immediate destinations (that is, "without quotation
marks"), as the unmediated expressions of his intentions'
(ibid.).[9] Poetry somehow overcomes the impossibility of unme-
diated speech and stages both the author's and his or her words'
unrefracted intentionality.[10] In poetry all traces of the social

---

[6] See also Levinas, 'La Réalité'; *TI* 222.

[7] See Benveniste, i. 328–9. Bakhtin was, after all, a trained classicist.

[8] By 'object' Bakhtin means both meaning and referent.

[9] See also *PPD* 415: 'Poetic speech requires the uniformity of all words, their reduction to one common denominator.'

[10] Bakhtin claims 'direct . . . intentionality' for the poet and for poetic language itself (*VLA* 99); while the poet presumably has unmediated intentional control over

diversity of speech and languages are erased in favour of a 'tense discursive unity' (111). Within the framework of Bakhtin's rapprochement between forms of utterance and forms of political authority—dialogue and monologue are correlative of non-repressive and (potentially) repressive political contexts, respectively (*VLA* 86, 154–8; *PPD* 285–8)—and his unambiguous advocation of personal freedom and incompleteness, poetry finds itself on the side of the implicitly repudiated official discourses of state and power:

At the time when major divisions of the poetic genres were developing under the influence of the unifying, centralizing, centripetal forces of verbal-ideological life, the novel and those artistic prose-genres that gravitate toward it were being historically shaped by the current of decentralizing, centrifugal forces. At the time when poetry was accomplishing the task of cultural, national, and political centralization of the verbal-ideological world on the higher official socio-ideological levels, on the lower levels, on the stages of local fairs and at spectacles the buffoonery of the diversity of speech and languages sounded forth, ridiculing all 'languages'; there developed the literature of the fabliaux and Schwänke, of street songs, folksayings, jokes, where there was no language-center at all, where there was to be found a lively play with the 'languages' of poets, scholars, monks, knights and others, where all languages were masks and where no language could claim to be . . . authentic [and authoritative, all of which ultimately led to and crystallized in the novelistic genre]. (*The Dialogic Imagination*, 272–3; trans. modified)[11]

Bakhtin's repudiation of poetry on the grounds of its putative monologicity raises several questions: if every word is born in dialogue, that is, if every word is internally and externally dialogic, how can there be utterances which would not be dialogic? Does poetry necessarily have to be monologic? Can it be that Bakhtin's axiological distinction between poetry and novelistic discourse is polemical rather than essentializing? What kind of notion of poetic language underlies Bakhtin's

his or her poetic utterances and the objects of these utterances, words within and between utterances in turn directly relate to each other and to their objects.

[11] Bakhtin's distinction between poetry and novelistic discourse is informed by a traditional, classical, and neoclassical concept of poetry—based on Horace's 'utilis urbi' (*Epistles*, ii. 124)—according to which poetry is in alliance with power and promulgates reigning or desired social and moral norms. For a concise discussion of the link between poetry and power, see also Attridge, *Peculiar Language*, 35–40.

view of poetry? Is Bakhtin's socio-political denigration of poetry not belied by such poetry which avowedly counteracts 'official' and 'centralizing' discourses, such as Mandel'shtam's famous anti-Stalinist poems (*MSS* iii: 29, 64)?[12]

The tension inherent in Bakhtin's stipulation of the irreducible dialogicity of language and his concurrent claim that certain forms of utterance are (relatively) monologic has—to the best of my knowledge—been most pointedly discussed by Ken Hirschkop. Insofar as any utterance is, according to Bakhtin, 'essentially dialogical' (Hirschkop, 23), poetry, too, Hirschkop argues, must be 'dialogical; it just pretends that this is not the case' (ibid.). Dialogicity, Hirschkop suggests, is not only possible in, but, in fact, always already constitutes poetry. Poetic monologicity reveals itself as a matter of functionalization and intention rather than essence or genre: poetry and novelistic discourse are two possibilities of an author's 'intention toward language' (Benjamin, 57); in poetry, the word's natural dialogicity, that is, the very dialogic make-up of co-existence does not become the 'principle of concrete poetic construction' (*PPD* 213), does not overtly manifest itself 'in poetic style' (*VLA* 98), does not define a poem's stylistic visage.

Poetry and novelistic discourse reveal themselves as the diametrically opposed modalities of literary discourse, marking, as it were, the lower and the upper limits, respectively, of the degree of an utterance's performance of co-existential dialogue, that is, an utterance's polyphony. Poetry is thus not discourse which, by adhering to certain, commonly accepted structural and prosodic criteria—such as stanzaic division, metrical arrangement, or simply linear discontinuity—quasi-automatically obtains its generic stamp; rather, it is discourse which 'produces or reproduces a relation of submission to an authoritative language, whereas [novelistic discourse] subverts this authority' (Hirschkop, 27). Consequently, as Bakhtin himself admits, novels can be monologic (*PPD* 262–3, 303, 395, 405–6), while poems can be just as 'novelistic', that is, polyphonic or dialogic as, say, Dostoevsky's novels: 'Of course, here [in poetry], too, works are possible which do not reduce their entire verbal material to one common denominator' (415); 'of course . . . even in strictly poetic

---

[12] All references to Mandel'shtam's poems follow the numeration in *MSS* and are cited according to the volume and poem number separated by a colon.

[utterances] . . . internally dialogic [that is, polyphonic] speech is possible' (*VLA* 138). All in all, Bakhtin's metalinguistic distinction between poetry and novelistic discourse testifies to a socio-political and functional rather than essentializing approach to poetic and novelistic discourse based on the 'difference of political effect' (Hirschkop, 32). Clark and Holquist pertinently note: 'Bakhtin assigns the term "novel" to whatever form of expression within a given literary [and socio-political] system reveals the limits of that system as inadequate, imposed, or arbitrary' (*MB* 276).

In conceding the possibility of dialogic, that is, polyphonic poetry, Bakhtin implicitly acknowledges the fundamentally dialogic constitution of poetry as a linguistic product and takes account of the historical facticity of poetry which does not reduce its 'verbal material to one common denominator': as 'Heine's, Barbier's, partially Nekrasov's and others' "prosaic" lyric poetry' (*PPD* 415) demonstrates, poetic works which stage polyphony are undeniably possible, and——although 'rare in the nineteenth century' (ibid.)—numerous in the twentieth, in which 'a radical prosaicization of lyric poetry occurs' (ibid.).[13] While Bakhtin, unfortunately, does not divulge which twentieth-century poetry he has in mind, he clearly indicates which poetry does not participate in the radical prosaicization of poetry and, thereby, reveals the deeply polemical character of his valorization of novelistic discourse. Poetry produced in the contexts of symbolism, futurism, dadaism, surrealism, and further 'analogous movements' (*VLA* 90), Bakhtin argues, obliterates the dialogic potential of language; rather than creatively engaging co-existential dialogue in its limitless varieties as the principle of poetic construction, all of these movements in one way or another advocate the hierarchically marked separation and isolation of a variously conceived poetic language from its everyday diversity and contexts. The language of poetry 'becomes authoritarian' (100), closes itself off from the 'impact of extraliterary social dialects' (ibid.). Therefore, Bakhtin continues,

such ideas as a special 'poetic language', a 'language of the gods', a 'priestly language of poetry' and so forth could flourish on poetic soil.

---

[13] See also *VLA* 91, 144; *MB* 277.

It is noteworthy that the poet, should he not accept the given literary language, will sooner resort to the artificial creation of a new language specifically for poetry rather than use actual, available social dialects [and] languages . . . filled with specific objects . . . Thus, when Russian prose writers at the beginning of the twentieth century began to show profound interest in dialects and *skaz*, the symbolists (Bal'mont, V. Ivanov) and later the futurists dreamed of creating a special 'language of poetry' and even made attempts at creating such a language (V. Khlebnikov). The idea of a special . . . language of poetry is a typical utopian philosopheme of poetic discourse: it is grounded in the actual conditions and demands of poetic style, which is always . . . informed by one directly intentional language. (*The Dialogic Imagination*, 287–8; trans. modified)

Bakhtin's attack is directed against Viacheslav Ivanov's (and other symbolists') claim that it is poetry's duty to remember and complete 'its primordial tasks' (Ivanov, 130), namely, to mediate 'between the world of divine essences and human beings' (131) by means of the 'language of the gods' (ibid.) in the face of the 'crowd, which demands an earthly language from the Poet' (130); against Velimir Khlebnikov's and Aleksandr Kruchenykh's (and other futurists') repudiation and 'insurmountable hatred of the language which existed before them [in the name of] arbitrary and derivative words',[14] of a 'personal . . . language, which does not have concrete meanings . . . which is trans-sensical', and by means of which the poet, 'like Adam, bestows his own names on everything';[15] and, finally, against the Russian formalists' emphasis on the distinctness of poetic language from 'practical' or 'prosaic' language, on poetry's separation from the actual diversity of speech and languages.[16] In addition to its pragmatic import, Bakhtin's apparently negative attitude toward poetry is informed by his overt subscription to the traditional notion of poetic speech as highly tropical, that is, to the very concept of poetry which was propagated by the symbolists: the poetic word, Bakhtin contends, is functionalized as a directly and singularly intentional symbol or metaphor

---

[14] Burliuk, Kruchenykh, Maiakovskii, and Khlebnikov, 'A Slap in the Face of Public Taste' (cited in Markov, 50–1).

[15] Kruchenykh, 'Declaration of the Word As Such' (cited in Markov, 63). Bakhtin explicitly inveighs against Kruchenykh's claim that the futurists 'destroyed the object' ('The Word's New Paths' (cited in Markov, 71)) by emphasizing that social languages are 'filled with specific objects'.

[16] See Medvedev; *R* 257–318; Shklovskii.

(*VLA* 137–45) and as such tends to be ambiguous or poly-
semous but not double-voiced or dialogic (141).[17]

The implicit contradiction in Bakhtin's oscillation between a
strictly monologic conception of poetry and the simultaneous
acknowledgement of the possibility and undeniable facticity of
dialogic, prosaicized poetry remains—like other inconsistencies
and thematic loose ends which inevitably emerge from the
conceptual, argumentative, and expository incompleteness of
many of his texts (*LKS* 531)—unresolved in his oeuvre. Instead
of criticizing and dismissing his ambivalent discourse on poetry
on logical grounds, however, I suggest exploring its heuristic
significance by engaging it productively in its very ambivalence.
If Bakhtin's claim that polyphony is possible and factually
observable and determinant in certain, prosaicized poetic utter-
ances—rather than his numerous implicit and explicit condem-
nations of poetry—is taken as the starting point for assessing his
attitude toward poetry, a positive view of poetry can be
uncovered in his writings—a view less clearly articulated than,
yet equally as pervasive as its denigrating mate. Foregrounding
the positive aspects of Bakhtin's heterogeneous view of poetry is
significant both theoretically and methodologically: on the one
hand it underscores the theoretical plausibility of engaging his
writings in the interpretation of poetry, on the other hand it
points to the dangers of reading Bakhtin monologically, that is,
in the light of a putative, clear-cut conceptual or argumentative
stance on Bakhtin's part.

The prosaicization of poetry, Bakhtin notes, depends on the
adoption of discursive strategies which shake up and subvert
putative authorial impositions and constraints, such as hybridi-
zation, the dialogized juxtaposition of languages, or the pre-
sentation of genuine dialogues (*VLA* 170–6). As an outstanding
case of prosaicized poetry Bakhtin adduces Pushkin's *Eugene
Onegin* (*VLA* 141–2; *LKS* 353–62), which exemplifies the
elusiveness of generic boundaries and the subversion of the
structural enactment of authorial intentionality and, thereby,
vindicates—from the metalinguistic point of view—its subtitle,

---

[17] See e.g. Aristotle, *Poetics*, 1457b-1459a. This view of poetry was, of course,
dominant in the symbolist movement. Bakhtin distinguishes novelistic 'double-
voicedness' (dvugolosost') (*VLA* 137) from poetic 'ambiguity' (dvusmylennost')
(141).

'A Novel in Verse'. In *Eugene Onegin*, Bakhtin notes, Pushkin engages in dialogue with Onegin's and the other protagonists' languages; he literally speaks to Onegin and the other protagonists. Pushkin's novel in verse is stylistically constructed like any 'genuine novel' (*LKS* 361): like any genuine novel it is a 'more or less dialogized system of . . . "languages", styles, and concrete . . . consciousnesses' (ibid.). However, *Eugene Onegin* can also be interpreted—if one is to apply Bakhtin's own criteria for monologicity—as one of *the* most poetic utterances, that is, as one of the most monologic and authoritative poetic utterances precisely because it creates the impression of polyphony, while all the more efficiently instantiating the author's control over the text: this control is effectuated by way of a consistently implemented isometric prosodic arrangement (iambic tetrameter), which 'strengthens and tightens the unity and self-enclosedness of . . . poetic style and the unitary language which it postulates' (*VLA* 110–11), thereby, rhythmically subduing and homogenizing the text's presumed polyphony, and, more importantly, by way of a stanzaic form—the famous Onegin-stanza—specifically invented for *Eugene Onegin*.[18] It is precisely this exacerbated interplay between utmost polyphony and utmost monologicity in *Eugene Onegin* which most palpably illustrates the prosaicization of poetry (or the poeticization of novelistic discourse).

Polyphony in poetry is always somewhat precarious and not as easy to achieve as in novelistic discourse, since dialogue in poetry must permanently counteract homogenizing forces. While these homogenizing forces may be viewed negatively in the light of Bakhtin's valorization of novelistic discourse, they reveal their fundamentally positive function in the light of his simultaneous insistence that precisely because the poet—in the narrow sense of the term—uses language in a presumably more individualized, more personal, more authoritative way than the polyphonic novelist, he is a fortiori answerable for 'every word

---

[18] *Eugene Onegin* is composed in fourteen-line, iambic, tetrametric stanzas with the following rhyme scheme: ababccddeffegg. The only exceptions are the two letters written by Onegin and Tatiana, respectively, which interrupt the formal arrangement of the text and thus underscore their independence from the author. Bakhtin's metalinguistic analysis of Pushkin's poem 'For the Shores of the Distant Homeland' (*R* 61–8; 73–83) equally points out the possibility of polyphony in poetry. Interestingly, Bakhtin never addresses the monologic aspects of *Eugene Onegin*.

as [if it were] his' (*VLA* 110). (And it will remembered that throughout his writings Bakhtin advocates answerability—one of his central ethical and socio-political categories.) It is import-ant to note that throughout 'The Word in the Novel' ('Slovo v romane') (*VLA* 72–233), that is, that text which critics mostly refer to when presenting Bakhtin's denigrating view of poetry, Bakhtin reiterates at least three times that the 'poet must . . . assume equal answerability for all aspects of his poetic utter-ances' (109),[19] while only once conceding—apologetically, as it were—that even in novelistic discourse 'all . . . discursive elements are, *of course*, also subject to authorial accentuation, are ultimately also determined by the author's artistic will, and entirely fall within the purview of the author's answerability' (227).[20] However, Bakhtin immediately clarifies (correcting himself, as it were) that in a truly polyphonic novel these elements actually 'do not belong to the author's language' (ibid.): the novelist's answerability is of a merely '*convention-ally-literary, conventionally-monologic*' (*PPD* 247) kind.[21]

Poetic speech, Bakhtin suggests, is not simply monologic and authoritative; precisely because it structurally tends toward monologicity, it sets a task before the poet, namely, the task of answerability: The poet 'must' (dolzhen) (*VLA* 109) become answerable for every element in his poetic utterance.[22] Thus, poetry reveals itself as that mode of speech which emphatically points to the poet's, that is, first and foremost, a person's, non-alibi in co-existence. Insofar as metalinguistics is grounded in the philosophy of the act, poetic speech reveals itself—ironically, given Bakhtin's putative repudiation of poetry on metalinguistic grounds—as metalinguistically more significant than novelistic discourse precisely because it turns a person's indelible answer-ability for his or her acts (including speech acts) into one of its artistically constitutive moments. Because the poet is answerable through and through for every element in his poetic utterance, Bakhtin suggests, he or she is both in a position of power with regard to his or her utterance(s) and all its constituents and, in a

[19] See also *VLA* 99, 109.
[20] See also *LKS* 360–1.
[21] Divisions into chapters and paragraphs, for instance, are indicative of an author's conventionally literary, conventionally monologic presence. See also *MPL* 111.
[22] 'Dolzhen', it will be remembered, translates the German 'sollen', the ethical 'ought'.

sense, powerless in view of the burden of answerability which this power imposes. While the poet may be on the side of state power and official discourses, he or she may equally—precisely because he or she does not simply enact the diversity of speech and languages, but an *emphatically* singular, answerable, and invested position within this diversity—criticize and reprehend those who are in power by way of his or her poetry. Unlike the polyphonic novelist, who may devolve the answerability for his or her discourse, which may or may not be in accord with the reigning official discourses, upon his or her characters, the poet has no such alibi. Undermining his earlier condemnation of poetry, Bakhtin points to the 'courage of the poet, who, in his own name, criticizes the princes' (*LKS* 518), a possibility unattainable for the polyphonic novelist, whom—if he spoke 'in his own name', that is, authoritatively—Bakhtin would brand as ideological, dogmatic, and monologic. Thus, poetry acquires socio-political significance as a potentially subversive and coun-ter-hegemonic force.

While the tendency of poetry to manifest itself in author-itatively mastered and presumably homogeneous utterances may play into the hands of 'cultural, national, and political centralization' (*VLA* 86), which is accomplished through the 'unifying, centralizing, [and] centripetal forces' (ibid.) of the official discourses of state and power, poetry also facilitates the creation and advancement of that communal language without which 'the decentralizing, centrifugal forces' (ibid.) of socio-political critique, which—as Bakhtin's own writings demon-strate—presupposes mutual understanding based on a commu-nal language, would be impossible. Bakhtin notes, thereby underscoring the thematic link between his early, philosophical and later, metalinguistic writings, that '[u]nitary language is never given but, essentially, always a task' (83). 'Unitary language' does not signify 'an abstract minimum of linguistic communality in the sense of a system of elementary forms (linguistic symbols)' (84). Perpetually counteracting the 'factual diversity of speech and languages' (ibid.), it is an 'ideologically saturated' (ibid.) force which constrains this diversity, which facilitates a 'maximum of mutual understanding in all spheres . . . of life' (ibid.) and which 'crystallizes in the real, if relative, unity of the reigning colloquial and literary language' (ibid.). Insofar as the development of consciousness is fundamentally dialogic and implies (mutual) understanding (158) the creation and consolidation of a communal language reveals itself as one of the most 'noble' and necessary co-existential tasks.

What has become clear in the course of my discussion is the highly ambiguous status of poetry in Bakhtin's writings. On the one hand, Bakhtin depicts poetry as repressive and hetero-phobic; on the other hand, he suggests that it is an exemplary mode of the enactment of co-existence precisely because it facilitates the completion of one of the most important co-existential tasks, namely, the creation of mutual understanding and, concurrently, the subversion of socio-political, potentially repressive, authority—a function explicitly ascribed to the novel. While I do not think that this dilemma, which exemplifies the heuristic and cognitive productivity of an author's 'blind-ness' with regard to the results and implications of his or her own argument, can—at least not within the present frame-work—or should be conclusively resolved, I hope to have shown that Bakhtin does provide sufficient grounds for the metalinguistic engagement of poetry.[23] The implications of Bakhtin's ambiguous stance regarding poetry are significant. If poetry implies the poet's answerability and non-alibi in co-existence, if it indeed facilitates mutual understanding by help-ing to bring about a communal language and thereby allows for socio-political critique, if it can, furthermore, be polyphonic (in addition to its 'natural dialogicity'), then poetry rather than novelistic discourse reveals itself as *the* metalinguistically exem-plary mode of speech: in contrast to polyphonic novelistic discourse, it not only evinces all of the above characteristics, but, moreover, most palpably instantiates the co-existential clashes between homogenizing and oppositional discourses in its very construction, by imposing a unifying organization on the voices of others, which is (quantitatively and qualitatively) less determinant in (non-'poeticized') novelistic discourse. *Eugene Onegin* rather than Dostoevsky's (and others') novels reveals itself as the polyphonic novel or poem par excellence—precisely because it enacts and maintains polyphony in the face of such '*conventionally-literary, conventionally-monologic*'

---

[23] See also Emerson, *The First Hundred Years*, 281.

(*PPD* 247) aspects of novelistic discourse as the division of a text into chapters *and* such traditionally monologizing aspects of poetry as stanzaic form, metre, rhyme, and so forth. While Bakhtin may or may not be right regarding the monologicity of certain poetic texts, he certainly allows for the polyphony of other, prosaicized poetic texts, especially, as he notes, of poetic texts produced in the twentieth century. A metalinguistic approach to Mandel'shtam's and Celan's poetry is thus all the more plausible.

EXCURSUS: BAKHTIN AND MANDEL'SHTAM

That both authors did indeed take notice of each others' works is indicated by references to acmeism[24] in Bakhtin's 'The Word in the Novel' (*VLA* 72–233) and by references to Bakhtin's Dostoevsky book in Mandel'shtam's 'Conversation About Dante' (*MSS* iii. 216–59). Terminological and conceptual parallels characterizing both authors' texts, furthermore, suggest, as I illustrate below, Mandel'shtam's potential influence on Bakhtin.[25] I should emphatically stress, however, that the question whether Bakhtin was or was not influenced by Mandel'shtam is ultimately irrelevant to the argumentative force of the two authors' conceptual rapprochement in the present context and is raised for heuristic purposes only, insofar as a positive answer to this question would allow for a historically grounded reassessment of Bakhtin's view of poetry.

In his 1923 essay, 'Storm and Stress' ('Buria i natisk'), Mandel'shtam writes: 'Andrei Belyi . . . enriched Russian poetry with sharp prosaicisms . . . In his book *Ashes* he skillfully

---

[24] The poetic movement with which Mandel'shtam was associated. For an excellently documented exposition and survey of acmeism, see Doherty.

[25] Notwithstanding these indices, Bakhtin's relation to acmeism and to Mandel'shtam in particular has hardly received critical attention. To the best of my knowledge, only Renate Lachmann and Jane Gary Harris have commented on acmeism and Bakhtin in the same context. In her essay, 'Bachtins Dialogizität', Lachmann simply notes that Bakhtin and Voloshinov 'did not take constructive notice of acmeism' (cited in Stierle and Warning, 490) and abandons the issue; Gary Harris suggests 'Bakhtin's possible influence' (Mandel'shtam, *The Complete Critical Prose*, 680, n. 30) on Mandel'shtam. While Harris's suggestion is, as I demonstrate below, factually mistaken, Lachmann does not take into consideration overt terminological and conceptual parallels between Mandel'shtam's and Bakhtin's texts.

introduces polyphony [polifoniia], that is, multi-voicedness [mnogogolosie], into the poetry of Nekrasov, whose themes undergo an idiosyncratic orchestration [orkestrovke]' (*MSS* ii. 291–2).[26] Although Mandel'shtam's use of some of Bakhtin's key terms[27] may be interpreted as a simple, albeit uncanny instance of metapoetic anticipation, it is—given the chronological precedence of Mandel'shtam's text with regard to Bakhtin's Dostoevsky book (1929), in which the metalinguistic approach to dialogue is introduced—by no means implausible to speculate that metalinguistics may in fact be informed by Mandel'shtam's poetics (and, therefore, especially 'applicable' to the latter).

In the context of his overall condemnation of poetry Bakhtin mentions acmeism in connection with those poetic movements which together with 'dadaism [and] surrealism' disregard the fundamentally dialogic character of the word (*VLA* 90). Two pages later Bakhtin notes that since 'any word is essentially dialogically oriented . . . [o]nly the mythical and lonely Adam, approaching the virginal, not-yet-spoken-about world with the first word, could have . . . avoided this dialogicity' (92). This unmarked allusion to Genesis 2: 19[28] acquires particular polemical significance in the light of Bakhtin's explicit repudiation of futurism and, more importantly, acmeism (*VLA* 90, 100–1). Both futurists and acmeists propelled the topos of Adam to the forefront of the literary debates of the times: while the futurists emphasized the baptismal powers of the poet, who, 'like Adam, bestows its own name on everything',[29] the acmeists valorized Adam's anti-symbolist 'manly, steady, and clear outlook on life' (Gumilev, i. 171).[30] More importantly, 'adamism' was another

---

[26] In 'The Noise of Time' ('Shum vremeni') (1925), Mandel'shtam twice uses the term 'diversity of voices' (raznogolositsa) (*MSS* ii. 364, 375), a term equally prominent in Bakhtin's texts (e.g. *VLA* 76). See also Mandel'shtam's poem ii: 15.

[27] Bakhtin uses 'polifoniia' throughout *PPD*; 'mnogogolosie', for instance, in *PPD* 219; 'orkestrovka', for instance, in *VLA* 88, 105.

[28] 'And out of the ground the Lord formed every beast of the field and every fowl of the air; and brought *them* unto Adam to see what he would call them: and whatsoever Adam called every living creature, that *was* the name thereof' (King James version).

[29] Kruchenykh, 'Declaration of the Word As Such' (cited in Markov, 63).

[30] A similar anti-symbolist plea for the assumption of the life of the here and now, of existence, can be found in Mandel'shtam's 'The Morning of Acmeism' ('Utro Akmeizma') (*MSS* i. 177–81), published in 1919 but probably written as early as 1913. The topos of 'virility' informs acmeist poetics throughout. Sergei

name used by members of that movement which became
prominent under the name of acmeism in reference to the
early stages of their movement's development: 'A new move-
ment comes to replace symbolism, whatever its name—acmeism
(derived from the word ἀκμή—the highest level of anything . . .)
or adamism' (ibid.).[31]

In view of Bakhtin's avowed familiarity with acmeism—and
this means, in particular, with those acmeist texts which were
published in the periodicals of the times before and during his
stint at Petersburg University in the mid-1910s and before and
during the period in which he first developed metalinguistics
(throughout the 1920s) and which culminated in the publica-
tion of his Dostoevsky book (1929),[32] his hostility toward
acmeism can only be interpreted in polemical and strategic
terms: the presumed novelty of his own conceptual and
terminological approach to literature would have been jeopar-
dized by the admission that other authors—poets, in particu-
lar—who did not belong to the Bakhtin circle, could have
come up with similar ideas—albeit on opposite grounds. After
all, it is hard to explain how Bakhtin can bluntly argue that
acmeism and 'analogous movements' facilitate the monologi-
city of poetry given Mandel'shtam's dictum that there is 'no
lyric poetry without dialogue' (*MSS* i. 187) and Gumilev's
claim that 'the poet always addresses someone, some listener'
(i. 179).

If Bakhtin's familiarity with (at least some of) the poeto-
logically central acmeist texts and his fundamentally opposi-
tional attitude toward the movement as a whole are granted *and*
taken seriously, Mandel'shtam's use of the terms 'polyphony',
'multi-voicedness', and 'orchestration' (*MSS* ii. 292) in particu-
lar connection with Belyi's 'prosaicisms' and Nekrasov's poetry

Gorodetskii emphasizes that 'this new Adam did not arrive on the sixth day of
creation into an untouched and virginal world but into the Russian historical
present' (Gorodetskii, 49).

[31] See also Gorodetskii, 48; *MSS* i. 229–30; Zhirmunskii, 106–32; Brown,
Mandelstam, 56; Doherty, 85.

[32] See e.g. Mandel'shtam's 'On the Interlocutor' ('O sobesednike') (1913), 'Storm
and Stress' ('Buria i natisk') (1923), 'The Noise of Time' ('Shum vremeni') (1925),
'The End of the Novel' ('Konets romana') (1928) (all in *MSS*), Gorodetskii's 'Some
Currents in Contemporary Russian Poetry' (1913), Gumilev's 'The Legacy of
Symbolism and Acmeism' ('Nasledie simvolizma i akmeizm') (1913) (i. 171–6), to
name only a few.

(ibid.) can be interpreted as informing Bakhtin's emphasis on the 'prosaic' character of Bely's (*R* 226) and Nekrasov's (*PPD* 415) writings. Concomitantly, Bakhtin's polemical attitude toward acmeism may be viewed as informed by the fact that in the 1928 essay 'The End of the Novel' Mandel'shtam already articulates one of Bakhtin's central conceptual metaphors, when he depicts the functioning of the novel as dependent on the interplay between centrifugal and centripetal forces and, more specifically, on the domination of the centrifugal over the centripetal force (*MSS* ii. 273–4). Finally, Bakhtin's concept of the superaddressee as constitutive of any utterance, located either in 'metaphysical distance or in historically distant time' (*BSS* 332) and embodied in such concepts as 'god, absolute truth, [or] the people' (ibid.) is uncannily reminiscent of both Mandel'shtam's notion of the 'reader in posterity' (*MSS* ii. 184) the 'secret interlocutor' (ii. 184, 275) in the future and, in particular, of Gumilev's 'mystical interlocutor [who may be] God, Nature, the People' (i. 179).

While a sophisticated critical evaluation of these parallels has to be relegated to future research, their recognition in itself proves valuable for an adequate assessment of certain aspects of Bakhtin's writings and underscores the particular suitability of metalinguistics as a backdrop for a discussion of acmeist and, in particular, Mandel'shtam's poetics and poetry. This suitability is further corroborated by Mandel'shtam's more or less overt polemical references to Bakhtin's Dostoevsky book (1929). When claiming that the 'concept of scandal in literature is much older than Dostoevsky, [that] in the thirteenth century—in Dante's work in particular—it was much stronger' (*MSS* iii. 223), and that it is 'absolutely inadequate to present . . . Dante's poem [i.e. the *Divine Comedy*] as a linear, monologic narrative' (iii. 225), Mandel'shtam implicitly polemicizes both against Bakhtin's general valorization of Dostoevsky's historical significance as the inventor of the polyphonic novel and, more specifically, against Bakhtin's valorization of Dostoevsky's polyphonic novels at the expense of Dante's *Divine Comedy*, which, although enacting a multiplicity of voices, ultimately remains, according to Bakhtin, merely formally polyphonic (*PPD* 42): although 'the world of Dostoevsky's novels is, in its own way, equally completed . . . as the world of Dante's *Divine Comedy*' (ibid.), Bakhtin notes, 'it would be futile to try to find in it the *systematico-monologic* . . . and dialectical, *philosophical* completeness' (ibid.) characterizing Dante's work. If Mandel'shtam's most comprehensive poetological manifesto, the 'Conversation About Dante', is interpreted as polemicizing—of course not exclusively—against Bakhtin in particular, the *Divine Comedy* emerges as an exemplary precursor of polyphony as both Mandel'shtam and Bakhtin understand it.

MANDEL'SHTAM'S POETICS OF DIALOGUE

Mandel'shtam's apodictic proclamation that there is 'no poetry without dialogue' poetologically replicates Levinas's and Bakhtin's insistence on the irreducibility of semethical and co-existential dialogue, respectively, and universalizes Bakhtin's metalinguistic concession that poetry can be dialogic. Poetic dialogue, which, according to Mandel'shtam, originally transpires in the form of dialogic relations between singularities by way of singular poetic utterances, manifests itself in singular poems in the form of—more or less visible, more or less displaced—traces of these relations. In what have probably become his most famous and most frequently quoted passages, Mandel'shtam writes:

In the critical moment a seafarer throws a sealed bottle containing his name and the description of his fate into the ocean waves. Many years later, roaming in the dunes, I find it in the sand, read the letter, learn about the date of the event [sobytie] and the last will of the one who died . . . The letter sealed in the bottle is addressed to the one who finds it. I found it. Consequently, I am the . . . addressee . . . Reading [a] poem, I experience the same feeling that I would experience if such a bottle had found its way into my hands . . . Two moments, expressed in an equally precise manner, can be discerned in . . . sending . . . the poem and the seafarer's act of throwing the bottle into the waves. Just like the poem, the letter is not addressed to anyone in particular. Nevertheless, both have an addressee: the letter—the one who happens to notice the bottle in the sand, the poem—the 'reader in posterity' . . . And everyone who is reached by [the poem], experiences himself as such a 'reader'—chosen, called by his own name . . . Even if singular poems (in the form of missives and dedications) may be addressed to concrete persons/visages [litsam], poetry as a whole is always directed toward a more or less distant, unknown interlocutor, whose existence the poet cannot doubt without doubting his own. (*MSS* i. 183–8)

These lines contain some of the central aspects of Mandel'shtam's poetics. Poetry is presented as transpiring in an originarily dialogic context. Similarly to Bakhtin, Mandel'shtam conceives the poem as an utterance—and, in particular, as a letter—addressed to a real, not merely implied reader or interlocutor.[33] (The metaphoric rapprochement between poetic utterance and letter culminates in the metaphoric transformation of the former into the latter, effectuated by the use of 'sending' in reference to poetry.) The poem's constitutive addressivity, which, I should stress, exceeds its structural make-up as involving an implied author and an implied reader, will have originarily grounded it in *at least two* absolutely distinct singular dates (the real author's and real reader's),[34] marking two co-existential events, which—by virtue of the thus created poem—form a new singular metalinguistic nexus: the interlocutor, who is necessarily futural, constitutively participates in the writing of the poem, that is, retroactively co-authors the poem. 'In poetry', Mandel'shtam writes, 'only performative understanding counts—not passive, reproductive or paraphrasing understanding' (*MSS* iii. 217). The interlocutor's performative, or, to use Bakhtin's term, 'active responsive understanding' is thus always already an act of co-authoring.[35] Poetically performative understanding exceeds the constitutive performativity of every act of understanding qua act. Analogously to Bakhtin's proleptic and futural conception of speech in general, Mandel'shtam conceives the dialogicity of poetic speech in particular as not merely factually accomplished but as constitutively proleptic, that is, as predicated on poetry's orientation toward its retroactive

---

[33] It will be remembered that Bakhtin classifies the letter as a primary speech genre. Mandel'shtam equates reader and interlocutor, thereby—similarly to Levinas and Bakhtin—subverting the oral–written dichotomy.

[34] 'Date' must be understood not as a punctual occurrence, but as temporally extended. Thus, one of the poem's dates would be the context of its production.

[35] Referring to poetry in general, Derek Attridge pertinently notes that the 'act of reading is a response to the act of writing [which] makes the "original" act happen, and happen differently with each such response' ('Literary Form', 245). I emphasize the interlocutor's role as co-author—notwithstanding the fact that this has become a commonplace of reader-response criticism (beginning with Sartre's *Qu'est-ce que la littérature?*)—due to its particular significance in the context of Celan's response to Mandel'shtam.

constitution through singular acts of performative understanding in the future. This manifests itself, Mandel'shtam suggests, most clearly in the semantic indeterminacy of poetry, which calls for an infinite 'commentary in futurum' (238). While this feature is of course structurally characteristic of any utterance, it assumes a dominant function in poetry, in which the dialogicity of speech becomes supremely self-conscious both in the form of concrete, more or less salient intertextuality and in the form of an irreducible dependence on future rereadings and, consequently, rewritings, predicated on its semantic concreteness *and* generality.[36]

The poem's interlocutor—whether concretely specified or non-specified—is never an impersonal entity, but a unique person, whose singularity is constituted precisely in the process of his or her interpellation by the poet through the poem. As Mandel'shtam's fellow acmeist Nikolai Gumilev points out: 'Poetry always addresses itself to the person. Even when a poet speaks to the crowd, he speaks to every member of the crowd in his or her unicity' (i. 178). Mandel'shtam's and Gumilev's insistence on the singularly co-existential character of poetic interlocution[37] is reminiscent of Bakhtin's observation that polyphony does not dialogically engage 'two [or more] *impersonal* linguistic consciousnesses (the correlates of different languages) but two [or more] *individualized* linguistic consciousnesses (the correlates of different utterances rather than different languages) and two [or more] *individualized* linguistic wills' (*VLA* 171; my emphasis).

In addition to responding to preceding utterances and addressing more or less immediate interlocutors, a poem always addresses itself to a not predetermined interlocutor in the future,[38] who *experiences* his or her interpellation as a kind of (re)baptism or (nominal) (re)creation—without, however, being actually called by his or her name. Mandel'shtam's conception of poetic interpellation as the *experience* of being

---

[36] See Ch. 1 59–60.

[37] Critics tend to overlook or downplay Mandel'shtam's attention to dialogic singularity, emphasizing his presumably impersonal and merely intertextual desire for (literary) 'culture' in general (see esp. Ivanovic, 216; Doherty, 7–8).

[38] Thus, Mandel'shtam's poems i: 188 and i: 190 (to name only two) are presumably addressed to Anna Akhmatova, without thereby being any less constitutively addressed to an interlocutor in the future.

called by own's name, that is, as the experience of one's co-existential singularization[39] and (re)creation without being actually phonically or graphically named, echoes the biblical, ethically exemplary instances of interpellation and, thus, parallels Levinas's depiction of semethical interpellation in the light of the biblical paradigm. The poetic interlocutor is in the same position as Moses in Exodus 3: 4, *experiencing* himself as being singularly constituted in response to the other's call without having been or being actually called by the other (insofar as 'call' implies the use of a human language, in which proper names signify).[40] Furthermore, Mandel'shtam's observation that, aside from involving proper names, poetic interpellation inevitably occurs on and from singular dates complements Bakhtin's depiction of the architectonic of co-existence as the 'world of proper names . . . and singular chronological dates' (*R* 51). It is precisely the fact of being interpellated which constitutes the person as an irreducible co-existential singularity, whereby the person is burdened with the answerability for—once the poem-letter has been retrieved from the bottle—co-authoring the poem and, concomitantly, its primary author's fate. In contrast to the reception of utterances which fall into the realm of primary speech genres and serve a more or less instrumental function, poetic co-authorship burdens, as it were, by obliging the co-author to participate in the (re)constitution of the fate of the poem's primary author, who in turn participates—through his or her poetry—in the interlocutor's fate.[41]

---

[39] Judith Butler notes that 'by being interpellated within the terms of language . . . a certain social existence . . . first becomes possible . . . One is, as it were, brought into social location and time through being named' (5, 29). Using the example of hailing ('Hey, you there'), Louis Althusser points out that interpellation need not transpire by way of actually articulating someone's proper name (180).

[40] Exodus 3: 4 reads: 'God called unto him out of the midst of the bush, and said, Moses, Moses' (King James version). Moses is not actually called by god in the language in which 'Moses' is a proper name. Rather, Moses *experiences* himself as being called. Already Dante points out that 'God need not . . . have used what we call speech' (*Literature*, 18).

[41] It is precisely such a performative and responsive understanding which informs Celan's encounter with Mandel'shtam (see below). Mandel'shtam's attention to the co-authoring interlocutor/reader calls to mind Derrida's notion of the 'counter-signature' (*Acts*, 69), which comes 'both to confirm, repeat and respect the . . . other' (ibid.), which 'is responsible (for itself and for the other)' (70). In contrast to

While Mandel'shtam apparently uses 'fate' in its loose, everyday sense, the term acquires metalinguistic significance: 'Fate', Bakhtin notes, 'is the artistic transcription of that trace in Being, which [singular] internally teleological life leaves behind, the artistic expression of the deposition in Being of [singular] internally sense-filled life' (*R* 228). Fate reveals itself as the very mode in which co-existence singularly objectivates itself poetically, in its unicity. In the light of Bakhtin's metalinguistic concept of fate, the term's poetological instrumentalization by Mandel'shtam and—as I illustrate below—by Celan loses its 'mystical' or divinatory character and vindicates Celan's dictum that whoever writes the poem 'remains given to it' (*GW* iii. 198). The poem can be read as the artistic trace of a person's trace in co-existence(s), or, to put it simply, as the artistic trace of a person's life. It is exemplarily a 'sign which holds itself in the trace [of] someone [e.g. its author(s)] who passes' (*DEHH* 200), and which, by virtue of its exemplary metalinguistic status as Said, is particularly capable of indicating its dialogic (semethical and co-existential) underpinnings. In line with his emphasis on the inseverability of author and utterance, which carries its author's fate, and in accordance with his stipulation of 'performative understanding', Mandel'shtam emphasizes that since the poem 'only exists in its performance [by its author *and* interlocutor(s)]' (*MSS* iii. 259), a 'completed poem is nothing but a calligraphic product, which inevitably remains as a result of the existential-performative impulse' (ibid.).[42]

Derrida's 'countersignature', however, which confirms in *repeating*, Mandel'shtam's interlocutor does not repeat the other('s text). The singularity of Mandel'shtam('s text) constitutes itself precisely in his diachronic extension toward an ever displaced reception by the other. For insightful and informative discussions of these issues, see Attridge, 'Singularities', 119–20.

[42] See Lehmann, 'Atmen', 187–99. Mandel'shtam's insistence on the existential groundedness of poetry in the 'real' world, in the 'real' life of its authors, is, of course, consonant with and constitutive of acmeist poetics and the acmeist world view, which explicitly opposes Russian symbolism as it manifests itself most pointedly in Viacheslav Ivanov's valorization of the 'realiora', the noumenal, the ontologically essential realm as opposed to the 'realia', the phenomenal or ontic realm (Ivanov, 134), and Aleksandr Blok's dictum that 'the poet's business is absolutely incommensurable with the order of the external world' (Blok, vi. 165). Mandel'shtam's emphasis on the inseverability of poetry and existence is not a covert continuation of symbolist-Nietzschean 'zhiznetvorchestvo' (Ivanov, 168), the aesthetic transformation of life with a tendency toward the 'otherworldly', but, on the contrary, an emphatic infusion of poetry with the here and now.

That such a performative response indeed involves the assignation and assumption of answerability is underscored by the fact that Mandel'shtam uses the term 'chosen' (*izbran*) to depict the experience of poetic interpellation, which places poetic dialogue in the context of biblical election and, more specifically, in the context of such socio-politically significant passages as the already mentioned 'encounter' between god and Moses in Exodus 3: 4. In contrast to interlocution involving primary speech genres, poetic interlocution involves the experience of being chosen, which, of course, poetologically complements Levinas's Torah-based depiction of semethics as a dynamic of 'election' (*TI* 276).[43] Poetic election indicates the semethical foundation of co-existence by reminding every interlocutor of his or her excessive answerability to and for the other, whose fate diachronically depends on the interlocutor. Because it is constitutively diachronic, that is, because responsive co-authoring is by definition futural with respect to poetic address, the latter constitutively passes to the interlocutor's principally futural time, thus exemplarily staging and indicating in the Said my semethical 'passage to the time of the Other' (*DEHH* 192). Mandel'shtam's emphasis on the originary co-existential processuality of poetry culminates in the conceptualization of poetry in terms of breathing,[44] the life-sustaining activity par excellence, which poetologically complements Levinas's insistence on the respiratory character of semethics (*AQE* 277–8). Mandel'shtam's respiratory conception of poetry is ostensibly informed by a long tradition, going back to Plato's depiction of the emergence of poetry and the concomitant constitution of the poetic subject through divine inspiration (Plato, 533a–534d). Its contextually most significant backdrop, however, is unmistakably Dante's poetic functionalization of the respiratory topos.[45] Dante, Mandel'shtam writes, thereby highlighting the co-existential *and* semethical underpinnings of poetry, 'conceives the beginning of poetry as taking a step . . . accompanied by breathing' (*MSS* iii. 219); concomitantly, the

[43] See also *AQE* 95, 195, 201; *EN* 239.

[44] See *MSS* i. 216; ii. 256; iii. 219; Lehmann, 'Atmen', 191; Brown, 'Into the Heart', 592, 594, 597. Mandel'shtam's conceptualization of poetry in respiratory terms exemplifies the overall acmeist conceptualization of poetry in physiological and organicist terms (see *MSS* i. 216, 323; Gumilev, i. 157–70, 185–9).

[45] See e.g. Dante, *The Divine Comedy*, 333.

movement of metrical feet, the very performance of poetry proceeds as 'inhalation and exhalation' (ibid.).

Dante's significance for Mandel'shtam by far exceeds his significance in the history of European literature in general, and in the context of modernism in particular.[46] Dante was not only an integral part of 'Mandel'shtam's self-image' (Gary Harris, 115) and the precursor of Mandel'shtam's own poetry of 'address-ivity' (obrashchaemost') and 'addressedness'/'transmutability' (obratimost') (*MSS* iii. 233)[47]—and all 'genuine poetry' (ibid.) is, according to Mandel'shtam, addressive and transmutable— but also the 'greatest and incontestable master of transmutable and addressive poetic matter' (iii. 245). Thus, similarly to Levinas's self-disclosing interpretation of Celan's poetics, Man-del'shtam's comments on Dante equally pertain to his own poetic practice.[48]

By 'transmutable and addressive' Mandel'shtam means both that poetry synthesizes and transforms previous poetic and non-poetic matter, regardless of its temporal distribution in history,

[46] Anna Akhmatova points to the significance of Dante for the acmeist movement and for Mandel'shtam in particular: 'For my friends and contemporaries Dante was the greatest . . . teacher . . . Osip Mandel'shtam devoted many years of his life to the study of the works of Dante' (Akhmatova, ii. 183).

[47] It is extremely difficult to translate the terms 'obrashchaemost'' and 'obrati-most''. 'Obrashchaemost'' is the substantivized form of the present passive participle of the imperfective—implying reiteration—verb 'obrashchat'' (lit. to convert, turn, direct, orient); 'obratimost'' is the substantivized form of the perfective—implying completed action—verb 'obratit'' (lit. to convert, turn, direct, orient). Furthermore, both verbs acquire the distinct meaning of dialogic address if the reflexive suffix 'sia' is added (*MSS* iii. 245). Thus their literal meanings may be best circumscribed as 'addressableness'/'addressivity'/'convertibility'/'transmutability' and 'addressed-ness'/'convertibility'/'transmutability', respectively, which comprise both poetry's dialogic orientation and its interpoetic or intertextual convertibility and adapt-ability. Gary Harris's and Link's translation of the two terms as 'convertibility or transmutability' (Mandel'shtam, *The Complete Critical Prose*, 414) unfortunately loses the dialogic aspects of Mandel'shtam's terms. Nikita Struve's French transla-tion of the terms as 'mutable et mutée' (Struve, 201) equally loses their dialogic import.

[48] Struve rightly points out that 'in the 1930s . . . Mandel'shtam studies the strategies of . . . the *Divine Comedy*, in order to elaborate a synthesis of his own poetics' (Struve, 200). (Mandel'shtam's 'Conversation About Dante' was written, probably, in the early 1930s.) Mandel'shtam's depiction of Dante's poetry and poetics in terms of breathing underscores his poetological identification with the Italian poet, insofar as he (Mandel'shtam) already develops a poetics of breathing in such texts as 'The Word and Culture' ('Slovo i kul'tura') (1921), 'Literary Moscow' ('Literaturnaia Moskva') (1922), and 'The Noise of Time' (1925) (all in *MSS*) without explicit references to Dante.

and, concurrently, continuously transforms itself in acts of absorption and transformation, in incessant acts of performative understanding. Mandel'shtam notes that '[t]ime for Dante [and Mandel'shtam himself] is the contents of history understood as a single synchronic act' (iii. 238), in which 'events, names and traditions separated by centuries are synchronized' (iii. 256)— without thereby being congealed or frozen into a static construct—within a single poetic utterance, the *Divine Comedy*. Thus, Dante's poetry emerges in the futurally oriented process of synthesizing and transforming others' utterances. 'It is unthinkable to read Dante's cantos', Mandel'shtam writes, 'without turning them to the present, for which they are created; they are missiles for capturing the future; they demand a commentary in futurum' (iii. 238). Mandel'shtam has been 'hit' by these missiles and offers such a commentary. Half a century later Celan will capture Mandel'shtam's missiles and offer his commentary.[49]

It is important to note that Mandel'shtam strictly opposes a mechanistic understanding of poetry; rather, he conceives it in chemical terms, as producing something completely new by bringing diverse materials to react to and with each other, that is, to form organic bonds and to transform themselves into qualitatively new matter.[50] Mandel'shtam's insistence on the chemical character of the transmutability and dialogic orientation of poetic speech is very much akin to Bakhtin's claim that 'an alien word, which is introduced into the context of singular speech, does not enter into mechanical contact with the surrounding speech context, but chemically merges with it' (*VLA* 152) and thematically anticipates Celan's use of the chemical topos in *Die Niemandsrose*.

In line with his emphasis on the constitutively dialogic and intertextual make-up of poetry, Mandel'shtam conceives the

[49] This fundamental performativity, diachronicity, and dialogicity of poetry is of course already spelled out in Mandel'shtam's earlier essay 'On the Interlocutor' (1913). The fact that Mandel'shtam reappraises his poetics by way of a rereading of Dante in the early 1930s underscores the overall continuity and dialogic quality of his poetics.

[50] Throughout 'Conversation About Dante' Mandel'shtam emphasizes the chemical character of poetic addressivity and transmutability. Struve points to Mandel'shtam's 'strict dismissal of a mechanistic approach' to poetry (Struve, 201), and suggests that his insistence on performance and transmutability 'stems . . . directly from [Bergson's] *l'Évolution créatrice*' (ibid.).

word itself as internally dialogic: 'Any word is a sheaf, and senses [and voices] stick out from within the word in different directions; they do not strive toward one official point. In articulating "sun" we undertake, as it were, a gigantic journey [from and to the other, through the word's infinite uses by infinite speakers], to which we have become so accustomed that we can accomplish it in our sleep' (*MSS* iii. 226).[51] Concomitantly, Mandel'shtam explains, it 'is crucial to consider any poetic period—be it a verse, a strophe, or a complete lyrical composition—as a single word' (ibid.). The conception of the word as a dialogic sheaf a fortiori pertains to poetry as the most dialogic of speech genres. Elaborating upon the dialogic constitution of any utterance and, in particular, of poetry, Mandel'shtam specifies that the genuine poet 'does not introduce even a single word of his own [into his poems]' (iii. 253) and that, consequently, genuine poetry is emphatically heterologous—an 'orgy of citations' (iii. 220)—whereby the poet's take on the diversity of voices, intonations, and accents, that is, his or her stylistic visage, constitutes itself in the process of the 'chemical' transformation and synthesis of others' (poetic) utterances. How does the acquisition of others' words transpire according to Mandel'shtam? How does the transmission of verbal material take place?

As I have mentioned earlier, 'Dante [and Mandel'shtam] conceiv[e] the beginning of poetry as taking a step . . . accompanied by breathing' (iii. 219); 'inhalation and exhalation' (ibid.) enact the movement of metrical feet. If, as Mandel'shtam points out, genuine poetry is originarily heterologous and if its source lies in breathing, it is constitutively inspired—albeit not in any mystical-biblical sense, but by others' words, which address themselves to the poet and are in turn transformed into and within his or her poetry. The genuine poet, Mandel'shtam argues, 'never forgets the origins of things [and words]' (iii. 255). Mandel'shtam transforms divine inspiration into poetic inspiration, which involves the real words of real co-existing persons:

---

[51] Similarly, in his autobiographical sketch 'The Noise of Time' Mandel'shtam speaks of his 'journey through the patriarchy of Russian literature' (ii. 391). Mandel'shtam's depiction of poetry as a journey, as 'always being on one's way' (iii. 226), anticipates Celan's conception of poetry as 'being on one's way' (Unterwegssein) (*GW* iii. 186).

the divine afflatus is superseded by the poetic afflatus. Pertinently, Mandel'shtam writes: 'When asked what the poet wanted to say, the critic can refuse to answer, but when asked, where does the poet come from, he must answer' (ii. 252).[52] Using the example of Dante, Mandel'shtam illustrates the co-existentially 'real' character of poetic inspiration by dismissing Socrates's view that poets are 'possessed . . . and . . . not in their senses when they make these lovely lyric poems' (Plato, 534a). Dante's and any genuine poet's secret, Mandel'shtam observes, resides in the fact that anything may incite him to write poems except the temptation to 'make things up, except inventiveness' (*MSS* iii. 253). Like any genuine poet, Mandel'shtam continues, 'Dante and [romantic] imagination are incompatible!' (ibid.); like any genuine poet, Dante 'writes to dictation, he is a copyist, a translator . . . completely bent over in the pose of the scribe, timorously casting a sidelong glance at the illuminated original, which he had borrowed from the prior's library' (ibid.). Only sometimes does Dante show 'us his writing tools: his quill [and] ink . . . The dictator-supervisor is far more important than the so-called poet' (ibid.). Rather than being possessed and inspired, the poet is not only 'in his senses' but evinces an even heightened awareness of and concentration on the process of poetic production, so as not to admit oversights and mistranslations into his text, which he copies from other texts. In contrast to Socrates's conceptualization of poetry as devoid of *technê* (Plato, 533d), Mandel'shtam depicts poetry as a craft requiring instruments, practice, and assiduousness: 'A new poetry of the word-object has come to replace symbolism, futurism, imaginism, the romantic, the idealist . . . the dreamer of pure symbols and an abstract verbal aesthetics; its creator is not the idealist Mozart, but the rigid and disciplined craftsman, master Salieri' (*MSS* i. 231).[53] The poet's inspiration is predicated on his craft and capacity to grasp preceding texts, which he or she translates, that is, absorbs and transforms into new poetry; it is informed by actual dialogue as binding two or more persons in the dialogic event of poetry;

[52] In the 1922 'Letter on Russian Poetry' Mandel'shtam equally stresses the significance of a poet's origins rather than the content of his (or her) poetry (*MSS* ii. 236–40).

[53] In opposition to symbolism and with explicit emphasis on craftsmanship such poets as Mandel'shtam, Akhmatova, Mikhail Zenkevich, and Vladimir Narbut formed the 'Poet's Guild' in 1910.

and, finally, as transcription and translation, it necessarily transpires as active performance, as active responsive understanding.

In taking a breath the copier-translator-poet inhales the words, voices, and intonations of others' utterances, potentially separated by centuries, synthesizing and 'chemically' transforming them; in exhaling the copier-translator-poet produces his or her own singular stylistic visage, translates his or her own singular position in co-existential dialogue. The poet's 'breath-turn' (Atemwende)—to use Celan's neologism—the transition from inhalation to exhalation is indispensable for the production of poetry. With every breath the poet takes, he remembers; with every act of exhalation he or she produces.[54] Although the poet does not make up anything new in the sense of absolute originality, he does create something new, albeit something 'chemically' new, in response to potentially limitless interpellations. Mandel'shtam's fine distinction between 'invention' (izobretenie) (ii. 258) and 'inventiveness' (izobretatel'stvo) (iii. 253) is significant.[55] While the poet does 'breathe through the mouth and through the nose . . . by way of recollection . . . and invention' (ii. 258), nothing of what he produces is the product of 'making up' or 'inventiveness', understood as a kind of originating ingenuity or genius in the romantic sense.[56] In contrast to Coleridge's 'synthetic' (Coleridge, ii. 12) poet, who is above all concerned with himself and his own state of being, who by way of 'that synthetic and magical power, to which we have exclusively appropriated the name of imagination [,] brings the whole soul of man into activity, with the subordination of its faculties to each other [and] diffuses a spirit of unity' (ibid.), Mandel'shtam's synthetic poet has nothing 'magical' about him, being an assiduous craftsman, whose 'inventions' consist in orchestrating previous discourses and sense-positions. Concomitantly, Mandel'shtam's poetic 'recollection' must be strictly distinguished from Wordsworth's and Coleridge's tranquil recollection 'of powerful feelings' (*Lyrical Ballads*, 'Preface',

---

[54] See also Lehmann, 'Atmen', 191.

[55] Unfortunately, Gary Harris and Link translate 'izobretenie' as 'inventiveness' (Mandel'shtam, *The Complete Critical Prose*, 147) and 'izobretatel'stvo' as 'invention', which is not only semantically dubious, but contextually misleading.

[56] It goes without saying that my brief account of romantic creativity is over-simplified and serves the function of a mere backdrop.

173), which gives rise to poetry; the romantic 'intertexture of . . . feelings' (172) yields to the intertext of singular utterances and voices. Poetic 'invention' must be understood as skilful instrumentation and orchestration of others' words, as a focused and highly conscious and intentional activity. Interestingly, Mandel'shtam's concepts of poetic recollection and invention are reminiscent of the classical rhetorical concept of 'inventio' as a constitutive moment in the construction of a speech: in analogy with the classical orator, who remembers and browses the gamut of available topoi in search of arguments, the poet remembers and browses others' poetic utterances in search of words, which he or she can appropriate by infusing them with idiosyncratic intentions, intonations, and accents.[57]

Mandel'shtam's depiction of poetic inspiration and production as breathing both through the nose and through the mouth (*MSS* ii. 258) points to his tacit recourse to Genesis 2: 7, according to which 'God . . . breathed into [Adam's] nostrils the breath of life' (King James version). However, Genesis neither mentions Adam's exhalation (through the mouth) nor specifies it as an originary act of verbal articulation. While Mandel'shtam's obvious displacement of this pre-text could be interpreted as indicative of his 'inventiveness', it reveals itself—in the light of his extensive dialogue with Dante—as an exemplary instance of 'invention', as yet another crucial absorption and transformation of the Italian poet's text. Throughout 'Conversation About Dante' Mandel'shtam emphasizes the poetic signficance of Dante's decision to use his 'native Italian idiom' (iii. 237) for the *Divine Comedy*. It is only plausible to interpret this reiterated emphasis as a tacit reference to Dante's own awareness of the significance of writing in Italian rather than in Latin, which he elaborates in *Eloquence in the Vernacular* (*De Vulgari Eloquentia*). In this unfinished treatise Dante argues for the institution of a literature in the vernacular. A short and inconclusive part of the fragment, however, does not seem to have any specific relevance to the project and stands apart within the text: a sketchy discussion of the nature of the linguistic sign and the origin of language.[58] After briefly defining

[57] See Cicero, 191; *MSS* i. 214–16, 222–5; ii. 259, 261–2, 266; iii. 216–59.

[58] 'The sign itself is the noble subject of our discussion' (signum est ipsum subiectum nobile de quo loquimur) (Dante, *De Vulgari Eloquentia*, 18).

the sign as consisting of sound and sense (*De Vulgari Eloquentia*, 18), he moves on to the question of the origin of language, stating that language originated 'by way of an [immediate] response' (per modum responsionis) (22) to divine inspiration, in the word 'El', the term for god. Adam responds to inspiration immediately after having received the divine 'breath' (afflatus) (26). Since, according to Genesis, Adam does not articulate any words in response to the divine afflatus, Dante's ascription of a response to Adam as a consequence of inspiration can only metaphorically designate Adam's first act of exhaling: by translating Adam's expiratory reaction into a verbal response, Dante pneumatizes language *and* discursivizes breathing thus anticipating Mandel'shtam's discursivization of exhalation. While Mandel'shtam narrows down Dante's conceptualization of the constitution of human existence through respiration and language to the constitution of the poetic subject, he implicitly posits the metalinguistic *and* semethical originariness of poetry by predicating 'breathing', the life-sustaining activity par excellence, in poetic terms.[59] Given that Levinas and Dante conceive the origin of language in my inspiration by the absolutely other and in my concomitant expiratory response against the backdrop of Genesis 2: 7, Mandel'shtam's reinterpretation of Genesis 2: 7 by way of Dante a fortiori justifies the rapprochement between his poetics and Levinasian ethics: if the divination of semethics depends on its indication by the Said, which in turn enacts co-existence, and if the poetic Said exemplarily indicates semethics, a poetics which views co-existence as fundamentally poetic[60] ideally complements Levinasian ethics. Mandel'shtam's conceptual proximity to both Levinas and Bakhtin is further underscored by his conceptualization of poetic dialogue in terms of translation.

Insofar as responding to the other's poetic interpellation burdens the interpellated with an answerability to and for the

[59] I adopt Harald Weinrich's non-Aristotelian theory of metaphor as implying semantic predication rather than substitution. Thus, Mandel'shtam's metaphoric equation of respiration and poetry engages both metaphoric poles in a dynamic of mutual predication. While poetry is pneumatized, respiration is necessarily poeticized. See Aristotle, *Poetics*, 1457b; Weinrich, 'Semantik der Metapher', 15; 'Semantik der kühnen Metapher', 337.

[60] Pertinently, Lehmann notes that Mandel'shtam 'strives toward . . . the fusion of poetry and existence' ('Atmen', 188).

other, engaging in poetry inevitably implies becoming answerable in socio-political terms. This comes to the fore clearly in the 'highest commandment of acmeism' (*MSS* i. 180), namely, that poetry must be emphatically oriented toward *this* world, toward actual co-existence (ibid.).[61] Consequently, the poet cannot avoid assuming answerability—his or her non-alibi in co-existence. Mandel'shtam reveals himself as the exemplary embodiment of Bakhtin's poet who 'in his own name, criticizes the princes' (*LKS* 518). After all, Mandel'shtam's arrest in 1934, which entailed his exile and, ultimately, led to his death in a Soviet transit camp in Siberia, was presumably the direct corollary of his anti-Stalinist poem (*MSS* iii. 64).[62] As Nadezhda Mandel'shtam, the poet's widow, notes, Mandel'shtam was painfully aware of and emphasized the socio-political significance of poetry:

O.M. had by chance learned about the alleged execution of five old men and was running about Moscow in a wild frenzy, demanding the reversal of the verdict. Since everybody was only shrugging their shoulders, he went directly to Bukharin, the only person susceptible to reasoning . . . As the ultimate reasonable means against execution, O. M. sent his *Poems*, which had just been published, to Bukharin, with the following epigraph: every line in this book speaks against what you are about to do. (*Vospominaniia*, 120)[63]

In opposition to the symbolists' emphasis on 'realiora' and Stalin's 'personality cult' which, according to Anna Akhmatova, he 'could hardly endure',[64] Mandel'shtam valorizes the co-existentially answerable poetic 'person' (lichnost'), who must assume the burden of *this* world with its 'weight' (ves) and immediate concerns.[65] Like Bakhtin's co-existential person, Mandel'shtam's poet-person is constituted dialogically, enacting his or her personhood in singular poetic utterances, whose stylistic visage consists precisely in the singular transformations

---

[61] The acmeist Gorodetskii depicts the struggle between acmeism and symbolism as the 'struggle for this world—a world that resounds, has colors, forms, weight and time—, for our planet, Earth' (Gorodetskii, 48).

[62] See Brown, *Mandelstam*, 131; Struve, 273.

[63] For an insightful critical discussion of Nadezhda Mandel'shtam's construction of a particular image of Mandel'shtam, see Coetzee, 78–81.

[64] Cited in the Struve/Filipoff edition of Mandel'shtam's works, i. 512.

[65] See e.g. *MSS* i. 179–180, 228–9; iii: 217–20; Gorodetskii, 48; Zhirmunskii, 106.

and orchestrations of others' innumerable poetic (and non-poetic) voices and utterances within singular acts of poetry.

Mandel'shtam's architectonic conceptualization of poetry presents yet another point of intersection between the poetics and the metalinguistics of dialogue. While Mandel'shtam's depiction of poet and poetry as 'builder' (zodchii) (*MSS* i. 178) and 'building' (zodchestvo) (i. 179), respectively, certainly draws on a long tradition going back to classical grammar and rhetoric, in which 'structura' (fut. act. part. of 'struere', lit. to build, to construct) refers to the construction of a text, and participates in the overall acmeist revival of the architectonic topos,[66] it reveals itself as metalinguistically significant in view of Mandel'shtam's poetological appropriation of the architectonic topos by way of an explicit displacement of Kantian architectonics, with which he had familiarized himself during a brief stint at the University of Heidelberg in 1909.[67] Mandel'shtam writes: 'The symbolists were bad house sitters . . . they did not like it in the cage of their organism and in that world cage which Kant had constructed with the help of his categories' (ibid.). In the name of acmeism, Mandel'shtam intends poetically to remedy this symbolist discontent with the here and now, with *this* world by reverting to and valorizing Kant's emphasis on concrete experience and its conditions. However, he simultaneously departs from Kant's transcendental approach to experience by pointing out that the acceptance and assumption of *this* world and *this* existence 'has nothing to do with metaphysics' (i. 240)[68] as a transcendental enterprise in the Kantian sense.[69] Mandel'shtam's insistence on the constitutive role of the—past and anticipated—interlocutor in the formation of the (poetic) subject subverts Kant's self-sufficient transcendental subject and displaces the latter's 'architectonics

---

[66] See also *MSS* i. 175–6, 224–5, 231; Gumilev, i. 173; Kuzmin, 6, 10; Gorodetskii, 46, 50; Zhirmunskii, 110–11; Doherty, 67, 112–14.

[67] See Struve, 258. Presumably Mandel'shtam visited lectures by Windelband and such other Neo-Kantians as Emil Lask (Brown, *Mandelstam*, 45–6). In 1916, while in Theodosia, Mandel'shtam asked his mother to send him 'Windelband's ancient philosophy' (letter to his mother (20 July 1916), cited in the Struve/Filipoff edn., iii. 196–7).

[68] Mandel'shtam, Struve/Filipoff edn. ii. 240.

[69] It will be remembered that by investigating the conditions of experience and the functioning of pure understanding Kant was working toward a '*metaphysics of nature*' in general (*Kritik der reinen Vernunft*, i. 18).

of pure reason' (*Kritik der reinen Vernunft*, ii. 695–709) along dialogico-poetic lines. It is important to note that, in addition to its historical and philosophical underpinnings, Mandel'shtam's poetological engagement of architecture is also a direct response to Fedor Ivanovich Tiutchev's (1803–73) poetic interpellation: 'Tiutchev's stone, which "came to rest in the valley after rolling down from the mountain, whether having torn itself from the top by its own force or having been thrown down by a thinking hand"—is the word. The voice of matter resounds in this unexpected fall . . . To this challenge one can only respond with architecture. Awestruck, the acmeists lift Tiutchev's stone and lay it down as the foundation for their edifice' (*MSS* i. 178).[70] Whereas Bakhtin transposes Kant's architectonics onto the interhuman plain, as descriptive of the co-existential constellations of dialogue, Mandel'shtam textualizes Kant's metaphysical edifice, thereby providing an intermediate link, as it were, between Bakhtin's radical dialogization of Kant's architectonics and the latter itself, insofar as dialogue most visibly manifests itself in and is indicated by utterances. Tiutchev's stone in Mandel'shtam's hands captures the intermediate status of poetic architectonics, as it reflects the concrete and singular dialogic encounter(s) between two or more poets and simultaneously provides the foundation for the Mandel'shtamian/acmeist 'poetic universe', which will have thus always been already truly polyphonic at its core.[71] Mandel'shtam's poetological appropriation of Kant's architectonics for the purposes of concrete poetic architecture avoids the trap of Bakhtin's initial phenomenological theoretism and in a sense elaborates a poetics of polyphony *avant la lettre*.

By conceptualizing the poetic word as a stone Mandel'shtam originarily ascribes 'weight' (ves) and 'gravity' (tiazhest') to it:[72]

---

[70] Mandel'shtam refers to Tyutchev's poem: 'After having rolled down the mountain a stone came to rest in the valley.—|How did it fall? nobody knows anymore—|Did it tear itself from the top by its *own* force,|Or was it thrown down by a *thinking* hand?|Century upon century has passed:|Nobody has yet resolved the question!' (Tiutchev, 131).

[71] Mandel'shtam is very clear about the socio-political implications of the acmeist 'poetic universe'. As he points out in 'The Morning of Acmeism', poetry is not isolated from socio-political reality, but, on the contrary, *is* this reality in condensed form, as it were, enhanced 'to the tenth power' (*MSS* i. 177). Poetic architecture, Mandel'shtam emphasizes, is part of the overall 'social architecture' (ii. 286).

[72] See Struve/Filipoff edn. ii. 236; *MSS* i. 175–8, 230; ii. 270–1; iii: 217–20.

the poetic word is heavy, grounded as it is in its authors' co-existences. This is consistent with the acmeist insistence on the acceptance of the world and the life of the here and now: 'The acmeis[t] . . . does not . . . reject his or her gravity but gladly accepts it' (*MSS* i. 178). Like the 'medieval human being' (i. 176), who 'considered himself as indispensable to and as connected with the building of the world as any stone in a Gothic construction' (ibid.), the acmeist valorizes the poet's and poem's 'earthly gravity' (Gumilev, i. 175), the poet's and poem's 'specific weight' (udel'nyi ves) (*MSS* i. 179)—a term also used by Bakhtin in reference to actual speech.[73] The axiological character of Mandel'shtam's (and other acmeists') valorization of existential[74] weight and gravity as informing poetic dialogue poetologically parallels and complements Bakhtin's co-existential emphasis on the 'axiological weight' (tsennostnyi ves) and 'axiological gravity' (tsennostnaia tiazhest') of the interhuman architectonic,[75] which in turn complements Levinas's ethical insistence on 'the pre-ontological weight/gravity of language' (le poids pré-ontologique du langage) (*AQE* 74). Bakhtin's co-existential attention to the architectonic 'axiological weight of *I* and *other*' (*R* 179) finds its poetological continuation in Mandel'shtam's conceptualization of poetry as a 'scales' on which the weight of ' "I" . . . and . . . "non-I" ' (ibid.),[76] respectively, is measured.

CELAN'S DIALOGIC POETICS

In contradistinction to Mandel'shtam's clearly marked poetological essays, in which a coherent and propositionally saturated poetics is elaborated, Celan's sparse prose oeuvre does not yield a clear-cut poetics.[77] Christoph Parry rightly emphasizes that in

---

[73] Bakhtin refers to the word's 'specific weight in the life of language' (*VLA* 82). The poetological and metalinguistic implementation of a technical term borrowed from chemistry corroborates Mandel'shtam's and Bakhtin's conceptualization of dialogue in chemical terms (see above). Of course, Mandel'shtam and his fellow acmeists read the Middle Ages extremely selectively. Thus, they only emphasize the palpable qualities of Gothic architecture, while not accepting its otherworldly connotations.

[74] By 'existential' I specifically refer to Mandel'shtam's injunction: 'Love existence [!]' (*MSS* i. 180).

[75] See e.g. *R* 179, 185, 240–1, 246–7, 251.

[76] Mandel'shtam, Struve/Filipoff edn. ii. 236.

[77] Aside from his two poetologically central speeches, delivered on the occasions

Celan's case the presentation of a presumably coherent poetics will always be the more or less convincing result of the interpreter's synthetic ingenuity and interpretative violence ('Meridian', 31). With this caveat in mind, it is nonetheless plausible to elaborate a Celanian poetics on the basis of such texts—to name only the central ones—as Celan's Bremen Prize speech (1958) and 'Der Meridian' (1960).[78] One of Celan's fundamental poetological tenets consists in the stipulation that poetry is dialogic: 'The poem [is] a manifestation of language and, therefore, essentially dialogic' (*GW* iii. 186). 'The poem', Celan reiterates, 'becomes . . . dialogue' (iii. 198).[79] While Celan's dialogic view of language may have many sources, his particular insistence of the dialogicity of poetry is unmistakably informed by Mandel'shtam's dictum that there is 'no lyric poetry without dialogue', from 'On the Interlocutor', which Celan had been familiar with ever since May 1957 when he bought the Struve-Filippov edition of Mandel'shtam's *Collected Works* (1955).[80] That Celan indeed elaborated both the Bremen Prize speech and 'Der Meridian'—which thematically continues the former and which he considered his 'most important contribution to modern poetics' (Mayer, 174)—in constant dialogue with Mandel'shtam's writings is most clearly evidenced by the fact that in the earlier speech Celan suggests—using Mandel'shtam's metaphor for poetry—that the 'poem can . . . be a message in the bottle, mailed in . . . the hope that some day and somewhere it might wash up on land' (*GW* iii. 186). Thus, Celan's stipulation

of being awarded literary prizes in Bremen and Darmstadt, respectively, letters written to various addressees, and a radio essay on Mandel'shtam, Celan's published prose oeuvre consists of several rather short prose pieces (see *GW* iii).

[78] 'Der Meridian' is Celan's 'speech on the occasion of being awarded the Georg Büchner Prize', delivered in Darmstadt on 22 October 1960. In what follows I focus on those moments of Celan's poetics which are relevant to the present context. For extensive discussions of 'Der Meridian', see e.g. Brierley; Mackey, 89–108.

[79] I should repeat that I use 'dialogicity' in the metalinguistic sense, that is, as a—more or less—mediated dynamic between singular persons, and not as 'intertextuality' in Kristeva's sense. Notwithstanding Celan's emphasis on the dialogic character of poetry, such critics as Ryan (281), Ziarek (150), and, most recently, Holger Gehle (in Böschenstein and Weigel, 126), have—surprisingly enough—attempted to reduce his view of poetry to a closeted monologicity. In contrast to Ryan, Ziarek, and Gehle, such critics as Mayer, Lehmann, Lyon, Fassbind, and Ivanovic, to name only a few, take Celan's stipulation of poetic dialogicity seriously.

[80] See Böschenstein, 'Celan', 156; Terras and Weimar, 359; Felstiner, 128; Ivanovic, 70–2.

of the fundamental dialogicity of poetry is itself already the emphatic enactment of a dialogue between singularities, a response to a singular interlocutor.

Celan's thematic proximity to Mandel'shtam's poetics is biographically grounded in the German poet's belief that he was Mandel'shtam's providential interlocutor, whom he considered and constructed as a 'brother' (*GW* i. 275) in fate.[81] As Christine Ivanovic observes:

> In addition to the significance of Celan's aesthetic dialogue with Mandel'shtam, which played a major role in Celan's explicit articulation of his poetics around 1960, the extremely subjective and emotional aspect of Celan's Mandel'shtam's reception . . . points to his existential and fatidic proximity to the Russian poet . . . Around 1960, Celan develops the conception of a constellation of fate(s), which can be interpreted as the common denominator of his and Mandel'shtam's biography . . . In the encounter with Mandel'shtam, Celan perceived the hope for a poetic response to Jewish fate [in light of the holocaust] (Ivanovic, 71, 82).[82]

It is, therefore, not surprising that Celan's 'encounter with Mandel'shtam's poetry',[83] and through it with its author, who, as Celan notes, necessarily 'remains given to it' (*GW* iii. 198),[84] should have been momentous for his own development as a poet and poetician: 'rarely', Celan writes to Gleb Struve, one of the editors of the first edition of Mandel'shtam's *Collected Works* (1955), 'have I had the feeling—as with his

---

[81] One of Celan's unpublished poems of the *Niemandsrose* period bears the title 'Brother Ossip' (see Ivanovic, 230, 244).

[82] In his poetry and biography, Mandel'shtam epitomized for Celan 'the deep and tragic accord with the epoch' (Mandel'shtam, *Gedichte*, 67). Like Celan, Mandel'shtam was Jewish, and had been persecuted and exiled. At the time when Celan developed his 'fatidic' view of and relation to Mandel'shtam, he assumed that Mandel'shtam had been killed by the Nazis (68); this assumption underscored Mandel'shtam's co-existential significance for Celan, who lost his own family to the Nazis and whose overall traumatic experience of the Holocaust indelibly traces his entire oeuvre.

[83] Celan in a letter to Gleb Struve (29 Jan. 1959), cited in Terras and Weimar, 361.

[84] Elsewhere, Celan notes: 'The poet is given to the poem as a person' (Dem Gedicht ist der Dichter als Person mitgegeben) (*Der Meridian*, 64). Celan does not distinguish between encountering the other and encountering the other through his or her utterances. Fred Lönker rightly notes: 'The encounter with the poem becomes for Celan an encounter with the person, who acquires linguistic gestalt in the linguistic constellation of reality' (Lönker, 223).

[i.e. Mandel'shtam's] poetry—of walking . . . alongside the Irrefutable and the True, and *thanks to him*'.[85]

These thematic and autobiographical references to Mandel'shtam as a poet, poetician, and person culminate in Celan's poetological subversion of a clear-cut distinction between his interpretation of Mandel'shtam's poetics and the articulation of his own. In 'Der Meridian', Celan literally takes up poetologically central passages from his radio broadcast on Mandel'shtam, 'The Poetry of Osip Mandel'shtam' ('Die Dichtung Ossip Mandelstamms')—aired on 19 March 1960, that is, after the Bremen Prize speech (26 January 1958) and before 'Der Meridian' (28 October 1960).[86] To single out only the most obvious instances, Celan writes with reference to Mandel'shtam:

Here the poem is the poem of the one who knows that he is speaking under the angle of inclination of his existence, that the language of his poem is neither 'correspondence' nor language as such, but *actualized* language, voiced and unvoiced at the same time, set free in the name of radical individuation, which, however, remembers the boundaries it is subjected to as well as the possibilities it is granted by language . . . The poem remains a creaturely phenomenon. It is a singularity's language having become gestalt . . . These poems are the poems of a perceiving and attentive [person], who is turned toward the phenomenal, which he interrogates and interpellates; they are *dialogue*. In the space of this dialogue the interpellated is constituted, and makes itself present around the I by which it is interpellated and named . . . into this presence the interpellated, which has, as it were, become a you by being named, brings its alterity and strangeness. Even in the here and now of the poem, even in this immediacy and proximity, the interpellated articulates its distance and preserves that which is uniquely its own: its time.

(Das Gedicht is hier das Gedicht dessen, der weiß daß er unter dem Neigungswinkel seiner Existenz spricht, daß die Sprache seines Gedichts weder 'Entsprechung' noch Sprache schlechthin ist, sondern *aktualisierte* Sprache, stimmhaft und stimmlos zugleich, freigesetzt im Zeichen einer zwar radikalen, aber gleichzeitig auch der ihr von der Sprache gesetzten Grenzen, der ihr von der Sprache erschlossenen Möglichkeiten eingedenk bleibenden Individuation . . . Das Gedicht bleibt . . . ein kreatürliches Phänomen. Es ist Gestalt gewordene

---

[85] Celan in a letter to Gleb Struve (29 Feb. 1960), cited in Terras and Weimar, 363.

[86] For a concise commentary on Celan's broadcast, which was written for the Norddeutscher Rundfunk, see, Ivanovic, 321–45.

Sprache eines Einzelnen . . . Diese Gedichte sind die Gedichte eines Wahrnehmenden und Aufmerksamen, dem Erscheinenden Zugewandten, das Erscheinende Befragenden und Ansprechenden; sie sind *Gespräch*. Im Raum dieses Gesprächs konstituiert sich das Angesprochene, vergegenwärtigt es sich um das es ansprechende und nennende Ich. Aber in diese Gegenwart bringt das Angesprochene und durch Nennung gleichsam zum *Du* Gewordene sein Anders- und Fremdsein mit. Noch im Hier und Jetzt des Gedichts, noch in dieser Unmittelbarkeit und Nähe läst es seine Ferne mitsprechen, bewahrt es das ihm Eigenste: seine Zeit.) ('Die Dichtung', 70–1)

Compare these lines with the following lines from 'Der Meridian':

The poem . . . can . . . only be a speaking. That is, not language as such and . . . not . . . 'correspondence'. Rather, it can only be actualized language, set free in the name of radical individuation, which, however, remembers the boundaries it is subjected to as well as the possibilities it is granted by language. This . . . can . . . only be found in the poem of the one who does not forget that he is speaking under the angle of inclination of his existence, under the angle of inclination of his creatureliness. Then the poem would be . . . a singularity's language having become gestalt . . . The poem becomes . . . dialogue. Only in the space of this dialogue is the interpellated constituted and gathers itself around the I by which it is interpellated and named . . . into this presence the interpellated, which has, as it were, become a you by being named, brings its alterity. Even in the here and now of the poem . . . even in this immediacy and proximity, the interpellated articulates that which is uniquely its, the Other's, own: its time

(Das Gedicht . . . kann . . . nur ein Sprechen sein. Also nicht Sprache schlechthin und . . . nicht . . . 'Entsprechung'. Sondern aktualisierte Sprache, freigesetzt unter dem Zeichen einer zwar radikalen, aber gleichzeitig auch der ihr von der Sprache gezogenen Grenzen, der ihr von der Sprache erschlossenen Möglichkeiten eingedenk bleibenden Individuation. Die[s] . . . kann . . . nur in dem Gedicht dessen zu finden sein, der nicht vergißt, daß er unter dem Neigungswinkel seines Daseins, dem Neigungswinkel seiner Kreatürlichkeit spricht. Dann wäre das Gedicht . . . gestaltgewordene Sprache eines Einzelnen . . . . Das Gedicht wird . . . Gespräch. Erst im Raum dieses Gesprächs konstituiert sich das Angesprochene, versammelt es sich um das es ansprechende und nennende Ich. Aber in diese Gegenwart bringt das Angesprochene und durch Nennung gleichsam zum Du Gewordene auch sein Anderssein mit. Noch im Hier und Jetzt des Gedichts . . .

noch in dieser Unmittelbarkeit und Nähe läßt es das ihm, dem Anderen Eigenste mitsprechen: dessen Zeit.) (*GW* iii. 197–9).

In view of the obvious, partially literal parallels characterizing both passages, Celan's assessment of Mandel'shtam and his poetry can be viewed as a fortiori pertaining to himself and his own poetry.[87] Celan's poetological identification with Mandel'shtam and his work, the poetological substitution, as it were, of himself and his poetry for Mandel'shtam and his poetry, anticipates the thematic substitution enacted in the poem 'Everything is different' ('Es ist alles anders'), from *Die Niemandsrose*: 'The Name Ossip comes toward you . . . | . . . | you sever one arm from his shoulder, the right one, the left one, | you attach your own in their place . . . | —what was torn apart grows together again' (*GW* i. 284).

However, Celan's insistence on the dialogicity of poetry is not only a positive response to Mandel'shtam, but also an ostensibly negative response to Gottfried Benn—one of the most influential post-war German poets, who, like Celan, had been awarded the Georg Büchner Prize in 1951—and to Martin Heidegger. In particular, Celan opposes Benn's dictum that 'poems are addressed to no one' (Benn, *Essays*, 502) and the concomitant stipulation of the fundamentally 'monologic character of poetry' (ibid.). By stating that 'there is no such thing, there cannot be such a thing' as the 'absolute poem' (*GW* iii. 199), Celan overtly criticizes Benn's conceptualization of the monologic poem as an 'absolute [i.e., absolutely monologic] poem . . . without belief . . . without hope' (Benn, *Essays*, 524). Celan also repudiates Benn's claim that 'the poem is made' (495), when he insists that poetry has nothing to do with 'making' understood as 'poiein' (*GW* iii. 178), since it is only a small step, according to Celan, from ' "making" through pretending to plotting' ('Machen' über die Mache . . . zur Machenschaft).

Celan's opposition to Benn's poetics is complemented by an equally strong critique of Heidegger. While seemingly an overt disavowal of—in particular Baudelairean—symbolism, Celan's

---

[87] In a letter to Brigitte and Gottfried Bermann Fischer (22 Nov. 1958), Celan employs the formula 'under the particular angle of inclination of his existence' (unter dem besonderen Neigungswinkel seiner Existenz) in reference to himself (cited in Böschenstein and Weigel, 33), thereby underscoring his identification with Mandel'shtam, whom the formula refers to in the subsequent radio broadcast.

stipulation that poetic language must not be understood as 'correspondence' (Entsprechung), that it is rather '[human] speaking' (Sprechen) and not 'language as such' (Sprache schlechthin), is an invective against Heidegger's ontological conception of language and poetry: Heidegger devaluates human speech in favour of an impersonal language, which he calls the 'house of Being' (*Wegmarken*, 333).[88] He specifies this impersonal language as 'correspondence to Being' (ibid.), while reducing actual human speech to the status of the 'correspondence to language' (*Unterwegs*, 32–3). Poetry, in this schema, becomes the monologic manifestation of the 'speaking of language' (16) by way of the poet, who—in a self-absorbed fashion—is oriented exclusively toward himself. In contrast to Heidegger's impersonal conception of language as 'correspondence to Being', Celan emphasizes the fundamentally dialogic character of language, which transpires in singular acts of actualized human speech addressed to the other, that is, not as the internal monologue of 'language as such': Heidegger's impersonal, ontologized language, Celan writes, is 'a language, not for you and not for me' (*GW* iii. 170). Whereas Heidegger considers poetic speech as most purely corresponding to the language of Being, Celan views poetry as the dialogic manifestation and embodiment of singular speech, as the 'the language of a singular human being having become gestalt' (gestaltgewordene Sprache eines Einzelnen) (iii. 197–8).[89] In contrast to Heidegger, who interprets the 'possibility and necessity of the most radical *individuation*' (*SuZ* 38) in reference to Dasein's assumption of its own existence, Celan considers 'radical . . . individuation' as

[88] In the same passage, Heidegger notes that 'when specifying the humanity of the human being it is crucial to keep in mind that it is not the human being who is essential but Being' (*Wegmarken*, 333–4).

[89] When claiming that, because the capitalization of the term 'der/ein Einzelne(r)' (lit. the/a singular (one)) is uncommon in reference to human beings in German, it must refer to the suprahuman in Celan's text, David Brierley does not take into account the simple possibility of capitalization for reasons of emphasis (Brierley, 210). Thus, Brierley finds himself stuck with a suprahuman entity which presumably speaks a human language. Brierley overlooks the fact that in his response to *Der Spiegel*, Celan equally capitalizes the term when unambiguously referring to the singular human being (*GW* iii. 179). Celan's use of 'Gestalt' (figure, form) is indebted to Martin Buber's term 'Gestaltigkeit' (figureness) (*DP* 29), which characterizes the encounter between human beings. Celan had been closely familiar with Buber's writings since at least 1944 (see *GW* iii. 185; Lyon; Chalfen, 140, 144; Felstiner, 161).

fundamentally interhuman and dialogic rather than ontological. While Heidegger states that 'it is not the human being who is essential . . . but Being' (*Wegmarken*, 333–4), Celan, like Levinas, foregrounds 'creatureliness' (Kreatürlichkeit) (*GW* iii. 197) and 'the human' (das Menschliche) (iii. 190), the singular 'I' as opposed to Heidegger's impersonal '*They*' (Man) (iii. 192).

By responding negatively to Benn and Heidegger in particular, Celan does not simply disavow the poetological and philosophical stipulation of the monologicity of (poetic) language on theoretical grounds, but, more importantly, he unambiguously condemns the presumed socio-political implications of Benn's and Heidegger's conceptual positions: both Benn and Heidegger had endorsed National Socialism after Hitler had been elected chancellor in 1933, and had thereby, in Celan's view, irrevocably compromised themselves and their writings.[90] For Celan, their insistence on the fundamentally monologic character of poetry and language, respectively, acquires definite socio-political significance in the context of the Third Reich, the most lethal manifestation of socio-political monologicity—the physical silencing of the other. Where not the human being is essential but Being, where not the interlocutor is essential but the self-absorbed poet,[91] the other will have been reduced to the same in Levinas's sense, will have, potentially, been physically exterminated. Celan's poetological critique of Benn and Heidegger reveals itself as a scathing socio-political commentary on the socio-political and cultural continuity between pre- and post-war Germany[92] and,

---

[90] In his famous speech 'The New State and the Intellectuals', which was broadcast on 24 April 1933, Benn applauded the 'genuine historical movement' of National Socialism and proclaimed that 'the human being wants to be great, this is his greatness; the human being inevitably strives toward the Absolute' (cited in *Gedichte*, 598–9). It is significant in this context that Benn uses the term 'absolute' both as an historico-political and a poetic category: while the poet strives for the 'absolute poem . . . without belief . . . without hope . . . addressed to no one' (*Essays*, 524), the National Socialist strives toward the socio-political and ideological 'absolute' (*Gedichte*, 599). Subsequently Benn completely reversed his position vis-à-vis National Socialism. Thus, in a letter to F. W. Oelze (24 July 1934) Benn writes: 'There are no words for this tragedy' (cited in *Gedichte*, 600). Heidegger's involvement with National Socialism is sufficiently well documented and in no need of further commentary at this point (see esp. Schneeberger).

[91] Benn notes: 'There is no other subject for poetry than the poet himself' (*Essays*, 510).

[92] It is well known that Celan never ceased to suspect post-war Germany of

in particular, on the lack of socio-political and ideological 'Aufarbeitung',[93] insofar as an initially Nazi-sympathizing poet could have been awarded one of the most prestigious German literary prizes and insofar as one of the most prominent and influential German philosophers failed to comment on his involvement with National Socialism.[94] Celan's implicit socio-political commentary is especially significant in view of the fact that Büchner himself had been an ardent critic of state power and exploitation and an advocate of human rights,[95] and in view of the fact that the reinstitution of the Büchner Prize after the war,[96] whose first post-war recipient was Benn, had been hailed as a landmark of radical socio-political and ideological changes in post-war Germany—as a 'cultural stimulation of the new country' (Johann, 7).

Like Mandel'shtam and Bakhtin, Celan emphasizes the 'dated-ness' of poetry, thereby underscoring its groundedness in singular 'co-existence' (Dasein):[97] 'Perhaps it is permissible to say that

National Socialist tendencies. This suspicion reached its peak in 1960–1, during the so called 'Goll affair', when Celan was publicly accused by Ivan Goll's widow Claire Goll of having plagiarized her husband's work (see Mackey, 179–80). In a letter to Alfred Margul-Sperber (2 Feb. 1962) Celan writes à propos Germany and the plagiarism charge: 'What is new about this Nazi renaissance is that they have found out how to do it "better" than Hitler . . . *Today*, the Goebbels collaborators do not publish in the "Reich" anymore—but you can find them in the Cologne-based "Germania Judaica" (as, for instance, Prof. Dr. Heselhaus)' ('Briefe an Alfred Margul-Sperber', 56). On 22 March 1962 Celan writes to Petre Solomon: 'The other day, I sent you a letter accompanied by a poem (which is the cry of a person *destroyed*—in the strongest sense of the term—by German neo nazis and their accomplices)' ('Briefwechsel mit Petre Solomon', 65). See also Böschenstein and Weigel, 86.

[93] Lit. working up. In the socio-political discourse of post-war Germany, this term implies the conscious, sincere, and productive assumption and assessment of the historical past and contrasts with Freudian repression.

[94] Gerhart Baumann documents Celan's expectations and disappointment with regard to Heidegger's position vis-à-vis his (Heidegger's) initial endorsement of and involvement with National Socialism: the poet hoped for a mitigating comment on the philosopher's part, for an apology perhaps; the philosopher, however, remained silent on the subject of his National Socialist past (Baumann, 51–78; esp. 68).

[95] See Büchner's famous pamphlet 'The Hessian Messenger' (1834) (*Werke*, 39–65).

[96] The Georg Büchner Prize was instituted in 1923 and was not awarded in 1933–45.

[97] See *GW* iii. 186, 201. Celan's use of 'Dasein' should not be rashly equated with Heidegger's ontological functionalization of the term, which conventionally signifies 'existence' in a non-Heideggerian sense. Thus, to give only one pertinent example, in his third Sonnet to Orpheus Rilke writes that 'Poetry is existence' (Gesang ist

in every poem its "January 20th" is inscribed' (*GW* iii. 196).[98]
Celan conceives the poem as an 'event' (Ereignis) (iii. 186)
having a merely 'singular, punctual presence' (einmalige, punk-
tuelle Gegenwart) (iii. 199); poetry witnesses both to the '*event
of co-existence*' (sobytie bytiia) (*R* 43; my emphasis) and the
underlying '*event* of semethics' (événement éthique) (*AQE* 227;
my emphasis).[99] 'January 20th' is a complex semantico-refer-
ential cluster: while it literally invokes Büchner's narrative
Lenz[100] and, as a token date, conveniently generalizes what
can by definition only be singular—co-existential datedness—it
is also a reference to an actual, historical, and, therefore,
singular January 20th, namely, to January 20th 1942, the day
on which the 'Final Solution of the Jewish Question' was
decided upon at the Wannsee Conference.[101] The poem, Celan
notes, subtly mingling the semantics of 'Dichtung' with
National Socialist vocabulary, commemorates such dates; it is
'a *concentration*, which remembers all our dates' (*GW* iii. 198;
my emphasis).[102] Poems are not only condensed utterances, they
are condensations of co-existential constellations. The gravity
and seriousness of Celan's stipulation of the datedness of poetry
is emphasized by his selection of 'January 20th'; this particular
date suggests that every poem is not only written or uttered on a
certain date and thus carries singular co-existential data with it,
that it is permeated from within by its author's dialogic relations

Dasein) (i. 488); in the eleventh Sonnet he writes that 'existence [Dasein] is still
magic to us' (i. 513). I translate Celan's 'Dasein' as 'co-existence' in order to
emphasize his thematic proximity to Mandel'shtam and Bakhtin: if, as Celan
suggests, the constitution of the subject is fundamentally dialogic, his 'Dasein'
reveals itself as indeed always already co-existential in Bakhtin's sense.

[98] On the significance of the 'date' in Celan's poetics and poetry, see Derrida,
'Shibboleth'; Böschenstein and Weigel, 89–90.

[99] Although Celan's stipulation of the poem's absolute singularity is invalid from
the linguistic point of view, which presupposes the constitutive universality of
language, it is metalinguistically justified in view of the constitutive 'iterability'
(Derrida, *Limited Inc*, 119) of utterance. Derrida's concept of iterability—the
'alterability of [the] same . . . in the singularity of the event . . . in this or that
speech act' (ibid.)—articulates with Bakhtin's metalinguistic approach to language.

[100] The first sentence of Büchner's text reads: 'On the 20th of January Lenz
wandered through the mountains' (*Lenz*, 3).

[101] Marlies Janz was the first to point to this haunting allusion by Celan (105; see
also Gellhaus, 'Erinnerung', 7).

[102] The German terms 'Dichtung' (poetry, seal) and 'Gedicht' (poem) contain the
stem *dicht*, which means 'dense'. 'Concentration' of course alludes to concentration
camp, in which human beings were 'condensed', as it were.

to others and others' utterances, but, more importantly, that it is dated from within mortal and moribund co-existence, from within the lives of singular human beings, who speak 'under the angle of inclination of [their] (co-)existence[s]' (iii. 197), and 'always pleads its own, very own cause' (iii. 196), which is ultimately the cause of sheer 'physical survival' (Janz, 11).[103] By virtue of its dialogic make-up, however, the poem also endeavours to plead *'the cause of an Other . . ., . . . of a wholly Other'* (*eines Anderen Sache . . ., . . . eines ganz Anderen Sache*) (ibid.). While Celan's use of Otto's term may suggest a reference to the divine—albeit not necessarily in ontologically immutable terms—it a fortiori implicates the absolutely other human being, insofar as poetry has been defined as fundamentally dialogic.[104] Celan's claim that 'the one who writes [the poem] remains given to it' (iii. 198) does not merely imply the significance of the poem's author as a displaced dialogic 'origin' but, more importantly, as a centre of answerability to and for the other—an answerability, which, Celan points out, 'begins . . . here and now with the singular human being' (iii. 179). By way of Büchner, Celan stresses the 'social and

---

[103] Celan's poetry is thus decidedly engaged, without thereby being propagandistic or ideological (see Janz, 11; Enzensberger, *Einzelheiten*, 133; Pöggeler, *Spur*, 119–20).

[104] Celan explains that by using the 'wholly Other' he is using a 'familiar auxiliary word' (*GW* iii. 199) rather than subscribing to Otto's onto-theological notion of the divine. Buber's critique of Otto's exclusively divine concept of the 'wholly Other'—Buber points out that the 'wholly Other' is equally 'the wholly present . . . which is closer to me than my I' (*DP* 80)—informs Celan's use of Otto's term (see Fassbind, 33–46, 77–96). The simplistic equation of Celan's reference to the 'wholly Other' with a presumed orientation toward 'god' as an immutable 'ontological presence' (DwL 31), whom the poet presumably wishes to encounter in a quasi-mystical or mystical union, is an inadequate interpretation of Celan's putative mysticism at best (see Wolosky, 364; Schulze; Schwarz, 17; Neumann, 77–8). If Celan's orientation toward god is viewed in the Jewish rather than the Christian context, god acquires a decidedly linguistic character, insofar as, according to the Jewish mystical tradition, god operates linguistically, creates through language (see Sholem, 18–19; Wolosky, 368). Thus, the relation to god reveals itself as an essentially linguistic relation. The fact that my relation to the wholly Other is linguistic in turn implies that the wholly Other is always already diachronically engaged, that, hence, a (mystical) union with the wholly Other is impossible (Wolosky, 369–70). Insofar as it is linguistically-diachronically engaged, furthermore, the wholly Other reveals itself as a dialogic sense-position, as an absolutely other interlocutor rather than a putatively supreme ontological entity. The poem's relation to the wholly Other can, consequently, be interpreted as its very dialogic-diachronic orientation. (See also n. 108 below.)

political roots' (iii. 191) of poetry in general and of his own poetry in particular and underscores the ethical function—in Levinas's sense—of poetry as the interruption of (necessarily totalizing) politics in the name of 'the human' (iii. 190). Celan's emphasis on the ethical function of poetry as the interruption of politics comes to the fore most clearly in his insistence that poetry is an 'act' (iii. 189) of protest, a risk-fraught 'counter-word' (Gegenwort) (ibid.) in the face of socio-political adversity, an act which testifies to the 'presence of the human' (Gegenwart des Menschlichen) (iii. 190) alongside the political.[105] Celan further specifies poetry as a 'step' (Schritt) (iii. 195), understood both as spatio-temporally oriented physical displacement *and* as a value-laden, ethically significant act. Poetry reveals itself as the metalinguistically exemplary mode of utterance in the light of Bakhtin's metalinguistic conception of speech as a 'step taken' (Emerson, 'Bakhtin', 108), as an act (postupok) in the co-existential sense. Celan emphasizes the co-existential and ethical significance of poetry by reiterating that it is concerned with 'reality' (*GW* iii. 186), that it endeavours to 'design reality' (ibid.) and that it is both 'sore from reality and searching for reality' (wirklichkeitswund und Wirklichkeit suchend) (ibid.).[106] Celan most poignantly captures the co-existential and ethical significance of his poetry in avowing that 'in those years and in the years that followed [I have tried] to write poems: in order to speak, in order to orient

---

[105] Celan elaborates this ethical concept of poetry on the basis of Lucile's pernicious utterance 'May the king live!' (Büchner, *Werke*, 133) at the end of *Danton's Death*. Lucile publicly utters these words immediately after the execution of Danton and her husband Camille by Robespierre. Lucile knows that by uttering these words at this particular moment and in this particular history she signs her own death warrant. Celan notes: 'Lucile's words may initially sound like a tribute to the "ancien régime". But they do not—allow me, who grew up with the writings of Piotr Kropotkin and Gustav Landauer, explicitly to stress this—pay tribute to monarchy or a conserving Yesterday. They pay tribute to the majesty of the absurd, which testifies to the presence of the human' (*GW* iii. 189–90). (Büchner's Camille and Lucile are fashioned after the historical Camille Desmoulins and Lucile Duplessis, both executed by Robespierre.) Celan's reference to the communist Pyotr A. Kropotkin (1842–1921) and the radical socialist Gustav Landauer (1870–1919) underscores the ethical import of his poetics and poetry.

[106] Celan's insistence on the groundedness of his poetry in reality is, in particular, directed against critics who in one way or another attempt to classify his poetry as 'obscure' and 'hermetic' (see Mayer, 170, 174–5; Mackey, 90–1; Buck, 12; Silbermann, 13, 17; Baumann, 115); it is also a positive response to Günter Eich's 1956 speech 'The Author and Reality', originally published in *Akzente*, 3 (1956).

myself, in order to explore where I was and where I was bound to, in order to design reality for myself' (ibid.).[107] Celan's view of the poetic Said as a means of orientation complements Levinas's ethical view of semethics as originary orientation. The 'one who writes the poem', however, must first be constituted as a poetic subject. Insofar as poetry is fundamentally dialogic, poetic speaking itself must be a fundamentally responsive process, that is, it must transpire in response to poetic interpellation. Celan stresses that it is only 'in the space of [poetic] dialogue [that] the interpellated [das Angesprochene] is constituted' (iii. 198), becomes a 'You' (Du) (ibid.), and thus capable of poetic response;[108] poetic response in turn transpires as a socio-politically exemplary act of protest, a 'counterword'. In close thematic proximity to Levinas, Bakhtin, and Mandel'shtam, Celan conceptualizes the dialogically constituted poetic subject as a 'person' (iii. 189, 194–5).[109] Similarly to Levinas, Celan specifies the fundamental constitution of the human interlocutor in terms of 'creatureliness' (Kreatürlichkeit); while pointing to the human condition, that is, to human mortality, 'Kreatürlichkeit' emphatically indicates my awareness and recognition of a 'feeling of fundamental dependence' (Otto, 22) on the (absolutely) other for my creation.[110]

The space of poetic interpellation opens itself in the encounter

[107] Celan refers to the years of the reign of National Socialism, during which he lost his parents. These lines invoke Eich's credo in 'The Author and Reality': 'I write poems in order to orient myself in reality' (Eich, iv. 441).

[108] Celan uses the neuter form 'das Angesprochene'. He notes that 'for the poem every thing, every human being is the figure of . . . th[e] Other' (GW iii. 198). The fact that Celan does not specify the poem's addressee as necessarily human distinguishes his poetics from Mandel'shtam's. Celan does not resolve the implicit contradiction between the claim that poetry is fundamentally dialogic and the possibility of poetic dialogue with objects or, potentially, with suprahuman agents. In the present context, I focus on the human aspect of Celan's poetics (see also Brierley, 189, 210).

[109] Insofar as the poem is the 'a singularity's language having become gestalt', and insofar as Celan implicitly equates 'gestalt' and 'person' when he writes, 'I am looking for Lenz . . . as a person, I am looking for his gestalt' (GW iii. 194), the poem reveals itself as the manifestation of 'person'. Celan's use of 'person'—like Levinas's—is informed by Buber's concept of 'person' as dialogic and opposed to 'being for itself' (Eigenwesen) (DP 65–6, 71).

[110] Celan's use of 'creature' throughout 'Der Meridian' invokes Büchner's use of the term as contrasting with 'art' in Woyzeck: 'Look at the creature as god made it, nothing, absolutely nothing. Look at art now, it walks upright, has coat and pants' (Büchner, Werke, 237). Celan calls Büchner the 'the poet of the creature' (GW iii. 192).

between the interpellated and the interpellator. In analogy with Levinas's ethical and Bakhtin's co-existential instrumentaliza-tion of the category of the encounter (*EN* 200–2, 239; *R* 160; *PPD* 186, 194; *AST* 340), Celan conceives poetic dialogue as an encounter (Begegnung) with the other in and through poetry. Echoing Mandel'shtam, Celan further submits that poetically encountering the other entails encountering oneself in and through the other (*GW* iii. 201).[111] This emphasis on self-encountering—which does not invalidate the constitutive ad-dressivity of poetry and always already presupposes a poem's actual or proleptic reception by the other—is not only signific-ant in the context of Celan's Mandel'shtam reception, but, more importantly, yet again underscores the thematic proximity between Celan's and Mandel'shtam's poetics and Bakhtin's text. The two poets' insight that my poetic encounter with the other involves my return to myself poetologically complements Bakhtin's insistence on my perseverance in my place in co-existence in the process of dialogic interaction. It is crucial to note, however, that encountering myself through the other always already implies encountering an ever displaced, an ever newly created 'I', an 'I' who is continuously authored by the other, who will have in turn been continuously authored by me.

The possibility of encountering the other through his or her poetry is based on the fact that the other, the poem's primary author, will have always remained in the poem as 'given to it', will have always left the trace of his or her passing in the poem, which will, in turn, have always transported a singular person's fate into the future: poetry, Celan explicates—thereby yet again underscoring both his thematic proximity to Levinas, Bakhtin, and Mandel'shtam *and* his construction of the latter as a 'brother in fate'—performs a person's 'orientation and fate' (Richtung und Schicksal) (iii. 188, 194). Moreover, Celan

---

[111] With particular reference to the composition of one of his own poems (*GW*, i, 147), Celan notes: 'I have . . . encountered myself' (iii. 201). Mandel'shtam equally suggests that poetic dialogue constitutively involves encountering oneself in and through the other: 'The only thing that drives us into the interlocutor's embrace is our desire to be surprised by our own words' (*MSS* i. 187). Ivanovic does not take Mandel'shtam's implicit stipulation of poetic encountering as self-encountering through the other into account, when she opposes Celan's presumed emphasis on 'self-encounter' (Ivanovic, 34, 219) to Mandel'shtam's 'integration and assimilation of others' voices' (ibid.).

suggests, the process of receiving, reading, in short, of co-authoring the poem, of encountering it and through it its primary author transpires as interpersonal contact, as shaking the other's hand: 'I do not see', Celan writes, 'any principal difference between a handshake and a poem' (iii. 177). Celan's poetic handshake exemplarily complements Levinas's ethical stipulation that semethics transpires as contact (*DEHH* 224; *AQE* 134–5).[112] Similarly to Levinas and Mandel'shtam, Celan points out that poetic dialogue allows the person to bring in that which is uniquely his or her own, namely, his or her 'time' (*GW* iii. 199). Insofar as poetic dialogue involves and textually enacts interpersonal diachronicity (in addition to the inevitable diachronicity of speech), poems are fundamentally extended in time, they are 'on the way' (iii. 186, 198), passing 'to the time of the Other' (*DEHH* 192). Celan illustrates the poem's extendedness in time by suggesting that 'poetry attempts to capture gestalt in its directedness, [that] poetry hastens forward' (*GW* iii. 194), that it is a 'sending oneself ahead' (iii. 201). In analogy with a certain technique of representing motion in the visual arts by way of a blurred, continuous, and unidirectional displacement of an initially clearly outlined object or person along the surface of the paper or canvas, poetry performs a singular person's motion through the 'space of time' and, in particular, beyond the singular person's death. Poetry exemplarily indicates the semethical fact that I am constitutively destined 'for-beyond-my-death' (pour-après-ma-mort) (*DEHH* 192)—not, however, for a presumably altered ontic or ontological state, but for the time and life of the other person. Like the light of certain stars which reaches the earth a long time after their actual extinction, carrying its respective source's gestalt with it, poetry transports its primary author's gestalt beyond the span of his or her life. Celan reiterates poetry's constitutive dynamism, its 'motion [and] being on the way' (*GW* iii. 186) by stressing that 'the poem is not timeless' (ibid.), that, while claiming infinity (ibid.), it 'strives to reach across [time], not to bypass it' (ibid.). Celan's rapprochement between poetry and 'utopia' (iii. 199, 200, 202) must be interpreted in the light of this attention to the poem's

---

[112] Celan's conceptualization of poetic dialogue as physical contact is indebted to Buber's notion of the dialogic touch, the 'touch of the You' (Berührung des Du) (*DP* 65).

constitutive spatio-temporal extendedness. While always already traced by singular co-existential constellations, poems—as secondary speech genres—stage secondary contexts,[113] which explode, as it were, the spatio-temporal constraints of actual co-existence. The spatio-temporal realms opened or created by poems are utopian in a literal sense, that is, constitutively without localizable and historically-geographically chartable points of reference in the 'real' world— 'un-spaces', in which interpersonal encounters that may have never taken and might never take place in history may and indeed do take place poetically. Celan's poetological stipulation of the utopian character of poetry complements Levinas's ethical insistence on the utopian character of semethics, which transcends 'space' (as an anthropological, existential, mathematical concept), transpiring 'in' a 'non-space' on the grounds of which 'space' originarily emerges (*EN* 242–3; DwL 32; *AQE* 279, 282–3).

---

[113] See Ch. 2., 'Central Concepts of Metalinguistics'.

PART II

Poethics

If, as Levinas argues, it is 'necessary . . . that Saying . . . manifests itself . . . in the indiscretion of the *Said*' (*AQE* 75, 243), if, furthermore, the architectonic of co-existence can only be witnessed by way of its discursive manifestations, and if, finally, the written Said—and, more specifically, the written poetic Said—is the 'pure Said' (264) par excellence, that is, semethically and metalinguistically exemplary, then recorded poetic utterances exemplarily enact and indicate semethics and co-existential dialogue. It is, therefore, contextually more than plausible to focus on Celan's reception of and response to Mandel'shtam's texts for the study of the actual poetic performance and indication of the semethical and co-existential moments of dialogue. In order to foreground the thematic specificity of my interpretation of Celan's response to Mandel'shtam, I henceforth employ the term *poethics*[1] and its cognate forms in reference to the two poets' dialogue *and* to my reading of this dialogue through the prism of Levinas's and Bakhtin's writings. Poethics signifies my unique attitude—in the phenomenological sense—toward a singular constellation of texts within the clearly delimited conceptual framework of my inquiry. The adoption of the poethic attitude allows me to disclose and capture the ethical and metalinguistic dimension of Celan's dialogue with Mandel'shtam with particular acuity.

[1] To the best of my knowledge, Richard Weisberg introduced the term 'poethics' in reference to the 'poetic substance' of literature as 'a unique source of learning for lawyers' (Weisberg, 34). The term has subsequently been used in the general sense of capturing the relation between ethics and poetry/aesthetics by Gerald Bruns and Joan Retallack (Perloff and Junkermann, 206, 243). I should stress that my understanding and use of the term is distinct from its use by Weisberg, Bruns, and Retallack.

CHAPTER 4

Encountering the Other

TRANSLATING THE OTHER

Celan's poetological response to Mandel'shtam points to a more originary response to the Russian poet on Celan's part—a response which must have transpired, minimally, as some kind of interpretative reception, and this means: as translation. This translational response underlies and informs Celan's more complex, less immediate poetic and poetological rejoinders to Mandel'shtam, which manifest themselves in Celan's extant theoretical texts and poetry—most significantly, in his Mandel'shtam-translations and the cycle *Die Niemandsrose*. While Celan need not have recorded his encounter with Mandel'shtam, he could not have possibly avoided *translating* the latter's interpellation, that is, being constituted as his interlocutor in and through translation.

Judging by his dated annotations in the margins of his copy of the 1955 edition of Mandel'shtam's collected works, Celan began translating Mandel'shtam's poetry in 1958.[2] In 1959 he published the majority of his Mandel'shtam translations.[3] Together with translations of Aleksandr Blok's and Sergei Esenin's poetry, Celan republished his Mandel'shtam translations in expanded form in 1963.[4] Although he continued translating Mandel'shtam's poetry until 1967,[5] the most intensive phase of his dialogue with the Russian poet chronologically coincides with the elaboration of his own poetics (1958–60) and its exemplary instantiation in *Die Niemandsrose*, which, although published in 1963, was begun as early as 1959, that is, precisely during that period in which Celan was deeply

---

[2] The copy is located at the Deutsches Literaturarchiv in Marbach am Neckar.
[3] See Mandel'shtam, *Gedichte*.
[4] See Celan, *Drei russische Dichter*.
[5] Mandel'shtam's poem i: 211 was published in Celan's translation in *Neue Züricher Zeitung* on 23 Dec. 1967.

immersed in Mandel′shtam's texts and in which he was work-
ing on 'Der Meridian'.[6]

The experience of reading Mandel′shtam's poetry underlies
Celan's emphatic valorization of poetic translation as the 'true'
and, hence, fundamental mode of encountering the other
human being. In a letter to Gleb Struve, the editor of the
1955 edition of Mandel′shtam's collected works, Celan depicts
his 'encounter with Mandel′shtam's poems [as] the experience
of the irrefutably true'[7]: encountering, that is, reading, under-
standing, and, consequently, translating Mandel′shtam's poetry
and through it the poet himself constitute 'truth' (Wahrheit)
(*GW* ii. 89). Insofar as Celan uses 'truth' in Kierkegaard's sense,
that is, in reference to the singular human being,[8] his momen-
tous encounter with Mandel′shtam vindicates Bakhtin's philo-
sophical stipulation that the constitution of the other as an
interpellating singularity depends on the interlocutor's respons-
ive, hence, translational act of co-existential authorship. Thus,
when Celan writes in *Atemwende* ('Breath Turn')—thereby
responding to Mandel′shtam's verses 'The air trembles with
similes.│No word is better than the other,│The earth booms
[*drozhit*] with metaphors' (*MSS* ii: 12, ll. 31–3)—

> EIN DRÖHNEN: es ist
> die Wahrheit selbst
> unter die Menschen
> getreten,
> mitten ins
> Metapherngestöber.
>
> (A BOOMING:
> truth itself
> among humans
> has stepped,
> into the midst of the
> flurry of metaphors.)
>
> (*GW* ii. 89)

---

[6] See Ivanovic, 76, 119, 235; Felstiner, 111–69.

[7] Cited in Terras and Weimar, 361.

[8] 'The singular human being . . . is . . . truth' (Kierkegaard, *Die Schriften*, 104).
While Celan could have plausibly had first-hand knowledge of Kierkegaard's
elaboration of his particular notion of truth, he most likely encountered it in *DP*
(210–11). See Chalfen, 140, 144; Felstiner 161; Ivanovic, 349, n. 8.

he implicitly addresses the dialogically, that is, translationally, constituted Mandel'shtam as 'truth' (note Celan's anthropomorphization of 'truth'); the Russian poet literally steps forth as 'gestalt . . . orientation and fate' (*GW* iii. 188) and introduces 'into the poem a [singular] name' (*MSS* ii: 12, l. 38), thereby dissipating the 'flurry of metaphors'.[9] The central significance of poetic translation for Celan is clearly documented in the fact that quantitatively poetic translations constitute more than half of his entire oeuvre.[10]

Under the influence of his encounter with Mandel'shtam, Celan obliterates any attempt at distinguishing between poetic creation and poetic translation, as both are grounded in the dialogic encounter with the other, which they manifest, objectivate, and indicate—albeit in different referential and generic modes.[11] The fact that Celan abandons the distinction between translation and original creation in particular connection with Mandel'shtam's poetry points to the metalinguistic inseverability of Celan's Mandel'shtam translations and his concomitant original poems dedicated to Mandel'shtam. Celan's Mandel'shtam translations and *Die Niemandsrose* enjoin their interpretation as the diachronically displaced objectivations of Celan's unitary response to Mandel'shtam's call.[12] Although critics have pointed to the intimate link between Celan's Mandel'shtam translations and *Die Niemandsrose*, the ethical and metalinguistic significance and cogency of this link have not been noted.[13] As I illustrate in the remainder of this book, together, the Mandel'shtam translations and *Die Niemandsrose* can be read as uniquely

---

[9] Celan's 'Dröhnen' (booming, roaring) phonologically replicates Mandel'shtam's 'drozhit' (booms).

[10] See Lehmann, 'Berührung', 85; Olschner, 322–6.

[11] See Lehmann, 'Berührung', 85; Ivanovic, 106, 230; Baumann, 40; Terras and Weimar, 365–7.

[12] Ivanovic pertinently notes that Celan's 'entire lyric oeuvre is . . . one single text' (Ivanovic, 123). Given the limited framework of the present study, I do not deal with the significance of Celan's encounter with Mandel'shtam for his cycle *Sprachgitter* (*Speech Grille*) (1959).

[13] See e.g. Olschner, 227; Ivanovic, 106–7; Lönker; Parry, *Mandelstam*, 139–226; Baumann, 36, 40; Lehmann, 'Intertextualität'; Rexheuser, 273. Following Pöggeler's suggestion that 'if one really needs a philosophy to read Celan's poems . . . one should look to E. Levinas' (*Spur*, 405, n. 10), Fassbind, Lesch, Wiemer (403–13), and Ziarek (133–80) interpret Celan's writings against the backdrop of Levinasian ethics; however, they do not take into consideration the translational underpinnings of Celan's Mandel'shtam-oriented poetry.

staging and indicating by way of the Said the dynamic of semethics and co-existence. Celan's Mandel'shtam-translations, in particular, exemplarily testify to the irreducibly translational character of semethics and co-existence: as objectivations of Celan's response to Mandel'shtam's interpellation they indicate semethical response-ability and asymmetry *and* co-existential answerability; as enactments of Celan's assumption of answer-ability for Mandel'shtam's poetry and fate through empathizing authorship from an irreducible distance, they point to the interlocutionary dynamic of semethical substitution predicated on infinite separation;[14] as constitutively responsive and hetero-nomous, they indicate semethical passivity, which, 'more passive than any passivity' (*AQE* 170), will have always already trans-formed itself into the 'ethical act [of] personal response' (acte éthique [de la] réponse personnelle) (*TI* 242) and, by extension, into answerability.

TOWARD THE OTHER

Celan's poetic cycle *Die Niemandsrose* is dedicated to Man-del'shtam. Aside from *Die Niemandsrose*, Celan dedicated only one other volume of poetry, *Von Schwelle zu Schwelle* (*From Threshold to Threshold*) (1955), in its entirety to another person, his spouse Gisèle Celan-Lestrange. However, Celan's dedication to his spouse lacks the poetic and poetological dimension which characterizes his dedication to Mandel'shtam: while the dedication 'Für Gisèle' (*GW* i. 81) replicates an infinite number of similar dedications—suggesting the author's grati-tude, reverence, respect, or affection with regard to a particular

---

[14] It will be remembered that Bakhtin conceives co-existential authoring in terms of empathy, that is, as my discursive substitution for the other *and* my return to my singular place in co-existence. The fact that Celan and Mandel'shtam never actually met 'face-to-face' by no means invalidates the exemplary character of their poetic encounter: insofar as semethics and the architectonic of co-existence always already depend on discursivity and, ideally, on poetic discursivity for their witnessability, their indication as the fundamental strata of dialogue will have been constitutively mediated; the degree of discursive mediation, that is, interlocu-tionary distance, is structurally irrelevant to the indication of the inseverability of Saying, co-existence, and Said. Ivanovic rightly notes that 'notwithstanding their utmost an indisputable proximity to the original' (Ivanovic, 139), Celan's trans-lations indicate their insurmountable distance from their pre-texts in placing 'idiosyncratic accents' (ibid.).

dedicatee[15]—and exhausts itself in its formulaic character, the dedication 'Dem Andenken Ossip Mandelstamms' (To the remembrance of Osip Mandel'shtam) by far exceeds its paratextual function. In addition to proclaiming a relation to the dedicatee, in addition to establishing a particular 'intellectual lineage' (Genette, *Paratexts*, 133), it captures in a nutshell the central themes and discourses of *Die Niemandsrose* and, thereby, subverts its paratextual status, plunging the reader into the midst of the poetic and poetological concerns of *Die Niemandsrose*.

The particular significance of Celan's dedication to Mandel'shtam is evidenced in its densely allusive and polyphonic character. 'Andenken' invokes: Friedrich Hölderlin's hymn 'Andenken', which concludes with the famous lines 'What remains, however, the poets found/give' (Was bleibet aber, stiften die Dichter); Heidegger's onto-theological, depersonalized, nationalistic interpretation of this hymn;[16] Celan's own poetological functionalization of the term in his Bremen Prize speech (*GW* iii. 185); and, finally, Celan's earlier poem, 'Andenken' (*GW* i. 121), which in turn refers to Hölderlin's hymn. This thematic and discursive nexus, which displaces the dedication's purely paratextual function, is further saturated by Celan's originary placement of the dedication as an overt and immediate response to Mandel'shtam and his poetry: before appearing at the head of *Die Niemandsrose* the dedication preceded six of Celan's separately published poems, which were subsequently included in *Die Niemandsrose* and which in their first publication in the journal *Die Neue Rundschau* (74/1 (1963)) immediately succeed two of Mandel'shtam's poems in Celan's translation.[17] Thus, Celan's dedication and the original

---

[15] Genette notes: 'The dedication always is a matter of demonstration, ostentation, exhibition: it proclaims a relationship, whether intellectual or personal, actual or symbolic' (*Paratexts*, 135). He adduces the 'minimal formula "To X, Y"' (140), whose 'modern variant [is] "*For X, Y*"' (ibid.). Using the same formula, Celan dedicated several of his poems to various people (*GW* i. 125, 138, 140).

[16] 'Andenken' (1943; in: Heidegger, *Erläuterungen*, 79–151). Heidegger comments: 'The . . . poets of Germany say the Holy. Hölderlin's *Andenken* is not concerned with his "personal experiences" . . . the poet [becomes] the founder of the history of a people . . . that is, in this case, of the history of the Germans' (86, 106).

[17] Celan's poems are: 'Eine Gauner- und Ganovenweise' ('A Rogues' and Swindlers' Ditty') (*GW* i. 229–30; I use John Felstiner's translation (Felstiner,

pre-published poems, which it introduces, directly respond to and continue, as it were, Mandel'shtam's poems; insofar as Celan's pre-published poems synecdochically anticipate *Die Niemandsrose* as a whole, the latter itself can plausibly be interpreted as inherently continuing its author's Mandel'shtam translations.

Celan's dedication, furthermore, acquires ethical force against the backdrop of Levinas's displacement of Celan's dictum that the poem's author 'remains given to it' (*GW* iii. 198). Insofar as any poem is constitutively 'on the way' (iii. 186) to the other, that is, 'dedicated' to the other, according to Levinas's reading of 'Der Meridian',[18] *Die Niemandsrose* as a complex, yet unitary and singular poetic utterance can be interpreted as a 'modality . . . of *otherwise than being*' (*NP* 50), that is, as staging and indicating semethics and thus as fundamentally poethic. My reinterpretation of Celan's dedication to Mandel'shtam by way of Levinas's 'misreading' of Celan's poetological dictum is all the more justified in view of Celan's own oblique depiction of poetry as a dynamic of dedication: 'The attention which the poem endeavours to dedicate to everything that it encounters' (Die Aufmerksamkeit, die das Gedicht allem ihm Begegnenden zu widmen versucht) (*GW* iii. 198) informs its dialogicity. Celan's use of the verb 'to dedicate' (widmen) in connection with 'attention' (Aufmerksamkeit)—although in itself idiomatically unmarked in German—acquires poethic significance in the present context[19] and, ironically, thematically vindicates Levinas's tendentious interpretation of Celan's stipulation of the author's inseverability from his or her poetic utterance.

Of course, the discursive character of Celan's diachronically extended, yet unitary poetic response to Mandel'shtam's inter-

---

174–5)); 'Tübingen, Jänner' ('Tübingen, January') (*GW* i. 226–7); 'Mandorla' (i. 244); 'Anabasis' (i. 256–7); 'Die Silbe Schmerz' ('The Syllable Pain') (i. 280–1); 'Was geschah?'('What occurred?') (i. 269). Mandel'shtam's poems are: *MSS* iii: 121, iii: 177a. Regarding Celan's particular attention to the order and placement of his Mandel'shtam-translations and original poems in *Die Neue Rundschau*, see Ivanovic, 315.

[18] It will be remembered that, following du Bouchet's translation of 'Der Meridian', Levinas observes that 'the I dedicates itself to the other' (le moi se dédie à l'autre) (*NP* 54) by way of the poem. See Ch. 1, 56.

[19] Celan might have equally used the verb 'schenken' (lit. to present with, to give as a present) in connection with 'Aufmerksamkeit' to express the same thought.

pellation necessarily implies its constitution as a heteronomous co-existential act, that is, as an utterance. It must have always been already by definition dialogic, since every word, according to Bakhtin, is 'born in dialogue'. In addition to its 'natural dialogicity', however, Celan's overall poetic response and, in particular, *Die Niemandsrose* reveal themselves as polyphonic: polyphony, I argue, is the very 'principle of [its] concrete poetic construction' (*PPD* 213).[20] This in turn implies that *Die Niemandsrose* must be punctured by the discourse of the third. The continuous presence of the third in Celan's dialogue with Mandel'shtam enacts the ethical and co-existential stipulation of the third in dialogue, while underscoring the cycle's systematic aspect as performed 'langue', in which 'all terms are interrelated' (Saussure, 159) according to the principle of justice (in the most general sense);[21] the polyphonic character of *Die Niemandsrose* reinforces its status as Said, on which both semethics and the architectonic of co-existence depend for their witnessability. Insofar as *Die Niemandsrose* is polyphonic, it must be a 'hybrid construction' (*VLA* 118), that is, an 'utterance which, although it belongs to one speaker grammatically (syntactically) and compositionally, comprises two [or more] utterances, two [or more] manners of speech, two [or more] styles, two [or more] "languages," two [or more] horizons of value and sense' (ibid.).[22]

In the two remaining chapters, which are devoted to the close examination of Celan's Mandel'shtam-translations and *Die Niemandsrose* in the light of Levinas's and Bakhtin's ethical philosophies, my poethic claims shall be concretely tested. I

[20] It will be remembered that 'polyphony' metalinguistically corresponds to and informs the concept of the architectonic of co-existence with all of its concomitant features and designates the entire range of aspects characteristic of interpersonal dialogue as it is uncovered by Bakhtin in Dostoevsky's novels. 'Polyphony' has been metalinguistically defined as the artistic enactment of the architectonic of co-existence, of a 'multiplicity of fully valid voices within the limits of one poetic work' (*PPD* 240).

[21] In the most general sense, 'justice' means, as Derek Attridge observes, the 'union of a singular occurrence and a general law' (cited in Derrida, *Acts*, 18).

[22] I should stress that hybridization is equally possible and prevalent, according to Bakhtin, in novelistic discourse. However, while it may perform a subsidiary function in novelistic discourse, which avails itself of additional strategies for staging polyphony (such as the concrete juxtaposition of languages and actual dialogues), it assumes the burden of responsibility, Bakhtin implies, for polyphony in poetry, a 'formally' monologic mode of utterance.

focus on those aspects of Celan's text which most overtly manifest its stylistic visage and, thereby, disclose its semethical and co-existential motivation. I should stress that in stipulating the specifically poethic import of Celan's response to Mandel'shtam, I do not suggest a poethic intention on Celan's part; rather, I endeavour to do justice to the indelibly ethical demands of Celan's and Mandel'shtam's poetics and poetry. From within the poethic attitude the constitutive features of Celan's response acquire unprecedented force and significance. Insofar as Celan's poetry emphatically 'arranges (almost choreographs) its reader into attitudes of reception' (Waters, 131), my poethic attitude testifies, as I have noted earlier, to my very personal critical approach. Poethics is my countersignature to, my unique 'inventive experience' (Derrida, *Acts*, 52) with Celan's, Mandel'shtam's, Bakhtin's, and Levinas's writings.[23] It is my way of becoming answerable to and for my interlocutors. After all, is it not the critic—and by 'critic' I mean the professional literary critic, in particular—who by definition assumes the interlocutor's role, who perpetually reconstitutes him- or herself as an ever displaced interpellated and, hence, ethical subject, without an alibi?

---

[23] Christoph Parry rightly observes that for an adequate critical engagement with Celan's poetry the context of its reception is equally—if not more—decisive than the context of its production ('Meridian', 41). Although this 'catalytic method' (49) may seem logically unfounded, Parry notes, 'its results are by no means inferior to more traditional methods' (ibid.).

CHAPTER FIVE

'. . . combien est-il donc difficile de traduire'. . .[1]

RENDERING GESTALT

Translating poetry is difficult, according to Celan, not only and not so much because 'poetry [is presumably] by definition untranslatable' (*SW* 362) on the grounds of any two languages' fundamental linguistic and prosodic incongruities, but, more importantly, because the translator should aim beyond the linguistic and the prosodic, striving 'to translate the poetic in the poem, to render the gestalt . . . of the speaker'.[2] Rendering gestalt is predicated on the translator's grasp and (re)enactment of the poetic performance of another person's co-existence, that is, his or her 'orientation and fate' (*GW* iii. 188) (notwithstanding the other person's structural absence and relative historical or geographical distance from his or her poetic utterance). Insofar as poetry 'attempts to see . . . gestalt in its directedness' (iii. 194), as it 'hastens forward [toward the other]' (ibid.), that is, insofar as poetry raises the multi-contextual and diachronic constitution of living speech to the status of an artistic principle, the translator of poetry must take into account at least two co-existential contexts, two times, two realities: the primary author's and his or her own. This means that it is the translator's task not simply to treat poems 'as [reproducible] givens' (Olschner, 101), but to approach them in terms of obligation, as 'given as a task', as to be dialogically (re)created. Celan insists that in writing poetry—and translating for Celan is equal to original creation—he does not merely rely on a presumably given reality—including the material and semantic reality of the poem—but, on the contrary, stipulates reality as something to

---

[1] '. . . how difficult it is, after all, to translate . . .'; Celan in a letter to G. Struve (26 Feb. 1959), cited in Terras and Weimar, 363.
[2] Celan in a letter to G. Struve (29 Jan. 1959), cited in Terras and Weimar, 362.

be dialogically 'designed' and 'attained'.[3] The reality of the poem to be translated is by no means codified or fixed; it is always yet to be achieved through its potentially infinite dialogic (re)enactments.

It is hardly surprising then that Celan's poetic translations— being methodical enactments of realities (including the material realities of the texts themselves) which are necessarily distinct from those realities which the originals, as graphically fixed historical documents, are presumed to possess—are not principally 'faithful' to their pre-texts in any conventional sense. Celan's displacement of traditional, semantically and stylistically based paradigms of poetic translation in favour of a co-existential conception of poetic translation predicated on dialogic encountering inevitably informs and manifests itself in his actual, poetologically motivated translational choices and strategies.[4] Although Celan by no means disregards or obliterates the original's semantics, he is willing to make it subservient to his particular poetological and poetic purposes, orienting his translations toward their pre-texts' respective semanticity rather than semantics.[5] Thus, to give a famous preliminary example, in his translation of Shakespeare's sonnet 105 ('Let not my love be called idolatry'), Celan departs from the original's semantics in any sense of literalness, transposing its theme ('constancy'), as Peter Szondi suggests, onto the material level of the text:

Let not my love be call'd idolatry,
Nor my beloved as an idol show,
Since all alike my songs and praises be
To one, of one, still such, and ever so.
Kind is my love today, tomorrow kind,
Still constant in a wondrous excellence;
Therefore my verse, to constancy confin'd,
One thing expressing leaves out difference.
'Fair, kind, and true' is all my argument—
'Fair, kind, and true' varying to other words;

[3] See Ch. 3, 'Celan's Dialogic Poetics'.

[4] For a synopsis of the history of poetic translation, see my '"Literal Translation"', 3–6. Lehmann notes that critical approaches which endorse a conception of poetic translation predicated on 'adequacy and lexical faithfulness . . . hardly do justice to Celan's texts' ('Intertextualität', 255).

[5] By 'semanticity' I mean an utterance's overall significance and signification as opposed to 'semantics', which I understand to be a structural category pertaining to an utterance's more or less clearly delimited level of meaning, to its signified or theme.

And in this change is my invention spent—
Three themes in one, which wondrous scope affords.
  'Fair, kind, and true' have often liv'd alone,
  Which three till now never kept seat in one.

              (Shakespeare, Sonnet 105)

Ihr sollt, den ich da lieb, nicht Abgott heißen,
Nicht Götzendienst, was ich da treib und trieb.
All dieses Singen hier, all dieses Preisen:
von ihm, an ihn und immer ihm zulieb.

Gut ist mein Freund, ists heute und ists morgen,
und keiner ist beständiger als er.
In der Beständigkeit, da bleibt mein Vers geborgen,
spricht von dem einen, schweift mir nicht umher.

'Schön, gut und treu', das singe ich und singe.
'Schön, gut, und treu'—stets anders und stets das.
Ich find, erfind—um sie in eins zu bringen,
sie einzubringen ohne Unterlaß.

'Schön, gut und treu' so oft getrennt, geschieden.
In einem will ich drei zusammenschmieden.

         (translation by Celan, GW v. 344–5)[6]

You shall, the one there whom I love, not name an idol,
not idolatry what I there *pursue and pursued*.
All this singing here, *all this* praising:
about him, to him and always for his sake.

Good is my friend, *is it* today and *is it* tomorrow,
and no one is more constant than he.
In constancy, there my verse remains sheltered,
speaks of the one, does not stray about.

'Fair, good, and true', this I *sing and sing*.
'Fair, good, and true'—*constantly* different and *constantly* this.
I *find, invent*—in order *to bring them into* one,
to bring them in without intermittence.

'Fair, good, and true' so often *separated, divorced*.
In one I want to forge three.

        (translation of Celan's translation; my italics)

---

[6] The stanzaic division is Celan's.

Szondi comments:

Constancy is the theme of Shakespeare's sonnet . . . Celan does not
have the poet speak of his *argument*, his *invention*, his *scope*; rather,
his verses adapt themselves to the requirements of theme and
intention. Celan does not have the poet claim that he obliterates
differences; rather, he has him speak a language which has obliter-
ated differences . . . In translating a poem whose theme is . . .
constancy . . . Celan . . . has replaced the traditional symbolist poem,
which deals with itself, which is its own theme, with a poem, which
does not deal with itself anymore, but which is itself. A poem which
does not speak about itself anymore, whose language is *sheltered* in
that which it ascribes to its subject, to itself: *in constancy*. (Szondi,
43–4)

Szondi's observations[7] articulate with Celan's insistence on
rendering gestalt through translation: the semanticity of Shake-
speare's poem—including its semantic, grammatical, and pro-
sodic features, in short, everything that makes it meaningful as
this singular utterance—acquires palpable, material gestalt in
Celan's (prosodically faithful) translation.[8] Insofar as Celan
conceives the poem as its primary author's diachronic extension
into the future, the speaker's poetic gestalt must be understood
as the poem itself—in its semanticity: gestalt reveals itself as an
emphatically metalinguistic concept, as a speaker's co-existence
viewed from within, or rather, by way of his or her (poetic)
utterances. By materially staging the original's gestalt, Celan
indeed succeeds in fulfilling his poetological stipulation and,
thereby, demonstrates its practical feasibility. Furthermore,
insofar as poetry qua utterance will have not only always been
already co-authored by its recipient but will have potentially
turned its natural dialogicity into an artistic principle, Celan's
idiosyncratic addenda and displacements not only testify to any
utterance's natural dialogicity, but, more importantly, hybridize
the original, thus creating a genuinely prosaicized, polyphonic
structure.

   Among his numerous poetic translations, Celan's transla-
tions of Mandel'shtam's poetry have received particular critical

---

[7] For an alternative interpretation, see Lönker, 212–13.
[8] Celan preserves Shakespeare's iambic pentameter and alternating rhyme scheme
(quartets abab, cdcd, efef; couplet: gg). His only alteration consists in breaking the
Shakespearean sonnet up into three discrete quartets and a discrete couplet, which
can be interpreted as the formal performance of constancy.

attention given his explicit proclamation of the Russian poet's significance for himself both as a person and as a poet. In contrast to Rexheuser's early condemnation of Celan's practice of poetic translation on the grounds of faithfulness, such critics as Lönker, Böschenstein, Lehmann, Olschner, Ivanovic, and, most recently, Parry have interpreted Celan's reception of Mandel'shtam's texts as an integral, poetologically motivated part of his poetic oeuvre and as immensely influential with regard to his immediately succeeding original poetry.[9] While building on these critics' linguistic and philological observations, I interpret Celan's reception of and response to Mandel'shtam from within a radically distinct, phenomenological attitude. Rather than merely explicating Celan's translational choices in the light of his poetics—thereby validating the latter by the former—or endeavouring to disclose an ever-expanding subtextual network underlying Celan's texts, I interrogate their poethic significance. Thus, from within the poethic attitude, Celan's perpetual 'unfaithfulness' to and displacements of Mandel'shtam's poems can plausibly be interpreted as pointing to and motivated by semethical and co-existential asymmetry.

It is important to note at this point that, although Celan's response to Mandel'shtam may share linguistic, stylistic, and prosodic features with his other translations and original poems, the mere observation of these features' presumed universality[10] is not only hermeneutically unproductive but, more importantly, obfuscates the fact that universality is principally grounded in singularity—in this case, in singular co-existential and semethical dialogue: if, as Celan suggests, his encounter with Mandel'shtam was *the* poetically central event in his life, those texts by Celan which explicitly testify to this encounter—his Mandel'shtam translations and *Die Niemandsrose*—demand an emphatically non-universalizing, poethic interpretation. Since poethics must perforce proceed by way of the Said in its attempt to elucidate the co-existential and semethical underpinnings of dialogue, it inevitably depends on and involves close reading and meticulous

[9] See Lönker; Böschenstein, 'Celan'; Lehmann, 'Berührung'; 'Intertextualität', 268–77; Olschner, 226–74; Ivanovic, 212–46; Parry, 'Übersetzung'.
[10] See esp. Rexheuser; Olschner, 57–136; Lönker; Turk.

textual description and analysis. In what follows I focus on the pragmatic and semantic features of Celan's Mandel'shtam translations. Insofar as metalinguistics deals with the semethically grounded architectonic of co-existence from the perspective of its poetic enactment, a pragmatic approach to Celan's translations is the logical point of entry into their overall poethic interpretation. For the sake of clarity and in order to provide the reader with a general impression and 'feel' of Celan's translations, I cite—sometimes at length—the relevant textual instances before describing and commenting on them.

DIALOGIZATION[11]

One of the first idiosyncrasies striking the reader of Celan's Mandel'shtam translations is his frequent use of deictic—personal, spatio-temporal, and demonstrative—markers, which are either absent or less prominent in the originals and thus constitute a textual pragmatics characteristic of the translations only.[12] The excessive presence of these deictic markers—especially personal pronouns—in Celan's translations is not explicable on the grounds of the respective linguistic and grammatical specificities of Russian and German.[13] Beginning my discussion of Celan's Mandel'shtam translations by focusing on person deixis, I elaborate Celan's consistent dialogization—and, hence, poethic displacement—of his Russian pre-texts.

---

[11] As will become clear in the course of my discussion, 'dialogization' encompasses all ethically and metalinguistically significant features of Celan's translations. It does not primarily signify the poetic staging of conventional dialogue.

[12] I use 'pragmatics' in its most general semiotic sense as designating the 'relation of signs to interpreters' (Morris, 6), that is, to speakers in particular spatio-temporal contexts (Carnap, 3). Pragmatics is inevitably linked to semantics, insofar as it constitutes part of an utterance's overall meaning.

[13] See Olschner, 117. Both Russian and German are inflected languages and thus indicate the person through the ending of the finite form of the verb. Although—in theory—both would, consequently, not require the use of personal pronouns (as is frequently the case in Polish, for instance), personal pronouns are conventionally used in both. However, while Russian may or may not call for the personal pronoun in certain speech contexts and genres (especially in elliptic, everyday speech), German always requires the use of the personal pronoun.

Between Persons

As the following examples illustrate,[14] two pronominal tendencies characterize Celan's response to Mandel'shtam: (1) he proliferates personal pronouns (first-, second-, and third-person), which occur much less frequently in the originals, and at times introduces first-person discourse completely absent in the originals; (2) he dramatically intensifies the originals' dialogic structure and at times introduces dialogic constructions which have no equivalents in the originals. Given that these tendencies are not sporadic but inform Celan's translations throughout, they can be considered the translations' constitutive organizing forces.[15]

In his translations of poems i: 77 ('How slowly [the] horses tread*'), i: 162 ('Sleeplessness. Homer. Taut sails'), and i: 197 ('Tristia'), Celan proliferates the first-person pronoun beyond the number of its occurrences—in various grammatical cases—in the originals. By thus intensifying Mandel'shtam's first-person pragmatics Celan highlights the significance of singular enunciation:

(i: 77, ll. 5–6, 9–12)	(GW v. 63)
(5) А я вверяюсь их заботе.	Ich bin umsorgt, *ich* bin es gerne,
(6) Мне холодно, я спать хочу	ich suche Schlaf, mich friert.
(9) Горячей головы качанье,	Der Kopf gewiegt, *ich* fühl ihn brennen.
(10) И нежный лед руки чужой,	Die fremde Hand, ihr sanftes Eis.
(11) И темных елей очертанье,	Der dunkle Umriß dort, die Tannen,

[14] I adduce the contextually most striking and relevant instances only. Mandel'shtam's and Celan's texts are presented as follows: Mandel'shtam's text (left column), Celan's translation (right column), followed by English translations of the Russian (left column) and the German (right column) texts. Celan's translations are cited according to GW, vol. 5, with page references. All italics are my own. I should stress that I provide crude, literal translations only and do not deal with Celan's deployment of rhyme in detail. Those instances in the English translations in which the definite and indefinite or the continuing and simple present could be used are marked with an asterisk.

[15] See Olschner, 83. I should stress that this and subsequent arguments are not quantitative. Only very few of Celan's translations (GW v. 49, 51, 55, 83, 117, 119) are pronominally unmarked.

(12) Еще невиданные мной.

von denen ich nichts weiß.

(5) But I entrust myself into their care.

I am taken care of, *I* enjoy* it,

(6) I am cold, I want to sleep;

I look* for sleep, I am cold.

(9) A* hot head's rocking,

The head rocked, I feel it burning.

(10) And the tender ice of a* strange hand,

The strange hand, its tender ice.

(11) And (the) dark fir trees' contours,

The dark silhouette, there, the fir trees,

(12) Not yet seen by me.

about which I don't know anything.

(i: 162, ll. 1–2, 7–8, 10–12)

(GW v. 91)

(1) Бессоница. Гомер. Тугие паруса.

Schlaflosigkeit. Homer. Die Segel, die sich strecken.

(2) Я список кораблей прочел до середины:

Ich las im Schiffsverzeichnis, *ich* las, *ich* kam nicht weit:

(7) Куда плывете вы? Когда бы не Елена,

Ihr schwebt, ihr schwimmt— wohin? Wär Helena nicht drüben,

(8) Что Троя вам одна, ахейские мужи?

Achäer, solch ein Troja, *ich* frag, was gält es euch?

(10) Кого же слушать мне? И вот Гомер молчит,

Wem lausch ich und wen hör *ich*? Sieh da, er schweigt, Homer.

(11) И море черное . . . шумит

Das Meer . . . an dieses Ufer schlägt es,

(12) И подходит . . . к изголовью.

zu Häupten hör *ich*s tosen . . .

---

(1) Sleeplessness. Homer. Taut sails.

Sleeplessness. Homer. The sails which stretch* themselves.

(2) I have read half of the list(ing) of ships:

I read* in the list(ing) of ships, *I* read*, *I* did not get* far:

(7) Where are you sailing? If it were not for Helen,

You float*, you swim—where to? If Helen were not over there,

(8) Would you care for Troy alone, Greek men?

Greeks, such a Troy, *I* ask, what would it mean to you?

(10) To whom should I listen? Look, Homer is silent,

To whom do *I* hearken*, and whom do I hear*? Look, there, he is silent, Homer.

(11) And the black sea . . .
    roars*

The sea . . . beats* against this
    shore,

(12) And reaches* . . . the
    pillow.

at my head *I* hear it roaring . . .

(i: 197 ('Tristia'), ll. 1–2, 5–6)

(*GW* v. 105)

(1) Я изучил науку расста-
    ванья

Ich lernte Abschied—eine Wissen-
    schaft;

(2) В . . . жалобах ночных.

ich lernt sie nachts, von Schmerz
    . . .

(5) И чту обряд той . . .
    ночи,

Und ich—*ich* halts wie in der
    Nacht . . .

(6) Когда, подныв . . .
    скорби груз,

da *ich*, den Gram geschultert . . .

(1) I have learnt the science of
    separation

I studied* separation—a science;

(2) In . . . nocturnal com-
    plaints.

I studied* it at night, from pain
    . . .

(5) And I honour the ritual of
    that . . . night,

And *I*—I do as in the night . . .

(6) When, having lifted . . . the
    load of sorrow,

when *I*, having shouldered the
    grief . . .

Celan's repetition of the identical first-person-singular-copula formula, 'I am . . ., I am' (Ich bin . . ., Ich bin) (l. 5) in i: 77 is immediately succeeded by yet another first-person-singular-predicate structure, 'I look* for' (Ich suche) (l. 6). A Germanic 'Stabreim' (strong-stress metre) ('bin . . . bin'), which prosodically reiterates the poem's transposition into the German idiom by pointing to the translation's specifically Germanic contextualization,[16] corroborates this rhetorical emphasis on the utterance's active, German-speaking source. Celan's pronominal anaphora in lines 5 and 6 as well as the prosodically[17] and semantically gratuitous second 'I' in line 5[18] foreground the

[16] The Germanic or Anglo-Saxon 'strong-stress meter' was characteristic of medieval and late medieval texts, such as *Beowulf*, *Edda*, and the Old High German *Hildebrandslied*.

[17] My subsequent attention to prosody pertains to the prosodic parameters established within Celan's translations. I take it for granted that Mandel'shtam's poems can be and have been translated in completely different ways (e. g. by Ralph Dutli), which do not accommodate such pronominal (and other) idiosyncrasies.

[18] In this case, the 'I' could easily be substituted by 'and' (und) without disrupting Mandel'shtam's iambic tetrameter—which Celan preserves in his translation—or departing from the verses' overall meaning.

translation's active first-person pragmatics. Celan's pragmatic displacement of the original culminates in lines 9–12, in which Mandel'shtam's static and almost impersonal description is replaced by the speaker's emphatically active experiencing: while lines 9–12, the poem's last stanza, do not contain a single predicate or an active subject in the original—the stanza's only verb ('to see') is given as a negated past participle ('Not . . . seen'), the only personal marker occurs in the instrumental case, 'mnoi' (by me), which emphasizes the speaker's passivity— Celan stresses the speaker's active perception and experience of his state and surroundings by introducing two active predicates, 'feel' (l. 9) and 'know' (l. 12), accompanied by two pronominally specified subjects.[19]

In contrast to its singular occurrence in the original, Celan uses the first-person singular pronoun five times in his translation of i: 162 (ll. 2, 8, 10, 12)—excluding the 'I' of 'To whom do I hearken*', which correctly translates the Russian 'Kogo zhe slushat' mne'. He repeats it three times in line 2 alone and thematizes the grammatical question of line 8, 'Would you care for Troy alone, Greek men?' (l. 8) in the parenthetic 'I ask'. This multiple use of the first-person-singular pronoun is not only prosodically unmotivated, but, in fact, interferes with the translation's iambic hexameter, which Celan suggests in line 1—in compliance with the original—as the translation's metric structure. Already in the second line Celan disrupts the poem's hexametric flow by positioning a caesura at its centre, thus breaking it up into two iambic trimeters. This is surprising, since a clean, caesuraless hexameter could have been preserved by simply omitting the second 'I'. Similarly, if Celan's third 'I' in line 2 is substituted by an 'and', the prosodically unnecessary pronominal repetition can easily be avoided without metric sacrifices whatsoever. This shows that if Celan had indeed been concerned with translating 'meaning' correctly in a prosodically 'regular' fashion, he could have, for instance, written: 'Ich las im Schiffsverzeichnis, las und kam nicht weit' (I read* in the list(ing) of ships, read* and did not get* far). The caesura between the third foot of the first trimeter and the first foot of the second trimeter in line 2 stresses the centrality of the 'I', thus

---

[19] The adverb 'there' (l. 11) equally contributes to the personalization and concretization of Mandel'shtam's poem (see below).

enhancing the impact of its triple repetition. A similar positioning of a prosodically unmotivated first-person-singular pronoun occurs in lines 8 and 10, whose central spaces are occupied by an 'I': in line 8, 'I ask' materially and thematically stages the caesura which it borders on the right as the first foot of the second trimeter; in line 10, the 'I' falls on the unstressed syllable of the last foot of the first trimeter immediately preceding the caesura. The anaphoric (ll. 1–2) and iterative (l. 5) placement of the first-person pronoun in Celan's rendition of 'Tristia' equally serves the function of emphasis. In all of these cases Celan positions the first-person singular pronoun in such ways that it coincides with a metrically unstressed syllable. The ensuing inversions of stress further underscore the first-person pronouns' significance.[20]

In his translations of poems i: 124 ('In a* tavern, a band of thieves') and i: 127 ('The bread is poisoned and drunk the air'), Celan intensifies the pragmatic value of first-person deixis by gratuitously introducing direct first-person discourse:

(i: 124, ll. 5–8)

(5) На башне спорили химеры:

(6) Которая из них урод?

(7) А утром проповедник серый

(8) В палатки призывал народ.

(GW v. 79)

Auf dem Turm: Chimären raufen:

'Ich bin häßlicher!'—*'Nein, ich!'*

Tag. Ein Prediger. Der Haufe

strömt ins Zelt, versammelt sich.

(5) On a* tower chimeras argued*:

(6) Which one among them is the ugly one?

(7) But in the morning a* grey preacher

(8) Called* the crowd into (the) tents.

On the tower: chimeras scuffle*:

'I am uglier!'—*'No, I!'*

Day. A preacher. The crowd

streams* into the tent, gathers* itself.

(i: 127, ll. 1–2, 9–12)

(1) Отравлен хлеб и воздух выпит.

(GW v. 81)

Die Luft—vertrunken, und das Brot—vergiftet.

---

[20] A similar proliferation of first-person singular pronouns can be observed in Celan's translations of Mandel'shtam's poems i: 45, l. 9 (GW v. 57); i: 46, ll. 6–7 (59); i: 86, l. 10 (71); i: 202, ll. 1, 8 (109); i: 206, l. 2 (111); i: 207, l. 19 (115); ii: 2, l. 12 (121).

(2)	Как трудно раны враче- вать!	Wie diese Wunden heilen? Schwer.
(9)	Немного нужно для наитий:	Nur wenig brauchts, und *du* durchschaust dein Leben:
(10)	Кто потерял в песке колчан,	—*Ich* fand den Köcher nicht mehr.—*Ich*
(11)	Кто выменял коня— событий	vertauscht mein Pferd.—Was sich begeben,
(12)	Рассеевается туман.	ist Nebel, und es lichtet sich.

(1)	(The) bread is poisoned and drunk the air.	The air—drunk, and the bread— poisoned.
(2)	How hard is it to treat (the) wounds!	How these wounds are healing? Hard.
(9)	Not much is needed for inspiration:	Little is needed, and you see through your life:
(10)	One (has) lost a* quiver in the sand,	—I did not find the quiver any- more.—I
(11)	One (has) exchanged a* horse—of (the) events	exchanged my horse—What (has) transpired,
(12)	The fog is clearing up.	is fog, and it is clearing up.

Celan's transformation of Mandel'shtam's pragmatically unspecified query in i: 124, l. 6, 'Which one among them is the ugly one?', into an overt dialogic exchange, ' "I am uglier!"—"No, I!" ', radically personalizes the translation. By allowing the chimeras to speak for themselves, this conventional literary dialogue indicates and suggests the implied speaker's situational immediacy with regard to the narrated events in the poem.[21]

In his translation of i: 127 Celan equally personalizes Mandel'shtam's fairly impersonal, epic 'narrative', which culminates in the proclamation:

И, если подлинно поется
И полной грудью, наконец,
Всё исчезает: остается
Пространство, звезды и певец!

And when it is genuinely sung
At the lungs' full capacity, in the end,
All vanishes: remains
Space, stars and a* singer!

---

[21] Poem i: 124 consists of four iambic tetrameter stanzas, which relate events in a balladesque fashion. The poem begins in the epic past and ends in the historical present. Celan's dialogized translation stresses the original's balladesque character.

While Mandel'shtam gnomically states that 'Not much is needed
for inspiration' (l. 9), providing two impersonal examples of this
thesis, 'One (has) lost a* quiver in the sand, I One (has) exchanged
a* horse . . .' (ll. 10–11), Celan introduces two direct utterances, 'I
did not find the quiver . . .—I I exchanged my horse . . .',[22] which
have the same function of immediatization as the conventional
literary dialogue in his translation of poem i: 124. Celan's implicit
emphasis on pragmatic immediacy—in the context of the nar-
rated events—on the part of the poetic witness is corroborated by
his displacement of Mandel'shtam's exclamation, 'How hard is it
to treat (the) wounds!' (l. 2). Although Mandel'shtam's exclama-
tion suggests an emotional enunciatory source, his implied
speaker—poem i:127 does not contain any first-person pronom-
inal references—remains pragmatically unspecified. Celan trans-
lates this line by way of an indirect question, 'How these wounds
are healing?', and an immediate response, 'Hard'. Whereas
Celan's dialogization of Mandel'shtam's poem i: 124 occurs on
an intrapragmatic plain, creating a fiction to the second degree, as
it were, this instance genuinely testifies to the implied speaker's
pragmatic stance vis-à-vis a presumed extratextual interpellation.
The question's syntax suggests its responsive character: syntactic-
ally, it is itself an indirect question in response to a presumed
interpellation, which it takes up for reasons of emphasis or
clarification, thus serving a metalingual, phatic and/or conative
function.[23] Without using any specifying deictic markers, Celan
unambiguously points to the heteronomous constitution of his
own poetic utterance, that is, to its constitution in response to
Mandel'shtam's interpellation. This subtle transformation of
Mandel'shtam's text evinces Celan's utterance as genuinely
double-voiced, hybrid, and, consequently, polyphonic, insofar
as hybridization is, according to Bakhtin, one of the poetic
manifestations of polyphony: Celan's indirect question is indeed
an 'utterance which belongs to one speaker . . . [but] which . . .

[22] These lines enact an intrapragmatic, fictional dialogue, as it were, within the
poem's overall pragmatics (the change of speakers, although not indicated by
quotation marks, is obvious in view of the original's 'One . . . I One . . .', which
clearly implies two discrete referents.

[23] See Jakobson, *Language*, 66–71. The position of 'healing' in Celan's transla-
tion unmistakably indicates the verse's indirect interrogatory character, since the
question's direct variant would grammatically require that the verb be in second
place (see below).

combines two utterances ... two horizons of valuation and sense'
(*VLA* 118). The responsive character of Celan's question is
underscored by the answer, 'Hard', which refers not so much to
Celan's indirect question, 'How these wounds are healing?', but
responds to and thus confirms Mandel'shtam's exclamation,
'How hard is it to heal (the) wounds!' Here, the '[d]ialogic
collision' (*PPD* 426) of two co-existentially singular utter-
ances—Mandel'shtam's and Celan's—has 'entered the inner
and most intricate elements of speech' (ibid.), thus making
Celan's response metalinguistically exemplary.[24]

   In these examples, too, Celan's choices cannot have been
prosodically motivated, since he could have opted for more
'faithful' translations without altering the German texts' re-
spective prosodic structures.[25] In i: 124, he could have, for
instance, written, 'Welche ist von beiden häßlich?' (Which one
among the two is ugly?). In i: 127 he could have simply phrased
the second line in the form of a direct question, 'Wie heilen diese
Wunden?' (How are these wounds healing?), thus precluding
the polyphony of its indirect variant. Similarly, he could have
translated lines 10–11 as, for instance, 'Den Köcher fand im
Sand wer nicht,|wer tauscht' sein Pferd.—Was sich begeben'
(The quiver someone did not find in the sand,|someone
exchanged his horse.—What (has) transpired).[26]

Celan further personalizes and, thereby, dialogizes Man-
del'shtam's text by staging the interlocutor's poetic significance
through the proliferation or introduction of pronominally
specified apostrophes.[27] While his use of first-person pronouns
foregrounds the factual dialogic emergence of a responsive,

---

[24] Celan's interrogative response to Mandel'shtam is pragmatically indistinguish-
able from the underground man's pre-emptive and anticipatory self-explications in
the first part of Dostoevsky's *Notes from Underground*, which Bakhtin adduces as
one of the successful stagings of polyphony.

[25] i: 124 : iambic tetrameter with alternating rhymes; i: 127 : iambic tetrameter
(exception: ll. 1, 5, 9, 13, and 16) with alternating rhymes.

[26] Interestingly, in his translation of Sergei Esenin's poem 'The autumn wind has
danced and wept', Celan does not dialogize Esenin's similar impersonal construc-
tion, 'Кто-то сядет, кто-то выгнет плечи' (Someone will sit down, someone will
shrug his or her shoulders), rendering it as: 'Es hockt da wer, ungläubig . . .
(Someone is sitting there, incredulously . . .) (*GW* v. 190–1). This *ex negativo*
highlights the dialogic significance of Mandel'shtam for Celan.

[27] See also Olschner, 117.

answerable 'I', his employment of second-person pronouns points to the interlocutor's, that is, interpellator's concomitant dialogic constitution:[28]

(i: 15, ll. 9–10)

(9) Запечатлеется на нем узор,

(10) Неузнаваемый с недавних пор.

(9) A* pattern will capture itself on it,

(10) Unrecognizable since not very long.

(GW v. 53)

Die Zeichnung auf dem Glas, die Schrift:

du liest sie nicht, *erkennst* sie nicht.

The drawing, on the pane, the writing:

you are do not read* it, do not recognize* it.

(i: 45 ('Silentium'), ll. 13–14)

(13) Останься пеной, Афродита,

(14) И слово в музыку вернись,

(13) Remain foam, Aphrodite,

(14) And word, return to music,

(GW v. 57)

Bleib, Aphrodite, dieses Schäumen,

du Wort, geh, bleib Musik.

Remain, Aphrodite, this foaming

you, word, go, remain music.

(i: 46, ll. 9–12)

(9) Я вижу месяц бездыханный,

(10) И небо мертвенней холста;

(11) Твой мир, болезненный и странный,

(12) Я принимаю, пустота!

(9) I see a* lifeless moon,

(10) And the sky/heaven (is) more dead than linen;

(11) Your world, dolorous and strange,

(12) I accept, emptiness!

(GW v. 81)

Du Himmel, weißestes der Hemden,

du Mond, entseelt, ich sehe *dich*.

Und, Leere, deine Welt, die fremde,

empfang ich, nehme ich!

You, sky/heaven, whitest of shirts,

you, moon, soulless, I see *you*.

And, emptiness, your world, the strange one,

I receive, I take!

(i: 127, ll. 13–16)

(13) И, если подлинно поется

(GW v. 81)

Und singst *du*, wahr, und hast getreu gesungen,

---

[28] In addition to the following examples, see also Celan's translations of poems i: 80 (GW v. 67), i: 86 (71), i: 157 (87).

(14) И полной грудью, нако-
    нец,

aus voller Brust, so merkst *du*:
    kaum

(15) Всё исчезает—остается

daß etwas blieb—es ist ge-
    schwunden,

(16) Пространство, звезды и
    певец!

bis auf den Sänger und den
    Sternenraum.

(13) And when it is genuinely
    sung

And if/when *you* sing, truly, and
    if/when you have sung faith-
    fully,

(14) At the lungs' full capacity,
    in the end,

at the lungs' full capacity, *you*
    notice: hardly

(15) All vanishes: remains

anything remained—it disap-
    peared,

(16) Space, stars and a* singer!

but for the singer and the star
    space.

(i: 193, ll. 5–6, 13–14, 19–21, 23)

(*GW* v. 103)

(5) Восходишь ты в глухие
    годы,—

In Finsternisse trittst du, taub
    und dicht,

(6) О солнце, судия народ.

du Volk, *du* Sonne-und-Gericht.

(13) Мы в легионы боевые

Dort, kampfbereit, die Phalanx—
    dort: die Schwalben!

(14) Связали ласточек—и вот

Wir schlossen sie zusammen,
    und—*ihr sehts*:

(19) Ну что ж, попробуем:
    огромный, неукюжый,

Nun, wir versuchen es: Herum
    das Steuer!

(20) Скрипучий поворот
    руля.

Es knirscht, *ihr Linkischen*,—los,
    reißts herum!

(21) Земля плывет. Мужай-
    тесь, мужи.

Die Erde schwimmt. Ihr
    Männer, Mut, aufs neue!

(23) Мы будем помнить и в
    летейской стуже,

Und denken, Lethe, noch wenn
    uns *dein* Frost durchfährt:

(5) You rise into deaf years,

You step* into darknesses, deaf
    and dense,

(6) Oh sun, judge, people.

you people, *you* sun-and-court.

(13) Into fighting legions we

There, ready to fight, the pha-
    lanx—there: the swallows!

(14) have tied (the) swallows—
    and there

We tied* them together, and—
    you see it:

(19) Okay, let's try: a* huge,
    clumsy,

So, we are trying it: around the
    rudder!

(20) Creaking turn of the rudder.	It creaks*, *you clumsy ones,*—go ahead, tear it around!
(21) The earth swims*. Man yourselves, men.	The earth swims*. You, men, courage, anew!
(23) We will remember even in Lethe's cold,	And [we] think*, Lethe, even when *your* frost permeates us:

(i: 197 ('Tristia'), ll. 9–12, 23–4)	(*GW* v. 105)
(9) Кто может знать при слове 'расставанье',	Wer, hört dies Wort er: Auseinandergehen,
(10) . . .	weiß . . .,
(11) Что нам сулит . . .	was es verheißt, wenn Flammen auf *dir* stehen,
(12) Когда огонь в акрополе горит,	Akropolis . . .?
(23) Всё было встарь, всё повторится снова,	Ach, nur Gewesnes kommt, zum andern Male:
(24) И сладок нам лишь узнаванья миг.	der Nu, da *du's* erkennst—*dein* Glück.

(9) Who can know, when hearing the word 'separation'	Who, hearing the word: separation,
(10) . . .	knows . . .,
(11) What is in store for us . . .	what it presages, when flames stand* on *you,*
(12) When fire burns* in the Acropolis,	Akropolis . . .?
(23) Everything was of old, everything will repeat itself,	Oh, only that which has been comes, a second time:
(24) And only the moment of recognition is sweet for us.	the moment, when *you* recognize it—*your* happiness.

(iii: 29, ll. 2–3)	(*GW* v. 153)
(2) За высокое племя людей,—	*dir*, Mensch, zur unsterblichen Glorie,
(3) Я лишился и чаши на пире отцов,	kam ich, als die Väter tafelten, um
(4) . . .	den Kelch . . . .
(2) For the high tribe of people,—	*for your*, human being, immortal glory,

(3) I have forfeited the chalice   I was deprived, when the fathers
     at the feast of the fathers,   were feasting,
(4) . . .   of the chalice . . .

Leonard Olschner pertinently notes that Celan's 'you-saying could be viewed as response in general: Celan considers and experiences himself as literally addressed in such a way that he responds by saying "you"—as if he had to hold on to the interpellating and in turn interpellated agent' (Olschner, 117). While the apostrophes in Celan's translations of poems i: 15, i: 127, and iii: 29 could be interpreted as conventionally-literary, that is, as 'projection[s] of the I' (Ryan, 280)[29]—without, therefore, being metalinguistically insignificant—the pronominal interpellations in Celan's translations of poems of i: 45, i: 46, i: 193, and i: 197 acquire emphatic metalinguistic significance both on an intratextually semantic and on an extratextual, interpersonal level.

In i: 45, Celan makes Mandel'shtam's interpellation of Aphrodite and the word, which is ordered to 'return to music', pronominally explicit: '*You*, word, go . . .' In his translation of poem i: 46, Celan does not only deictically reinforce the interpellation of 'sky/heaven' and 'moon', but transforms the original's pragmatics by momentarily shifting the 'deictic center' (Levinson, 64) away from the pronominally specified speaker ('I see a* lifeless moon') to the interlocutors ('moon', 'sky/heaven'), before moving it back to the speaker, the 'I'. A similar deictic reinforcement and shift occur in Celan's translation of poem i: 193, in which the second-person pronoun is proliferated (ll. 5–6, 20–1) and Mandel'shtam's hortative and affirmative first-person utterances, 'Okay, let's try . . | . . . | We will remember even in Lethe's cold' (ll. 19–20, 23) are turned into explicit addresses: '. . . you clumsy ones,—go ahead, tear it

---

[29] In rewriting Mandel'shtam's reflexive construction, 'A* pattern will capture itself on it, | Unrecognizable since not very long', as 'The drawing, on the pane, the writing: | you do not read* it, do not recognize* it', Celan introduces conventionally dialogic rhetoric into the poem. A similar 'dialogization' occurs in Celan's translation of poem i: 127 , in which the speaker's second-person singular apostrophes, directed at no one in particular, reinforce his own belief in the durability of 'genuine' poetry. In his translation of poem iii: 29, finally, Celan unambiguously addresses the common name of an entire species, 'human being', by way of a second-person singular pronoun in the dative case, thus underscoring the apostrophe's rhetoricity.

around! | . . . | . . . | And we think, Lethe, even when your frost permeates . . .'. Celan, thereby, intensifies the dialogic character of the poem's last stanza (ll. 19–24).

Whereas the preceding instances of dialogization occur within the poems' 'fictional' worlds, Celan's dialogic displacement of Mandel'shtam's 'Tristia' suggests genuinely co-existential interlocution. Celan's affirmation that 'only that which has been comes, a second time: the moment, when you recognize it—your happiness',[30] can plausibly be interpreted as genuinely addressing Mandel'shtam—the person and poet—himself, insofar as the latter will have always already relied on the future reception and, consequently, (re)enactment of his poetry, which will have consequently 'com[e], a second time' by way of the other. In this sense, Celan's translation can indeed be called Mandel'shtam's 'happiness': after all, it is Mandel'shtam's 'desire to be surprised at [his] own words, to be captivated by their novelty and unexpectedness' (*MSS* i. 187) through their re- and co-articulation by (a) futural interlocutor(s). Significantly, Celan's pronominal address in poem i: 197, l. 24 corroborates and qualitatively modifies Olschner's observation in that it performs not only—and not so much—'response in general', but, more importantly, an emphatically singular and singularly oriented response.

As with his use of first-person pronouns, Celan's placement of second-person pronouns cannot be accounted for prosodically, since even within the respective prosodic parameters of Celan's translations, other—pronominally unmarked and semantically more 'faithful'—options would have been possible. Without modifying the texts' respective prosodic structures, Celan could have translated i: 15, l. 10 (iambic tetrameter) as 'erkennbar ist seit kurzem nicht' or 'seit kurzem ist erkennbar nicht' (unrecognizable since not very long); i: 45, l. 14 (iambic trimeter) as 'und Wort, geh, bleib Musik' (and word, go, remain music); i: 46, ll. 9–10 (iambic tetrameters) as '(Der/den) Himmel, weißestes der Hemden, | den atemlosen Mond seh ich' ((The) sky/heaven, the whitest of shirts, | the lifeless moon I see); i: 127, ll. 13–14 (iambic pentameter, iambic tetrameter) as 'Und singt man, wahr, und hat getreu gesungen, | aus voller

---

[30] It has rhetorically been set up by the preceding personal interpellation of 'Acropolis' (ll. 11–12).

Brust, so merkt man: kaum' (And if/when one sings, truly, and if/when one has sung faithfully, I at the lungs' full capacity, one notices: hardly); i: 193, l. 6 (iambic tetrameter) as 'O Volk, du Sonne-und-Gericht' (O people, you sun-and-court);[31] i: 193, l. 14 (iambic pentameter) as 'Wir schlossen sie zusammen, und—da/dort sehts' (We tied them together, and—there, see it); i: 193, l. 20 (iambic pentameter) as 'Es knirscht, das Linkische,—los reißts herum' (It creaks*, the clumsy one,—go ahead, tear it around);[32] and i: 193, l. 23 (iambic hexameter) as 'Und werden denken, wenn uns Lethes Frost durchfährt' (And [we] will think when Lethe's cold permeates us).

Celan's idiosyncratic implementation of third-person pronouns further underscores the translations' dialogic pragmatics by making it more vivid, as it were, by emphasizing the speech situations' metalinguistic immediacy:[33]

(i: 15, ll. 9–10)	(GW v. 53)
(9) Запечатлеется на нем узор,	Die Zeichnung auf dem Glas, die Schrift:
(10) Неузнаваемый с недавних пор.	du liest *sie* nicht, erkennst *sie* nicht.
(9) A* pattern will capture itself on it,	The drawing, on the pane, the writing:

---

[31] The fact that this variant would still have one too many second-person singular pronouns does not invalidate the gratuity of Celan's pronominal interpellation of 'sun'.

[32] Mandel'shtam's 'неуклюжий' (clumsy) (l. 19) can be read as referring both to those who are called on to turn the rudder and to the rudder's movement itself.

[33] See also Olschner, 111. In addition to the examples provided below, see e.g. Celan's translations of poems i: 77 (GW v. 63), i: 86 (71), i: 156 (89). I should stress that notwithstanding the presumed linguistic differences between the first- and second-person pronouns and the third-person pronoun (Benveniste, i. 255), all three pronouns—irrespective of their grammatical number—function analogically from a pragmatic and, by extension, metalinguistic point of view. Émile Benveniste conceptually distinguishes between the first- and second-person pronouns and the third-person pronoun. He claims that in contrast to the first- and second-person pronouns the third-person pronoun 'represents . . . the non-person' (ibid.), since it does not directly refer to the 'instance of enunciation' (ibid.), that is, the speaker. Without engaging in a critique of Benveniste, suffice it to say that his unsubstantiated claim only makes sense if it pertains to the conventional literary use of the third-person pronoun as a narrative device. If, however, Benveniste implies an essential pragmatic distinction, his verdict equally applies to the second-person pronoun. I argue that all three pronouns indicate a certain degree of situational concreteness, a certain degree of immediacy between a speaker and his or her pronominal referent (him- or herself in the case of the first-person pronoun singular).

(10) Unrecognizable since not very long.

you do not read* it, do not recognize* it.

(i: 31 , ll. 1–4)

(GW v. 55)

(1) Ни о чем не нужно говорить,

Keine Worte, keinerlei.

(2) Ни чему не следует учить,

Nichts, das es zu lehren gilt.

(3) И печальна так и хороша

Sie ist Tier und Dunkelheit,

(4) Темная звериная душа:

sie, die Seele, gramgestillt.

(1) There is no need to talk about anything,

No words, nothing.

(2) There is nothing that should be taught,

Nothing, which should be taught.

(3) And so sad and good/pretty

It is animal and darkness,

(4) Is a* dark animal soul:

it, the soul, stilled/breast-fed with grief.

(i: 80 ('Shell'), ll. 5–8)

(GW v. 67)

(5) Ты равнодушно волны пенишь

Du Unbeteiligte, du rollst

(6) И несговорчиво поешь;

dein Meer, du hörst nicht, singst, singst fort.

(7) Но ты полюбишь, ты оценишь

Doch sie, die leer und unnütz ist, du sollst

(8) Ненужной раковины ложь.

sie lieben, deine Muschel dort.

(5) You foam* (the) waves indifferently

You indifferent one, you roll*

(6) and sing* intractably;

your sea, you don't hear* it, sing*, sing* on.

(7) But you will love, you will value

But it, which is empty and use-less, you ought to

(8) The lies of a* superfluous shell.

love it, your shell, there.

(#161,[34] ll. 17–18)

(GW v. 77)

(17) И, болезненно, накануне казни,

Ich, unnütz, seh dies, hörs, ich fühl den Schauer,

---

[34] This poem is cited according to the numeration of the expanded Struve/Filipoff edition of Mandel'shtam's works used by Celan. (In the 1955 Struve/Filipoff edition, this poem is #173.)

(18) Видением и пеньем потрясен,	hörs, seh's am Abend vor dem letzten Tag.
(17) And, dolorously, on the eve of execution,	I, useless, see* this, hear* *it*, I feel* the shiver,
(18) Shaken by vision and sing- ing.	hear* *it*, see* *it* on the evening before the last day.

The use of personal pronouns in general by definition effectuates an utterance's pragmatic specification: by indicating a certain degree of the speaker's familiarity with his or her pronominal referent, that is, by highlighting his or her relation to another (co-)existent, personal pronouns, more or less directly, singular- ize and metalinguistically concretize both utterance and speaker. Notwithstanding their universal applicability to any instance of pronominal deixis—from everyday utterances to, say, Browning's dramatic monologues—these pragmatic obser- vations acquire particular metalinguistic significance in the specific context of Celan's dialogue with Mandel'shtam, that is, precisely because the pronominal deixis of Celan's transla- tions constitutes itself within a singular poetico-poetological framework, which, as I have been arguing, dialogically comple- ments metalinguistics. Only as the 'result' of and testimony to Celan's co-existential relation with Mandel'shtam do Celan's pronominal and other translational choices (see below) make their emphatically metalinguistic interpretation plausible, with- out rendering the latter vulnerable to the objection of voluntar- ism. In other words, while Celan's use of pronominal deixis is certainly not unique from a structural, linguistic, or traditionally stylistic point of view, it is unique insofar as it enacts Celan's co- existential, poetic response to Mandel'shtam—insofar as it manifests Celan's singular twist on a decisive moment in the dialogic reality of his own life.[35]

Although Celan's translations by no means reflect or represent their 'author's intention' in any simplistic manner, they do trace the contours of a stylistic visage which points to the author's

---

[35] One might object that even this uniqueness is fundamentally universal, since any linguistically embodied response in one way or another points to the respon- dent's co-existential facticity as always already interpellated. While being structu- rally valid, this objection misses its mark: it succumbs to what might be called the metaleptic fallacy in that it stipulates the logical anteriority of universality, which is always already diachronically informed by singularity.

awareness of the subject-constituting function of dialogue: Celan's constant personalization—and, hence, dialogization— of Mandel'shtam's text palpably stages his metalinguistically significant claim that the interpellated is constituted 'only in the space of [poetic] dialogue' (*GW* iii. 198). His complementary use of the first- and second-person pronouns poetically performs and thus metalinguistically indicates the co-existential singularity of his encounter with Mandel'shtam, the factually 'interpellating I' (ibid.): Celan's first-person pronouns point to his dialogic constitution through the Russian poet, his second-person pronouns point to Mandel'shtam's proleptic dependence on his own retroactive co-constitution by Celan (or other interlocutors). In further concretizing the translations' pragmatics Celan's use of the third-person pronoun contributes to the adumbration of the two poets' singular co-existential situatedness *and* the participation and role of the third in their dialogue.

Celan's metalinguistically exemplary pronominal strategies must also necessarily be ethically significant, given that metalinguistics and ethics have been established as dialogically complementary. Consequently, Celan's excessive implementation of personal pronouns can plausibly be interpreted as staging and indicating semethical interpellation. As 'shifters',[36] personal pronouns are functionally predicated on the interplay between singularity and universality, since their 'general meaning . . . cannot be defined without a reference to the message' (*SW* 131), that is, without a reference to their singular enunciation in singular circumstances. Shifters are necessarily systematic and rule governed—symbolic in Peirce's terms—*and* functionally dependent on their relation to a referent (speaker or object).[37] If semethics is both the foundation and the continuous interruption of systematicity and if it can only be glimpsed by way of the Said, shifters ideally indicate semethics by systematically—through the Said—enacting absolute discursive singularity, by participating in and transcending systematicity. As Levinas suggests, personal pronouns in particular—and a fortiori personal pronouns poetically employed—must overtly

---

[36] See *SW* 130–47.
[37] Adopting Peircean terminology, Jakobson refers to shifters as 'indexical symbols' (*SW* 132). See Peirce, ii. 247, ii. 259, ii. 260, ii. 305.

indicate semethics: 'Denomination, here, is nothing but pro-nomination . . . The pronoun already dissimulates the unique one who speaks [or is spoken to], subsumes him under a concept, only designating the mask . . . of the unique one, the mask which is left by the I who evades conceptuality, that is, by the I of saying in the first person, absolutely nonconvertible into a noun, a sign given of this giving of the sign, exposition of the self to the other' (AQE 94–5).[38] My poethic interpretation of Celan's pronominal strategies as part of an overall poethic interpretation of his response to Mandel'shtam is ultimately grounded in Celan's insistence on the inseverability between poetry and the 'person and fate of the one who writes it' (Ivanovic, 337).[39] Contrary to its apparent formality and con-ventionality, Celan's dialogic rhetoric is informed by the 'exis-tential necessity' (ibid.) poetically to articulate his traumatic experience of being interpellated by Mandel'shtam, poetically to perform his co-existential dependence on and need for the singular other.[40]

The poethic seriousness[41] of Celan's Mandel'shtam transla-tions comes to the fore most overtly in his complex use of caesurae, which serve several contextually crucial functions: they highlight Celan's pronominal strategies; by interrupting metric continuity they subvert (poetic) systematicity and, thereby, help to indicate semethics;[42] most importantly, however, they serve a pneumatic, physiological function. Owing to caesurae the speaker's respiration becomes an integral part of poetic perform-ance and, conversely, poetic performance becomes an integral part of respiration. Celan's poetologically motivated pneumatiza-tion of Mandel'shtam's text acquires ethical significance given

---

[38] Elsewhere, Levinas refers to the 'self without concept . . . signifying itself in the first person, that is, precisely designating the level of Saying, pro-ducing itself in Saying me [moi] or I [je], that is, [as] absolutely different from any other me [moi]' (AQE 182).

[39] Badiou, Rambach, and Wiedemann equally stress the 'personal, all too personal dimension [of Celan's] poems' ('Editorisches Nachwort', in: Celan, Gedichte aus dem Nachlass, 333).

[40] Levinas explicitly characterizes semethics as 'traumatisme' (AQE 31).

[41] Celan's and Mandel'shtam's poems palpably disprove the influential philo-sophical view that poetry is a 'non-serious' mode of discourse (see esp. Frege, Kleine Schriften, 347; Austin, 9, 22, 104, 122).

[42] See also Olschner, 106. Insofar as the poetic text is a system within the system of language, its subversion necessarily performs the subversion of systematicity.

that semethics transpires fundamentally as inspiration and expiration. Those instances, in particular, in which Celan places the first-person singular pronoun immediately following a caesura—such as i: 162, ll. 2, 8 (*GW* v. 91)—most palpably indicate semethics by linking the diachronic emergence and pronominal articulation of the responding subject to the factual transition from inspiration to expiration. My poethic valorization of Celan's caesurae is corroborated by Celan's attention to the essential significance of caesurae for Mandel'shtam and, consequently, for himself as Mandel'shtam's interlocutor. As Jürgen Lehmann notes, 'the caesura is . . . for Mandel'shtam the expression of an essential experience of time; the absence of words—in the caesura—confers upon the poem [a certain] tension' ('Berührung und Dialog', 92), which is the result of the interplay between the ' "Now" and the "Once", between the time of the speaker and the [time of] the addressee' (ibid.). Postponing my discussion of 'time' in Celan's Mandel'shtam translations, suffice it to point out that by staging temporality through the use of caesurae, Celan congenially responds to the principally diachronic constitution of Mandel'shtam and his poetry.

Celan further dialogizes Mandel'shtam's text by pragmatic displacements on the local and temporal deictic levels: while the translations' place deixis poetically instantiates their primary author's singular place in co-existence as Mandel'shtam's interlocutor, their time deixis stages and indicates Mandel'shtam's passage to the time of the other, that is, to Celan's time.

My Place in Co-Existence

As the following examples illustrate, Celan is far more precise than Mandel'shtam in providing intratextual place deixis. Similarly to his excessive use of personal pronouns, he introduces and proliferates local deictic markers. The radically personalized speakers of Celan's translations find themselves in deictically specified situational contexts:

(i: 77, ll. 9–12)	(*GW* v. 63)
(9) Горячей головы качанье,	Der Kopf gewiegt, ich fühl ihn brennen.
(10) И нежный лед руки чужой,	Die fremde Hand, ihr sanftes Eis.

(11) И темных елей очертанье,

Der dunkle Umriß *dort*, die Tannen,

(12) Еще невиданные мной.

von denen ich nichts weiß.

(9) A* hot head's rocking,

The head rocked, I feel it burning.

(10) And the tender ice of a* strange hand,

The strange hand, its tender ice.

(11) And (the) dark fir trees' contours,

The dark silhouette, *there*, the fir tress,

(12) Not yet seen by me.

about which I don't know anything.

(i: 80 ('Shell'), ll. 5–9)

(*GW* v. 67)

(5) Ты равнодушно волны пенишь

Du Unbeteiligte, du rollst

(6) . . .

dein Meer . . .

(7) Но ты полюбишь, ты оценишь

Doch sie, die leer und unnütz ist, du sollst

(8) Ненужной раковины ложь.

sie lieben, deine Muschel *dort*.

(9) Ты на песок с ней рядом ляжешь,

Im Sand, *da* liegt ihr, dein Gewand

(5) You foam* (the) waves indifferently

You indifferent one, you roll*

(6) . . .

your sea . . .

(7) But you will love, you will value

But it, which is empty and useless, you ought to

(8) The lies of a* superfluous shell.

love it, your shell, *there*.

(9) You will lie down in the sand by its side,

In the sand, *there* you lie*, your cloak

(i: 86, ll. 7–8, 13–16)

(*GW* v. 71)

(7) Неба пустую грудь

Geh, grab dich, nadelfein,

(8) Тонкой иглою рань.

ins Leere *über mir*.

(13) Или, свой путь и срок

Die Bahn, die Frist . . . Ich kehr,

(14) Я, исчерпав, вернусь:

wer weiß, zurück ins *Hier*.

(15) Там—я любить не мог,

Die Liebe: dort zu schwer,

(16) Здесь—я любить боюсь . . .

und hier: die Angst vor ihr . . .

(7) The sky's/heaven's empty breast/chest

Go, dig yourself, like a fine needle,

(8) Wound with a thin needle. | Into the empty (space) *above me.*

(13) Or, my path and time | The path, the span . . . I come,
(14) Having used up, I will return: | who knows, back into the *here.*

(15) There—I could not love, | Love: there to heavy,
(16) Here—I am afraid to love . . . | and here: the fear of it . . .

(i: 173, ll. 1–4, 7–8)

(GW v. 93)

(1) В Петрополе прозрач-
ном мы умрем,

Petropolis, diaphan: *hier* gehen
wir zugrunde,

(2) Где властвует над нами
Прозерпина.

hier herrscht sie über uns: Pro-
serpina.

(3) Мы в каждом вздохе
смертный воздух пьем,

Sooft die Uhr schlägt, schlägt die
Todesstunde,

(4) И каждый час нам смерт-
ная година.

wir trinken Tod aus jedem
Lufthauch *da.*

(7) В Петрополе прозрач-
ном мы умрем,—

Petropolis, diaphan: *hier* gehen
wir zugrunde,

(8) Здесь царствуешь не ты,
а Прозерпина.

nicht du regierst—hier herrscht
Proserpina.

(1) In transparent Petropolis
we will die,

Petropolis, diaphanous: *here* we
die*,

(2) Where Proserpina rules
over us.

here she rules over us: Proser-
pina.

(3) With each/every breath we
drink (the) mortal air,

Whenever the clock strikes, the
hour of death strikes,

(4) And each/every hour is an*
hour of (our) death.

we drink* death out of every
whiff of air *there.*

(7) In transparent Petropolis
we will die,—

Petropolis, diaphanous: *here* we
die*,

(8) Here not you rule but Pro-
serpina.

Not you rule—here rules Proser-
pina.

(i: 191, ll. 9–12)

(GW v. 99)

(9) Что на крыше дождь
бормочет—

Dächerhin die Regenworte

(10) Это черный шелк горит,

—schwarze Seide brennt—, doch
blieb

(11) Но черемуха услышит

er, der's hört, der Faulbaum,
drunten,

(12) И на дне морском:
    прости.

(9) What [the] rain is mumbling
    on the roof—
(10) It is black silk burning,

(11) But the black-alder tree will
    hear
(12) Even on the ocean floor:
    forgive (me).

tief im Meer, das Wort: Vergib.

Toward the roofs the rain
    words
—black silk is burning—, but
    remained
he, who hears* it, the black-
    alder tree *down there*,
deep in the sea, the word: for-
    give.

(i: 193, ll. 1–2, 13–21, 23)
 (1) Прославим, братья,
    сумерки свободы,
 (2) Великий сумеречный
    год.
(13) Мы в легионы боевые

(14) Связали ласточек—и вот

(15) Не видно солнца; вся
    стихия
(16) Щебечет, движитсы,
    живет;
(17) Сквозь сети—сумерки
    густые—
(18) Не видно солнца и земля
    плывет.
(19) Ну что ж, попробуем:
    огромный, неуклюжый,
(20) Скрипучий поворот
    руля.
(21) Земля плывет. Мужай-
    тесь, мужи.
(23) Мы быдем помнить и в
    летейской стуже,

(GW v. 103)
Die Freiheit, die *da* dämmert,
    lasst uns preisen,
dies große, dieses Dämmerjahr.

Dort, kampfbereit, die Phalanx
    —*dort*: die Schwalben!
Wir schlossen sie zusammen,
    und—ihr sehts:
Die Sonne—unsichtbar. Die Ele-
    mente alle:
lebendig, vogelstimmig, unter-
    wegs.
Das Netz, die Dämmrung: dicht.
    Und nichts erglimmt.
Die Sonne—unsichtbar. Die Erde
    schwimmt.
Nun, wir versuchen es: Herum
    das Steuer!
Es knirscht, ihr Linkischen,—los,
    reißts herum!
Die Erde schwimmt. Ihr
    Männer, Mut, aufs neue!
Und denken, Lethe, noch wenn
    uns dein dein Frost durchfährt:

 (1) Let us glorify, brothers, the
    twilight of freedom,
 (2) The great twilight year!
(13) Into fighting legions we
    have

The freedom, in the twilight,
    there, let us glorify,
this great, this twilight year.
There, ready to fight, the pha-
    lanx—*there*: the swallows!

(14) Tied (the) swallows—and now | We tied them together, and—you see it:

(15) The sun is invisible; all elements | The sun—invisible. The elements, all:

(16) chirp*, move*, live; | alive, birdvoiced, underway.

(17) Through the nets—dense twilight— | The net, the twilight: dense. And nothing glimmers*.

(18) The sun is invisible and the earth swims*. | The sun—invisible. The earth swims*.

(19) Okay, let's try: a* huge, clumsy, | So, we are trying it: around the rudder!

(20) Creaking turn of the rudder. | It creaks*, you clumsy ones,—go ahead, tear it around!

(21) The earth swims*. Man yourselves, men. | The earth swims*. You, men, courage, anew!

(23) We will remember even in Lethe's cold, | And [we] think, Lethe, even when your frost permeates us:

(ii: 1, ll. 1–4) | (GW v. 125)

(1) Умывался ночью на дворе. | Nachts *vorm* Haus, *da* wusch ich mich—

(2) Твердь сияла грубыми звездами. | Grobgestirnter Himmel strahlt.

(3) Звездный лучь, как соль на топоре. | Auf der Axt, wie Salz, steht Sternenlicht.

(4) Стынет бочка с полными краями. | *Hier* die Tonne: randvoll, kalt.

(1) I was washing my face in the courtyard— | At night *in front of* the house, *there* I was washing myself—

(2) The firmament was shining with coarse stars. | (The) coarse-starred sky/heaven is shining.

(3) Starlight, like salt on an* axe. | On the axe, like salt, starlight is standing.

(4) A* barrel is cold, filled to the rims. | *Here*, the barrel: filled to the rims, cold.

(ii: 17, ll. 29–32) | (GW v. 147)

(29) Мне хочется бежать от моего порога. | Die Schwelle *hier*: ich wollt, ich könn sie lassen.

(30) Куда? На улице темно, | Wohin? Die Straße—Dunkelheit.

(31) И, словно, сыплют соль мощеною дорогой, | Und, als wärs Salz, so weiß, *dort* auf dem Pflaster,

(32) Белеет совесть предо
      мной.

liegt mein Gewissen *vor mich*
hingestreut.

(29) I feel the urge to run from
      my threshold.

The threshold *here*: I wish, I
could leave it.

(30) Whereto? In the street it is
      dark,

Whereto? The street—darkness.

(31) And my conscience
      whitens* before me,

And, as if it were salt, so white,
there on the pavement,

(32) Literally, like salt spread
      along a* cobblestone
      road.

lies* my conscience spread
before me.

(ii: 18, ll. 17–18)

(GW v. 151)

(17) Среди скрипучего
      похода мирового—

Der Welten Rasselschritt, und
dies, inmitten:

(18) Какая легкая кровать!

dies Bett *hier* . . .

(17) Among the screeching
      world march—

The worlds' rattlestep, and this,
amidst:

(18) What a light bed!

this bed, *here.*

In contrast to his pre-texts Celan consistently divides the pragmatic space of his translations into a 'here' and a 'there' (i: 77, i: 80, i: 86, i: 173, i: 193, ii: 1, ii: 18).[43] This division parallels Celan's continuous personalization of his translations, that is, the creation of multiple, pronominally marked pragmatic centres of activity. It is complemented by more specific adverbial deictica, such as 'above (me)' (i: 86, l. 8), 'Toward the roofs' (i: 191, l. 9),[44] 'down there' (i: 191, l. 11), 'in front of' (ii: 1, l. 1), 'before (me)' (ii: 17, l. 32).

These specifications are particularly significant and effective in those poems in which they accompany personal specification. Thus, in i: 77, ll. 9–12 the deictic specification of the speaker's pragmatic context underscores his grammatically personalized, active perception and experiencing (see above). The adverb

[43] See also Celan's translations of Mandel'shtam's poems i: 75 (GW v. 65), i: 83 (69), i: 91 (75), i: 140 (85), i: 197 (105), ii: 11 (127–9), ii: 13 (139–43). 'There' translates both the German 'da' and 'dort'. While both 'da' and 'dort' suggest the immediacy of a given situation, 'da' may also signify non-deictically (Levinson, 66), that is, without particular pragmatic reference, as in: 'Im Kerker Welt, da bin ich nicht allein' (In the dungeon, world, there I am not alone) (i: 15, l. 6). ('Da' can also function as a causal conjunction, meaning 'as' or 'since'.)

[44] 'Dächerhin' is one of Celan's numerous neologisms (see Neumann, 7–27).

'there' creates a degree of immediacy incommensurable with the original. In the process of translation, a passive, pragmatically non-specified enunciatory source is transformed into an active, observing, experiencing, and communicating subject.

Similarly, in his translation of 'Shell' (i: 80) Celan combines personalization (ll. 7–10) with local specification, thereby concretizing the poem's pragmatics. In this instance, in particular, the interplay between space and person deixis radically alters the original's semantics. 'Shell' stages the speaker's apostrophe of 'Night'. In the first stanza, the pronominally identified speaker, 'I' (ll. 1, 4) declares his resemblance to a stranded shell: 'Like a shell without pearls, I I am hurled out onto your [night's] shore' (Как раковина без жемчужин, I Я выброшен на берег твой). In the three remaining stanzas the speaker obliterates pronominal self-references, yet continues nominally and pronominally to talk about the shell (e.g. ll. 7–10), suggesting his tacit identification with it. It is important to note the mere suggestion, rather than actual accomplishment of identification: literally, the speaker simply shifts his referential focus from himself to the shell.

In his version of the poem, Celan makes two crucial changes on the semantic and deictic levels:[45] (1) he displaces Mandel'shtam's simile: instead of merely likening the speaker to a shell, he ontologically identifies him with it (' . . . an empty shell, I I lie* on the edge of your bay' (eine Muschel hohl, I lieg ich am Rande deiner Bucht)), (ll. 3–4); (2) by subsequently using the adverbs 'dort' (there) and 'da' (there) (ll. 8–9) he alters the poem's pragmatic—and, consequently, semantic—configuration. Both alterations acquire particular significance in light of each other. While Mandel'shtam's comparative rapprochement between speaker and shell does not pragmatically concretize the speaker, leaving his co-existential place in the poem's secondary speech context unspecified, Celan's metaphoric identification of speaker and shell unambiguously situates the speaker-shell on the shore.[46] Celan reduces the original's semantic and pragmatic entropy

---

[45] Celan preserves the original's stanzaic (four quartets) and metric (iambic tetrameter with alternating rhymes) parameters.

[46] Rexheuser notes Celan's tendency to transform similes into metaphors in his translations (Rexheuser, 283–5). See also Terras and Weimar, 356. Following Harald Weinrich, I take metaphors to be ontologically predicating structures rather than abbreviated similes.

through metaphoric identification, creating a pragmatically singularized subject. In the process of translation, Mandel'shtam's rhetorically destabilized, oscillating speaker gains ontological and geographic concreteness and unicity. Upon completing this first step of singularization, however, Celan's speaker sheds the skin of metaphoric identity—it is left lying on the shore—and (re)emerges as the scene's witness: by employing the local adverbs 'dort' and 'da' (ll. 8, 9) with reference to the shell lying on the shore, Celan removes the speaker from his embodiment in the shell and situates him unambiguously outside the shell. Furthermore, in alliance with Celan's syncopation of 'hörst es' (hear it) into 'hörsts' (hear't) (l. 6) and the concomitant deployment of personal pronouns, which suggest the speaker's familiarity with and proximity to both night and stranded shell, in lines 5–10—'Du' (you; sing.), 'es' (it), 'sie' (her), 'ihr' (you; pl.)—these deictic markers help to cement the impression of situational immediacy. While Celan's speaker remains pragmatically unspecified in any direct fashion, his co-ordinates are nonetheless clearly staked out: he is located close to the shell on the shore.

In his version of poem i: 193, which displays Mandel'shtam's fundamentally ambiguous assessment of the Russian Revolution and its socio-political aftermath,[47] Celan combines local deictic specification with pronominal apostrophe, thus concretizing both the poem's speaker, who remains part of an unidentified collective in the original, and his (or her) interlocutors.[48] While the original presents a fraternal collective's self-agitation to 'glorify the twilight of freedom', dispensing with any pragmatic specifications with the exception of the grammatically and semantically ambiguous lexeme 'there/so' (вот) (l. 14)—it may function both as a deictic marker and as a mere interjection—Celan from the beginning clearly reduces the original's pragmatic vagueness by localizing the twilight 'there' (l. 1), that is, within the speaker's (immediate) external purview, thereby anticipating and proleptically intensifying Mandel'shtam's own subsequent depiction of perceptional immediacy (ll. 14–

---

[47] Regarding Mandel'shtam's ambivalent relation to the Russian Revolution, see e.g. Brown, *Mandelstam*, 267–9; Gary Harris 31–5; N. Mandel'shtam, 120.

[48] The interlocutors are: 'people' (l. 6), 'sun-and-court' (l. 6), 'you' (pl.) (ll. 14, 20), 'Lethe' (l. 23).

18). Celan's iteration of the adverb 'there' in line 13 further contributes to the poem's pragmatic specification. Together with such other devices as the idiosyncratic use of exclamation marks (ll. 13, 19–21), demonstrative pronouns (l. 2), and the present instead of the original's future tense (l. 23), Celan creates (the impression of) a situation of pressing immediacy and emotional excitement on the speaker's part, who—in contrast to his (or her) poised and almost matter-of-fact counterpart in the original—emerges as an emphatically engaged participant in and eyewitness to the depicted events.

Celan's excessive implementation of place deixis facilitates the pragmatic concretization and singularization of the poem's agents. Celan thus realizes his poetological stipulation—which is itself informed by Mandel'shtam's programmatic poetico-poetological emphasis on 'the place of the human being in the universe' (i: 140, l. 4)—that the poetically interpellated subject constitutes him- or herself in bringing his or her own 'here' (GW iii. 198) into poetic dialogue.[49] Metalinguistically, this pragmatic concretization can be interpreted as performing both Mandel'shtam's and Celan's situatedness in co-existence, which constitutes itself in and through their poetic dialogue and from within which Celan responds to Mandel'shtam's interpellation. The contextual plausibility of establishing this link between poetry and metalinguistics is borne out thematically: while Celan's singularizing version of Mandel'shtam's 'revolution' poem (i: 211) instantiates his belief that 'the revolution . . . begins . . . here and today, with the singular person' (GW iii. 179), his rendition of poem i: 80 ('Shell') subtly intertwines poetry and poetics, thus highlighting the metalinguistic significance of his poetic dialogue with Mandel'shtam.

If, as Clarence Brown has suggested, Mandel'shtam's 'Shell' is interpreted as an emphatically poetological text—whereby 'shell' and 'pearls' (l. 3) correspond to poet and poetic word, respectively,[50] and keeping in mind that any translation

[49] Celan's division of his translations' pragmatic space into 'here' and 'there' underscores the specification of either term by delimiting it in relation to its opposite.

[50] 'The Shell', Clarence Brown notes, is 'wholly typical of Mandel'shtam's early poems . . . in that it is about poetry' (*Mandelstam*, 163). The poet, Brown continues, 'is [the] shell' (ibid.). Mandel'shtam had a long tradition of the metaphoric identification of poetry with jewellery to draw on. See e.g. Mallarmé's comparison of poetry with 'gems' (Mallarmé, 366).

originarily signifies by way of its pre-text, which functions both as its primary referent and its primary signified, Celan's 'Muschel' (shell) originarily signifies the original 'Shell' and the shell in the original, that is, the poeticized shell-like Mandel'shtam himself, who undergoes a metaphoric identification with the shell in the course of being translated by Celan (ll. 3–4). As I have mentioned earlier, upon completing his metaphoric transformation, Celan's speaker sheds the skin of his newly acquired metaphoric identity to situate himself on the shore in close proximity to the shell. Given the semantic and referential groundedness of Celan's translation in its pre-text, the local deictica 'dort' (l. 8) and 'da' (l. 9) can be viewed as spilling over the translation's boundaries: in addition to establishing an intratextual pragmatics, these deictica also refer to the original—saying, as it were, 'there, in the original!' Consequently, when Celan writes, ' . . . you shall I love it, your shell, there. ‖ In the sand, there you lie*' (ll. 8–9), it is as if the speaker were insisting that 'you' love the Russian shell over 'there', the stranded, metaphorically transformed Mandel'shtam, lying on the shore. In responding to Mandel'shtam, Celan (re)creates a scene—a person situated on a shore indicating an object in the sand—which hauntingly resembles another scene, central to the poetics of both Mandel'shtam and Celan, and which, in a nutshell, captures the dialogic and co-existential dimension of poetry: a person wandering along the shore, finding a poet's message in the bottle. In view of Celan's diachronic identification of poet and poem—the latter being the poet's gestalt in its directedness, in its movement into the future (*GW* iii. 194)—his references to Mandel'shtam's shell can be read as staging and indicating his factual encounter with Mandel'shtam and his poetry. In finding the 'Shell' Celan has indeed found the diachronically extended Mandel'shtam himself.[51]

---

[51] Similarly to his use of person deixis, Celan's use of place deixis is not reducible to prosodic concerns. His excessive implementation of demonstrative pronouns equally contributes to the translations' pragmatic concretization and specification. See e.g. i: 40, l. 3 (*GW* v. 61); i: 83, l. 4 (69); i: 157, l. 11 (87); i: 193, l. 2 (103); i: 206, l. 21 (111); ii: 11, l. 17 (127); ii: 17, l. 16 (145); ii: 18, ll. 17–18 (151).

The Time of the Other

While Celan's use of place and demonstrative deixis facilitates the speaker's spatial singularization, his idiosyncratic employment of time deixis indicates semethical diachronicity by way of attending to the co-existential distinction between 'my time and the time of the other' (*R* 185). As the following examples illustrate, Celan radically displaces the originals' temporal structures:

(i: 80 ('Shell'), ll. 5–8, 9–10, 13–16	(*GW* v. 67)
(5) Ты равнодушно волны пенишь	Du Unbeteiligte, du rollst
(6) И несговорчиво поешь;	dein Meer, du hörsts nicht, singst, singst fort.
(7) Но ты *полюбишь,* ты *оценишь*	Doch sie, die leer und unnütz ist, du *sollst*
(8) Ненужной раковины ложь.	sie lieben, deine Muschel dort.
(9) Ты на песок с ней рядом *ляжешь,*	Im Sand, da *liegt* ihr, dein Gewand
(10) *Оденешь* ризою своей,	*schlägst* du um sie, die zu dir schlüpft.
(13) И хрупкой раковины стены,—	Die Wände—brüchig; dieses Haus
(14) Как нежилого сердца дом,—	*ist unbewohnt,* wie's Herzen sind.
(15) *Наполнишь* шопотами пены, . . .	Du *füllsts* mit Schaumgeflüster aus,

(5) You foam* (the) waves indifferently	You indifferent one, you roll*
(6) And sing* intractably;	your sea, you don't hear* it, sing,* sing* on.
(7) But you *will love,* you *will value*	But it, which is empty and useless, you *ought to*
(8) The lies of a* superfluous shell.	love it, your shell, there.
(9) You *will lie* down in the sand by its side,	In the sand, there you *lie*,* your cloak
(10) *Will clothe* it into your cloak,	you throw* around it, which slips* to you.

(13) And the fragile shell's walls,—

(14) Like an uninhabited heart's house,—

(15) You *will fill* with (the) whispers of (the) foam,

The walls—brittle; this house

is *uninhabited*, the way hearts are.

You *fill* it with foam whispering,

(i: 211, ll. 1, 3–8, 11–12, 15–16, 21–4, 31–2)

(GW v. 159–61)

(1) В Петербурге мы *сойдемся* снова,

Petersburg: es *führt* uns neu zusammen,

(3) И блаженное, бессмылен- ное слово

und es *tritt*, zum erstenmal uns auf die Lippen

(4) В первый раз *произнесем*.

jenes selge, deutungslose Wort.

(5) В черном бархате советс- кой ночи,

In jener Jännernacht, in ihrer Sammetschwärze,

(6) В бархате всемирной пустоты,

Und im Samt der Leere welten- weit

(7) Всё поют блаженных жен родные очи,

singen sie, der selgen Frauen traute Augen,

(8) Всё цветут бессмертные цветы.

Und es blüht die Blume ohne Tod und Zeit.

(11) Только злой мотор во мгле *промчится*

nur ein böser Motor *saust* noch durch den Nebel,

(12) И кукушкой *прокричит*

und du *hörst*, wie er, mit Kuck- ucksstimme, *schreit*.

(15) За блаженное, бессмы- сленное слово

für das Wort, das selig-deutung- slose,

(16) Я в ночи советской *помо- люсь*.

bete ich, die Jännernacht hin- durch.

(21) У костра мы греемсы от скуки,

Wir, gelangweilt, wärmen uns am Feuer,

(22) Может быть века *прой- дут*

und es *ziehn*, wer weiß, Jahrhun- derte *vorbei*,

(23) И блаженных жен родные руки

und der selgen Frauen traute Hände

(24) Легкий пепел *соберут*

sammeln sie, die leichte Asche, *ein*.

(31) Всё поют блаженных жен крутые плечи,

Sie, der selgen Frauen jähe Schultern singen,

(32) А ночного слонца не *заметишь* ты.

und die nächtge Sonne, du *bemerkst* sie nicht.

(1) In Petersburg we *will meet* again,

Petersburg: it *brings* us newly together,

(3) And a* blissful, senseless word

and for the first time *comes* to our lips

(4) We *will pronounce* for the first time.

that blissful, senseless word.

(5) In the black velvet of the Soviet night,

In the January night, in its velvet blackness,

(6) In the velvet of universal emptiness

and in the velvet of the emptiness worldwide

(7) Still sing* blissful women's familiar eyes,

they sing*, blissful women's familiar eyes,

(8) Still bloom* immortal flowers.

and the flower blooms* without death or time.

(11) Only an angry motor *will rush* by in the haze

only an evil motor *still rushes** through the fog,

(12) And *will shout* like a cuckoo.

and you hear how it, with a cuckoo's voice, *shouts**.

(15) For a* blissful senseless word

for the word, the blissful-senseless one,

(16) I *will pray* in the Soviet night.

I *pray** through the January night.

(21) We warm* ourselves by a* campfire from boredom,

We, bored, warm* ourselves by a* campfire,

(22) Maybe (the) ages *will pass*,

and, who knows, centuries *pass**,

(23) And (the)blissful women's familiar/beloved hands

and the blissful women's familiar hands

(24) *Will gather* (the) light ashes.

*gather** them, the light ashes.

(31) And (the) blessed women's steep shoulders sing* on,

They, the blissful women's wuthering shoulders sing*,

(32) But you *will* not *notice* the night sun.

and the night sun, you *do* not *notice* it.

While preserving the originals' present tenses,[52] Celan consistently converts their future tenses into present tenses; in fact, throughout his Mandel'shtam translations, Celan does not—with the exception of two prosodically motivated instances (ii: 17, l. 65 (*GW* v. 149) and ii: 18, l. 7 (*GW* v. 151))—use the

[52] See above i: 80, ll. 1–4; i; 211, ll. 7–11. See also Celan's translations of such poems as i: 7, ll. 1–4 (*GW* v. 51); i: 15, ll. 1–6 (53); i: 31 (55); i: 45, ll. 1–8, 13–16 (57); i: 46 (59); i: 77, ll. 1–7 (63); i: 75, ll. 15–16 (65); i: 80, ll. 1–2 (67); i: 86, ll. 1–8 (71); i: 91, ll. 2 (75); i: 127, ll. 7–16 (81); i: 140 (85); i: 157 (87); i: 162, ll. 9–12 (91); i: 202 (109); iii: 121, ll. 1–4, 10–13 (155); iii: 177, ll. 1–8 (157).

future tense at all. Metalinguistically, this poetic emphasis on the present, stages the 'arrival' of Mandel′shtam's 'bottled messages' in Celan's hands (especially in poem i: 80): the Russian poet's futurally oriented missives have found their providential reader in Celan, who co-authors them—thereby co-existentially co-constituting their primary author—in his own present, in his 'Now' (*GW* iii. 198).[53] As Celan points out, the poetic interlocutor necessarily infuses poetic dialogue with 'that which is uniquely his own' (iii. 199), namely, with his own 'time' (ibid.). It is this irreducible temporality of poetry, its principal diachronicity, which Celan suggests when he stipulates that 'in every poem its "20th of January" remains inscribed' (iii. 196), that a poem is 'a concentration which remembers all our [singular] dates' (iii. 198). Notwithstanding their constitutively future orientation, their 'being on the way' (iii. 186), poems exist only in 'respective singularities' 'one, unique, [and] punctual presence' (iii. 199), that is, they transpire in singular enactments. Celan's transposition of Mandel′shtam's poems into the present grammatically stages this performative unicity, thereby poetically staging and indicating both the co-existential incongruity between persons' respective 'times' (*R* 185), and a person's inevitable semethical 'passage to the time of the Other' (*DEHH* 192). The ethical dimension of Celan's response to Mandel′shtam is evidenced most overtly in Celan's use of the verb 'sollen' (ought) in i: 80, l. 7. Celan's ethical injunction addressed to 'night', 'you ought to l love it, your shell, there', indirectly points to Celan's own poethic 'ought' with regard to Mandel′shtam. Thus, the 'said of this poetic saying' (*NP* 53), which is Celan's translational response to Mandel′shtam, reveals itself as an exemplary 'figur[e] of th[e] movement' (ibid.) of Mandel′shtam's passage into Celan's hands.

Paradoxically, Celan must be textually unfaithful to Man-

---

[53] Although Celan occasionally replicates Mandel′shtam's past-tense constructions, especially, when the past tense is used epically (e.g. in his translations of poems i: 15 , l. 1 (*GW* v. 53); i: 89, ll. 2–5 (73); i: 135, ll. 9–10 (83)), the tendency to transpose Mandel′shtam's poems into the present characterizes the vast majority of his translations. In his translations of the following poems, Celan consistently converts the future into the present tense: i: 15, ll. 9–10 (*GW* v. 53); i: 45, ll. 9–10 (57); i: 75, ll. 9–12 (65); i: 83, l. 1 (69); i: 86, ll. 13–16 (71); i: 135, ll. 5–7 (83); i: 173, ll. 1, 7 (93); i: 188, l. 3 (97); i: 193, ll. 21–4 (103); i: 197, ll. 10, 25 (105–7); i: 207, ll. 17–20 (115); ii: 13, l. 49–56 (143); iii: 29, l. 15–16 (153).

del'shtam's poetry in order to make his response genuinely personal in the ethical and metalinguistic senses, that is, in order to be poethically 'faithful' to the Russian poet. 'Unfaithfully', Celan writes, 'am I faithful to you' (*GW* i. 33). He must transpose Mandel'shtam's text into his dialogically constituted co-existential context, into his very personal situation, in order poetically to enact his co-existential answerability to and for Mandel'shtam and his text, in order to do justice to Mandel'shtam's and his own unicity. Celan's versions of poems i: 175 and i: 211 exemplarily illustrate the fundamentally personal character of his translational response to Mandel'shtam: Celan translates Mandel'shtam's experiences into his own, thereby palpably (re)creating both Mandel'shtam and himself within the parameters of his response. Transposing Mandel'shtam's post-revolutionary meditation on a futural encounter in the 'Soviet night' into the present of his response (i: 211, ll. 1, 3, 11–12, 16, 22, 24, 32), Celan stages, as it were, the fulfillment of Mandel'shtam's anticipation, whereby Celan's 'us' (l. 1) refers as much to Mandel'shtam's unspecified 'we' as it suggests his encounter with Mandel'shtam through the poem, which Celan titles 'In Petersburg': thus, when Celan states that 'Petersburg . . . brings us newly together' he literally refers to his own poetic translation, which de facto performs his poetic encounter with Mandel'shtam.[54] Through Celan's response, in the process of which the respondent emerges as Mandel'shtam's poetic interlocutor, Mandel'shtam and his text are 'newly' authored in the light of Celan's singular take on co-existence. Celan poetically underscores this fact by explicitly linking his translation to his co-existential situation, which is evidenced most overtly in his replacement of Mandel'shtam's 'Soviet night' (ll. 5, 16) by 'January night'. As I have mentioned earlier, the 'date' 'January' occupies a very specific place in Celan's poetic and co-existential universe:[55] It metonymically invokes the socio-political ramifications of the Wannsee Conference (20 January 1942). Concomitantly, 'night' does not only metaphorically signify the

---

[54] It is significant that Celan does not translate Mandel'shtam's 'snova' (again) as 'wieder' (again), but as 'neu' (newly), which—while semantically replicating the core of Mandel'shtam's term—'-nov-' (new)—suggests not a repetition but a genuinely novel experience: not so much 'aufs neue' (anew) as 'auf eine neue Weise' (in a new way). [55] See Ch. 3., 'Celan's Dialogic Poetics'.

period between 1933 and 1945, but relates to a momentous incident in Celan's personal life: during a nocturnal raid in June 1942 Celan's parents were arrested in their apartment in Czernowitz, while he himself was hiding in a nearby cosmetics factory; this arrest led to the parents' deportation and subsequent death at the hands of the SS.[56] Israel Chalfen notes that as a result Celan suffered from 'a profound feeling of guilt for being alive, while his parents died a gruesome death' (Chalfen, 128–9). Thus, 'January night' captures both Celan's continuous awareness of being a survivor and witness and his memory of his victimized parents, whom he presumably 'deserted' by saving himself. This idiosyncratic displacement of the original's reference to 'Soviet night' is thematically warranted by Mandel'shtam's invocation of 'blissful women' in connection with death (ll. 7–8, 23), which yields itself easily to its appropriation by Celan with particular regard to the murder of his own mother— poetically commemorated as one of the 'blissful women'.[57] From Celan's perspective, furthermore, Mandel'shtam's dead mother, to whom the latter devoted poem i: 175, is also one of the 'blissful women'. In the present of Celan's poem, which testifies to the continuous presence of the private and public significance of 'January night', both Mandel'shtam's and Celan's mothers come to life.

Celan's translation of poem i: 175, which precedes and informs his version of poem i: 211, transposes Mandel'shtam's treatment of his mother's funeral into the present:

(i: 175)	(GW v. 95)
(1) Эта ночь непоправима,	Diese Nacht: nicht gutzumachen
(2) А у вас еще светло.	bei euch: Licht, trotzdem.
(3) У ворот Ерусалима	Sonnen, schwarz, die *sich entfachen*
(4) Солнце черное *взошло.*	vor Jerusalem.
(5) Солнце желтое страшнее,—	Sonnen, gelb: größres Entsetzen—
(6) Баю баюшки баю,—	schlaf eiapopei.
(7) В светлом храме иудеи	Helles Judenhaus: *sie setzen*
(8) *Хоронили* мать мою.	meine Mutter bei.

[56] See Chalfen, 119–29; Felstiner, 14–19.
[57] It is important to note that the German word 'selig' (blissful) is conventionally applied to dead people in the sense of 'God bless'.

(9) Благодати не имея	Sie, die nicht mehr priesterlichen,
(10) И священства лишены,	gnad- und heilsberaubt,
(11) В светлом храме иудеи	*singen* aus der Welt, im Lichte,
(12) *Отпевали* прах жены.	eines Weibes Staub.
(13) И над матерью *звенели*	Judenstimmen, die nicht schwie-gen,
(14) Голоса израильтян.	Mutter, wie *es schallt*.
(15) Я *проснулся* в колыбели—	Ich *erwach* in meiner Wiege,
(16) Черным солнцем осиян.	sonnenschwarz umstrahlt.

(1) This night cannot be cor-rected,	This night: not to be repaired
(2) and where you are it is still light.	where you are: light, nonethe-less.
(3) By the gates of Jerusalem	Suns, black, which *are kindling** themselves
(4) A black sun has risen.	before Jerusalem.
(5) A* yellow sun is more frightening—	Suns, yellow: greater horror—
(6) Hush baby, hush—	sleep, eiapopei.
(7) In a* bright temple (the) Jews	Bright Jew house: they *are bury-ing**
(8) *Were burying** my mother.	my mother.
(9) Not having (the) bliss	They, the ones who are not priestly anymore,
(10) And deprived of priest-hood,	deprived of grace and salvation,
(11) In a* bright temple, (the) Jews	*are singing** from this world, in light,
(12) *Were conducting* service for the woman's ashes.	a woman's dust.
(13) And above (my) mother *resounded**	Jew voices, which did not remain silent,
(14) (The) voices of (the) Israe-lites.	Mother, how it *echoes*.
(15) I *have woken up* in a* cradle—	I *wake up** in my cradle,
(16) shone on by a* black sun.	surrounded by sunblack rays.

Commenting on Celan's translation, Olschner rightly notes that 'Celan rewrote [the poem] remembering his own mother, whose hour of death and grave he could not have possibly known—through an act of identification with Mandelstam, as it were'

(Olschner, 260). Olschner's thematically motivated insight is corroborated pragmatically.[58] Whereas Mandel'shtam unmistakably situates his mother's funeral in the past, remembers or dreams of the past event of his mother's funeral, as a result of which a 'black sun has risen',[59] Celan witnesses the funeral in actu: 'are burying' (l.7) replaces 'were burying'; 'are singing' (l. 11) replaces 'were conducting service'; 'echoes' (l. 14) replaces 'resounded'; past perfective constructions—'A black sun has arisen' (l. 4), 'I have woken up' (l. 15)—yield to present tense constructions: 'Suns, black . . . are kindling themselves' and 'I wake up'. Obviously, Celan succeeds in creating the impression of utter immediacy, of poetically re-enacting and participating in the irreversibly past event of his mother's death. By pragmatically/grammatically personalizing his translation, Celan performs what is thematically and historically 'not to be repaired': the 'night' of his mother's— and, concurrently, the 'January night' of millions of others'— violent death. In his traumatic encounter with Mandel'shtam, in and through Mandel'shtam's words Celan (re)articulates his traumatic experience of the Holocaust and its continuous significance for himself. Celan's response hauntingly stages and indicates semethical 'traumatism' (*AQE* 31), which opens up the possibility of speech and memory. With particular attention to Celan's poetic heteronomy and Levinasian ethics, Elisabeth Weber notes that

the trauma which in the encounter with the other recalls an earlier trauma, is trauma because it is reminiscent of an immemorial trauma. But then it breaks . . . the impossibility of remembering this speechlessness. In the trauma of this opening *there are words* . . . and only *because* there are words is it reminiscent of the absolute lack of words. This trauma is trauma because it opens anamnesis . . . The encounter with the other is called 'traumatic' because it is the sole path of anamnesis of the trauma of persecution . . . The connection between

[58] Surprisingly, Olschner does not comment on the temporal structure of Celan's translation.

[59] Regarding Mandel'shtam's image of the 'black sun', which may have had numerous sources—such as Revelation 6: 12, Matthew 24: 29, Mark 13: 24—see Brown, *Mandelstam*, 216–17; Taranovsky, 54–5; Olschner, 260–1. Taranovsky suggests that most likely Mandel'shtam borrowed the term from 'the then sensational *Salomé* of Oscar Wilde: "En ce jour là le soleil deviendra noir . . ."' (Taranovsky, 54).

[the trauma of] persecution and [the trauma of encountering the] other allows . . . the possibility of mourning . . . Only in this opening are anamnesis and bearing witness possible. (Peperzak, *Ethics*, 74–5)

Through Mandel'shtam's poetic interpellation Celan performs a deeply personal act of testimony. Concurrently, by retroactively infusing Mandel'shtam's text with the weight of his own mother's death, that is, by emphatically co-authoring Mandel'shtam's text in the light of his particular place and time in co-existence Celan exemplarily assumes answerability for the Russian text and its author.

I have been arguing that Celan's translational response to Mandel'shtam lends itself to a poethic interpretation, insofar as some of its constitutive textual strategies articulate with and can, consequently, be shown to stage semethics and the architectonic of co-existence. Celan's idiosyncratic use of person, place, and time deixis, in particular, facilitate the dialogization of Mandel'shtam's text, whereby 'dialogization' implies not so much the construction of conventional dialogue as the poethic displacement of Mandel'shtam's text: Celan's interpellation by and response to Mandel'shtam—themselves irreducibly grounded in semethical interlocution—become the very principle governing the construction of Celan's translations. The pragmatic make-up of Celan's translations delineates their primary author's singular place in co-existence, constitutes and indicates him as an always already interpellated and, hence, answerable and response-able singularity.[60] By displacing Mandel'shtam's text, that is, by being unfaithful to it, Celan enacts not only the necessary differences between original and translation, but, contextually, the irreducible co-existential and semethical distance between Mandel'shtam and himself, his irreducible non-alibi in co-existence, his unicity as an answerable and response-able person. Celan's translational unfaithfulness reveals itself as fundamental poethic faithfulness; he co-authors Mandel'shtam and his text not in any historically or philologically veridic sense, but as an ever-changing, diachronic gestalt, as the gestalt which Mandel'shtam assumes in the

---

[60] It will be remembered that answerability and response-ability pertain to co-existence and semethics, respectively.

context of and through Celan's response. In an almost trivial sense, one could say that Celan (re)creates Mandel'shtam—while being himself (re)created by Mandel'shtam—in the only way that Mandel'shtam could possibly acquire gestalt in German, written by Celan in, say, 1959.

Before shifting my attention to Celan's 'original' poetry some further characteristics of his translations, which warrant and thus corroborate their poethic interpretation, must be taken account of. Insofar as dialogic relations—both co-existential and semethical—permeate any utterance from within, the poethicity of Celan's response must be observable on textual levels exceeding intra- and extratextual pragmatics.

SAYING THE SAID

Celan does not content himself with concretizing his pre-text on the level of textual pragmatics, that is, personally and spatio-temporally. The irreducible singularity of his response finds its most subtle expression in those instances in which pragmatic specification contaminates the utterances' materiality itself, in which it moves from the text's 'fictional world' to its very semioticity, thereby highlighting the unicity of Celan's response in the very process of its articulation:

(i: 40)

(1) Душный сумрак кроет ложе,

(2) Напряженно дышет грудь . . .

(3) Может, мне всего дороже

(4) Тонкий крест и тайный путь.

(GW v. 61)

Bett aus schwülen Finsternissen,

Lasten auf die Brust gelegt . . .

Dies vielleicht ist mir das Liebste:

Schmales Kreuz, geheimer Weg.

(1) Smothering darkness covers* the bed,

(2) The breast breathes* hard . . .

(3) Maybe, most valuable to me is

(4) A* thin cross and a* secret path.

Bed of sultry darkenesses,

burdens laid on the breast . . .

This is perhaps what I love most:

Narrow cross, secret path.

(i: 184, ll. 11–12)

(11) И семисвещником
     тяжелым освещали
(12) Ерусалима ночь и чад
     небытия.

(11) And with a heavy seven-
     handed lamp [we] lit *
(12) Jerusalem's night and the
     smoke of non-being.

(GW v. 105)

der Siebenleuchter flammte,
     erhellte *dies hier:*
die Nacht Jerusalems, den
     Qualm des Wesenlosen.

the seven-handed lamp was flam-
     ing, it [illuminated* *this here:*
the night of Jerusalem, the
     smoke of the substanceless.

(i: 197, l. 9)

(9) Кто может знать при
     слове 'расставанье'

(9) Who can know by the
     word 'separation'

(GW v. 10)

Wer hört *dies* Wort er: Ausein-
     andergehen,

Whoever hears *this* word: separ-
     ation,

(i: 208, l. 7)

(7) Нам остаются только
     поцелуи,

(7) Only kisses remain for us,

(GW v. 117)

Uns bleibt nur *dies:* die . . .
     Küsse,

For us remains only *this:* the . . .
     kisses,

(ii: 18, ll. 17–18)

(17) Среди скрипучего
     похода мирового—
(18) Какая легкая кровать!

(17) Amidst the screeching
     march of the world—
(18) What a light bed.

(GW v. 151)

Der Welten Rasselschritt, und
     dies, inmitten:
dies Bett hier, leicht, so leicht.

The worlds' rattlestep, and *this,*
     amidst:
this bed here, light, so light.

(#161,[61] l. 11)

(11) Нет . . . слов для жалоб
     и признаний,

(11) There are no . . . words for
     complaints and confes-
     sions,

(GW v. 77)

Kein Wort für *dies hier:* Klagen
     und Bekennen . . .

No word for *this here:* com-
     plaining and confessing . . .

In all of these instances Celan transposes the pragmatic speci-
fication of his translations onto the discursive level itself by
employing demonstrative pronouns and interpunctuation:

---

[61] As I have mentioned earlier, this poem is cited according to the expanded
Struve/Filipoff edition of Mandel'shtam's works used by Celan.

through the implementation of discourse deixis,[62] Celan yet again underscores the metalinguistic and, by extension, ethical singularity of his response. It is crucial to note Celan's use of cola (i: 40 , l. 3; i: 184, l. 11; ii: 18, l. 17), which evince the discursive orientation of the preceding demonstratives and without which the demonstratives could be interpreted as operating on the pragmatic textual level.[63] Celan's rendition of ii: 18, ll. 17–18 clearly illustrates the difference between the functionalization of demonstratives as pragmatic deictica in general as opposed to discursive deictica in particular. The first 'this' and its apposition 'amidst' emphatically point to that part of speech which succeeds the colon, namely, 'this bed here'. Conversely, the demonstrative pronoun immediately preceding 'bed'—just like the latter itself and the apposite adverb 'here'—pertains to the text's pragmatics proper, that is, constitutes the text's spatio-temporal make-up.

PERFORMING SENSE

The poethicity of Celan's response to Mandel'shtam is not restricted to pragmatics, but palpably manifests itself in the texts' semantics proper. This is evidenced in particular by several consistently maintained textual strategies, which self-consciously enact the translations' semanticity, thereby exemplarily performing poethic sense: in other words, the translational constitution of Celan's response becomes its own, that is, the translations', governing semantic principle. In contrast to 'meaning' in the narrow linguistic sense, poethic sense constitutes itself originarily in response to poetic address, that is, in and through the poetic encounter between persons or between the objectivations of—more or less—mediated or unmediated poetic encounters between persons.[64] Poethic

---

[62] The term 'discourse deixis' designates the 'use of expressions within some utterance to refer to some portion of . . . that utterance (including that utterance itself)' (Levinson, 85).

[63] This is the case in the following of Celan's translations: i: 83, l. 4 (GW v. 69); i: 157, l. 11 (87); i: 193, l. 2 (103); i: 206, l. 21 (111); ii: 11, l. 17 (127); ii: 17, l. 16 (145).

[64] It will be remembered that both Bakhtin and Levinas distinguish between 'sense' and (linguistic) 'meaning' proper. Whereas 'meaning', according to Bakhtin, is the abstract-semantic correlate of a dictionary word, which is itself only an artificial abstraction from the word's actual and originary dialogic use, 'sense'

sense thus testifies to 'the originary semantic situation in which the human being receives sense' (*EN* 199), in which the interpellated acquires 'orientation and fate' (*GW* iii. 188) in translating the Other.

Semiosis

The first of the three poethically constitutive semantic strategies characterizing Celan's response can be called the intradiscursive or intralingual enactment of semiosis, that is, the intradiscursive enactment of translation *tout court*, which in itself—as *the* fundamental semiotic dynamic—performs and indicates a central component of both the co-existential and semethical moments of dialogue. Two modes of intradiscursive translation can be witnessed in Celan's response: (1) the consecutive syntagmatic placement of paradigmatically (semantically) similar expressions, whereby the first is translated into a presumably equivalent, alternative sign;[65] (2) the semantic development of lexemes (especially personal pronouns), that is, their intratextual translation into 'more developed sign[s]' (Peirce, ii. 228). In both cases, Celan's proliferation of poetic material has no apparent—material or semantic—basis in Mandel'shtam's text.

In each of the following examples, Celan substitutes two semantically contiguous expressions, separated by a comma, for a singular original expression:

(i: 46, ll. 11–12)	(*GW* v. 59)
(11) Твой мир, болезненный и странный,	Und Leere, deine Welt, die fremde,
(12) Я принимаю, пустота!	*empfang ich, nehme ich*!
(11) Your world, dolorous and strange,	And emptiness, your world, the strange one,
(12) I accept, emptiness!	I *receive*, I *take*!
(i: 77, l. 1)	(*GW* v. 63)
(1) Как кони медленно ступают,	Der Schritt der Pferde, *sacht, gemessen.*

transpires between dialogically oriented persons (*VLA* 94; *BSS* 189, 321, 336–7). Bakhtin's valorization of the co-existential significance of sense as dialogically enacted parallels Levinas's valorization of the semethical signficance of sense as originary dialogic orientation (*AQE* 26; *TI* 193).

[65] See Peirce, ii. 228; *SW* 261.

(1) How slowly (the) horses stride*,	The step of the horses, *gentle, measured.*
(i: 75 , l. 13)	(*GW* v. 65)
(13) Небо тусклое с отсветом странным—	Himmelsflor, *verblüht, hinweg-gerafft*—
(13) The sky is murky with a strange reflection—	The sky's filigree, *out of bloom, completely faded*—
(i: 127, ll. 3–4)	(*GW* v. 81)
(3) Иосиф, проданный в Египет,	Die Schwermut Josephs, in Ägypten,
(4) Не мог сильнее тоско-вать!	Sie war nicht *schwerer, lasten-der.*
(3) Joseph, sold to Egypt,	Joseph's grief, in Egypt,
(4) Could not have grieved stronger!	It was not *heavier, more burden-some.*
(i: 157, l. 2)	(*GW* v. 87)
(2) Сухую жизнь мою,	Mein *trocknes, morsches* Sein:
(2) My dry life,—	My *dry, brittle* Being:
(i: 206, ll. 7, 16)	(*GW* v. 111)
(7) Всех кладут в кипарис-ные носилки,	Man hebt sie auf die *Sänften,* auf das Zypressen*bett,*
(16) И прекрасное лицо.	Das menschliche, *das Antlitz, das* herrliche *Gesicht.*
(7) All are being lain on cypress stretchers,	They are being lifted onto the *sedans,* onto the cypress *bed,*
(16) And a wonderful face.	The human, *the visage, the* won-derful *face.*
(ii: 17, l. 4)	(*GW* v. 145)
(4) В сугроб пшеничный за окном.	im hochgehäuften *Weizen,* im *Getreid.*
(4) In the wheat drift outside the window.	in the high-piled *wheat,* in the *grain.*

In i: 46, ll. 11–12, Celan doubles the original 'I accept' into 'I receive, I take!'; in i: 77, l. 1, Mandel'shtam's adverb 'slowly' yields to the two apposite attributes, 'gentle, measured'; in i: 75, l. 13, the apposite predicate noun 'murky' turns into 'out of bloom, completely faded'; in i: 127, ll. 3–4, Joseph's grief gains in intensity, becoming 'heavier, more burdensome'; in i: 157, l. 2, the dryness of Mandel'shtam's life is enriched by the quality of brittleness; the 'cypress stretchers' of i: 206, l. 7 become 'sedans' and 'cypress bed', while the 'face' of line 16 is split into 'visage' and 'face'; similarly, the 'wheat drift' of ii: 17, l. 4 is transformed into 'high-piled wheat' and 'grain'.[66] By offering paradigmatically contiguous expressions as possible translations for singular lexemes in the original, Celan syntagmatically points to any translation's paradoxical semantico-referential status, as constitutively implying the constitutively impossible equivalence between utterances.

This semantico-lexematic proliferation is complemented by the intratextual semantic development of speech elements:

(i: 31, ll. 3–4)	(GW v. 55)
(3) И печальна так и хороша	Sie ist Tier und Dunkelheit,
(4) Теманая звериная душа:	sie, die Seele, gramgestillt.
(3) And so sad and good	It is animal and darkness,
(4) Is the dark animal soul:	it, the soul, imbued with grief.

(i: 80, l. 2)	(GW v. 67)
(2) . . . из пучины мировой,	. . . Aus ihr, der Weltenschlucht,
(2) . . . from the abyss of the world,	. . . From it, the world abyss,

(i: 156, ll. 5–6)	(GW v. 89)
(5) И ласточки, когда летели	Und sie, die nach Ägypten flogen,
(6) В Египет водяным путем,	die Schwalben . . .
(5) And swallows, when they flew*	And they, who flew* to Egypt,
(6) To Egypt along the water-way,	the swallows . . .

(i: 191, ll. 15–16)	(GW v. 99)
(15) Что в горячке соловьи-ной	Darum glühts, das Herz, in seinem
(16) Сердце теплое еще.	Nachtigallenschein.

[66] See also Celan's translations of Mandel'shtam's poems i: 45, l. 1 (GW v. 57); i: 156, l. 3 (89); ii: 13, l. 17 (139); ii: 17, l. 54 (149); ii: 18, l. 24 (151); iii: 29, l. 5 (153).

(15) That in nightingale fever

Therefore it glows, the heart, in its

(16) The heart is still warm.

nightingale shine.

(ii: 11, l. 21)

(GW v. 127)

(21) Это век волну колышит

Sie, die Zeit, bewegt die Welle,

(21) That's (the) age rocking the wave
(There, (the) age rocks* the wave)

It, the time, moves* the wave,

(ii: 17, l. 18)

(GW v. 145)

(18) Боюсь, лишь тот поймет тебя,

Nur dem, ich fürcht, erschließt er sich, dein Sinn,

(18) I fear, only the one will understand you,

To the one only, I fear, it discloses itself, your sense,

In all of these instances a respective apposite noun—'soul', 'world abyss', 'swallows', 'heart', 'time', and 'sense'—translates, thereby specifying, a preceding personal pronoun—'sie' (fem. nom. sing.), 'ihr' (fem. dat. sing.), 'sie' (fem. nom. pl.), 'es' (neutr. nom. sing.), 'Sie' (fem. nom. sing.), 'er' (masc. nom. sing.).[67] This diachronic analysis of linguistic material most palpably enacts the diachronicity of speech and, hence, the diachronicity of sense constitution. It thus intradiscursively reiterates the dialogic significance of Celan's translations with regard to their pre-texts' semanticity, which principally depends on its diachronic translational realization.

Figures of Contiguity

Translation is predicated on the referential—if not spatial or graphic—contiguity of utterances. This contiguity may be suppressed—yet not eliminated—by the translation's pretence to substitute itself for its pre-text on the grounds of a variously conceived notion of equivalence. Insofar as the stipulation of equivalence can only be advanced within the linguistic attitude, it necessarily diverts attention from an utterance's metalinguistic singularity, which, according to Bakhtin, principally entails both axiological unicity and the unicity of sense. Utterances cannot

---

[67] See also Celan's translations of poems i: 175, ll. 9–10 (GW v. 95); i: 211, l. 24 (159).

possibly be equi*v*alent. Translation exemplarily stages the tension between the linguistic stipulation of semantic equivalence and the metalinguistic facticity of irreducible difference, which—as I have been arguing—is itself dialogically grounded in semethics. Two of Celan's translational strategies, in particular, palpably enact this dichotomy between a translation's and its pre-text's stipulated semantic congruity *and* principal metalinguistic incongruity: the inversely complementary devices of 'compounding' and 'syndetic doubling'. The former signifies the translational transformation of lexematic pairs into singular lexemes; the latter signifies the translational transformation of singular lexemes into conjunctionally—by way of 'and'—linked lexematic pairs:

1. (i: 7, l. 2)[68]

(2) Как мало в фонарях огня!

(2) How little light there is in the lanterns!

(*GW* v. 63)
Laternenlicht—nicht viel.

Lanternlight—not much.

2. (i: 75 , l. 7)

(7) Я участвую в сумрачной жизни

(7) I participate* in gloomy life

(*GW* v. 65)
Dämmerleben. Ich—ich bin dabei

Twilightlife. I—I am in

3. (i: 83, l. 4)

(4) Немного дыма и немного пепла!

(4) A little smoke and a few ashes!

(*GW* v. 69)
zu diesem bißchen Rauch, zu diesem *Aschenrest*!

to this little amount of smoke, to this *ashesremainder*!

4. (i: 127, l. 16)

(16) Пространство, звезды и певец!

(16) Space, stars and the singer!

(*GW* v. 81)
bis auf den Sänger und den *Sternenraum.*

but the singer and the *starspace.*

5. (i: 208, l. 13)

(13) Возьми ж на радость дикий мой подарок,

(13) Take, for the sake of joy, my wild present.

(*GW* v. 117)
So nimm dies *Waldgeschenk,* nimms, dich zu freuen:

So take this *forestpresent*, take it, to be joyful:

[68] In order to highlight Celan's translational idiosyncrasies I depart from conventional English orthography.

6. (ii: 18, ll. 5–6, 12, 17)

(5) Два сонных яблока у
   века—властелина
(6) И глиняный прекрасный
   рот,
(12) Ход воспаленных тяжб
   людских.
(17) Среди скрипучего
   похода мирового—

(5) Two sleepy apples has ruler
   age
(6) And a beautiful clay
   mouth,
(12) The course of heated
   human litigations.
(17) Amid the screeching course
   of the world—

(GW v. 151)
Zwei *Schlummeräpfel* nennt die
   Zeit ihr eigen,
ihr *Herrschermund* ist lehmig-
   schön.
wie *Menschenzwist* entbrannte,
Jahr um Jahr.
Der Welten *Rasselschritt* und
   dies, inmitten:

Two *snoozeapples* the time calls
   its own,
its *rulermouth* is clay-beautiful.

how *humanfeud* ignited, year
   after year.
The worlds' *rattlestep* and this,
   amidst:

7. (i: 45, ll. 15–16)

(15) И, сердце, сердца усты-
   дись,
(16) С первоосновой жизни
   слито!

(15) And, heart, be ashamed of
   heart
(16) With life's foundation
   blent!

(GW v. 57)
Des Herzens schäm dich, Herz,
   das seinem
Beginn und Grund entstieg.

Of the heart be ashamed, heart,
   that
has left its *beginning and
   ground*.

8. (i: 124, ll. 15–16)

(15) И недовольный, о
   ночлеге
(16) Монах рассказывает
   ложь!

(15) And unhappy, about his
   lodging for the night
(16) The monk is telling lies!

(GW v. 79)
Unbequem dem Mönch das
   Lager.
Seine Rede: *Lug und Trug*.

Uncomfortable the monk finds
   the lodging (for the night).
His speech: *lies and deception*.

9. (i: 157, l. 10)

(10) Стучите, молотки,

(10) Rap, hammers,

(GW v. 87)
du Hammer, *poch und stoß*:

you hammer, *pant and pound*:

10. (i: 208, l. 11)

(11) Их родина—дремучий
         лес . . .

(11) Their homeland—the deep
         forest . . .

(GW v. 117)

Der dichte Wald . . .: *die Heimat
und die Herkunft.*

The thick forest . . .: the *home-
land and the origin.*

11. (ii: 11, l. 25)

(25) И . . . набухнут почки,

(25) And . . . buds will swell,

(GW v. 129)

Blatt und Schößling treiben . . .

Leaf and shoot sprout* . . .

12. (ii: 12 ('The Horse Shoe
         Finder'), ll. 10–12)

(10) И мореплаватель,

(11) В необузданной жажде
         пространства,

(12) . . .

(10) And the seafarer,

(11) In his unbridled thirst for
         space,

(12) . . .

(GW v. 131)

. . .

Und der Sefahrer,

Unbezähmbar in seinem Durst
nach *Weite und Raum,*

. . .

And the seafarer,

Unbridled in his thirst for *open-
ness and space,*

Celan's oscillation between compounding (1–6) and syndetic
doubling (7–12) throughout his translations[69] materially stages
any translation's constitutive linguistico-metalinguistic tension:
the fusion of lexematic pairs into singular lexemes[70] performs

---

[69] For further instances of compounding, see Celan's translations of Mandel'sh-
tam's poems: i: 6, l. 4 (GW v. 49); i: 46, l. 8 (59); i: 80, ll. 2, 15–16 (67); i: 86, l. 9
(71); i: 157, l. 8 (87); i: 156, ll. 3–4 (89); i: 162, ll. 6, 10 (91); i: 175, ll. 7–16 (95);
i: 191, ll. 2, 5, 7 (99); i: 193, ll. 2 (103); i: 197, l. 28 (107); i: 207, l. 2 (115); ii: 2,
ll. 6, 7, 9–11, 13–15 (121); ii: 1, l. 9 (125); ii: 11, l. 5, 11 (127); ii: 13, l. 53 (143);
ii: 17, ll. 54, 64 (149); iii: 29, ll. 8, 11 (153). For further instances of syndetic
doubling, see Celan's translations of Mandel'shtam's poems i: 45, l. 4 (57); i: 89, l.
7 (73); i: 140, l. 3 (85); i: 162, l. 4 (91); i: 193, l. 5 (103); i: 197, ll. 10, 21 (105); i:
206, l. 17 (111); ii: 17, ll. 6, 22, (145, 147, 149). Frequently, the oscillation
between compounding and syndetic doubling occurs within one poem, as in
Celan's translations of Mandel'shtam's poems: i: 157, ll. 8, 10 (GW v. 87); i:
193, ll. 2, 5 (103); i: 197, ll. 10, 21, 28 (105); ii: 11, ll. 5, 11, 25 (127, 129); ii: 17,
ll. 6, 22, 54, 64 (145, 149).
[70] 1. light + lantern → Lanternlight; 2. gloomy + life → Twilightlife; 3. a few +
ashes → ashesremainder; 4. Space + stars → starspace; 5. wild + present → forestpre-
sent; 6. sleepy + apples → snoozeapples, ruler + mouth → rulermouth, human + litiga-
tions → humanfeud, screeching + course → rattlestep.

the presumed semantic congruence of translation and original; the concomitant intralingual multiplication of singular original lexemes[71] indicates the irreducible metalinguistic incongruity between utterances, between translation and pre-text.

Both modes of rendition create two distinct kinds of material and conceptual contiguity. Compounding produces semantic contiguity within material identity by fusing initially discrete lexemes into material (morphological and phonological) units; syndetic doubling produces semantic and material contiguity within internally heterogeneous units, which are constituted by absolutely separated, yet conjunctionally bound lexemes. Both modes introduce seemingly gratuitous—from a purely linguistic perspective—instances of figuralness into Celan's response: metaphor and hendiadyoin. While the metaphorization of Mandel'shtam's text stages the mutually predicating relation between translation and original as contiguous utterances, the use of hendiadyoin stages—in contrast to the asyndetic concatenation of paradigmatically contiguous expressions,[72] which function as discrete translational alternatives rather than integral units—the inherently heterologous, that is, polyphonic character of translation, by joining discrete terms into complex rhetorical units.[73] The semantic and rhetorical significance of Celan's excessive use of figures of speech fulfils his poetological stipulation of the figuralness of poetry as gestalt: the poem as such is its author's, or rather authors', figure. Metaphor and hendiadyoin, in particular, enact poetry's character as textual gestalt by complementarily indicating the principally heterologous, dialogic constitution of any utterance.

Being translationally significant and performing gestalt, metaphor and hendiadyoin acquire emphatic metalinguistic and ethical force, insofar as both co-existence and semethics are predicated on interpersonal translation and insofar as poetic dialogic gestalt is necessarily grounded in co-existence. Through

---

[71] 7. foundation → beginning and ground; 8. lies → lies and deception; 9. rap → pant and pound; 10. homeland → homeland and origin; 11. buds → leaf and shoot; 12. space → openness and space.

[72] See section 'Semiosis' above. It is significant that in all of the above examples the semantically contiguous expressions are separated by commas.

[73] Olschner addresses Celan's penchant for 'doubling' (Olschner, 108) and interprets it as part of Celan's overall poetologically and existentially motivated device of 'emphasis' (101–14, esp. 102).

metaphor and hendiadyoin Celan poetically stages a person's constitutive dialogicity, a person's heterologous constitution *and* his or her simultaneous unicity, his or her absolute non-alibi in co-existence. Concurrently, by embodying semiotic contact *and* separation, respectively, metaphor and hendiadyoin exemplarily indicate semethical contiguity: if semethics 'is contact' (*DEHH* 224) in separation and if it 'acquires sense . . . in the space of contiguity' (prend un sens . . . dans l'espace de la contiguité) (*AQE* 245), metaphor and hendiadyoin in Celan's translations palpably perform the tactile, yet distally contiguous emergence of sense.

CHAPTER SIX

Continued Response:
Die Niemandsrose

Given that Celan's Mandel'shtam translations and *Die Nie-mandsrose* can be read as one complex, diachronically displaced, yet unitary response, *Die Niemandsrose* must be materially linked to Celan's Mandel'shtam translations.[1] While the structural inseverability of Celan's translations and original poetry is most clearly indicated by their concomitant dedicatory publication in *Die Neue Rundschau*,[2] their organic interdependence—whose demonstration is the condition for the unitary dialogic treatment of both bodies of text—can only be established by way of a detailed analysis of *Die Niemandsrose* itself. In the following three sections I elaborate the material groundedness of *Die Niemandsrose* in Mandel'shtam's poetry (and poetics). *Die Niemandsrose* consists of a dedication and fifty-three poems, which are divided into four internal cycles.[3]

THE TITLE

Already the title—*Die Niemandsrose* (*The No One's Rose*)—points to the cycle's intricate connection to Mandel'shtam's poetry *and* its translation by Celan: both constituents of the title's compound noun, 'Niemands-' (gen. sing.) and '-rose', materially instantiate Mandel'shtam's text.

'Niemands-'

'No one's' figures in Mandel'shtam's very personal and poetologically central poem ii: 18, whose first line, 'No, never have I

---

[1] By 'materiality' I mean here and subsequently 'in terms of the verbal material itself'.

[2] See *Die Neue Rundschau*, 74/1 (1963), 54–60.

[3] Regarding the cyclical character of *Die Niemandsrose*, see Witte. For an overall commentary on the cycle, see Lehmann, *Kommentar*.

been anyone's contemporary' (Net, nikogda nichei ia ne byl sovremennik),[4] Celan renders as 'Was no one's contemporary, was it in no way' (War niemands Zeitgenosse, wars in keiner Weise) (*GW* v. 151). Significantly, poem ii: 18 concludes the original volume of Celan's Mandel′shtam-translations.[5] By placing 'Niemands' at the head of *Die Niemandsrose*, Celan picks up where his translations leave off, as it were; he, thereby, materially links the entire cycle to Mandel′shtam's poetry and highlights the continuity between his translations and *Die Niemandsrose*.

'Niemand-'[6] acquires further significance in the light of Mandel′shtam's poetics and the co-existential context informing Celan's response. In his essay 'On the Interlocutor' Mandel′shtam suggests that the poem-letter in the bottle 'is addressed to no one [ni k komu] in particular' (*MSS* i. 184) and that 'this "anyone"/ "someone" ['nekto'] is precisely [the poet's] secret interlocutor' (i. 275). Mandel′shtam exploits the paronomastic and oxymoronic interplay between the semantically diametrically opposed Russian lexemes 'nikto' (no one, nobody)—used in the dative case ('ni k komu')—and 'nekto' (anyone, someone, somebody). Given that *Die Niemandsrose* is emphatically—by way of its dedication—addressed to Mandel′shtam, 'Niemand' can be interpreted as invoking Mandel′shtam's word-play by figuring both as a referring proper name and as a constitutively referentless pronoun: as the owner of '-rose', 'Niemand-' inevitably reveals him(- or herself) as 'someone' named 'Niemand'.[7]

That Celan indeed foregrounds the semantic indeterminacy of the term 'niemand'—as an indefinite pronoun and as a proper

[4] Lit. 'No, never no one's have I not been a* contemporary.' For an analysis of this poem, see: Ronen, *An Approach*, 331–63; see also Brown, *Mandelstam*, 113–20. The topos of 'time' and 'contemporaneity' is, as I have illustrated in Ch. 3, central to Mandel′shtam's poetics. If the poet is the contemporary of 'events, names and traditions separated by centuries' (*MSS* iii. 256), he or she is indeed 'no one's contemporary' by virtue of being everyone's contemporary, as poem iii: 38, l. 42 ('Midnight in Moscow') suggests.

[5] See Mandel′shtam, *Gedichte*.

[6] The letter 's' between 'Niemand' and 'rose', the so called connective 's', is irrelevant to the discrete meanings of both lexemes, functioning as a conventional connective in nominal genitive compounds.

[7] The positive functionalization of 'no one' as a proper name is, of course, sufficiently familiar from the *Odyssee's* Polyphemus-episode, which, incidentally, Celan reread during his work on *Die Niemandsrose* in its particular reinterpretation by Horkheimer and Adorno in *Dialektik der Aufklärung* (see Lehmann, *Kommentar*, 23).

name—is suggested by its functionalization in such poems from *Die Niemandsrose* as 'There was earth in them' (Es war Erde in ihnen) (*GW* i. 211)—the cycle's opening poem—and 'Psalm' (i. 225), which contains the noun 'Niemandsrose' (ll. 12–13).[8] In 'There was earth in them' Celan semantically deploys the term's referential ambiguity into its positive and negative components, thereby underscoring their simultaneous valorization: 'O one, o nobody, o no one, o you' (O einer, o keiner, o niemand, o du) (l. 15). 'Niemand' is thus both 'one' and 'nobody', whereby its positive signification outweighs the negative one, given the prosodically accentuated placement of a 'you' at the end of the line: 'niemand' is an interlocutor. Similarly, in 'Psalm' 'Niemand' is depicted as an active agent and interlocutor: 'No one kneads us again from earth and clay,|no one conjures our dust.| . . .||Praised be you, No One' (Niemand knetet uns wieder aus Erde und Lehm,|niemand bespricht unsern Staub.| . . .||Gelobt seist du, Niemand) (ll. 1–4).[9] The plausibility of stipulating Celan's valorization of the semantic ambiguity of 'niemand' is further corroborated by the term's fundamentally heteroglot contextual constitution. It must not be forgotten that, living in Paris, Celan was immersed in the French idiom, which more or less overtly provides a dialogizing background to his German poetry. The use of the German nouns 'Neige' (slant, waning) and 'Schnee' (snow) in the *Niemandsrose* poem 'Over wine and lostness' (Bei Wein und Verlorenheit) (i. 213, ll. 2–3) clearly illustrates the two languages' interdependence in Celan's poems: without obliterating its German signification, 'Neige' reveals itself as anticipating and announcing 'Schnee' if read as the French 'neige' (snow).[10] A similar

[8] See also Celan's earlier poem, 'Count the almonds' (Zähle die Mandeln) (*GW* i. 78), and his prose text, 'Conversation in the Mountains' (Gespräch im Gebirg), in both of which the pronominal/nominal ambiguity of 'niemand' is played out.

[9] Whereas the capitalization of 'niemand' in line 1 may be attributed to grammatical necessity ('Niemand' is the poem's first word), the capitalization of 'Niemand' in line 4 unambiguously personalizes the indefinite pronoun. Regarding the religious and theological connotations of Celan's use of 'Niemand', see e.g. Scholem, 'Die Schöpfung aus Nichts'; *Die jüdische Mystik*, 27, 236–41; Neumann, 53–4; Wienold; Wolosky; Felstiner 168–9; Lehmann, *Kommentar*, 23.

[10] Martine Broda was the first to point out Celan's poetic valorization of his co-existential linguistic situation, which she pertinently refers to as a 'linguistic bath' (*Dans la main*, 19, 68). Jean Bollack's critique of such interpretative linkages as 'unfounded' ('Chanson à boire', 28) remains unsubstantiated.

interlingual oscillation constitutes Celan's use of 'niemand', whose nominal and pronominal significations are most palpably conjoined in its French correlate 'personne', which means both 'person' and 'no one'.[11] This 'circumstantial evidence', as it were, is validated by Celan's consideration—and ultimate dismissal—of 'The Everyone's/Anyone's Rose' (Die Jedermannsrose) as the cycle's title.[12]

The interpretation of the titular 'Niemand-' against the backdrop of Celan's dialogue with Mandel'shtam is all the more justified in view of Celan's subversion of Gottfried Benn's poetics of monologue. Insofar as Celan developed his dialogic poetics with explicit recourse to Mandel'shtam's conception of poetry as dialogue and in opposition to Benn's stipulation that 'poems are addressed to no one [an niemanden]' (*Essays*, 502)—whereby both Mandel'shtam and Benn use 'no one' in mutually exclusive senses[13]—his placement of 'Niemand' in the title of that poetic cycle which he dedicates—thus underscoring the facticity of dialogue—to Mandel'shtam, unmistakably suggests the term's rootedness in Mandel'shtam's text.[14]

'-rose'

This term, too, materially ties Celan's text to Mandel'shtam's poetry—in particular, to poem i: 202 (translated by Celan, *GW* v. 109), the final stanza of which abounds with 'roses':

Словно темную воду, я пью помутившийся воздух. Время вспахано плугом, и роза землею была.	Ich trink die Luft wie Wasser, trink Trübes, Strahlenloses. Die Zeit—gepflügt, die Rose, die nun zu Erde ward . . .

---

[11] See Broda, *Dans la main*, 68.

[12] See Gellhaus, 'Erinnerung', 7.

[13] While Mandel'shtam's 'nikto' implies 'no one in particular', that is, 'anyone', Benn's 'niemand' is predicated on the apodictic postulate of the monologicity of poetry.

[14] I should also point to a deeply co-existential dimension of Celan's 'Niemand-', which further corroborates its dialogic significance. In a letter to his mentor Alfred Margul-Sperber (9 March 1962), Celan writes: 'Not only in the Federal Republic of Germany,—here [in Paris], too, we have no one [haben wir niemanden]' ('Briefe an Alfred Margul-Sperber', 57). The bitterness of this intimately personal revelation, Celan's resignation to having 'niemanden' (acc. sing.), provide the immediate co-existential interpretative context for the following passage from the same letter, in which 'niemand' undergoes a poetic transformation: 'I have almost completed a new volume of poetry; I intend to call it "Die Niemandsrose"' (ibid.).

В медленном водовороте
  тяыжелые нежные розы,
Розы тяжесть и нежность в
  двойные венки заплела!

Still drehn sich mit den Wassern
  die schweren zarten Rosen—
zum Doppelkranz geflochten die
  Rosen Schwer und Zart!

Like dark water, I drink* the
  air, which has grown muddy.

I drink* (the) air like water,
  drink* something that is
  muddy, beamless.

Time is ploughed up, and a*
  rose was earth/soil.

The time—ploughed, the rose,
  that now turned into earth/soil
  . . .

In the slow whirlpool heavy
  tender roses,

Softly turn* with the waters the
  heavy tender roses—

(The) roses heaviness and tender-
ness it has braided into double
wreaths!

braided into a double wreath the
  roses Heavy and Tender!¹⁵

In the context of the two poets' dialogue, the term may equally be interpreted as invoking Mandel′shtam's poetological function-alization of 'rose': 'Let us consider "rose" and "sun" for example . . . For a symbolist these images are not interesting in themselves; the rose is like the sun, the sun is like the rose . . . Acmeism emerged in opposition to symbolism: ". . . hail the living rose!" . . . was its initial password [lozung]' (*MSS* i. 227, 229).¹⁶

Of course these references are themselves imbued with a vast array of cultural, historical, and poetic significations of 'rose', which in part already underlie Mandel′shtam's use of the term.¹⁷ Suffice it to single out only two of the term's contextually pertinent connotations at this point. In the early poem 'The Last Banner' (Die letzte Fahne) (*GW* i. 23, l. 5) Celan employs the metaphor 'rose of exile' (Rose der Fremde), which echoes

---

¹⁵ For further occurrences of 'rose' in Mandel′shtam's poetry, see e.g. poems i: 183, i: 210, iii: 3, iii: 6, all of which Celan was familiar with.

¹⁶ Mandel′shtam's fellow acmeist Gumilev also comments on the symbolic function of the rose: 'the poets of the middle ages viewed the rose as a symbol of love and beauty . . . in Viacheslav Ivanov's writings the rose becomes a mystical value' (Gumilev, i. 191). Blok's 'heavenly roses' (Blok, v. 427–8) provide a good example of the symbolist use of 'rose'.

¹⁷ For the symbolic meanings of 'rose' in the Christian context, see: Lurker, 630; Schwarz, 32–3; Stiehler 22; Brierley, 305–7. For the symbolic meanings of 'rose' in the Jewish context, see: Killy, 318–20; Brierley, 307. For Celan's uses of 'rose' throughout his poetry, see Winkler.

the biblical and kabbalistic uses of 'rose' with reference to the exiled 'community of Israel',[18] and which informs Celan's functionalization of 'rose' in *Die Niemandsrose* in particular, insofar as the latter is the response of one exiled Jew to another.[19] 'Rose' thus acquires the status of a co-existential *chiffre*, a shibboleth or password, addressed—in times of adversity and distress—to a 'brother', to 'Bruder Ossip'.[20] It is, to use Voloshinov's term, a 'social enthymeme' (DLDA 101), 'mak[ing] myriad connections with the extraverbal context of [Celan's] life' (ibid.). Equally relevant in the present context is the traditional functionalization of the *flower* 'rose' as a symbol or metaphor for language and poetry.[21]

[18] See Song of Solomon, 2: 1–2; Hosea 14: 6. Despite the fact that in the Hebrew original, in the Septuagint, and in the Vulgate '(white) lily' (Heb.: 'chavatselet' or 'shoshana' (the latter has come to mean 'rose' in colloquial Hebrew); Gr.: 'krinon'; Lat.: 'lilium') is used in both passages, Luther, whose Bible translation became canonical in the German context, opts for 'rose' in both Song of Solomon, 2: 1–2: 'Ich bin eine Blume zu Saron | und eine Rosen im Thal. Wie eine Rose unter den Dornen so ist meine Freundin unter den Töchtern' (I am a flower of Sharon and a rose in the valley. Like a rose among the thorns so is my girlfriend among the daughters) and in Hosea, 14: 6: 'Ich will Israel wie ein Taw sein das er sol blühen wie eine Rose und seine Wurzeln sollen ausschlagen wie Libanon' (I want to be like dew for Israel so that he may bloom like a rose and his roots shall spread like Lebanon). Martin Buber's translation of the Old Testament, with which Celan was intimately familiar, is not helpful in this instance, since Buber renders Hosea's 'lily' as 'Rotanemone' (red anemone) (*Das Buch*, 41). The standard Church Slavonic editions of the Bible available to Mandel'shtam—incidentally, the bible was re-edited in 1904 in Moscow—have, in line with the Septuagint's 'krinon', 'krin' in the passages in question. Regarding the allegorical interpretation of 'rose of Sharon' as 'Israel', see: Scholem, 'Kabbalah und Mythus', 315–16; Brierley, 307. For a synoptic overview of the passages in question, see *Biblia Hexaglotta*, vols. 3 and 4. In the *Sohar* 'rose' is equated with Israel: 'What does the *word* rose mean? It means the community of Israel' (cited in Broda, *Dans la main*, 23).

[19] Both Mandel'shtam and Celan were exiles. Suffice it to mention Mandel'shtam's exile in Voronezh and, eventually, Siberia, where he died, and Celan's exilic existence in Paris (see Chalfen; Pajevic).

[20] It must be remembered that the composition of *Die Niemandsrose* historically overlaps with the so called Goll affair (see Ch. 3). One of Celan's unpublished poems of the *Niemandsrose* period bears the title 'Bruder Ossip'. Regarding Celan's view of Mandel'shtam as a 'brother', see e.g. Ivanovic, 230, 244. Regarding Celan's explicit functionalization of certain key words as shibboleths, see his poems 'Schibboleth' (*GW* i. 131) and 'In One' (In Eins) (*GW* i. 270). Of course, 'shibboleth' will have always already been rife with socio-political signification (see Judges 12: 6).

[21] See Lehmann, *Kommentar*, 40. In his hymn 'Germanien' Hölderlin calls language in general and, presumably, poetry in particular the 'flower of the mouth' (Blume des Mundes) (l. 72, cited in Hölderlin, *Gedichte*, 152–5). Celan's use of 'rose' implicitly opposes Heidegger's ontological functionalization of 'rose' as symbolizing Being (*Der Satz*, 102).

THE DEDICATION

'*Dem Andenken Ossip Mandelstamms*' (To the remembrance of Ossip Mandelstamm). Similarly to Levinas's epigraphic function-alization of Celan's poem 'In Praise of Remoteness' (Lob der Ferne),[22] Celan's dedicatory epigraph stakes out the thematic parameters against the backdrop of which the subsequent poems signify and are presumably to be interpreted. Insofar as it is identical with Celan's earlier dedication to Mandel'shtam in *Die Neue Rundschau*, it reveals the entire cycle as grounded in and emerging from Celan's translational response to the Russian poet.[23] The repetition of (parts of) Mandel'shtam's name throughout *Die Niemandsrose* further testifies to the entire cycle's proximity to the Russian poet and his texts.[24]

As I have suggested earlier, this link is saturated by the dedication's allusive, intertextual, and polyphonic character.[25] Its dialogic significance reveals itself most clearly if it is interpreted as a subtle, yet decisive displacement of Hölderlin's hymn 'Andenken' in its particular refraction through Heideg-ger. Heidegger reads the hymn in impersonal, universally historical terms: rather than being concerned with his or her own co-existence, the poet must assume an essentially hieratic and prophetic destiny,[26] which consists in 'stak[ing] out the premises for the house . . . in which the gods shall be visiting' (*Erläuterungen*, 148), thereby paving the way for the return of the 'absconded gods'.[27] The poet accomplishes this task 'in remembering the past' (ibid.) while working toward 'that which is to come' (107). Exacerbating Hölderlin's attention to the role of Germany as the facilitator of the return of the 'gods',[28] Heidegger reads Hölderlin's text in overtly national-

---

[22] See Ch. 1, 'Ethics and Poetry'.   [23] See Ch. 4, 'Toward the Other'.
[24] See the following *Niemandsrose* poems: 'A Rogues' and Swindlers' Ditty' (Eine Gauner- und Ganovenweise) (*GW* i. 229–30, ll. 16–18); 'Afternoon with Circus and Citadel' (Nachmittag mit Zirkus und Zitadelle) (i. 261, l. 4); 'Everything is different' (Es ist alles anders) (i. 284–6, l. 12).
[25] See Ch. 4, 'Toward the Other'.   [26] See Heidegger, *Erläuterungen*, 114.
[27] See Hölderlin's hymn 'Germanien' (esp. ll. 17–32, cited in Hölderlin, *Gedichte* 152–5), in which the poet is called 'priest' (l. 21) and which informs Heidegger's reading of 'Andenken'. See also Heidegger's 'Wozu Dichter?', in which a similar argument is developed, and 'Nachwort zu "Was ist Metaphysik?"' (both in *Wegmar-ken*), in which Heidegger summarizes the poet's task as: 'The poet says the holy' (312).
[28] See esp. the last stanza of Hölderlin's 'Germanien'. My treatment of Hölderlin

istic terms—in the context of the 'history of the Germans' (106), who—with their poets' help—are presumably destined to host the expected 'gods', thus bringing about 'salvation' (Rettung) (114).[29]

Celan dislocates Heidegger's Hölderlin-based stipulation of the German poet's presumed destiny as the depersonalized harbinger of the 'absconded gods': Celan's German poet, that is, Celan himself, emphasizes the fundamentally personal character of his poetry, which—far from being concerned with the return of the 'gods' (onto German soil)—is a means of personal response and co-existential orientation (ibid.).[30] This does not mean, however, that *Die Niemandsrose* can or should be reduced to the realm of the 'merely' personal and private. Such a reduction would neither take into account the linguistic and, hence, universal aspect of any utterance (including *Die Niemandsrose*) nor—and more importantly—the socio-political and historical dimension of Celan's poetry as a response to the Holocaust. Nowhere does the interplay between the singular and the universal in Celan's poetry come to the fore as poignantly as in his use of Mandel′shtam's very name.

Celan spells Mandel′shtam's name as 'Ossip Mandelstamm'; in Russian the poet's name is spelled 'Osip Mandel′shtam' (Осип Мандельштам). Celan's orthographic alterations seem to be motivated by the name's Russian pronunciation: the reduplication of the 's' in 'Ossip' moves the stress unequivocally to the 'O-'; the reduplication of the 'm' in 'Mandelstamm' indicates a stress on '-stamm'.[31] While Celan's spelling of the poet's given name

is avowedly tendentious. It is contextually justified in view of Celan's idiosyncratic reception of Hölderlin's poetry.

[29] Incidentally the poets are aided by 'German women': 'The German women save the appearance [retten das Erscheinen] of the gods . . . The German women save the arrival of the gods' (Heidegger, *Erläuterungen*, 107). It is, of course, no coincidence that Heidegger published his discussion of Hölderlin's 'Andenken' in 1943.

[30] While the complex question of Celan's 'poetic nationality' may be irrelevant in itself, it is productive in the present context. Neither Celan's self-characterization—by way of an ecclesiastical technical term—as a 'Russkij poët in partibus nemetskich infidelium [sic!]' (Russian poet in the parts of the German infidels) (letter to Margul-Sperber (9 March 1962)) nor Claude David's designation of Celan as 'the greatest French poet of the German language' ('Préambule', 239) alter the fact that German was Celan's mother tongue and poetic idiom. Thus, in a letter to Edith Silbermann Celan writes: 'My position as a Jew and a German author is not an easy one' (cited in Buck, 8).

[31] In Russian, the stresses in 'Osip Mandel′shtam' fall on 'Ó-' and '-shtám';

exhausts itself in phonological considerations, his spelling of the poet's last name testifies—in addition to its phonological motivation—to the name's German roots: 'Mandel'shtam'/'Mandelstamm' is a speaking proper name consisting of the lexemes 'Mandel' and 'shtam', which in German mean 'almond' and 'trunk/tribe', respectively.[32] Celan thus foregrounds both the singularity of 'Mandelstamm', the bearer of a particular proper name, *and* the latter's universality as the generic designation of the 'almond tribe', which, in the context of Celan's poetry, must be interpreted as referring to the Jewish people.[33] By virtue of its co-existentially singular orientation toward another exiled Jewish poet, Celan's dedication reveals itself as commemorating an entire people. Incidentally, the Russian poet's given name,

'Mandel-' is unstressed. In order to indicate this pronunciation in German, a double consonant must succeed the 'O-' in 'Ossip' and the '-a-' in '-stamm', since in German the vowel preceding a double consonant is necessarily short and stressed. Unlike its Russian counterpart, the German 'Mandel' requires a stress. If the name were transliterated as 'Osip Mandelstam', it could be pronounced as 'Osíp Mándelstam'. (The German '-st-' is automatically pronounced as 'sht', at least in most parts of Germany, and thus neatly replicates the Russian 'sht'.)

[32] Since the Russian spelling of non-Russian words is phonologically motivated, the Russian variant of the German 'Mandelstamm' requires a soft sign after the 'l', while not requiring a second 'm'. I should stress that my attention to the morphology of Mandel'shtam's name is motivated and legitimated by Celan's frequent use of the possibilities of verbal and semantic permutation. Beginning with the transformation of his own last name, 'Antschel', into 'Celan', he uses similar verbal techniques throughout his poetry, as the following lines illustrate: 'Mandelbaum. | Mandelbaum, Bandelmaum. | Mandeltraum . . .' (Almond tree. | Almond tree, Talmond aree. | Almond dream) (*GW* i. 229–30). Celan's ironic play with 'Stämme und Bäume und Stammbäume' (trunks and trees and genealogical trees) (undated letter to Margul-Sperber (between March and September 1962)) further corroborates the plausibility of claiming Celan's valorization of the semantic possibilities of 'Mandelstamm'.

[33] Focusing on Celan's poem 'Count the Almonds' (*GW* i. 78), John Felstiner summarizes the significance of 'almond' in Celan's oeuvre beginning with *Mohn und Gedächtnis* (*Poppy and Memory*) (1952): 'The poet is speaking to his mother. Later he called her an "almond-eyed shadow" and recollected "the almond eye of the dead" [in the poem 'Andenken'; *GW* i. 110, 121]. The *Mandeln* he wants to be numbered among call to mind the almonds she [i.e. Celan's mother] baked in breads and cakes, as well as the Yiddish lullaby about Zion's widowed daughter, "Raisins and Almonds", from Goldfaden's operetta *Shulamis*. Blooming earliest in Israel, yielding sweet nuts and bitter, oval like the Levantine eye, almonds now betoken Jewishness for Celan. The Israelites' menorah in the wilderness has almond blossom designs (Exod. 25: 33), and Aaron's rod bears ripe almonds (Num. 17: 23). When the prophet Jeremiah is summoned, a play on "almond" (*shaked*) proves that the Lord will "keep watch [*shoked*] over My word to perform it" (Jer. 1: 11). This pun surfaces in 1952—"Count the almonds,/count what was bitter and kept you waking"—after the lapse of the divine promise' (Felstiner, 63–4). See also Broda, *Dans la main*, 13–22; Lehmann, *Kommentar*, 46, 179.

'Osip/Ossip', indirectly corroborates the generic significance of 'Mandelstamm', insofar as its constitutive morphemes, 'Os-' and '-sip', implicate the contextually significant lexemes 'os' (осъ (axis)) (with a soft sign at the end) and 'Sippe' (kin, tribe, family), the German synonym for 'Stamm'; both implicata pertain to the semantic field 'link', 'connection', 'relation', and thus complement 'Stamm'.[34]

The structural irony informing Celan's dependence on the 'language of the murderers' for his response to the Holocaust, is compounded by the irony of the fact that his disavowal of Heidegger's (and Hölderlin's) perilous nationalistic views of poet and poetry in the name of the other—the non-German, the Russian-Jewish poet—only throws him back into the realm of the German: Mandel'shtam—for Celan, the exemplary other of any kind of totalitarianism (whether Stalinism or National Socialism) and a dialogic escape route, as it were, from the 'injustices' (especially the Goll affair) which he presumably experienced in the West and which he linked to fascism[35]—has a German name and is—from a historical point of view—German by virtue of being an Ashkenazic Jew![36] Celan's attempts to distance himself from the German—geographically, by settling in France, poetically, by subverting its socio-politically compromised idiom (see below), co-existentially, by seeking 'hope' in the East, that is, first

---

[34] That Celan was indeed aware of these implications is indicated by his use of 'Sippen' (pl.) in the emphatically Mandel'shtam-oriented *Niemandsrose* poem 'The Syllable Pain' (Die Silbe Schmerz) (*GW* iii. 280–1, l. 35) and in his emphasis on the 'Achsenton' [axis sound] 'O' in the *Niemandsrose* poem 'Huhediblu' (i. 275–7, ll. 32, 36, 40–3). Celan's attention to the 'axis sound' is informed by Mandel'shtam's play on 'os'' (axis) (with a soft sign at the end) and 'os' ((the) wasps') (without a soft sign at the end), which Celan encountered in Mandel'shtam's late Voronezh poem (iii: 160), 'Equipped with the vision of narrow wasps, | who suck* the earth's axis, the earth's axis' (Вооруженный зреньем узких ос, | Сосущих ось земную, ось земную) (ll. 1–2). This poem was published in the second volume of the journal *Aerial Ways*, 58 (New York, 1961), which Celan owned. See also Ivanovic, 242–3; Taranovsky, 83–114; Werberger, 19.

[35] See Celan's letters to Petre Solomon (22 Mar. 1962; 5 Sept. 1962) and to A. Margul-Sperber (8 Feb. 1962). See also Pajevic, 150–1.

[36] In a letter to Reinhard Federmann (14 Mar. 1962), Celan emphasizes his own Ashkenazic heritage (cited in Lehmann, *Kommentar*, 132). It should be remembered that the designation 'Ashkenaz' has been the Hebrew term for 'Germany' since the middle ages. The Ashkenazic Jews are those Jews, who, in the 14th century, began to migrate to eastern Europe from the German-speaking parts of central Europe, thus, in a sense, going into exile. For a discussion of the biblical roots of the term 'ashkenaz' and its application to eastern European Jewry ('Ashkenazim'), see Halévi, 119–22, 333.

and foremost, in Mandel'shtam and (to a lesser extent) in such poets as Marina Cvetaeva and Sergei Esenin[37]—lead him, ironically, back to 'where [he] started, [to] the [linguistic] realm of [his own] origin' (*GW* iii. 202): to the German (language), embodied in Mandel'shtam's very name. This return to himself by way of the other, this recovery of the German in the Jew, however, does not by any means imply 'failure' on Celan's part, but, on the contrary, demonstrates the disconcerting, paradoxical complexity of being a European—and, in particular, German—Jew 'after Auschwitz'. If the Jew was the National Socialist's 'negative image [and] counteridentity' (Rentschler, 159), to be repressed and reduced at any cost, yet, simultaneously, an indispensable element of the German self, then—Celan suggests in an almost perverse psychological reversal by valorizing the semantic possibilities of Mandel'shtam's very name—the German— and a fortiori the National Socialist German—has in turn become the post-Holocaust Jew's irreducible alter ego.

THE POEMS

All poems of *Die Niemandsrose* more or less overtly materially relate to Mandel'shtam's poetry and, in particular, to the poems translated by Celan. While critics acknowledge the intertextual importance of Mandel'shtam and his texts for an adequate reception of Celan's poems,[38] the comprehensive material significance of Mandel'shtam's poetic oeuvre for the poems of *Die Niemandsrose* has—to my knowledge—not been sufficiently noted. I should stress that by highlighting the constitutive function of Mandel'shtam's text (in Celan's translation) for *Die Niemandsrose* I do not aim at diminishing the role of others' voices (see below) for Celan's poems. I do argue, however, that Mandel'shtam ought to be viewed as *Die Niemandsrose*'s central

---

[37] 'My hope is in the East—*it is there*', Celan writes to Petre Solomon on 22 March 1962. Celan did not endorse the totalitarianism practised by the Warsaw Pact states. His 'East' was the imagined East of the past. As Marko Pajevic poignantly notes: 'His points of reference in the East were fixed. However, they were from a different time. Mandel'shtam, Cvetaeva and Esenin were not the poetic representatives of contemporary Eastern Europe . . . The more aggravating his experience of the West became, the more he thought back to his time in the East. His adolescence and youth in the East became the place, where "true friends", whom he could never find in the West, still existed' (Pajevic, 150).

[38] See esp. Broda, *Dans la main*, 13; Olschner, 29; Lehmann, *Kommentar*, 27.

interlocutor, in constant reference to whom Celan's other (poetic) interlocutors[39] situate themselves in dynamic dialogic constellations. Forgoing a detailed intertextual analysis of the cycle in its entirety, suffice it to point out only some of those instances in which the cycle's groundedness in Mandel'shtam's poetry (in Celan's translation) comes to the fore most saliently.

In addition to containing the lexeme 'no one' (l. 15),[40] which links the poem to Celan's translation of Mandel'shtam's poem ii: 18 and the essay 'On the Interlocutor', the cycle's introductory poem, 'There was earth in them', lexematically instantiates the semantics of the first poem of Mandel'shtam's first collection of poetry, *The Stone* (1913), in Celan's translation: the accumulation of the 'o sound' (Oh-Ton) (*GW* i. 276) in lines 15 and 17—'O one, o nobody, o no one, o you:|...|O you dig* ...'— materially realizes the 'hollow sound' (hohle Laut) of the first line of Celan's translation of Mandel'shtam's poem i: 6.[41] Of course, in the present context the 'axis sound' 'o' synecdochically invokes (the given name of) Os(s)ip Mandel'shtam, whose verbal gestalt thus palpably permeates Celan's introductory poem.[42] The structural parallelism, which Celan establishes between his translations, *Die Niemandsrose*, and Mandel'shtam's *Stone*, underscores the mutual affinities informing the three bodies of texts.

The cycle's second poem, 'The word of going-to-the-depth' (Das Wort vom Zur-Tiefe-Gehn) (i. 212) further cements the introductory segments' (title, dedication, introductory poem)— and thus, synecdochically, the entire cycle's—orientation toward Mandel'shtam by almost literally invoking line 12 from

---

[39] Such as Nelly Sachs, Hölderlin, and Rilke, to name only a few.

[40] For further occurrences of the indefinite pronoun in *Die Niemandsrose*, see the following poems: 'Psalm' (*GW* i. 225, ll. 1–4, 13); 'Radix, Matrix' (i. 239–40, l. 23); 'Snuggling no one' (An niemand geschmiegt) (i. 245).

[41] It is crucial to note that 'hollow sound' does not occur in the original, which has 'Звук . . . глухой' (A* deaf . . . sound) (l. 1) instead. Further (cumulative) occurrences of 'o' sounds throughout *Die Niemandsrose* (*GW* i. 217, 219, 225, 234, 239, 276, 283) must be interpreted in the light of this initial reference.

[42] See n. 34. To my knowledge, only two critics deal with the phoneme 'o' in 'There was earth in them', without, however, exploring its dialogic implications: David Brierley interprets the 'o' in the light of the 'Ring' of the poem's last line as a 'sign of the covenant between god and humankind' (Brierley, 308); Hendrik Birus, the poem's most recent commentator, contents himself with noting the presence of the 'apostrophic particle "o"' (cited in Lehmann, *Kommentar*, 55).

Mandel'shtam's poem i: 193, 'How your ship goes* to the bottom [of the sea]' (Как твой корабль ко дну идет), which Celan renders as '. . . your ship, which goes to the depth' (dein Schiff, das zur Tiefe geht) (*GW* v. 103).[43] Notwithstanding the line's simultaneous reference to Georg Heym's poem 'Your lashes, the long ones' (Deine Wimpern, die langen),[44] in whose fourth line the poem's unidentified speaker says, 'Let me go to the depth' (Laß mich zur Tiefe gehn), and which thus reveals itself as a subtext for both Celan's original poem and Mandel'shtam translation, its occurrence in the second poem of *Die Niemandsrose* testifies to the latter's material link to Celan's translational response to Mandel'shtam—without, thereby, diminishing the role of the 'third'—in this instance, Heym—in the two poets' dialogue (see below).

Such contextually contiguous and related poems as 'Radix, Matrix' (i 239–40) 'Black earth' (Schwarzerde) (i. 241), 'Mandorla' (i. 244), and 'Snuggling no one' (An niemand geschmiegt) (i. 245), which form a tight-knit web of references to Mandel'shtam and his text, equally indicate the cycle's material debt to the Russian poet.[45] 'Radix, Matrix' stages an extended comparison (ll. 1–2, 25–6, 28–9), which is parenthetically punctured by an unidentified speaker's appeal to and interrogation of a grammatically feminine interlocutor ('Ver-|schwis-terte' (en-|sistered); 'Zu-|geschleuderte' (hurled); 'Be-|gegnete' (en-|countered)):

(1) Wie man zum Stein spricht, wie	As one speaks to (a*) stone,[46] as
(2) du	you
(3) mir vom Abgrund her, von	who to me from an abyss, from
(4) einer Heimat her Ver-	an homeland en-
(5) schwisterte, Zu-	sistered,

[43] The literal translation of Mandel'shtam's 'ко дну идет' (ko dnu idet) would be 'zu Grunde geht'.

[44] Cited in Pinthus, 108.

[45] Lehmann notes the internal organization of *Die Niemandsrose* into clusters or chains of poems (*Kommentar*, 31–4; see also Witte).

[46] Although the German 'zum'—the abbreviated version of the syntagmatic concatenation of the preposition 'zu' (to) and 'dem' (def. art. masc./neutr. dat. sing.)—implies specificity, it may equally signify generality in connection with an unspecified common noun. Thus, 'to stone' would, in this particular context, be an adequate translation of Celan's 'zum Stein'. See Michael Hamburger's translation of this poem in Celan, *Poems*, 152–5.

(6) geschleuderte, du,	hurled, you,
(7) du mir vorzeiten,	you, who ages ago,
(8) du mir im Nichts einer Nacht,	you, who in the Nothing of a night,
(9) du in der [N]acht Be-	you, who in the [n]ight en-
(10) gegnete, du	countered me, you
(11) [D]u—:	[Y]ou—:
(12) Damals, da ich nicht da war,	Then, when I was not there,
(13) damals, da du	then, when you
(14) den Acker abschrittst, allein:	paced* the ploughed acre,[47] alone:
(15) Wer,	Who,
(16) wer wars, jenes	who was it, that
(17) Geschlecht, jenes gemor- dete, jenes	race, that murdered, that
(18) schwarz in den Himmel ste- hende:	which stood black into the sky:
(19) Rute und Hode—?	rod and testicle—?
(20) (Wurzel.	(Root.
(21) Wurzel Abrahams. Wurzel Jesse. Niemandes	Root of Abraham. Root of Jesse. No One's
(22) Wurzel—o	root—o
(23) unser.)	our.)
(24) Ja,	Yes,
(25) wie man zum Stein spricht, wie	as one speaks to (a*) stone, as
(26) du	you
(27) mit meinen Händen dorthin	with my hands therein
(28) und ins Nichts greifst, so	and into the Nothing grasps*, so
(29) ist, was hier ist:	is, what is here:
(30) auch dieser	also this
(31) Fruchtboden klafft . . .	fertile soil gapes* . . .

Since an even tentatively exhaustive discussion of the socio-historical and theological implications of this poem would exceed the thematic boundaries of the present section, I address only some of its contextually relevant aspects.[48] Relying on the unquestioned assumption that the poetic addressee's grammatical

---

[47] 'Acker' necessarily implies that it has been ploughed and cultivated.

[48] For interpretations of this poem, see e.g. Broda, *Dans la main*, 37–9; Hamacher and Menninghaus, 101–12; Felstiner, 175–7; Lehmann, *Kommentar*, 163–9.

gender co-existentially implies a female addressee, critics tend to single out and focus on the German-Jewish poet Nelly Sachs as the poem's interlocutor, whom Celan indeed used to address as 'sister' (Shoham and Witte, 196) and who—as I illustrate below—is an important dialogic partner throughout *Die Nie-mandsrose*.[49] This one-sided concern with Nelly Sachs, however, obfuscates the poem's simultaneous orientation toward Mandel'shtam.[50]

By implicitly positing the facticity of addressing '(a*) stone' (l. 1),[51] Celan not only thematizes his factual reception of and response to Mandel'shtam's first collection of poetry, *Stone*, many poems from which he translated, but, metonymically, names the Russian poet himself as his interlocutor. That Celan's reference to 'stone' is indeed a dialogic appeal to Mandel'shtam and his text is unambiguously corroborated by the prosodically emphasized occurrence in the poem of the indefinite pronoun 'no one' (l. 21) and the 'hollow sound' 'o' (l. 22), which, together with 'stone', form a continuum of material references to Celan's translations of Mandel'shtam's poems i: 6 and ii: 18. (The indefinite pronoun's genitive case underscores its link to poem ii: 18.[52]) Who is Celan's grammatically feminine, 'ensistered', 'hurled', 'encountered' addressee? In view of the poem's continuity with Mandel'shtam's text, the grammatically feminine interlocutor can plausibly be read as Mandel'shtam's 'shell' (rakovina), which is grammatically feminine both in German ('Muschel') and in Russian and which is 'hurled' during the 'night' onto the 'shore' from the 'world abyss' in Mandel'shtam's poem i: 80 ('Shell'). As I have noted earlier, in his translation of poem i: 80 Celan metaphorically identifies Mandel'shtam's similaically functionalized 'shell' with the origi-

---

[49] See Lehmann, *Kommentar*, 34, 163–4; Felstiner, 175–7. See also Sachs's letter to Celan (24 Mar. 1960), in which she writes: 'You have grasped the root of language as Abraham grasped the root of faith' (*Celan/Sachs*, 31).

[50] Even Germinal Civikov, the poem's most recent commentator, does not investigate the poem's dialogic orientation toward Mandel'shtam beyond its reference to the Russian poet's collection of poems *Stone* (cited in Lehmann, *Kommentar* 163–9).

[51] The comparative statement '[a]s one speaks to (a*) stone' suggests—by virtue of its indicative, gnomic present tense (3rd pers. sing. pres. ind. act.)—that speaking to (a*) stone is a fact.

[52] It will be remembered that in ii: 18, l. 1 'no one' (nikto) is also used in the genitive case (nichei) (see above, my discussion of the cycle's title).

nal's speaker, that is, with Mandel'shtam,[53] who reveals himself as the 'shell' encountered by Celan 'there': thematically—'on the shore'; dialogically—in and through Mandel'shtam's very poem and, by extension, in the poetically transmitted Mandel'shtam himself. In the light of Mandel'shtam's poem i: 80 and, a fortiori, in the light of Celan's idiosyncratic translational response to this poem, Mandel'shtam and his poetry emerge as the reiterated—the repetition of the poem's first two lines in ll. 25–6 is preceded by an emphatic 'Yes' (Ja) (l. 24)—addressees of 'Radix, Matrix': the 'you' (l. 2), which Celan encounters 'from the abyss' 'in the [n]ight' materially instantiates Celan's encounter with Mandel'shtam's poem i: 80 and through it with Mandel'shtam himself. If Mandel'shtam's 'shell' is granted as Celan's addressee in 'Radix, Matrix', then 'en-|sistered' (Ver-|schwisterte) may be interpreted as capturing Celan's fraternization with the grammatically feminine 'shell', that is, with 'Bruder Ossip'. The valorization of Mandel'shtam as Celan's interlocutor in 'Radix, Matrix' is further corroborated by the interlocutor's appropriation of Celan's hands (ll. 26–7), a transaction which—as the poem 'Everything is different' (i. 284–6, ll. 12–15) documents—occurs explicitly between Celan and Mandel'shtam and not between Celan and Sachs.

The immediately succeeding poem, 'Black earth', which overtly cites Mandel'shtam's 'black earth' (e.g. poems ii: 12, l. 52, iii: 97 ('Black Earth'), l. 15),[54] unambiguously contextualizes the 'fertile soil' (Fruchtboden) in 'Radix, Matrix' (l. 31), and underscores the latter's orientation toward Mandel'shtam. Given the poetologically central place which 'black earth' occupies in Mandel'shtam's oeuvre—it is time's most fundamental layer, brought to the surface by the plough of poetry[55]—Celan's 'fertile soil' reveals itself as the poetic thematization of memory or 'Andenken', performed in and through the poem

---

[53] It will be remembered that Mandel'shtam's poem i: 80 is a highly self-reflexive, poetological text, in which Mandel'shtam thematizes his existence as a poet (see Ch. 5; Brown, *Mandelstam*, 163).

[54] Celan translated poem ii: 12. Poem iii: 97 was published posthumously in 1962 and was thus also available to Celan (see Struve/Filipoff edn. of Mandel'shtam's works, i. 520).

[55] Mandel'shtam writes: 'Poetry—is a plough, ploughing time in such a way that its most fundamental layers, its black earth, find themselves on the surface' (*MSS* i. 213).

itself.[56] 'Mandorla', in which 'Mandel' (almond) is repeated five times, and 'Snuggling *no one*' (my italics) further testify to Mandel'shtam's presence in *Die Niemandsrose*. These material and thematic references to Mandel'shtam's text, which witness to the cycle's continuity with Celan's Mandel'shtam translations, are complemented by the formal trace of Mandel'shtam's (poetic) gestalt in *Die Niemandsrose*.[57] In the balladesque role poem 'A Rogues' and Swindlers' Ditty' (Eine Gauner- und Ganovenweise) (i. 229–30), the interplay between material, thematic and formal references to Mandel'shtam comes to the fore with particular acuity:

Eine Gauner- und Ganovenweise	A Rogues' and Swindlers' Ditty
Gesungen zu Paris Emprès Pontoise	Sung in Paris Emprès Pontoise
Von Paul Celan	By Paul Celan
Aus Czernowitz bei Sadagora	From Czernowitz Near Sadagora

> *Manchmal nur, in*
> *dunkeln Zeiten,*
> Heinrich Heine, An
> Edom

> *Sometimes only, in*
> *dark times,*
> Heinrich Heine, To
> Edom

(1) Damals, als es noch Galgen gab,	Then, when there still were gallows trees,
(2) da, nicht wahr, gab es	then, isn't it true, there was
(3) ein Oben.	an above.
(4) Wo bleibt mein Bart, Wind, wo,	Where is my beard, wind, where
(5) mein Judenfleck, wo	my Jew spot, where
(6) mein Bart, den Du raufst?	my beard, which you pull*?
(7) Krumm war der Weg, den ich ging,	Crooked was the way that I took,
(8) krumm war er, ja,	crooked was it, yes,

---

[56] See also Lehmann, *Kommentar*, 168. Accordingly, Celan's observation that his interlocutor 'was pacing/paced the ploughed acre' can be interpreted poetologically.

[57] Further instances of material contact between *Die Niemandsrose* and Mandel'shtam's poems include: 'Over wine and lostness' (Bei Wein und Verlorenheit) (*GW* i. 213, l. 13), 'Twelve Years' (Zwölf Jahre) (i. 220, ll. 6–7) and poem ii: 12 ('The Horse Shoe Finder'), ll. 31–3, 38–40; '(With) the Three of Us, the Four of Us' (Selbdritt, Selbviert) (i. 216, ll. 1, 11) and poem i: 208, l. 12. Celan's frequent recourse to such motifs as 'name', 'breath', 'clay', 'earth', 'almond', 'stone', and 'rose' throughout *Die Niemandsrose* equally invokes Mandel'shtam's texts (e.g. poems i: 127, l. 1; i: 202, ll. 2, 6, 10–12; ii: 12, ll. 52, 38–40; ii: 17, l. 17).

(9) denn, ja,	for, yes,
(10) er war gerade.	it was straight.
(11) Heia.	Heia.
(12) Krumm, so wird meine Nase.	Crooked, so becomes my nose.
(13) Nase.	Nose.
(14) . . .	. . .
(15) . . .	. . .
(16) Denn es blühte der Mandel-baum.	For the almond tree bloomed*.
(17) Mandelbaum, Bandelmaum.	Almond tree, talmond aree.
(18) Mandeltraum, Trandel-maum.	Almond dream, dalmond aream.
(19) Und auch der Machandel-baum.	And also the juniper tree.
(20) Chandelbaum.	Chandel tree.
(21) . . .	. . .
(22) . . .	. . .
(23) *Envoi*	*Envoi*
(24) Aber,	But,
(25) aber er bäumt sich, der Baum. Er,	but it is resists*, the tree. It,
(26) auch er	it, too,
(27) steht gegen	is stands* against
(28) *die Pest.*	*the Plague.*

In this poem Celan subtly intertwines 'public' and 'private' history by being attentive to the manifestations of anti-Semitism both from an 'universalist' *and* a 'singularist' perspective: while the Heine-motto and the concluding reference to Camus's *The Plague* create a universal historical framework spanning antiquity and the immediate past,[58] the citation of the Grimm brothers' fairy tale, 'The Juniper Tree' (Vom Machandelboom), invokes the violent death of Celan's own mother.[59] One of the

---

[58] 'Edom' was one of Israel's neighbour states, which participated in the destruction of the temple (587 BCE). In Heine's text, 'Edom' is a *chiffre* for the anti-Semite. The epigraph is taken from Heine's dedicatory poem in *The Rabbi of Bacharach*. Celan's reference to Camus's allegory on National Socialism underscores the historical continuity of anti-Semitism and testifies to the poem's (pan)historical perspective (see also Felman and Laub, 8).

[59] It will be remembered that in this gruesome fairy tale a mother is killed off twice.

poem's interlocutionary points of reference is, not surprisingly, the indirectly named (ll. 16–17) Mandel'shtam: insofar as 'Stamm' (trunk) synecdochically signifies 'Baum' (tree), Mandelbaum can be interpreted as a thematically and rhetorically motivated, displaced reference to the Russian poet.[60] This appeal to Mandel'shtam is further underscored by Celan's initial intention to use Mandel'shtam's words as an epigraph to the poem,[61] and by the fact that it immediately follows Celan's original dedication of five pre-published poems from *Die Niemandsrose* in *Die Neue Rundschau* (1963). The thus established spatial contiguity between the Russian poet's name and Celan's ditty cements the link between 'Mandelbaum' and 'Mandelstamm' (in Celan's spelling). The poem's orientation toward Mandel'shtam, the observation that '[c]rooked, so becomes my nose' (l. 12)—before proceeding to the morphological play with the constituents of 'Mandelbaum' (ll. 17–20), can be interpreted as more than the ironic invocation of a stereotype commonly associated with a presumably homogeneous Semitic and, in particular, Jewish—including Celan's own—physiognomy:[62] it can plausibly be read as thematizing the physiognomy of Mandel'shtam, whose famously 'crooked' profile Celan intended to have reproduced on one of the preliminary pages of the first edition of *Die Niemandsrose.*[63] (Incidentally, the poem's third stanza (ll. 7–10) calls to mind Mandel'shtam's own poetic meditation on the crookedness of his name:

> Это какая улица?
> Улица Мандельштама.
> Что за фамилия чертова!—
> Как ее не вывертывай,

[60] 'Baum' continues the theme of 'Galgen' (gallows) (l. 1), as the English 'gallows tree' clearly illustrates. The first letters of the two nominal constituents of 'Mandelbaum', 'M-' and '-b', lend themselves to a semantically significant paronomastic exchange: 'Bandelmaum' invokes 'Band' (band, ribbon, rope), hence, 'noose', and 'gallows', as well as 'bandeln' (hang, dangle). See also Broda, *Dans la main,* 19–20; Lehmann, *Kommentar,* 134.

[61] Celan was considering poems iii: 27 ('I will tell you with utmost l straightforwardness') and iii: 95 ('Let me go . . . Voronezh'), in particular (see *Die Niemandsrose* (Tübingen edn.), 42–3).

[62] See Lehmann, *Kommentar,* 134; *Der Meridian* (Tübingen edn.), 127–9.

[63] See Lehmann, *Kommentar,* 20. For Mandel'shtam's profile, see e.g. the covers of the Struve/Filipoff edn. of his works. This interpretation implies that lines 12–13 of Celan's role poem are spoken by 'Mandel'shtam'.

> Криво звучит а не прямо.
> What street is this?
> Mandel'shtam Street.
> What a devilish last name!—
> Whichever way you turn it,
> It sounds crooked and not straight.
>
> (iii: 92, ll. 1–5)[64]

If Celan's invocation of Mandel'shtam's physical gestalt is granted, stanzas 3–5 (ll. 7–13) reveal themselves as graphically staging the 'crookedness' of Mandel'shtam's 'nose' (ll. 12–13): the 'crooked' distribution of verses

> Krumm war der Weg, den ich ging,
> krumm war er, ja,
> . . .
> er war gerade.
> Heia.
> Krumm, so wird meine Nase.

formally replicates Celan's thematic emphasis on 'krumm' and creates the impression of the contours of a 'crooked' human nose in the negative (in the photographic sense), as it were.[65]

In addition to corroborating *Die Niemandsrose*'s continuity with Celan's translational encounter with Mandel'shtam, the latter's physical presence in Celan's text acquires ethical significance. Being marked by the singular other's palpable trace, that is, by Mandel'shtam's profile, in its very figure, in its very gestalt, Celan's poem can be interpreted as indicating the

---

[64] I should stress that, most likely, Celan did not know poem iii: 92 while working on *Die Niemandsrose*, since it was published for the first time in 1964, that is, after the publication of *Die Niemandsrose* (1963). As so often, the interpretation of Celan's text depends more on the context of its reception than on the context of its production (Parry, 'Meridian', 41). Reading Celan's and Mandel'shtam's poems in conjunction is all the more justified given both poets' implicit (ironic) reference to Isaiah 40: 3–4: 'Prepare ye the way of the Lord, make straight in the desert a highway for our God. [A]nd the crooked shall be made straight.'

[65] I am well aware of the speculative character of my physiognomic, 'pictorial' interpretation, which in part depends on the reader's imaginative 'good will'. Since it is not by any means essential to the viability of my overall argument regarding the groundedness of *Die Niemandsrose* in Mandel'shtam's text, my argument remains completely intact even if my physiognomic interpretation is dismissed on the grounds of insufficient evidence. I simply cannot resist suggesting this graphic, physiognomic connection, given Celan's explicit thematization of physiognomy and given his intention to place Mandel'shtam's profile at the head of *Die Niemandsrose*.

dynamic of that other trace—the trace of the infinite (in Levinas's ethical sense)—which will have always already meta-leptically marked and informed semethics and which may be glimpsed, according to Levinas, only indirectly, in profile:

> The signifiance of the trace places us within a lateral relationship which cannot be converted into straightforwardness [rectitude] and which responds to an irreversible past . . . If the signifiance of the trace does not transform itself . . . into the straightforwardness [rectitude] which marks . . . the [linguistic] sign it is because the trace signifies beyond Being. The personal order to which [the other's] visage obligates us is . . . of a radical irrectitude [manifesting itself in] profile . . . by way of the trace. (*DEHH* 198)

Celan's thematic oscillation between straightness/rectitude and crookedness/irrectitude provides a propitious semantic foil for the indirect semanticity of his poem's gestalt, in whose trace the poem's verbal material can indeed be seen as holding itself.[66]

INTRODUCING THE THIRD

Celan's dialogue with Mandel'shtam is continuously punctured by the voice of the third[67]—not merely by way of intertextuality, however, which testifies to Celan's 'absorption and transforma-tion' of a presumably more or less depersonalized, more or less readily available cultural heritage, but in the form of concrete utterances issued by identifiable, co-existentially significant—for Celan, that is—singularities; thus, in addition to being constitu-tively intertextual, Celan's poetry is polyphonic in the Bakhtinian sense.[68] It is important to keep in mind that notwithstanding the

---

[66] I should stress that my rapprochement between Celan's suggested indication of Mandel'shtam's profile and Levinas's conceptualization of the trace of the infinite as appearing in profile is poethically motivated and not the upshot of a simplistic valorization of Celan's and Levinas's conceptual or terminological proximity. Insofar as Levinas's depictions of semethics are philosophical, that is, apophantic, Celan's poetic practice can plausibly be interpreted as (non-apophantically) enacting Levinas's stipulations. In those instances in which Celan thematically approximates Levinasian ethics, which—as I have illustrated—is itself thematically indebted to Celan, a poethic approach to his poetry is all the more justified.

[67] As I have pointed out earlier, 'third' does not imply numerical specificity.

[68] Lehmann rightly notes that Kristeva's depersonalized concept of intertextuality is inapplicable to Celan's poetics and poetry, insofar as he valorizes the (speaking and breathing) subject as a centre of answerability (*Kommentar*, 27). It will be remembered that Kristeva, misreading Bakhtin, stipulates the originary intertex-tuality of any text, 'which constitutes itself as a mosaic of citations, [in and through] the absorption and transformation of another text' (Kristeva, 87).

plethora of cultural, literary, and theological connotations and symbolic contexts invoked by such characteristic Celanian lexemes and motifs as 'stone', 'breath', 'star', and 'rose', to name only a few, Celan's texts—*Die Niemandsrose* in particular—self-consciously instantiate their inevitably dialogic constitution in response to concrete interpellations by concrete persons, thereby exemplarily evincing their poethicity and lending themselves to poethic scrutiny. I should stress that the disclosure of the polyphony and multivoicedness of *Die Niemandsrose* does not so much serve the purpose of uncovering sources and influences— which would presumably guarantee a certain coherence of meaning—but the delineation of a singular style (in the metalinguistic sense), that is, of Celan's singular poetic testimony to his unique position in dialogue, as part of the overall depiction of Celan's stylistic visage as it manifests itself in his complex response to Mandel'shtam.[69] I should equally stress that, since—as Levinas and Bakhtin point out—dialogue always already involves the third, that is, since dialogue between two persons always already transpires as a polylogue, 'introducing the third' at this point testifies to my particular approach to Celan's response to Mandel'shtam rather than to its presumably sequential constitution, progressing from dialogue proper to polylogue. Celan's continuous 'reference to the [singular and co-existentially significant] third' (*TI* 313) throughout *Die Niemandsrose*, poetically stages and indicates both the triadic character of semethics and co-existence, which is predicated on the internal dialogization of every word. Focusing on a limited number of instances in *Die Niemandsrose*, I single out the voices of some of Celan's most significant interlocutionary thirds, who accompany his response to Mandel'shtam.

Beginning with the cycle's very title, singular thirds can be heard refracting Celan's response to Mandel'shtam through the din of the title's vast array of cultural, historical, and literary significations. Two voices in particular stand out within the title's polylogue: Rainer Maria Rilke's and Nelly Sachs's. As is well

---

[69] It will be remembered that the metalinguistic concepts of 'style' and 'stylistic visage' are not equivalent. While an utterance's stylistic visage comprises all of its discursive aspects, insofar as they make it singular and meaningful, an utterance's style consists in its singular orchestration of voices, sense positions, and languages 'into the higher unity of the work'.

known, both poets—Rilke especially—had a significant impact on Celan's development and self-definition as a poet.[70] Celan was particularly fascinated by Rilke's insistence on the inseverability of poetry and existence[71]—this became one of the cornerstones of Celan's poetics—by his 'sense of death as the richly present other side of life' (Felstiner, 72), and—given Celan's own co-existential orientation toward eastern Europe from within the 'homeland' of the German language (Pajevic, 147–54)—by Rilke's 'passionate love for Russia' (Mason, 30).[72] Furthermore, Rilke had preceded Celan as an exile in Paris and thus might have been perceived by Celan as an alter ego of sorts. In the German-Jewish poet Nelly Sachs, who, like Celan, survived the Holocaust, whose poetry he had been aware of since 1953, and whom he subsequently referred to as 'sister'—being himself called 'brother' by Sachs— Celan found a congenial living interlocutor and poetic witness to the historical trauma which both—along with millions of others—had undergone during the Third Reich.[73] Sachs's voice manifests itself throughout *Die Niemandsrose*.[74]

Celan's 'Niemandsrose' orchestrates contextually pertinent utterances by both Rilke and Sachs. In particular, Rilke's epitaph—'Rose, oh pure contradiction, desire, | No one's sleep to be under so many | Lids' (Rose, oh reiner Widerspruch, Lust, | Niemandes Schlaf zu sein unter soviel | Lidern)[75]—the

[70] See e.g. Chalfen 68–9, 99, 104; Felstiner 72, 199.

[71] See esp. the following lines by Rilke: 'If only once you had | seen how fate enters the verses (wie Schicksal in die Verse eingeht)' ('Requiem für Graf von Kalckreuth', cited in Rilke, i. 419); 'Poetry is existence' (Gesang ist Dasein) (third 'Sonnet to Orpheus', l. 7, cited in i. 488).

[72] Rilke travelled to Russia twice, in 1899 (April–June) and in 1900 (May–August), and thought of himself as a 'deeply Slavic person' (cited in Mason, 30). Rilke's friendship with the poet Marina Cvetaeva, who was to become one of Celan's own poetic points of reference, might also have contributed to the significance of Rilke for Celan (see: Brodsky, 'On Daring to be a Poet'; Ivanovic, 288–305; Lehmann, 'Dichten').

[73] See *Celan/Sachs*; Felstiner, 158–63. As early as 1959 Hans Magnus Enzensberger singled out Nelly Sachs (followed by Celan and Erich Fried) as the 'greatest poet writing today in the German language' ('Die Steine', 771), viewing her as the exemplary living refutation of Adorno's dictum that it is 'barbaric to write poetry after Auschwitz' (*Prismen*, 26). Adorno subsequently modified his dictum in response to Enzensberger (*Noten*, 243). The majority of Sachs's work is devoted to the commemoration of the Holocaust and its victims.

[74] See e.g. the poem 'Zurich, At the Stork' (Zürich, Zum Storchen) (*GW* i. 214–15), which is 'Für Nelly Sachs'. See also Lehmann, *Kommentar*, 34, 65–72; Shoham and Witte, 195–210.

[75] See Winkler; Lehmann, *Kommentar*, 39–42.

fifth sonnet to Orpheus—'Erect no memorial stone. Let the rose I bloom every year for his sake' (Errichtet keinen Denkstein. Laßt die Rose I nur jedes Jahr zu seinen Gunsten blühn) (ll. 1–2; cited in *Werke*, i. 489), and lines from the cycle 'Les Roses' (*Werke*, ii. 327–38)—especially, 'every petal a shroud' (chaque pétale un linceul) (xiii, l. 6)—fuse with Sachs's poem 'The Spinoza Scholar' (Der Spinozaforscher) (Sachs, 36),[76] in which the 'encounter' (Begegnung) with 'the past' (das Vergangene) (l. 8) is associated with a 'farewell rose' (Abschiedsrose) (l. 2). Significantly, all of these texts relate the rose to death and memory: echoing Rilke's epitaph, the 'Sonnets to Orpheus' are subtitled 'tombstone' (Grab-Mal); 'Les Roses' presents the rose as the apparel of death, and, finally, Sachs's poem is part of the subcycle 'Epitaphs Written in the Air' (Grabschriften in die Luft geschrieben) from her collection of poems, *In the Dwellings of Death* (*In den Wohnungen des Todes*) (1947).[77]

The intertextuality of *Die Niemandsrose* undergoes an emphatic, co-existentially motivated singularization through Celan's unique take on the cultural and discursive heritage available to him. In poetically foregrounding personal voices and sense positions in a presumably depersonalized 'intertextual space' (Kristeva, 196), that is, in highlighting the polyphonic, intersubjective ground of intertextuality, Celan not only testifies to his principal co-existential responsiveness to and answerability to and for Mandel'shtam and others, but makes this responsiveness and answerability the very principle of, to invoke Bakhtin's terms, 'concrete poetic construction'. While certainly engaging the infinite significations of 'Niemandsrose'—ranging from 'people of Israel' to 'rose de personne' (see above)—Celan develops his very personal style in clearly staking out his singular place in co-existential dialogue, in juxtaposing and orchestrating singular voices in a singular mode.

This initial involvement of the third in Celan's response to Mandel'shtam continues throughout *Die Niemandsrose*. Suffice it to point to two further significant instances. In the cycle's introductory poem, 'There was earth in them', which—as I have illustrated above—unmistakably conjoins *Die Niemandsrose* with Celan's Mandel'shtam translations and *The Stone*,

[76] Sachs uses 'rose' in various contexts and constellations throughout her oeuvre.
[77] Cited in Sachs, 5–68.

Mandel′shtam's first collection of poetry, Mandel′shtam's voice is clearly punctured by Nelly Sachs's poetic commemoration of the dead. Thus, Celan's lines

(13) Ich grabe, du gräbst, und es
gräbt auch der Wurm,

(14) und das Singende dort sagt:
Sie graben.

(15) O einer, o keiner, o nie-
mand, o du:

(16) Wohin ging's, da's nir-
gendhing ging?

(17) O du gräbst und ich grab,
und ich grab mich dir zu,

(18) und am Ende erwacht uns
der Ring.

I dig*, you dig*, and the worm,
too, digs*,

and the singing there says*: they
dig*.

O one, o nobody, o no one, o
you:

Where did it go* to, when it
went* nowhere?

O you dig* and I dig*, and I
dig* myself to you,

and on the finger the ring awa-
kens to us.

displace and recontextualize the following verses from Sachs's 'The Hour of Endor' (Die Stunde zu Endor)[78] (214–23), which commemorates the victims of the Holocaust by staging 'encounters with the dead' (Begegnungen mit den Toten) (217): 'Touched/churned is the worm, | it digs* the end without sound - ‖ O, o music from disintegrating skeletons, | Fingers on the . . . gadgets of dying' (Angerührt ist der Wurm, | der gräbt lautlos das Ende - ‖ O, o Musik aus zerfallenen Gerippen, | Finger an den . . . Geräten des Sterbens) (220).[79] That Celan indeed absorbs and transforms Sachs's text is further evidenced by such subsequent *Niemandsrose* poems as 'Zürich, At the Stork' (*GW* i. 214–15) and '(With) the Three of Us, (with) the Four of Us' (Selbdritt, Selbviert) (i. 216), both of which were composed immediately after Celan's momentous encounter with Sachs in Zürich—at the hotel 'Zum Storchen'—in May 1960.[80] Thus, in Celan's 'You | and But-You (Du | und Aber-Du) ('Zürich, Zum Storchen', ll. 2–3) resounds Sachs's 'But you again, | but you' (Aber du, | aber du) (225) from 'Untergänge'[81] (224–36), which

---

[78] See 1 Samuel 28: 7. 'Die Stunde zu Endor' is a section in Sachs's collection of poems, *And no one knows how to go on* (Und niemand weiß weiter) (1957) (cited in Sachs, 155–249).

[79] In his commentary on 'There was earth in them', Hendrik Birus does not deal with Sachs's subtext (in Lehmann, *Kommentar*, 51–6).

[80] See Felstiner, 156–69; Lehmann, *Kommentar*, 65–73.

[81] A section from *Und niemand weiß weiter*. 'Untergänge' is the plural of 'Untergang' (decline, downfall, demise, peril, setting, sinking). In his commentary

immediately follows 'Die Stunde zu Endor'; concomitantly, 'Selbdritt, Selbviert' is punctured by 'Untergänge' (l. 8) and displaces Sachs's 'Blut-Krause-Minze'[82] (218): 'Ruffled mint, mint, ruffled' (Krauseminze, Minze, krause) (*GW* i. 216, ll. 1, 11).

Finally, in the second poem of *Die Niemandsrose*, 'The word of going-to-the-depth' (Das Wort vom Zur-Tiefe-Gehn) (i. 212), Celan's response to Mandel'shtam is permeated from within by the voice of Georg Heym (1887–1912), a German expressionist poet, and via Heym, by an entire 'symphony' of poetic voices: the 'word of going-to-the-depth' is a literal reference to Heym's poem 'Your lashes, the long ones' (Deine Wimpern, die langen), which Kurt Pinthus included in his seminal anthology *Twilight of Humanity: A Symphony of Recent Poetry* (Pinthus, 108–9),[83] and in whose first stanza an unidentified speaker desires to dive into the 'dark waters' (dunkele Wasser) of the beloved's eyes (l. 2): 'Let me dive therein,|Let me go* to the depth' (Laß mich tauchen darein,|Laß mich zur Tiefe gehn) (ll. 3–4). As commentators have noted, 'Das Wort vom Zur-Tiefe-Gehn' is an autobiographical testimony to Celan's attempts to teach his wife German by way of poetry.[84] The poem's second verse, 'which we have read' (das wir gelesen haben), corroborates the poem's autobiographically testimonial character. Notwithstanding the poem's autobiographical roots, its first line equally recalls Celan's translation of Mandel'shtam's 'revolution poem' i: 193, 'Let us glorify, brothers, the twilight of freedom' (Прославим, братья, сумерки свободы): Celan renders 'Who has a heart must hear, time,|How your ship goes* to the bottom (of the sea) (В ком сердце есть, тот должен слышать, время,|Как твой корабль ко дну идет) (ll. 11–12) as 'Who, time, has a heart, hears with it, under-stands:|he hears your ship, time, which goes* to the depth'

---

on 'Zürich, Zum Storchen', Thomas Sparr (in Lehmann, *Kommentar*, 66) does not mention the proximity between Celan's 'Du|Aber-Du' and Sachs's 'Aber du,|aber du'.

[82] Lit. 'blood-ruffled-mint'. 'Krauseminze' is the general name for a variety of mint plants.

[83] Pinthus edited and published *Menschheitsdämmerung: Symphonie jüngster Dichtung* in 1919. Celan owned a copy of this anthology.

[84] See Lehmann, *Kommentar*, 57. The poem's provisional title was 'The German Lesson' (La leçon d'allemand) (*Die Niemandsrose* (Tübingen edn.), 11).

(Wer, Zeit, ein Herz hat, hört damit, versteht: | er hört dein Schiff, Zeit, das zur Tiefe geht) (*GW* v. 103). In the light of *Die Niemandsrose*'s overall status as a continued performance and manifestation of Celan's response to Mandel'shtam, Heym's vocal presence in Celan's text yet again underscores the impossibility of responding to the other without, at the same time, responding and, indeed, having always already responded to a third. This constitutive 'reference of every dialogue to the third' (*TI* 313) comes to the fore most visibly in Celan's translation of Mandel'shtam's poem i: 193: by using Heym's words to translate Mandel'shtam's text,[85] Celan not only exemplarily stages the originary heterological make-up of any utterance, but clearly marks his unique personal style, his singular perspective on and position within the heterogeneity and multiplicity of dialogic exchanges, his singular twist on co-existential dialogue.

How and in what sense exactly, one might ask, does Celan's stylistic unicity manifest itself? How and in what sense does Celan impose a singular twist on co-existential dialogue? How do I know in reading Celan's poetry that, to use Levinas's terms, 'someone passes—pure and simple' (*DEHH* 200), that a unique person, with his unique 'orientation and fate' (*GW* iii. 188) traces the text? From a merely 'structural'—in the common sense of the term—point of view, Celan's singular concatenation of voices, styles (in the linguistic and rhetorical senses), and languages alone would suffice to warrant the observation of stylistic (in the metalinguistic sense) unicity.[86] However, insofar as 'style' is a 'social phenomenon' (DLDA 109), a merely 'structural' approach—although a heuristically necessary first step—fails to capture the co-existential significance of style as always already imbued with sense and valuation, with 'orientation and fate'. Keeping in mind Bakhtin's crucial philosophical distinction

---

[85] Celan's translation of Mandel'shtam's 'goes* to the bottom (of the sea)' as 'zur Tiefe geht' is an interesting mixture of literalism and citation. Celan's 'zur Tiefe geht' almost literally renders the Russian original; however, 'Tiefe' (depth) does not quite correspond to the original's 'bottom' and thus corroborates the version's interpretation as a slightly altered citation of Heym's poem, which contains the infinitival 'zur Tiefe gehen' (with a syncopated 'gehn').

[86] In addition to the poems cited above, see e.g. the following *Niemandsrose* poems: 'Tübingen, January' (*GW* i. 226), in which Celan literally quotes Hölderlin; 'Benedicta' (i. 249) and 'Anabasis' (i. 256), in which Celan uses Yiddish, Latin, and Greek; 'In One' (In Eins) (i. 270), in which Celan cites Büchner and Mandel'shtam, and juxtaposes Hebrew, French, and Spanish.

between linguistic or lexical 'meaning' and co-existential or dialogic 'sense', style—which emerges in and through a person's responsive and axiological stance toward and singular appropriation of the surrounding heterogeneity of singular voices and languages—reveals itself as inherently bound up with sense. Thus, an utterance's style can only be somewhat comprehensively grasped by way of its sense, its unique axiological orientation within dialogue. What kind of sense, what kind of axiological orientation can be witnessed in Celan's poems, whose intertextual and heteroglot constitution must be metalinguistically attributed to a valuating, co-existing, responding consciousness? In other words, what does it mean that Celan orchestrates his continuous response to Mandel'shtam in engaging such voices as Rilke's, Sachs's, and Heym's, to name only a few?

Rilke's and Sachs's voices co-constitute and underscore *Die Niemandsrose*'s significance as an epitaph and farewell missive to Mandel'shtam, saturating it with singular co-existential weight and value. Through Celan's 'Andenken', through his polyphonic testimony, Mandel'shtam—who died in a transit camp in Siberia and whose burial site remains unknown—receives a proper burial, as it were, is literally enveloped in the shroud made from the poems/petals of *Die Niemandsrose*. Celan co-existentially personalizes both Rilke's poetic injunction regarding the mythical Orpheus and Sachs's universal farewell to the victims of the Holocaust (see above) by planting a 'poetic rose', as it were, for the sake of, or—as Celan puts it—to 'the remembrance of' Mandel'shtam. *Die Niemandsrose*: Mandel'shtam's rose, insofar as Mandel'shtam himself was the 'no one', the providential interlocutor, of so many poets. *Die Niemandsrose*: a 'farewell rose'—joining the singular (Mandel'shtam) and the universal (the people of Israel, the Jews perished in the Holocaust), thereby instantiating the paradoxical status of poetry as simultaneously totalizing qua language *and* ethical qua 'unheard of modality of *otherwise than being*'. Sachs's voice in particular allows Celan to respond to and author Mandel'shtam from within his co-existential situation as a Holocaust survivor: Mandel'shtam's/Celan's 'hollow sound',[87] which materially informs Celan's 'There was earth in them'

---

[87] It will be remembered that Celan translates Mandel'shtam's '(A*) sound,

bonds with Sachs's 'round emptiness in the air' (runde Leere in der Luft) ('Die Stunde zu Endor', l. 1)—a metonymic reference to millions of burnt bodies. With the help of Sachs's voice, Celan authors Mandel'shtam and his text from within his unique post-Holocaustian co-existential situation, retroactively injecting both with his unique, emotionally and axiologically imbued sense position. By engaging Heym in responding to Mandel'shtam—both in his translation of poem i: 193 and in *Die Niemandsrose*—Celan manages, furthermore, to (re)create and author Mandel'shtam and his text within the emotional and axiological parameters of his private, conjugal co-existence, thereby underscoring Mandel'shtam's intimately personal significance for himself. In addition to this autobiographical (re)contextualization of Mandel'shtam, Heym's voice in Celan's response points to Celan's fundamentally ethical concerns. This becomes clear if the inclusion of Heym's poem 'Your lashes, the long ones' in Pinthus's anthology *Twilight of Humanity*, which it synecdochically invokes in its entirety, is taken into account. (That Celan indeed functionalizes Heym's poem synecdochically is borne out by the fact that he refers to it in his translation of that poem by Mandel'shtam in which the lexeme 'twilight' plays a thematically central role.)[88] More specifically, it is Pinthus's famous preface to the anthology which deserves particular attention at this point. In his preface, Pinthus adumbrates the anthologized poets' shared co-existential plight:

[It was their] fate . . . to live with the terrible awareness of decline among an ignorant and hopeless humanity [during] the wildest and most desolate period of world history [pp. xvi, vi]. All poems gathered in this book spring from the lament over humanity, the yearning for humanity . . . These poets experienced . . . how the human being sank into twilight . . . into the night of decline . . . in order to emerge into the clearing twilight of a new day. In this book the human being consciously turns away from the imposed twilight of a devouring past and present

---

careful and deaf (Звук осторожный и глухой] (i: 6, l. 1) as 'The hollow sound, careful . . .' (Der hohle Laut, behutsam . . .) (*GW*, v. 49).

[88] In poem i: 193 Mandel'shtam gives poetic expression to his ambivalent stance regarding the socio-political changes in Russia in 1917–18 (and in pre- and post-war Europe in general). Mandel'shtam's 'twilight [sumerki] of freedom' is ambiguous, since it can mean both 'dusk' and 'dawn' of freedom. The rising sun in lines 5–6 suggests morning twilight, that is, 'dawn'. However, the sun rises, as Mandel'shtam notes, into 'deaf [glukhie] years' (l. 5), into an age, in which freedom is 'muted'.

toward the saving twilight of a [poetically] self-created future . . . The human being can only be saved by the human being . . . And since salvation cannot come from outside—from there war and destruction had been anticipated long before the world war—but only from the human being's inner forces, the great turn toward the ethical occurred. (pp. vi–xii).

Celan must have perceived these words as an apt—if not all-too lenient—depiction of his own co-existential situation: similarly to the poets anthologized by Pinthus, Celan had lived through the 'most desolate period of . . . history'—whose atrocities Pinthus could have hardly imagined—and was constantly haunted by a 'devouring past and present'; similarly to Pinthus, who presumably speaks for the anthologized poets, Celan believed—while not wholeheartedly sharing Pinthus's unsubdued optimism—that 'salvation' can only be achieved through interhuman means, that is, through the ethical—beginning 'here and now, with the singular human being' (*GW* iii. 179).[89] By orchestrating his response to Mandel'shtam synecdochically alongside Pinthus's poetic symphony, Celan subtly stresses the ethicity of poetic dialogue and, more importantly, the co-existential necessity of the poetic enactment of ethics.

POETHIC THEMES

As Levinas's central Celan-motto and commentary unmistakably suggest, Celan's themes in particular contribute to the poethic exemplarity of his texts.[90] After having elaborated the poethicity of Celan's poetics, I now turn to the poethically significant themes in Celan's poetry itself. In this section, I discuss three of Celan's poethically prominent themes— 'weight', 'substitution', and 'contradiction'—by looking at a limited number of textual instances.

[89] An in-depth discussion of Celan's religious beliefs and 'personal theology' exceeds the boundaries of my inquiry. Suffice it to note that such poems as 'Tenebrae' (*GW* i. 163), 'Zürich, Zum Storchen' (i. 214–15), and 'Psalm' (i. 225) suggest Celan's fundamental scepticism with regard to and, in fact, implicit disavowal of the reliance on 'god' for 'salvation'. Thus, Klaus Manger speaks of Celan's 'negation of salvation history' (in Lehmann, *Kommentar*, 114; see also Janz, 129–38; Wienold; Felstiner, 167–9).

[90] See Ch. 1, 'Ethics and Poetry'; *AQE* 156; *NP* 49–56. By 'theme' I mean recurrent motifs and topoi in Celan's texts.

'weight'

Such *Niemandsrose* poems as 'So many galaxies' (Soviel Gestirne) (*GW* i. 217), 'It is no more' (Es ist nicht mehr) (i. 238), 'What occurred?' (Was geschah?) (i. 269), and 'In the air' (In der Luft) (i. 290–1), clearly demonstrate that the topos of weight occupies a central place throughout *Die Niemandsrose*. In contrast to its emphatically obituary and emotional function in the overall context of remembering and mourning the victims of the Holocaust in Celan's earlier poetry,[91] 'weight' acquires poethic significance in the avowedly dialogic context of *Die Niemandsrose*. This comes to the fore most overtly in the poem 'Was geschah?':

(1) Was geschah? Der Stein trat aus dem Berge.	What occurred? The stone stepped forth from the mountain.
(2) Wer erwachte? Du und ich.	Who awakened? You and I.
(3) Sprache, Sprache. Mit-Stern. Neben-Erde.	Language, language. Co-star/planet. Parallel-earth.
(4) Ärmer. Offen. Heimatlich.	Poorer. Open. Homelandly.
(5) Wohin gings? Gen Unver-klungen.	Where did we go? Toward Unverklungen.[92]
(6) Mit dem Stein gings, mit uns zwein.	With the stone, with the two of us.
(7) Herz und Herz. Zu schwer befunden.	Heart and Heart. Found too heavy.
(8) Schwerer werden. Leichter sein.	Becoming heavier. Being lighter.[93]

In this poem, Celan responds to Mandel'shtam's poetics and poetry, invoking both Mandel'shtam's poetological conception of the poetic word as 'stone'—as the material for constructing the acmeist poetic edifice—and its poetic realization in *Stone*.[94]

---

[91] See esp. the poems 'The hand full of hours' (Die Hand voller Stunden) and 'The Secret of (the) Ferns' (Das Geheimnis der Farne) in *Mohn und Gedächtnis* (*GW* i. 17, 21).

[92] 'Unverklungen' does not have an operable English equivalent. The noun 'Unverklungen' is a neologism. It consists of the negative prefix 'un-' and the past participle 'verklungen', which derives from the infinitive 'verklingen' (subside, peter out (in reference to sound)). Thus, 'Unverklungen' signifies 'unsubsided resounding' or 'continuous resounding'.

[93] My translation is partially based on Michael Hamburger's translation of the same poem (Celan, *Poems* 169).

[94] In his programmatic essay 'The Morning of Acmeism' Mandel'shtam observes

Following Mandel'shtam, Celan in turn picks up Tiutchev's/
Mandel'shtam's stone and uses it for the edifice of his own text.
The dialogic 'challenge' (vyzov) issuing forth through Tiutchev's
stone and resounding—in amplified form—in Mandel'shtam's
poetry, leads, among other things, to the emergence of 'You and
I' in Celan's poem.[95] These two are then reported to have
travelled toward 'Unverklungen', that is, in the direction of
continuous dialogue, having been synecdochically—by way of
'Heart and heart'—assessed as 'too heavy'.[96] Celan's depiction
of 'You and I' in terms of weight directly relates to
Mandel'shtam's constant poetological emphasis on 'gravity'
(tiazhest') (*MSS* i. 178), to his attribution of a 'specific weight'
(udel'nyi ves) to the poet (i. 179), and, more specifically, to his
conceptualization of the relation between (the poetic) self and
(the poetic) other in terms of 'lightness' and 'heaviness'. In the
programmatic essay 'On the Interlocutor', Mandel'shtam con-
demns poetry in which the ' "I" . . . unjustly outweigh[s] . . . the
"non-I", which reveal[s] itself as too light',[97] advocating a 'just'
balance between the respective weight/gravity of self and other.
In view of Mandel'shtam's attention to the topos of weight/
gravity, the last two verses of Celan's poem can be interpreted as

that 'Tiutchev's stone, which "came to rest in the valley after rolling down from the
mountain, whether having torn itself from the top by its own force or having been
thrown down by a thinking hand"—is the word. The voice of matter resounds in this
unexpected fall . . . To this challenge one can only respond with architecture.
Awestruck, the acmeists lift Tiutchev's stone and lay it down as the foundation for
their edifice' (*MSS* i. 178). Celan's 'Der Stein trat aus dem Berge' is a liberal
adaptation of Tiutchev's line quoted by Mandel'shtam. Ivanovic's claim that Celan
had presumably read 'The Morning of Acmeism' for the first time in the Struve-
Filippov edition of Mandel'shtam's works only after the publication of *Die
Niemandsrose* in 1963 (Ivanovic, 259) is implausible given the essay's public
availability since 1919: it was originally published in *Sirena*, 4–5 (30 Jan. 1919)
and republished in *Literaturnye manifesty: Ot simvolizma k Oktiabriu* (Moscow,
1929). The rapprochement between 'stone' and language is also characteristic of
Nelly Sachs's poetry (see esp. Sachs, 58–9), which, as I have noted, significantly
informs *Die Niemandsrose*. Most recently, Marina Dmitrieva-Einhorn has sug-
gested—without substantiating her claim—that 'Was geschah?' also addresses itself
to Celan's childhood friend Erich Einhorn (Dmitrieva-Einhorn, 9).

[95] I dispense with an exhaustive thematic analysis of this poem, focusing on its
contextually most relevant aspects only. The awakening of 'You and I' is accompan-
ied by the awakening of 'language', characterized as a planet—as 'Parallel-earth',
which displaces the 'real' earth as the interlocutors' home(land).

[96] Throughout his poetry, Celan uses the device of synecdoche in reference to
persons and bodies.

[97] Struve/Filipoff edn. of Mandel'shtam's works, ii. 236–7.

enacting precisely the opposite of what Mandel'shtam condemns: rather than being 'too light', Celan's interlocutors are assessed as 'too heavy'; it is precisely in *becoming* 'heavier' that both can be 'lighter'.

But—in what sense can 'Heart and heart', that is, 'You and I', be 'lighter' in growing 'heavier'? Insofar as Mandel'shtam's poetological valorization of weight/gravity dialogically complements Bakhtin's emphasis on co-existential 'axiological weight' (tsennostnyi ves) and 'axiological gravity' (tsennostnaia tiazhest') (*R* 179, 185, 240–1, 246–7, 251) and Levinas's stipulation of 'the pre-ontological weight/gravity of language' (le poids pré-ontologique du langage) (*AQE* 74), Celan's use of the topos of weight in response to Mandel'shtam calls for an emphatically poethic reading. From within the poethic attitude, the coupling of 'Becoming heavier' with 'Being lighter' can be read as implying the dependence of an 'easier' life (in the common sense of the term), as it were, on the 'heaviness' or weight of co-existence and semethics.[98] Celan subtly displaces—without disavowing its fundamental purport—Buber's observation that the encounter with the other does not make 'one's life easier in any way' (einem das Leben irgend erleichterte) (*DP* 111), but, on the contrary, significantly 'heavier . . . heavy with sense' (schwerer . . . sinnschwer) (ibid.). Together, 'You and I' indeed become heavier—by assuming the burden of answerability to and for each other, the burden of co-existential authoring—than they would be in isolation. However, it is only thanks to this burden—thanks to the other's (infinite) excess of answerability and aesthetic task with regard to me and vice versa—that my life and the other's life, my co-existence and the other's co-existence are also lighter, easier, as it were. By thus thematizing weight/gravity, Celan poetically stages the dynamic of co-existential, axiological weight/gravity *and* indicates the 'pre-ontological weight/gravity of language', that is, semethics.

'substitution'

It will be remembered that Levinas singles out Celan's poetry as an outstanding interruption of philosophical ethics precisely

---

[98] 'Leichter' can also mean 'easier'.

because Celan exemplarily addresses the problem of ethical substitution in the verse: 'I am you, when I am I' (Ich bin du, wenn ich ich bin) (*GW* i. 33), from the poem 'In Praise of Remoteness' (l. 10). The question of substitution—poignantly thematized in this early poem—undergoes an intensified treatment in *Die Niemandsrose*,[99] culminating in Celan's 'physical' substitution for Mandel'shtam in the poem 'Everything is different' (Es ist alles anders) (*GW* i. 284–5):

(12) der Name Ossip kommt auf dich zu, . . .	the name Ossip approaches* you, . . .
(14) du löst ihm den Arm von der Schulter, den rechten, den linken,	you remove his arm from his shoulder, the right one, the left one,
(15) du heftest die deinen an ihre Stelle, mit Händen, mit Fingern . . .,	you attach your own arms in their stead, with hands, with fingers . . .,
(16)—was abriß, wächst wieder zusammen—	—what tore away, grows* together again—

In the present context, this synecdochically performed substitution on Celan's part can be read as staging and indicating both co-existential and semethical substitution. It is important to note that Celan's emphasis on Mandel'shtam's name as the mode of the latter's poetic presence is based on the realization that the Russian poet can indeed only present himself to the 'reader in posterity'—in this instance to Celan—textually, that is, not 'in person': by opting for the approaching 'name Ossip', Celan engages in a phenomenologically cogent depiction of the poetic 'encounter with a dead person' through his or her textual gestalt—of which the person's name is a constitutive part; by way of his name, Mandel'shtam acquires physical presence in and through Celan's text.

'contradiction'

Critics have noted Celan's penchant for semantic and thematic contradictions and paradoxes.[100] Paradigmatically articulated in the line, 'But do not separate the No from the Yes' (Doch scheide

[99] See e.g. the poems 'Radix, Matrix' (*GW* i. 239–40) and 'The Syllable Pain' (Die Silbe Schmerz) (i. 280–1).

[100] See above, esp. my discussion of the pronoun 'niemand'; see also Lehmann, *Kommentar*, 39, 374.

das Nein nicht vom Ja) (*GW* i. 135, l. 5), this penchant blatantly manifests itself in the title *Die Niemandsrose* and reveals itself as a constitutive principle throughout the cycle. These are some of the most significant instances: 'O one, o nobody, o no one, o you' (O einer, o keiner, o niemand, o du) (i. 211), 'No one kneads* us from earth and clay' (Niemand knetet uns . . . aus Erde und Lehm) (i. 225), 'Crooked was the way . . . | crooked was it, yes, | for, yes, | it was straight' (Krumm war der Weg . . . | krumm war er, ja, | denn, ja, | er war gerade) (i. 229), 'Lost was not-lost' (Verloren war Unverloren) (i. 261), 'Becoming heavier. Being lighter' (Schwerer werden. Leichter sein) (i. 269).

In the light of his overall endeavour to deconstruct the historically compromised German idiom (see below), Celan's continuous thematic subversion of 'logically plausible' meaning, which must presumably comply with Aristotle's law of non-contradiction, can be interpreted as a programmatic repudiation of apophansis—whose devastating exacerbation Celan had personally experienced in the National Socialist rationalization and practical execution of the Final Solution.[101] Celan's programmatic dislocation of the law of non-contradiction through poetry vindicates Levinas's ethical valorization of poetry as non-apophantic discourse and exemplarily indicates semethics, which, as Levinas points out, transpires 'prior to the negative or affirmative proposition [and] in which neither the "no" nor the "yes" is the first word' (*TI* 32).

DECONSTRUCTING LANGUAGE

Fated to write in the 'language of the murderers', that is, in the historically compromised German idiom,[102] Celan engages—particularly in his middle and late oeuvre—in the programmatic deconstruction of his mother tongue, with the presumably cath-

[101] Celan's disavowal of apophansis comes to the fore most poignantly in the *Niemandsrose* poem 'Tübingen, January' (*GW* i. 226), in which Celan aligns himself with late Hölderlin's 'mad' as opposed to his early 'sane', that is, 'rational' discourse (see esp. Gellhaus, 'Erinnerung', 13).

[102] See Buck, 14. My psychologistic imputation is based on Celan's strict distinction between his mother tongue, that is, German, in which he wrote, and the other languages which he was exposed to in the course of his life, such as Hebrew, French, Romanian, and Russian (Chalfen, 39–41). Celan's linguistic distinction is informed by his fundamental belief that a poet can only write truthfully in one language—presumably, in his mother tongue: 'I do not believe in bilingualism in poetry . . . Poetry—that is the fatedly unique of language' (*GW* iii. 175).

artic objective of facilitating its recovery from the infection of National Socialism.[103] Celan's deconstructive 'intention toward language' results in the creation of an idiosyncratic, displaced idiom, which disrupts the 'totality' of German as an accepted, coherent, and normative linguistic system, thereby exemplarily staging the ethical function of poetry as an 'unheard of modality of *otherwise than being*' (and, ironically, vindicating Adorno's dictum that 'it is barbaric to write a poem after Auschwitz' (*Prismen*, 26)):[104] in deconstructing his mother tongue Celan enacts the socio-politically performative and transformative power of poetry as the disruptive potential haunting any—linguistic, conceptual, or socio-political—system.[105] In none of Celan's works does the transformative potential of poetry come to the fore as palpably as in *Die Niemandsrose*—Celan's most intertextual and heteroglot collection.

I should like to conclude my inquiry by looking at two of Celan's most prominent deconstructive devices: the orchestration and juxtaposition of different national languages and the decomposition of the verbal material itself.[106] In addition to being constitutively polyphonic, *Die Niemandsrose* is constitutively heteroglot: the juxtaposition of different languages, which breaks up the presumed integrity (or homogeneity) of German as a delimited language system, reveals itself as one of the cycle's

---

[103] See esp. Celan's *Sprachgitter* (*Speech Grille*) (1959), *Die Niemandsrose* (1963), *Atemwende* (*Breath Turn*) (1967), and *Fadensonnen* (*Thread Suns*) (1968), as well as several posthumously published collections of poetry. I use 'deconstruction' in Derrida's methodological sense, that is, as signifying the performance of a fundamental interrogation and, consequently, critique (*Marges*, 13–15, 392). I should stress that Derrida's methodological concept of deconstruction—in line with its Heideggerian precursor (*SuZ* 22)—involves a positive component, as the prefix '-con-' indicates.

[104] The language of Celan's poetry *is* indeed barbaric—in the Greek sense of the term—with regard to 'standard' German. (See Liddell-Scott: 'βαρβαρίζω . . . speak like a barbarian . . . violate the laws of speech . . . βαρβαρισμός . . . use of a foreign tongue or of one's own tongue amiss' (306).)

[105] See Attridge, 'Singularities', 114. In contrast to Paul de Man's concept of rhetorical 'blindness' (141), however, poetry is not always already co-opted by, always already incorporated into the system which it disrupts. Celan thematizes the deconstructive force of his poetry in the poetologically programmatic poem 'Wordpilingup' (Wortaufschüttung) (*GW* ii. 29).

[106] Lehmann uses the term 'Dekompositionsverfahren' (devices of decomposition) in reference to *Die Niemandsrose* (*Kommentar*, 29). Other deconstructive strategies employed by Celan in *Die Niemandsrose* include: the disruption of the German syntax by way of frequent hyperbata and aposiopeses; the subversion of semantic coherence by way of oxymoronic structures (see above).

constructive principles. Aside from selecting non-German titles
for individual poems—'Radix, Matrix' (root, placenta, matrix
(Lat.)) (*GW* i. 239), 'Mandorla' (almond (Ital.)) (i. 244), 'Ben-
edicta' (the blessed (Lat.)) (i. 249), 'À la pointe acérée'
(i. 251),[107] 'Anabasis' (rise, mounting (Gr.)) (i. 256), 'Hawda-
lah'[108] (i. 259), 'Le menhir' (the Menhir (Fr.)) (i. 260), 'Les
globes' (the spheres, globes, eyeballs (Fr.)) (i. 274), 'Huhedi-
blu'[109] (i. 275), 'La contrescarpe' (moat wall (Fr.)) (i. 282)[110]—
Celan continuously punctures the poems' textual fabric proper
with foreign idioms. These are some of the significant instances:

Die Schleuse (The Sluice), ll. 12–20 (*GW* i. 222)

(12) An	To
(13) die Vielgötterei	paganism
(14) Verlor ich ein Wort, das mich suchte:	I lost a word, that was looking* for me:
(15) *Kaddisch.*	*Kaddish.*
(16) Durch	Through
(17) die Schleuse mußt ich,	the sluice I had to go,
(18) das Wort in die Salzflut zurück-	to save the word into the salt flow
(19) und hinaus- und hinüber- zuretten:	back, out, and across:
(20) *Jiskor.*	*Yizkor.*[111]

Kermorvan, ll. 9–12 (*GW* i. 262)

(9) Ein Spruch spricht—zu wem? Zu sich selber:	A saying speaks*—to whom? To itself:
(10) *Servir Dieu est régner,*—ich kann	*Servir Dieu est régner,*—I can
(11) ihn lesen, ich kann, es wird heller,	read it, I can, it is becoming lighter,
(12) fort aus Kannitverstan.	away from Kannitverstan.[112]

[107] 'To/at/with the sharp/pointed tip'. Celan alludes to Baudelaire's 'il n'est pas de
pointe plus acérée que celle de l'Infini' (there is no tip which would be sharper/more
pointed than that of the Infinite) (Baudelaire, 37).

[108] Lit. 'distinguishing' (Heb.); blessing said at the end of Shabbat or a holiday.

[109] Nonsense word deriving from the playful permutation of 'blühen die' (bloom
the) (l. 16) through 'hühendiblüh' (ibid.) into 'Huhediblu'.

[110] Celan lived close to the Place de la Contrescarpe in Paris.

[111] 'Kaddish' (holy (Aram.))) and 'Yizkor' (may he remember (Hebr.)) are ritual
prayers for the dead. See Felstiner, 161–3.

[112] 'Servir Dieu est régner' (To serve god is to reign) is part of the coat of arms
above the entry to Kermorvan, a castle in Trébabu, Brittany (see *Die Niemandsrose*
(Tübingen edn.), 96). 'Kannitverstan' (I don't understand (presumably Dutch)), is
the title of a famous story by Johann Peter Hebel (Hebel, 121–3).

In Eins (In One), ll. 1–4 (*GW* i. 270)

(1) Dreizehnter Feber.[113] Im Herzmund	Thirteenth of February. In the heart mouth
(2) erwachtes Schibboleth. Mit dir,	awakened Shibboleth. With you
(3) Peuple	Peuple
(4) de Paris. *No passarán.*	de Paris. *No passarán.*[114]

Huhediblu, ll. 19, 58–62 (*GW* i. 275–7)

(19) Hüh—on tue . . . Ja wann?	Hüh—on tue . . . But when?
(58) das Julchen, das Julchen:	the Julchen, the Julchen:
(59) daseinsfest rülpst,	steady in existence belches*,
(60) rülpst es das Fallbeil los,— call it (hott!)	belches* the guillotine off,—call it (hott!)
(61) love	love
(62) Oh quand refleuriront, oh roses, vos septembres?	Oh quand refleuriront, oh roses, vos septembres?[115]

Celan continues and intensifies the interlingual disruption of his poetic utterance intralingually—by performing the decomposition of the verbal material itself. As the following examples illustrate, three modes of intralingual decomposition are particularly prevalent throughout *Die Niemandsrose*: the separation of prefixes and suffixes from their verbal stems, the splitting of compound terms into their nominal, adjectival, and verbal constituents, and, finally, the breaking up of non-compound terms into morphemic entities:

Chymisch (Alchemically), ll. 16–17, 31–4 (*GW* i. 227–8)

(16) Große. Graue. Schlacken-	Great [one]. Grey [one]. Cinder/ Slag/Waste-

---

[113] Celan uses the Austrian 'Feber' instead of the 'regular' German 'Februar' (February) in order to commemorate the Viennese workers' uprising (13–14 Feb. 1934) against the fascist regime of chancellor Dollfuß.

[114] Regarding 'shibboleth', see Judges 12: 4–6. 'Peuple de Paris' (people of Paris), an allusion to the public addresses to Parisians during the Paris commune in 1871. 'No passarán' (they will not pass (Span.)) was the password of the International Brigades during the Spanish Civil War.

[115] '[O]n tue . . .' (they kill) is an allusion to the dictum: 'On tue les poètes pour les citer après' (they kill the poets in order to cite them afterwards); 'Call it Love' is the title of a poem by Hans Magnus Enzensberger (*Verteidigung*, 19). 'Oh quand refleuriront, oh roses, vos septembres' (Oh when will bloom again, oh roses, your Septembers) is an inversion of Paul Verlaine's line: 'Ah! quand refleuriront les roses de septembre!' (Ah! When will the roses of September bloom again!) (Verlaine, 192).

(17) lose.	less [one].
(31) Große. Graue. Fährte-	Great [one]. Grey [one]. Trace-
(32) lose.	less [one].
(33) König-	King-
(34) liche.	ly [one].

Benedicta, ll. 20–5 (GW i. 249–50)

(20) Ge-	Dr-
(21) trunken.	unk.
(22) Ge-	Bl-
(23) segnet.	essed
(24) Ge-	Ge-
(25) *bentscht.*	*bentscht.*[116]

Ein Wurfholz (A piece of throwwood), ll. 8–12 (GW i. 258)

(8) . . . Zeitstaub, mit-	. . . timedust, with-
(9) verwaisend mit euch,	orphaning with you,
(10) Lapilli, ver-	lapilli, per-
(11) zwergt, verwinzigt, ver-	dwarfed, permidgeted, an-
(12) nichtet,	nihilated,[117]

Ich habe Bambus geschnitten (I have cut bamboo), ll. 4–5, 15–17 (GW i. 264)

(4) Diese morgen fort-	This tomorrow away-
(5) getragene Hütte . . .	carried hut . . .
(15) . . . wohin dich	. . . wherever
(16) die Seele auch hinspielt im Un-	the soul may play you in the un-
(17) gebundenen.	bound.

Huhediblu, ll. 24–7, 48–9 (GW i. 275–6)

(24) . . . du liest,	. . . you read*,
(25) dies hier, dies:	this here, this:
(26) Dis-	Something dis-
(27) parates . . .	parate . . .
(48) ad-	ad-
(49) jektivisch . . .	jectivally . . .

Die Silbe Schmerz (The Syllable Pain), ll. 13–16 (GW i. 280)

| (13) . . . aus- | . . . ri-[118] |

---

[116] 'Gebentscht' means 'blessed' in Yiddish.

[117] The German prefix 'ver-' implies 'carrying through', 'carrying out', in short, the accomplishment of an activity. The prefix 'per-' most neatly captures these meanings in English. In the case of 'ver-|nichtet' I decided upon 'an-|nihilated' so as to replicate morphologically and semantically the German 'nichtet' (lit.: nihilates, nothings).

[118] I use 'ri-' as a prefix, since the implied signification of 'out-ripened', which

(14) gereift und	pened and
(15) rück- und fort-	back- and away-
(16) verwandelt	transformed

In all of these poems composite lexemes—nouns, verbs and adjectives—undergo processes of internal disjunction: suffixes ('-lose' (less), and '-liche' (ly) in 'Chymisch') and prefixes ('Ge-'[119] in 'Benedicta'; 'mit-' (with-), 'ver-' (per-/an-) in 'Ein Wurfholz'; 'fort-' (away-) and 'Un-' (un-) in 'Ich habe Bambus geschnitten'; 'Dis-' and 'ad-' in 'Huhediblu'; 'aus-' (ri-), 'rück-(back-)', and 'fort- (away-)' in 'Die Silbe Schmerz') are either raised to the status of self-standing prosodic units, which constitute entire verses after having been severed from their verbal stems ('Chymisch', 'Benedicta', 'Huhediblu'), or become discrete syntactical elements in verses ('Ein Wurfholz', 'Ich habe Bambus geschnitten', 'Die Silbe Schmerz').[120]

In the following instances both compound and non-compound terms are subjected to internal disjunction:

... Rauscht der Brunnen (Plashes the Fountain), ll. 1–2, 10–11, 17–19 (*GW* i. 237)

(1) Ihr gebet-, ihr lästerungs-, ihr	You prayer-, you slander-, you
(2) gebetscharfen Messer	prayersharp knives
(10) mein täglich wahr- und wahrer-	my daily true- and truer-
(11) geschundenes Später	grounddown later
(17) Wir werden das Kinderlied singen, das,	We will sing the nursery song, the one
(18) hörst du, das	you hear, the one
(19) mit den Men, mit den Schen, mit den Menschen ...	with the hum, with the ans, with the humans ...

Einem, der ... (To (the) one who ...), ll. 27, 29 (*GW* i. 243)

| (27) Wirf auch die Abendtür zu, Rabbi. | Throw the evening door shut, too, rabbi. |

morphologically corresponds to its German counterpart, is semantically incompatible with 'ausgereift' (fully ripe).

[119] In German, the prefix 'ge-' is added to the word stem in the past participle passive form of a verb, as in: 'trinken' (drink) → 'getrunken' (drunk); 'suchen' (to look for, to search for, to seek (after)) → 'gesucht' (looked for, searched for, sought (after)).

[120] See also the following *Niemandsrose* poems: 'Tübingen, Jänner', ll. 1–2; 'Anabasis', ll. 21–3; 'Die Silbe Schmerz', ll. 22–3; 'La contrescarpe', ll. 47–8; 'In der Luft', ll. 45–6. The functionalization of prepositions as prefixes is common in German.

(29) Reiß die Morgentür auf,	Tear the morning door open,
Ra—	ra—

Ein Wurfholz, ll. 1–8 (GW i. 258)

(1) Ein Wurfholz , auf Atemwe-	A piece of throwwood, on
gen,	breathways,
(2) so wanderts, das Flügel-	so it wanders, the wing-
(3) mächtige. Das	mighty. The
(4) Wahre. Auf	true. On
(5) Sternen-	star-
(6) bahnen, von Welten-	paths, by world-
(7) splittern geküßt, von Zeit-	splinters kissed, by time-
(8) körnern genarbt . . .	seeds scarred . . .

Kolon, ll. 12–15 (GW i. 265)

(12) Fühlst du, wir liegen	Do you feel, we lie*
(13) weiß von Tausend-	white with the thousand-
(14) farbenem, Tausend-	coloured, thousand-
(15) mündigem . . .	mouthed . . .

Huhediblu, ll. 1–3, 17–18 (GW i. 275)

(1) Schwer-, Schwer-, Schwer-	Heavy-, heavy-, heavy-
(2) fälliges auf	legged on
(3) Wortwegen . . .	wordways . . .
(17) huhediblu, ja sie, die Sep-	huhediblu, yes they, the Septem-
tember-	ber-
(18) rosen?	roses?

Die Silbe Schmerz, ll. 39–42, 44–6 (GW i. 281)

(39) . . . ein	. . . a
(40) Knoten	knot
(41) (und Wider- und Gegen-	(and counter- and against- and
und Aber- und Zwillings-	but- and twin- and thou-
und Tau-	
(42) sendknoten) . . .	sandknot[s]) . . .
(44) . . . im Abgrund	. . . in the abyss
(45) buch-, buch-, buch-	was spell-, spell-, spell-
(46) stabierte, stabierte.	ing, ing.

The splitting of compounds into their nominal, adjectival, and prepositional constituents ('. . . Rauscht der Brunnen', ll. 1–2; 'Ein Wurfholz', ll. 2–3, 6–8; 'Kolon', ll. 13–15; 'Huhediblu', ll. 1–2, 17–18; 'Die Silbe Schmerz', ll. 41–2, 45–6) gives way to the splitting of non-compounds into their syllabic units ('. . . Rauscht der Brunnen', l. 19; 'Einem, der . . .', l. 29; 'Die Silbe Schmerz', ll. 41–2).[121] These devices of de*com*position are—as I have indicated—not simply destructive, but de*con*structive, that is, positively 'barbaric' in that they perform a *radical* remapping and reconfiguration of the language system they subvert: the cleansing of the 'language of the murderers' must begin at its roots, as it were. Thus, in the examples given above, 'Menschen [humans]' ('. . . Rauscht der Brunnen', l. 19) multiplies into its syllabic constituents, giving birth to the neologisms 'Men' and 'Schen'; 'Rabbi' ('Einem, der . . .', l. 27) yields to its circumcised replica 'Ra-' (l. 29); the severed prefix 'ver-' ('Ein Wurfholz', l. 10) is reattached to verbs which do not allow for composite derivations involving the prefix 'ver-', thus entailing the emergence of such neologisms as 'verwinzigt' (permidgeted) and 'verzwergt' (perdwarfed) (ll. 10–11); similarly, the prepositions '[w]ider' (counter) and '[g]egen' (against), as well as the conjunction '[a]ber' (but) are linked, in neologistic manner, to the noun '[K]noten' (knot) ('Die Silbe Schmerz', ll. 41–2).[122]

Celan's idiosyncratic poetic idiom explodes the linguistic system(s) which it engages, on whose resources it constantly draws, without, however, ceasing to be traced and haunted by it (them). Although words like 'permidgeted', 'perdwarfed', or 'againstknots' do not signify as tokens of a paradigmatic dictionary entry, that is, conceptually (in the Hegelian sense) and systematically, they do engage the dislocated systematic meanings of their lexematic and morphemic constituents: while signifying 'something, which would not be without this [singular] appellation and which is attainable only for *this singular* word' (Neumann, 9), Celan's poetic word equally points to, commemorates, as it were, its origin in a system, in a totality. It thus palpably enacts the 'haunting' concatenation of singularity and universality, which has traditionally been associated with poetic language, and, thereby, yet again corroborates the poethic significance of the poetic Said.

---

[121] See also the following *Niemandsrose* poems: 'Zwölf Jahre', ll. 1–3; 'Anabasis', ll. 7–8, 12–13, 16–17; 'Hawdalah', ll. 12–13; 'La contrescarpe', ll. 25–6; 'Es ist alles anders', ll. 66–7; 'Und mit dem Buch aus Tarussa' (And with the Book from Tarussa), ll. 26–7, 40–1, 48–9, 78–9.

[122] Since Neumann provides a fairly comprehensive survey of Celan's deconstructive 'solecisms' (Neumann, 7–27), I dispense with further examples.

Conclusion:
Toward a Metapoethics

My inquiry into dialogue necessitated the development and performance of what I call poethics. As I have pointed out earlier, I distinguish between two aspects of poethics: (1) poethics as my synoptic engagement of Levinas's, Bakhtin's, Mandel'shtam's, and Celan's writings—as my approach to Celan's dialogue with Mandel'shtam in the light of Levinas's and Bakhtin's ethical philosophies, that is, as a form of criticism; (2) poethics as the 'theme' of my critical discourse, that is, Celan's idiosyncratic mode of responding to Mandel'shtam's interpellation. By 'criticism' I mean—following Roland Barthes—'a series of intellectual acts profoundly engaged in the existence . . . of the person who accomplishes them [and bearing] upon discourse' (*Essais*, 254–5). If we accept with Barthes that 'every criticism is a criticism of the work and a criticism of itself' (254), my interpretation of Celan's dialogue with Mandel'shtam cannot avoid the critical task of interrogating itself in its very performance. As a form of criticism, as the performance of a speech genre, my approach faces (at least) two fundamental queries, which inevitably arise in view of its status as dialogic and self-reflexive: (1) Can it be 'applied' to texts other than Celan's and Mandel'shtam's poetry and prose? (2) What is its relation to other forms of critical activity? Since the elaboration of even tentative answers to these questions exceeds the scope of these concluding remarks, I would merely like to stake out at this point a path for future inquiry.

The universa(lizabi)lity of poethics as a methodologically and/or thematically delimited critical approach depends on the viability and operability of what could be called Bakhtino-Levinasian or ethico-metalinguistic criticism (in analogy with Freudian, Lacanian, and other forms of criticism) beyond the circumscribed context of its emergence in connection with Celan's and Mandel'shtam's writings. In other words, the stipulation of poethics as a general critical approach implies its functional independence from the dialogue between Celan and Mandel'shtam, which directly contributes to its articulation. Given that both Levinas and Bakhtin posit and describe presumably universal *structures* of dialogue, their insights must be universally valid and, consequently, heuristically instrumentalizable in a potentially unlimited number of discursive contexts. Further research will have to probe the extent to which poethics must (be able to afford to) suppress its constitutive debt to Celan and Mandel'shtam without undermining itself. It is safe to say already at this early stage, however, that against the grain of Levinas's, Bakhtin's, Mandel'shtam's, and Celan's insistence on enunciatory and ethical singularity, their synoptic engagement generates a philosophical framework for the development of critical questions and conceptual parameters which would allow for the practice of the poethic approach on a more general level. This approach would be predicated on the interpretation of poetry in the light of its singular responsiveness, in the light of the particular ways in which an author's responsiveness to and answerability to and for another text and its author organizes his or her poetic response.

As a mode of criticism poethics cannot avoid being hermeneutic and structuralist to the extent that it involves the 'reconstruction' or, rather, co-constitution of its 'object' or interlocutor. It is also ethical in the broad sense of testifying to a person's—in this instance, the critic's—particular ethos (*NE* 1103a14–20, 1142a24–30, 1143a25–b6). Consequently—and irrespective of its dialogicity—poethics falls into the realm of what Michel Foucault calls 'technologies of the self', that is, critical practices 'which permit individuals to effect by their own means, or with the help of others, a certain number of operations on their own bodies and souls, thoughts, conduct, and way of being, so as to transform themselves' (*Ethics*, 225),[1] and which accomplish, 'to use an expression that one finds in Plutarch, an *ethopoietic* function' (209). These practices include reading and writing, which more than other occupations

---

[1] Foucault fashions his 'technologies of the self' after the classical notions of 'the art of living, the *tekhnê tou biou* [and] *askêsis* . . . understood as a training of the self by oneself' (*Ethics*, 208). Notwithstanding the pertinence of Foucault's writings at this point, I should stress that his definition of ethics as 'relation to oneself' (263) is diametrically opposed to Levinas's and Bakhtin's notions of ethics as dialogue.

facilitate the 'transformation of truth into *ethos*' (ibid.). Further research will have to probe the significance of poethics with regard to other ethopoietic practices and determine its contribution to our understanding of criticism in general. These are only some of the tasks paving the way toward what may aptly be called a metapoethics.

Bibliography

ADLAM, CAROL, et al. (eds.), *Face to Face: Bakhtin in Russia and the West* (Sheffield: Sheffield Academic Press, 1997).

ADORNO, THEODOR W., *Prismen: Kulturkritik und Gesellschaft*, ed. R. Tiedemann, 4th edn. (Frankfurt a.M.: Suhrkamp, 1992).

—— *Noten zur Literatur*, ed. R. Tiedemann, 6th edn. (Frankfurt a.M.: Suhrkamp, 1994).

AIZLEWOOD, ROBIN, and DIANA MYERS (eds.), *Stoletie Mandel'shtama: Materialy simpoziuma/Mandelstam Centenary Conference*, Materials from the Mandelstam Centenary Conference, School of Slavonic and East European Studies, London 1991 (Tenafly, NJ: Hermitage, 1994).

AKHMATOVA, ANNA ANDREEVNA, *Sochineniia*, ed. E. G. Gershtein *et al.*, 2 vols. (Moscow: Khudozhestvennaia literatura, 1986).

ALTHUSSER, LOUIS, *Lenin and Philosophy*, trans. B. Brewster (London: Verso, 1971).

APEL, KARL-OTTO (ed.), *Sprachpragmatik und Philosophie: Beiträge von K. O. Apel, J. Habermas, S. Kanngießer, H. Schnelle, D. Wunderlich* (Frankfurt a.M.: Suhrkamp, 1976).

—— *Selected Essays I: Towards a Transcendental Semiotics*, ed. E. Mendieta (Atlantic Highlands, NJ: Humanities Press, 1994).

ARISTOTLE, *The Nicomachean Ethics*, trans. H. Rackham (London: Heinemann; New York: Putnam's 1926).

—— *The Metaphysics*, trans. H. Tredennick and G. C. Armstrong, 2 vols. (London: Heinemann; New York: Putnam's; Cambridge, Mass.: Harvard University Press, 1933, 1936).

—— *The Organon I: The Categories, On Interpretation, Prior Analytics*, trans. H. P. Cooke and H. Tredennick (Cambridge, Mass.: Harvard University Press; London: Heinemann, 1938).

—— *Politics*, trans. H. Rackham (London: Heinemann; Cambridge, Mass.: Harvard University Press, 1944).

ATTRIDGE, DEREK, 'Closing Statement: Linguistics and Poetics in Retrospect', in N. Fabb *et al.* (eds.), *The Linguistics of Writing: Arguments Between Language and Literature* (New York: Methuen, 1987), 15–32.

—— *Peculiar Language: Literature as Difference from the Renaissance to James Joyce* (Ithaca, NY: Cornell University Press, 1988).

—— 'Literary Form and the Demands of Politics: Otherness in J. M.

Coetzee's *Age of Iron*', in G. Levine (ed.), *Aesthetics and Ideology* (New Brunswick, NJ: Rutgers University Press, 1994), 243–63.

—— 'Trusting the Other: Ethics and Politics in J. M. Coetzee's *Age of Iron*', *South Atlantic Quarterly*, 93/1 (Winter 1994), 59–82.

—— 'Singularities, Responsibilities: Derrida, Deconstruction, and Literary Criticism', in C. Caruth and D. Esch (eds.), *Critical Encounters: Reference and Responsibility in Deconstructive Writing* (New Brunswick, NJ: Rutgers University Press, 1995), 106–26.

AUGUSTINE, *The Confessions*, trans. F. J. Sheed (New York: Sheed and Ward, 1943).

AUSTIN, J. L., *How to Do Things With Words*, ed. J. O. Urmson and M. Sbisà, 2nd edn. (Cambridge, Mass.: Harvard University Press, 1975).

BAKHTIN, MIKHAIL M., *Voprosy literatury i estetiki: issledovaniia raznykh let* (Moscow: Khudozhestvennaia literatura, 1975).

—— *Estetika slovesnogo tvorchestva*, ed. S. G. Bocharov (Moscow: Iskusstvo, 1979).

—— *Literaturno-kriticheskie stat'i*, ed. S. G. Bocharov and V. V. Kozhinov (Moscow: Khudozhestvennaia literatura, 1986).

—— *Art and Answerability: Early Philosophical Essays by M. M. Bakhtin*, trans. V. Liapunov, suppl. trans. K. Brostrom, ed. M. Holquist and V. Liapunov (Austin: University of Texas Press, 1990).

—— *The Dialogic Imagination: Four Essays*, trans. C. Emerson and M. Holquist, ed. M. Holquist (Austin: University of Texas Press, 1992).

—— *Toward a Philosophy of the Act*, trans. V. Liapunov, ed. V. Liapunov and M. Holquist (Austin: The University of Texas Press, 1993).

—— *Problemy poetiki-tvorchestva Dostoevskogo*, ed. O. V. Garun (Kiev: Next, 1994).

—— *Roboty 1920–x godov*, ed. D. A. Tatarnikov (Kiev: Next, 1994).

[——] *Bakhtinologiia: issledovaniia, perevody, publikatsii*, ed. A. P. Valitskaia *et al.* (St. Petersburg: Aleteiia, 1995).

—— *Sobranie sochinenii v semi tomakh*, v. *Raboty 1940–x—nachala 1960–x godov*, ed. S. G. Bocharov and L. A. Gogotishvily (Moscow: Russkie Slovari, 1996).

BAMBACH, CHARLES E., *Heidegger, Dilthey, and the Crisis of Historicism* (Ithaca, NY: Cornell University Press, 1995).

BARTHES, ROLAND, *Essais critiques* (Paris: Seuil, 1964).

—— 'Theory of the Text', in R. Young (ed.), *Untying the Text: A Poststructuralist Reader* (Boston, Mass.: Routledge and Kegan Paul, 1981), 31–47.

—— 'The Death of the Author', in D. Lodge (ed.), *Modern Criticism and Literary Theory* (London and New York: Longman, 1988), 167–72.

—— *The Semiotic Challenge*, trans. R. Howard (Oxford: Blackwell, 1988).

BAUDELAIRE, CHARLES, *Petits poèmes en prose (Le spleen de Paris)* (Paris: Garnier-Flammarion, 1967).

BAUMANN, GERHART, *Erinnerungen an Paul Celan* (Frankfurt a.M.: Suhrkamp, 1986).

BENJAMIN, WALTER, *Illuminationen: Ausgewählte Schriften I* (Frankfurt a.M.: Suhrkamp, 1977).

BENN, GOTTFRIED, *Essays, Reden, Vorträge*, ed. D. Wellershoff, 2nd edn. (Wiesbaden: Limes, 1962).

—— *Gedichte*, ed. B. Hillebrand (Frankfurt a.M.: Fischer, 1982).

BENVENISTE, ÉMILE, *Problèmes de linguistique générale*, 2 vols. (Paris: Gallimard, 1966, 1974).

BERGSON, HENRI, *L'Évolution créatrice*, 156th edn. (Paris: Quadrige/Presses Universitaires de France, 1986).

—— *Essai sur les données immédiates de la conscience*, 5th edn. (Paris: Quadrige/Presses Universitaires de France, 1993).

—— *Matière et mémoire: Essai sur la relation du corps à l'esprit*, 4th edn. (Paris: Quadrige/Presses Universitaires de France, 1993).

BERNASCONI, ROBERT, and SIMON CRITCHLEY (eds.), *Re-Reading Levinas* (Bloomington: Indiana University Press, 1991).

BHABHA, HOMI K., *The Location of Culture* (London and New York: Routledge, 1994).

Bibila Hexaglotta continentia Scripturas Sacras Veteris and Novi Testamenti, ed. Edward Riches de Levante, 6 vols. (London: Dickinson and Higham, 1874).

Biblia Sacra Latina ex Biblia Sacra Vulgatae Editionis Sixti V. et Clementis VIII (London: Bagster & Sons, 1794).

BIRUS, HENDRIK, '*Introite, nam et heic Dii sunt!*': Einiges über Lessings Mottoverwendung und das Motto zum Nathan', *Euphorion*, 75 (1981), 379–410.

BLOK, ALEKSANDR, *Sobranie sochinenii*, ed. V. N. Orlov *et al.*, 8 vols. (Moscow and Leningrad: Gosudarstvennoe izdatel'stvo khudozhestvennoi literatury, 1962).

BLONDEL, MAURICE, *Action (1893): Essay on a Critique of Life and a Science of Practice*, trans. O. Blanchette (Notre Dame, Ind.: University of Notre Dame Press, 1984).

BLOOM, HAROLD, *The Anxiety of Influence: A Theory of Poetry* (London: Oxford University Press, 1973).

BOCCACCIO, GIOVANNI, *Boccaccio on Poetry: Being the Preface and the Fourteenth and Fifteenth Books of Boccaccio's 'Genealogiae Deorum Gentilium'*, trans. C. G. Osgood (Princeton, NJ: Princeton University Press, 1930).

BOCHAROV, SERGEI. G., 'Ob odnom razgovore i vokrug nego', *Novoe Literaturnoe Obozrenie*, 2 (1993), 70–89.

BÖSCHENSTEIN, BERNHARD, 'Celan und Mandelstamm: Beobachtungen zu ihrem Verhältnis', *Celan-Jahrbuch*, 2 (1988), 155–68.

—— and SIGRID WEIGEL (eds.), *Ingeborg Bachmann und Paul Celan: Poetische Korrespondenzen. Vierzehn Beiträge* (Frankfurt a.M.: Suhrkamp, 1997).

BOLLACK, JEAN, 'Chanson à boire. Über das Gedicht "Bei Wein und Verlorenheit"', *Celan-Jahrbuch*, 3 (1989), 23–35.

BOOTH, WAYNE C., *The Rhetoric of Fiction*, 2nd edn. (Harmondsworth: Penguin, 1987).

BRIERLEY, DAVID, *'Der Meridian': Ein Versuch zur Poetik und Dichtung Paul Celans* (Frankfurt a.M.: Lang, 1984).

BRODA, MARTINE (ed.), *Contre-Jour: Études sur Paul Celan* (Paris: Cerf, 1986).

—— *Dans la main de personne: Essai sur Paul Celan* (Paris: Cerf, 1986).

BRODSKY, PATRICIA POLLOCK, 'On Daring to Be a Poet: Rilke and Marina Cvetaeva', *Germano-Slavica*, 3/4 (Fall 1980), 261–9.

BROWN, CLARENCE, 'Into the Heart of Darkness: Mandelstam's Ode to Stalin', *Slavic Review*, 26/4 (Dec. 1967), 584–604.

—— 'Mandelstam's Notes Towards a Supreme Fiction', *Delos*, 1 (1968), 32–43.

—— *Mandelstam* (Cambridge: Cambridge University Press, 1973).

BROYDE, STEVEN JOSEPH, 'Osip Mandel'stam's "Našedsij Podkovu"', in R. Jakobson, C. H. van Schooneveld, and Dean S. Worth (eds.), *Slavic Poetics: Essays in Honor of Kiril Taranovsky* (The Hague: Mouton, 1973), 49–66.

BUBER, MARTIN (trans.), *Das Buch der Zwölf* (Berlin: Schocken, 1926).

—— *Das dialogische Prinzip: Ich und Du, Zwiesprache, Die Frage an den Einzelnen, Elemente des Zwischenmenschlichen, Zur Geschichte des dialogischen Prinzips*, 5th edn. (Heidelberg: Lambert Schneider, 1984).

BÜCHNER, GEORG, *Lenz, Der Hessische Landbote* (Stuttgart: Reclam, 1990).

—— *Werke und Briefe*, 2nd edn. (Munich: DTV, 1990).

BUCK, THEO, *Muttersprache, Mördersprache: Celan-Studien I* (Aachen: Rimbaud, 1993).

BURGGRAEVE, ROGER, *Emmanuel Levinas: Une bibliographie primaire et secondaire (1929–1985) avec Complement 1985–1989* (Leuven: Peeters, 1990).

BUTLER, JUDITH, *Excitable Speech: A Politics of the Performative* (New York and London: Routledge, 1997).

CARNAP, RUDOLF, *Foundations of Logic and Mathematics* (Chicago: University of Chicago Press, 1939).

CAVANAGH, CLARE, *Osip Mandelstam and the Creation of Modernist Tradition* (Princeton, NJ: Princeton University Press, 1995).

CELAN, PAUL (trans.), *Drei russische Dichter—Alexander Blok, Ossip Mandelstamm, Sergej Jessenin.* (Frankfurt a.M: Fischer, 1963).

——*Strette: 'Poèmes' suivis du Méridien' et d'"Entretien dans la montagne'*, trans. A. du Bouchet (Mesnil-sur-l'Estrée: Mercure de France, 1971).

——'Briefe an Alfred Margul-Sperber', *Neue Literatur*, 26/7 (1975), 50–63.

——*Poems: A Bilingual Edition*, trans. M. Hamburger (New York: Persea Books, 1980).

——*Gesammelte Werke*, ed. B. Allemann, S. Reichert, and R. Bücher, 5 vols. (Frankfurt a.M.: Suhrkamp, 1986).

——'Die Dichtung Ossip Mandelstamms', in R. Dutli (ed.), *Im Luftgrab* (Zürich: Ammann, 1988), 69–81.

——*Das Frühwerk*, ed. B. Wiedemann (Frankfurt a.M.: Suhrkamp, 1989).

[——] *Paul Celan/Nelly Sachs Briefwechsel*, ed. B. Wiedemann, 3rd edn. (Frankfurt a.M.: Suhrkamp, 1994).

——*Die Niemandsrose: Vorstufen, Textgenese, Endfassung*, ed. J. Wertheimer, Tübingen edn. (Frankfurt a.M.: Suhrkamp, 1996).

——*Die Gedichte aus dem Nachlass*, ed. B. Badiou, J.-C. Rambach, and B. Wiedemann (Frankfurt a.M.: Suhrkamp 1997).

——*Der Meridian: Endfassung, Vorstufen, Materialien*, ed. B. Böschentsein and H. Schmull, Tübingen edn. (Frankfurt a.M.: Suhrkamp, 1999).

CHALFEN, ISRAEL, *Paul Celan: Eine Biographie seiner Jugend* (Frankfurt a.M.: Suhrkamp, 1983).

CICERO, MARCUS TULLIUS, *De Oratore III. De Fato. Paradoxa Stoicorum. De Partitione Oratoria*, trans. H. Rackham (Cambridge, Mass.: Harvard University Press; London: Heinemann, 1968).

CLARK, KATERINA, and MICHAEL HOLQUIST, *Mikhail Bakhtin* (Cambridge, Mass., and London: Harvard University Press, 1984).

——and MICHAEL HOLQUIST, 'A Continuing Dialogue', *Slavic and East European Journal*, 30/1 (Spring 1986), 96–102.

COATES, RUTH, *Christianity in Bakhtin* (Cambridge: Cambridge University Press, 1998).

COETZEE, J. M., 'Osip Mandelstam and the Ode to Stalin', *representations*, 35 (Summer 1991), 72–83.

COHEN, HERMANN, *Ethik des reinen Willens*, 2nd edn. (Berlin: Cassirer, 1907).

COLERIDGE, SAMUEL TAYLOR, *Biographia Literaria*, ed. J. Shawcross, 2 vols. (Oxford: Oxford University Press, 1962).

COLIN, AMY D. (ed.), *Argumentum e Silentio: International Paul Celan Symposium/Internationales Paul Celan-Symposium* (Berlin and New York: de Gruyter, 1987).

DANTE ALIGHIERI, *De Vulgari Eloquentia*, trans. A. Margio, 3rd edn. (Florence: Felice Le Monnier, 1957).

—— *Literature in the Vernacular (De Vulgari Eloquentia)*, trans. S. Purcell (Manchester: Carcanet New Press, 1981).

—— *The Divine Comedy*, trans. H. R. Huse (New York and Toronto: Reinhart, 1955).

DAVID, CLAUDE, 'Préambule', *Études Germaniques* (July-Sept. 1970), 239–41.

DE CERTEAU, MICHEL, *Heterologies: Discourse on the Other*, trans. B. Massumi (Minneapolis and London: University of Minnesota Press, 1995).

DE MAN, PAUL, *Blindness and Insight: Essays in the Rhetoric of Contemporary Criticism*, 2nd edn. (Minneapolis: University of Minnesota Press, 1983).

DERRIDA, JACQUES, *L'Écriture et la différence* (Paris: Seuil, 1967).

—— *Marges de la philosophie* (Paris: Minuit, 1972).

—— *Of Grammatology*, trans. G. C. Spivak (Baltimore and London: Johns Hopkins University Press, 1976).

—— *Psyché: Inventions de l'autre* (Paris: Galilée, 1987).

—— *Limited Inc* (Evanston: Northwestern University Press, 1988).

—— *Acts of Literature*, ed. D. Attridge (New York and London: Routledge, 1992).

—— 'At This Very Moment In This Work Here I Am', in R. Bernasconi and S. Critchley (eds.), *Re-Reading Levinas* (Bloomington: Indiana University Press, 1991), 11–48.

—— *La Voix et le phénomène: Introduction au problème du signe dans la phénoménologie de Husserl* (Paris: Quadrige/Presses Universitaires de France, 1993).

—— 'Shibboleth: For Paul Celan', in A. Fioretos (ed.), *Word Traces: Readings of Paul Celan* (Baltimore and London: The Johns Hopkins University Press, 1994), 3–72.

—— *Adieu à Emmanuel Lévinas* (Paris: Galiée, 1997).

DESCARTES, RENÉ, *Meditationes de Prima Philosophia*, trans. G. Schmidt (Stuttgart: Reclam, 1986).

——*Discours de la méthode suivi d'extraits de la Dioptrique, des Météores, de la vie de Descartes par Baillet, du Monde, de l'Homme et de Lettres*, ed. G. Rodi-Lewis (Paris: Garnier-Flammarion, 1992).

DIELS, HERMANN, and WALTHER KRANZ (eds.), *Die Fragmente der Vorsokratiker*, trans. H. Diels, 6th edn., 2 vols. (Berlin: Weidman, 1951).

DILTHEY, WILHELM, *Die Philosophie des Lebens: Eine Auswahl aus seinen Schriften 1867–1910* ed. H.-G. Gadamer (Frankfurt a.M.: Klostermann, 1946).

——*Das Erlebnis und die Dichtung: Lessing, Goethe, Novalis, Hölderlin*, 2nd edn. (Reclam: Leipzig, 1991).

DIOGENES LAERTIUS, *Lives of Eminent Philosophers*, trans. R. D. Hicks, 2 vols. (London: Heinemann; New York: Putnam's, 1925).

DMITRIEVA-EINHORN, MARINA, ' "Einhorn: du weißt um die Steine . . ." Zum Briefwechsel Paul Celans mit Erich Einhorn', *Celan-Jahrbuch*, 7 (1997/8), 7–22.

DOHERTY, JUSTIN, *The Acmeist Movement in Russian Poetry: Culture and the Word* (Oxford: Clarendon Press, 1995).

DOSTOEVSKY, FEDOR M., *Zimnie zapiski o letnikh vpechatleniakh*, in *Proizvedeniia 1862–1869* (Moscow: Gosudarstvennoe izdatel'stvo khudozhestvennoi literatury, 1956).

——*Brat'ia Karamazovy*, 2 vols. (Moscow: Khudozhestvennaia literatura, 1972).

——*Stat'i i zametki 1845–1861* (Leningrad: Nauka, 1978).

DRIVER, SAM, 'Acmeism', *Slavic and East European Journal*, 12/2 (Summer 1968), 141–56.

EAGLESTONE, ROBERT, *Ethical Criticism: Reading After Levinas* (Edinburgh: Edinburgh University Press, 1997).

ECO, UMBERTO, *Einführung in die Semiotik*, trans. J. Trabant, 5th edn. (Munich: Fink, 1985).

EICH, GÜNTER, *Gesammelte Werke*, ed. H. F. Schafroth, 4 vols. (Frankfurt a.M.: Suhrkamp, 1973).

EMERSON, CARYL, 'Editor's Preface', in Mikhail Bakhtin, *Problems of Dostoevsky's Poetics*, trans. C. Emerson (Minneapolis: University of Minnesota Press, 1984), pp. xxix–xliii.

——'Bakhtin at 100: Looking Back at the Very Early Years', *The Russian Review*, 54/1 (Jan. 1995), 107–14.

——*The First Hundred Years of Mikhail Bakhtin* (Princeton, NJ: Princeton University Press, 1997).

——'A Bakhtin for the Twenty-first Century: Double-voiced, Double-faced, Face to Face', *Slavonic and East European Review*, 77/2 (Ap. 1999), 280–94.

ENZENSBERGER, HANS MAGNUS, *Verteidigung der Wölfe* (Frankfurt a.M.: Suhrkamp, 1957).

—— 'Die Steine der Freiheit', *Merkur*, 13/8 (1959), 770–5.

ESKIN, MICHAEL, 'Introduction', in L. P. Yakubinsky, 'On Dialogic Speech', *PMLA*, 112/2 (March 1997), 243–8.

—— ' "Literal Translation": The Semiotic Significance of Nabokov's Conception of Poetic Translation', *Interdisciplinary Journal for Germanic Linguistics and Semiotic Analysis*, 2/1 (Spring 1997), 1–32.

—— 'A Language Before Words—Levinas's Ethics as a Semiotic Problem' (forthcoming in *Semiotica*).

—— 'Translating the Other: Celan's Encounter with Mandel'shtam' *Germano-Slavica*, 11 (1999): 27–38.

FASSBIND, BERNARD, *Poetik des Dialogs: Voraussetzungen dialogischer Poesie bei Paul Celan und Konzepte von Intersubjektivität bei Martin Buber, Martin Heidegger und Emmanuel Levinas* (Munich: Fink, 1995).

FELMAN, SHOSHANA, and DORI LAUB, *Testimony: Crises of Witnessing in Literature, Psychoanalysis, and History* (New York and London: Routledge, 1992).

FELSTINER, JOHN, *Paul Celan: Poet, Survivor, Jew* (New Haven and London: Yale University Press, 1995).

FOUCAULT, MICHEL, *L'Archéologie du savoir* (Paris: Gallimard, 1969).

—— *L'Ordre du discours: Leçon inaugurale au Collège de France prononcée le 2 décembre 1970* (Paris: Gallimard, 1971).

—— *L'Histoire de la sexualité I: La volonté de savoir* (Paris: Gallimard, 1976).

—— 'What is an Author?', in *Language, Counter-Memory, Practice: Selected Essays and Interviews*, ed. Donald F. Bouchard (Ithaca, NY: Cornell University Press, 1992), 113–38.

—— *Ethics: Subjectivity and Truth*, trans. R. Hurley *et al.*, ed. P. Rabinow (New York: New York Press, 1997).

FRANK, JOSEPH, *Dostoevsky: The Stir of Liberation 1860–1865* (Princeton, NJ.: Princeton University Press, 1986).

FREGE, GOTTLOB, 'Über Sinn und Bedeutung', *Zeitschrift für Philosophie und philosophische Kritik*, 100 (1892), 25–50.

—— *Kleine Schriften*, ed. I. Angelelli (Hildesheim: Olms, 1967).

FUNK, RUDOLF, *Sprache und Transzendenz im Denken von Emmanuel Lévinas: Zur Frage einer neuen philosophischen Rede von Gott* (Freiburg and Munich: Alber, 1989).

GADAMER, HANS-GEORG, *Wahrheit und Methode: Grundzüge einer philosophischen Hermeneutik* (Tübingen: Mohr, 1960).

GARY HARRIS, JANE, *Osip Mandelstam* (Boston: Twayne Publishers, 1988).

GELLHAUS, AXEL, 'Erinnerung an schwimmende Hölderlintürme: Paul Celan—"Tübingen, Jänner"', *Spuren*, 24 (Dec. 1993), 1–16.

—— 'Die Polarisierung von "Poesie" und "Kunst" bei Paul Celan', *Celan-Jahrbuch*, 6 (1995), 51–91.

GENETTE, GÉRARD, *Fiction and Diction*, trans. C. Porter (Ithaca and London: Cornell University Press, 1991).

—— *Paratexts: Thresholds of Interpretation*, trans. J. E. Lewin (Cambridge: Cambridge University Press, 1997).

GOGOTISHVILY, L. A., and P. S. GOUREVITCH (eds.), *M. M. Bakhtin kak filosof* (Moscow: Nauka, 1992).

GOLTSCHNIGG, DIETMAR, 'Das Zitat in Celans Dichtergedichten', in J. P. Strelka (ed.), *Literary Theory and Criticism: Festschrift Presented to René Wellek in Honor of His Eightieth Birthday* (Bern: Lang, 1984), 50–63.

GORODETSKII, SERGEI, 'Nekotoryia techeniia v′ sovremennoi russkoi poezii', *Apollon*, 1 (1913), 46–50.

GREISCH, JEAN, AND JACQUES ROLLAND (eds.), *Emmanuel Levinas: L'Éthique comme philosophie première* (Paris: Cerf, 1993).

GUMILEV, NIKOLAI STEPANOVICH, *Sobranie sochinenii*, ed. G. P. Struve and B. A. Filippov, 4 vols. (Washington: Kamkin, 1968).

HABERMAS, JÜRGEN, *Moralbewußtsein und kommunikatives Handeln*, 3rd edn. (Frankfurt a.M.: Suhrkamp, 1988).

HALÉVI, ILAN, *Auf der Suche nach dem gelobten Land: Die Geschichte der Juden und der Palästina-Konflikt* (Hamburg: Junius, 1986).

HALLIDAY, M. A. K., *Language as Social Semiotic: The Social Interpretation of Language and Meaning* (London: Arnold, 1978).

HAMACHER, WERNER, and WINFRIED MENNINGHAUS (eds.), *Paul Celan* (Frankfurt a.M.: Suhrkamp, 1988).

HAND, SEÁN (ed.), *Facing the Other: The Ethics of Emmanuel Levinas* (Richmond: Curzon, 1996).

HEBEL, JOHANN PETER, *Schatzkästlein des rheinischen Hausfreundes*, ed. D. Behagel (Berlin and Stuttgart: Spemann, 1811).

HEGEL, GEORG WILHELM FRIEDRICH, *Wissenschaft der Logik*, ed. H. Glockner, 3rd edn., 2 vols. (Stuttgart: Frommanns, 1958).

—— *Phänomenologie des Geistes* (Stuttgart: Reclam, 1987).

HEIDEGGER, MARTIN, *Der Satz vom Grund* (Pfullingen: Neske, 1957).

—— *Wegmarken*, ed. F.-W. v. Herrmann (Frankfurt a.M.: Klostermann, 1976).

—— *Prolegomena zur Geschichte des Zeitbegriffs*, ed. P. Jaeger (Frankfurt a.M.: Klostermann, 1979).

—— *Holzwege*, 6th edn. (Frankfurt a.M.: Klostermann, 1980).

—— *Erläuterungen zu Hölderlins Dichtung* (Frankfurt a.M.: Klostermann, 1981).

HEIDEGGER, MARTIN, *Sein und Zeit*, 16th edn. (Tübingen: Niemeyer, 1986).

——*Identität und Differenz*, 9th edn. (Pfullingen: Neske, 1990).

——*Unterwegs zur Sprache*, 9th edn. (Pfullingen: Neske, 1990).

——*Vorträge und Aufsätze*, 6th edn. (Pfullingen: Neske, 1990).

HERDER, JOHANN GOTTFRIED, *Abhandlung über den Ursprung der Sprache* (Stuttgart: Reclam, 1993).

HILLIS MILLER, J., *The Ethics of Reading: Kant, de Man, Eliot, Trollope, James, and Benjamin* (New York: Columbia University Press, 1987).

HIRSCHKOP, KEN, 'Dialogism as a Challenge to Literary Criticism', in C. Kelly, M. Makin, and D. Shepherd (eds.), *Discontinuous Discourses in Modern Russian Literature* (New York: St. Martin's Press, 1989), 19–35.

HITCHCOCK, PETER, 'Introduction: Bakhtin/"Bakhtin"', *South Atlantic Quarterly*, 97/3–4 (Summer/Fall 1998), 511–36.

HOBBES, THOMAS, *Leviathan* (New York and London: Macmillan and Collier, 1989).

HÖLDERLIN, FRIEDRICH, *Gedichte*, ed. K. Nussbächer (Stuttgart: Reclam, 1963).

HOLQUIST, MICHAEL, *Dostoevsky and the Novel* (Princeton, NJ.: Princeton University Press, 1977).

——'Answering as Authoring: Mikhail Bakhtin's Trans-Linguistics', *Critical Inquiry*, 10/2 (Dec. 1983), 307–19.

——*Dialogism: Bakhtin and His World* (London and New York: Routledge, 1990).

[HORACE] QUINTUS HORATIUS FLACCUS, *Satires, Epistles and Ars Poetica*, trans. H. R. Fairclough (Cambridge, Mass.: Harvard University Press; London: Heinemann, 1966).

HUSSERL, EDMUND, *Ideen zu einer reinen Phänomenologie und phänomenologischen Philosophie I*, ed. W. Biemel (The Hague: Nijhoff, 1950).

——*Recherches logiques*, trans. H. Elie, A. L. Kelkel, and R. Scherer, vol. 2/1 (Paris: Presses Universitaires de France, 1961).

——*Philosophie der Arithmetik*, ed. L. Eley (The Hague: Nijhoff, 1970).

——*Logische Untersuchungen II/1: Untersuchungen zur Phänomenologie und Theorie der Erkenntnis*, ed. U. Panzer (The Hague: Nijhoff, 1984).

——*Die phänomenologische Methode: Ausgewählte Texte I*, ed. K. Held (Stuttgart: Reclam, 1985).

——*Phänomenologie der Lebenswelt: Ausgewählte Texte II*, ed. K. Held (Stuttgart: Reclam, 1986).

—— *Vorlesungen über Ethik und Wertelehre: 1908–1914*, ed. U. Melle (Dordrecht: Kluwer, 1988).

IAKUBINSKII, LEV P., *Izbrannye raboty: iazyk i ego funktsionirovanie*, ed. A. A. Leont'ev (Moscow: Nauka, 1986).

IVANOV, VIACHESLAV, *Borozdy i mezhi* (Letchworth: Bradda Books, 1971).

IVANOVIĆ, CHRISTINE, *Das Gedicht im Geheimnis der Begegnung: Dichtung und Poetik Celans im Kontext seiner russischen Lektüren* (Tübingen: Niemeyer, 1996).

JAKOBSON, ROMAN, *Selected Writings II: Word and Language* (The Hague and Paris: Mouton, 1971).

—— *Language in Literature*, ed. K. Pomorska and S. Rudy (Cambridge, Mass., and London: Belknap Press of Harvard University Press, 1978).

JANZ, MARLIES, *Vom Engagement absoluter Poesie: Zur Lyrik und Ästhetik Paul Celans* (Frankfurt a.M.: Athenäum, 1984).

JAMES, WILLIAM, *Writings 1902–1910: The Varieties of Religious Experience, Pragmatism, A Pluralistic Universe, The Meaning of Truth, Some Problems of Philosophy, Essays*, ed. B. Kuklick (n.p: Library of America, 1988).

JAMME, CHRISTOPH, and OTTO PÖGGELER (eds.), *'Der glühende Leertext': Annäherungen an Paul Celans Dichtung* (Munich: Fink, 1993).

JOHANN, ERNST, 'VORWORT', in *Büchner-Preis-Reden 1951–1971* (Stuttgart: Reclam, 1987), 5–9.

KANT, IMMANUEL, *Kritik der Urteilskraft*, ed. G. Lehmann (Stuttgart: Reclam, 1963).

—— *Kritik der reinen Vernunft*, ed. W. Weischedel, 2 vols. (Frankfurt a.M.: Suhrkamp, 1974).

—— *Kritik der praktischen Vernunft. Grundlegung der Metaphysik der Sitten*, ed. M. Thom, 3rd edn. (Leipzig: Reclam, 1989).

KIERKEGAARD, SØREN, *Die Schriften über sich selbst*, trans. E. Hirsch (Düsseldorf and Köln: Diederichs, 1964).

—— *Furcht und Zittern*, trans. L. Richter, 2nd edn. (Frankfurt a.M.: Athenäum, 1984).

KILLY, WALTHER, ' "Psalm" von Paul Celan', in Walter Urbanek (ed.), *Begegnung mit Gedichten: 66 Interpretationen vom Mittelalter bis zur Gegenwart*, 3rd edn. (Bamberg: Buchners, 1977), 315–23.

KRISTEVA, JULIA, Σημειωτική: *Recherches pour une sémanalyse* (Paris: Seuil, 1969).

KUZMIN, MIKHAIL, 'O prekrasnoi iasnosti: zametki o proze', *Apollon*, 4 (1910), 5–10.

LACHMANN, RENATE (ed.), *Dialogizität*, (Munich: Fink, 1982).

LACOUE-LABARTHE, PHILIPPE, *La Poésie comme expérience* (Breteuil-sur-Iton: Bourgois, 1986).

LALANDE, ANDRÉ, *Vocabulaire technique et critique de la philosophie*, 5th edn. (Paris: Presses Universitaires de France, 1947).

LEHMANN, JÜRGEN, 'Ambivalenz und Dialogizität. Zur Theorie der Rede bei Michail Bachtin', in *Urszenen: Literaturwissenschaft als Diskursanalyse und Diskurskritik*, ed. F. A. Kittler and H. Turk (Frankfurt a.M.: Suhrkamp, 1977), 355–80.

——'Intertextualität als Problem der Übersetzung: Die Mandel'stam-Übersetzungen Paul Celans', *Poetica*, 19/3–4 (1987), 238–60.

——'Atmen und Verstummen: Anmerkungen zu einem Motivkomplex bei Mandel'stam und Celan', in G. Buhr and R. Reuß (eds.), *'Atemwende': Materialien* (Würzburg: Königshausen & Neumann, 1991), 187–99.

——'Berührung und Dialog: Zu einer unbekannten Mandel'stam-Übersetzung Paul Celans', *Celan-Jahrbuch*, 4 (1991), 83–99.

——' "Dichten heißt immer unterwegs sein": Literarische Grenzüberschreitungen am Beispiel Paul Celans', *arcadia*, 28/2 (1993), 113–30.

——(ed.), *Kommentar zu Paul Celans 'Die Niemandsrose'* (Heidelberg: Winter, 1997).

LESCH, WALTER, 'Die Schriftspur des Anderen: Emmanuel Levinas als Leser von Paul Celan', *Freiburger Zeitschrift für Philosophie und Theologie*, 35 (1988), 449–68.

LEVINAS, EMMANUEL, 'Phénoménologie', *Revue philosophique de la France et de l'étranger*, 118 (1934), 414–20.

——'De l'évasion', *Recherches philosophiques*, 5 (1935/6), 373–92.

——'La réalité et son ombre', *Les Temps Modernes*, 38 (Nov. 1948), 769–89.

——'L'ontologie est-elle fondamentale?', *Revue de Métaphysique et de Morale*, 56/1 (Jan.-Mar. 1951), 88–98.

——'Liberté et commandement', *Revue de Métaphysique et de Morale*, 58/3 (July–Sept. 1953), 264–72.

——'La Philosophie et l'idée de l'infini', *Revue de Métaphysique et de Morale*, 62/3 (July–Sept. 1957), 241–53.

——'La Signification et le sens', *Revue de Métaphysique et de Morale*, 69/2 (Apr.–June 1964), 125–56.

——'La Substitution', *Revue philosophique de Louvain*, 66/91 (Aug. 1968), 487–508.

——'Au-delà de l'essence', *Revue de Métaphysique et de Morale*, 75/3 (July–Sept. 1970), 265–83.

——'Le Dit et le Dire', *Le Nouveau Commerce*, 18–19 (1971), 20–48.

——*En découvrant l'existence avec Husserl et Heidegger*, 3rd edn. (Paris: Vrin, 1974).

—— *Sur Maurice Blanchot* (Montpellier: Fata Morgana, 1975).
—— *L'Au delà du verset: lectures et discours talmudiques* (Paris: Minuit, 1982).
—— *De dieu qui vient à l'idée*, 2nd edn. (Paris: Vrin, 1986).
—— and RICHARD KEARNEY, 'Dialogue with Emmanuel Levinas', in R. Cohen A. (ed.), *Face to Face with Levinas* (Albany, NY: State University of New York Press, 1986), 13–33.
—— 'Language and Proximity', in *Collected Philosophical Papers*, trans. Alphonso Lingis (Dordrecht: Nijhoff, 1987), 109–26.
—— *Noms propres* [1976], (Paris: Fata Morgana, 1987).
—— 'Ethics as First Philosophy', in S. Hand (ed.),*The Levinas Reader* (Oxford: Blackwell, 1989), 75–87.
—— *Autrement qu'être ou au-delà de l'essence* [1974] (Dordrecht: Kluwer, 1990).
—— *Difficile liberté: essais sur le judaïsme* [1963] (Paris: Albin Michel, 1990).
—— *Éthique et infini: dialogues avec Philippe Nemo* [1982] (Paris: Fayard, 1992).
—— *Totalité et infini: essai sur l'extériorité* [1961] (Dordrecht: Kluwer, 1992).
—— *De l'éxistence à l'éxistant* [1947], 2nd edn. (Paris: Vrin, 1993).
—— *Entre nous: essais sur le penser-à-l'autre* (Paris: Grasset, 1993).
—— *Altérité et transcendance* (Paris: Fata Morgana, 1995).
—— *Dieu, la mort et le temps*, ed. J. Rolland (Paris: Grasset, 1995).
—— *Le Temps et l'autre* [1948], 6th edn. (Paris: Presses Universitaires de France, 1996).
LEVINSON, STEPHEN C., *Pragmatics* (Cambridge: Cambridge University Press, 1983).
LLEWELYN, JOHN, *Emmanuel Levinas: The Genealogy of Ethics* (London and New York: Routledge, 1995).
—— 'Approaches to Semioethics', in H. J. Silverman (ed.), *Cultural Semiosis: Tracing the Signifier* (New York and London: Routledge, 1998), 196–218.
LÖNKER, FRED, 'Überlegungen zu Paul Celans Poetik der Übersetzung', in Chaim Shoham and Bernd Witte (eds.), *Datum und Zitat bei Paul Celan* (Bern: Lang, 1987), 211–28.
LURKER, MANFRED (ed.),*Wörterbuch der Symbolik* (Stuttgart: Kröner, 1991).
LUTHER, MARTIN (trans.), *Biblia. Das ist Die ganze Heilige Schrift* (Wittenberg: Seuberlich, 1603).
LYON, JAMES K., 'Paul Celan and Martin Buber: Poetry as Dialogue', *PMLA*, 86/1 (Jan. 1971), 110–20.
MACKEY, CINDY, *Dichter der Bezogenheit: A Study of Paul Celan's*

Poetry with Special Reference to 'Die Niemandsrose' (Stuttgart: Heinz, 1997).

MALINOWSKI, BRONISLAW, 'The Problem of Meaning in Primitive Languages', in C. K. Ogden and I. A. Richards, *The Meaning of Meaning: A Study of the Influence of Language upon Thought and of the Science of Symbolism*, 10th edn. (London: Routledge and Kegan Paul, 1969), 296–336.

MALLARMÉ, STÉPHANE, *Oeuvres complètes* (Paris: Gallimard, 1965).

MANDELKER, AMY (ed.), *Bakhtin in Contexts: Across the Disciplines* (Evanston, Ill.: Northwestern University Press, 1995).

MANDEL'SHTAM, NADEZHDA, *Vospominaniia* (New York: Chekhov Press, 1970).

MANDEL'SHTAM, OSIP EMILEVICH, *Sobranie Sochinenii*, ed. G. Struve and B. Filipoff (New York: Izdatel'stvo imeni Tchekhova, 1955).

——*Sobranie sochinenii*, ed. G. Struve and B. Filipoff. 2nd edn., 3 vols. (New York, Washington: Inter-Language Literary Associates, 1967–71; vol. 4. (supplementary volume), ed. G. Struve, N. Struve, and B. Filipoff (Paris: YMCA-Press, 1981)).

——*The Complete Critical Prose and Letters*, trans. J. G. Harris and C. Link (Ann Arbor, Mich.: Ardis, 1979).

——*Der Stein*, trans. Ralph Dutli (Zürich: Ammann, 1988).

——*Gedichte*, trans. Paul Celan [1959] (Frankfurt a.M.: Fischer, 1988).

——*Tristia: Gedichte 1916–1925*, trans. Ralph Dutli (Zürich: Ammann, 1993).

——*Sobranie sochinenii*, ed. Pavel Nerler *et al.*, Mandelshtam Society edn., 4 vols. (Moscow: Art-Biznes-Tsentr, 1993–7).

MARKOV, VLADIMIR (ed.), *Manifesty i programmy russkikh futuristov/ Die Manifeste und Programmschriften der russischen Futuristen* (Munich: Fink, 1967).

MASON, EUDO C., *Rainer Maria Rilke: Sein Leben und sein Werk* (Göttingen: Vandenhoeck & Ruprecht, 1964).

MAYER, HANS, *Der Repräsentant und der Märtyrer: Konstellationen der Literatur* (Frankfurt a.M.: Suhrkamp, 1971).

MEDVEDEV, PAVEL N., *Formal'nyi metod v literaturovedenii* (Moscow: Labirint, 1993).

MERLEAU-PONTY, MAURICE, *Signes* (Paris: Gallimard, 1960).

MORRIS, CHARLES W., *Foundations of the Theory of Signs* (Chicago: University of Chicago Press, 1938).

MORSON, GARY SAUL, 'The Baxtin Industry', *Slavic and East European Journal*, 30/1 (Spring 1986), 81–90.

——and CARYL EMERSON, *Mikhail Bakhtin: The Creation of a Prosaics* (Stanford, Cal.: Stanford University Press, 1990).

NEALON, JEFFREY T., *Alterity Politics: Ethics and Performative Subjectivity* (Durham and London: Duke University Press, 1998).

NEUMANN, PETER HORST, *Zur Lyrik Paul Celans: Eine Einführung*, 2nd edn. (Göttingen: Vandenhoeck & Ruprecht, 1990).

NUSSBAUM, MARTHA, *Love's Knowledge: Essays on Philosophy and Literature* (New York and Oxford: Oxford University Press, 1990).

OCKHAM, WILLIAM OF, *Summa Logicae*, ed. P. Boehner *et al.* (St Bonaventurae, NY: St Bonaventurae, 1974).

OLLIG, HANS-LUDWIG, *Der Neukantianismus* (Stuttgart: Metzler, 1979).

OLSCHNER, LEONARD MOORE, *Der feste Buchstab: Erläuterungen zu Paul Celans Gedichtübertragungen* (Göttingen and Zürich: Vandenhoeck & Ruprecht, 1985).

OTTO, RUDOLF, *Das Heilige: Über das Irrationale in der Idee des Göttlichen und sein Verhältnis zum Rationalen* (Breslau: Trewendt und Granier, 1917).

PAJEVIC, MARKO, 'Erfahrungen, Orte, Aufenthalte und die Sorge um das Selbst', *arcadia*, 32/1 (1997), 148–61.

PARRY, CHRISTOPH, 'Mandelstam der Dichter und der erdichtete Mandelstam im Werk Paul Celans: Versuch zur Beleuchtung einer literarischen Beziehung', Ph.D thesis, Marburg University, 1978.

—— 'Meridian und Flaschenpost: Intertextualität als Provokation des Lesers bei Paul Celan', *Celan-Jahrbuch*, 6 (1995), 25–50.

—— 'Übersetzung als poetische Begegnung: Paul Celan als Übersetzer und als Gegenstand von Übersetzung', *Jahrbuch Deutsch als Fremdsprache: Intercultural German Studies*, 24 (1998), 159–84.

PEIRCE, CHARLES SANDERS, *Collected Papers of Charles Sanders Peirce*, ed. C. Hartshorne and P. Weiss, 8 vols. (Cambridge, Mass.: Harvard University Press, 1932–1966).

—— *Philosophical Writings*, ed. J. Buchler (New York: Dover Publications, 1955).

—— *Selected Writings (Values in a Universe of Chance)*, ed. P. Wiener (New York: Dover Publications, 1966).

PEPERZAK, ADRIAAN T., 'From Intentionality to Responsibility: On Levinas's Philosophy of Language', in A. B. Dallery and C. E. Scott (eds.), *The Question of the Other: Essays in Contemporary Continental Philosophy* (Albany: State University of New York Press, 1989), 3–21.

—— *To the Other: An Introduction to the Philosophy of Emmanuel Levinas* (West Lafayette, Ind.: Purdue University Press, 1993).

—— (ed.) *Ethics as First Philosophy: The Significance of Emmanuel Levinas for Philosophy, Literature and Religion* (New York and London: Routledge, 1995).

PERLINA, NINA, 'Mikhail Bakhtin and Martin Buber: Problems of Dialogic Imagination', *Studies in Twentieth Century Literature*, 9/1 (Fall 1984), 13–28.

PERLOFF, MARJORIE, and CHARLES JUNKERMAN (eds.), *John Cage: Composed in America* (Chicago and London: University of Chicago Press, 1994).

PINTHUS, KURT (ed.), *Menschheitsdämmerung: Symphonie jüngster Dichtung* (Berlin: Rowohlt, 1920).

PIROG, GERALD, 'Bakhtin and Freud on the Ego', in D. Rancour Lafferriere (ed.), *Russian Literature and Psychoanalysis* (Amsterdam and Philadelphia: Benjamins, 1989), 401–15.

——'The Bakhtin Circle's Freud: From Positivism to Hermeneutics', *Poetics Today*, 8/3–4 (1987), 591–610.

PLATO, *The Collected Dialogues including the Letters*, ed. E. Hamilton and H. Cairns (Princeton, NJ: Princeton University Press, 1996).

PÖGGELER, OTTO, ' "—Ach, die Kunst!" ', in D. Meinecke (ed.), *Über Paul Celan*, 2nd edn. (Frankfurt a.M.: Suhrkamp, 1973), 77–94.

——*Spur des Worts: Zur Lyrik Paul Celans* (Freiburg and Munich: Alber, 1986).

PONZIO, AUGUSTO, 'Semiotics between Peirce and Bakhtin', *Kodikas/Code*, 8/1–2 (1985), 11–28.

——'The Relation of Otherness in Bakhtin, Blanchot, Levinas', *Recherches sémiotiques/Semiotic Inquiry*, 7/1 (1987), 1–20.

——*Man as a Sign: Essays on the Philosophy of Language* (Berlin and New York: Mouton de Gruyter, 1990).

——'Bachtin e Lévinas: Scrittura, Opera e Alterita', in P. Jachia and A. Ponzio (eds.), *Bachtin e . . .: Averincev, Benjamin, Freud, Greimas, Lévinas, Marx, Peirce, Valéry, Welby, Yourcenar con inediti di M. Bachtin* (Bari: Laterza, 1993), 119–36.

PUSHKIN, ALEKSANDR S., *Sochineniia*, ed. D. D. Blagoy, 3 vols. (Moscow: Gosudarstvennoe izdatel'stvo khudozhestvennoi literatury, 1955).

RENTSCHLER, ERIC, *The Ministry of Illusion: Nazi Cinema and Its Afterlife* (Cambridge, Mass.: Harvard University Press, 1996).

REXHEUSER, ADELHEID, 'Die poetische Technik Paul Celans in seinen Übersetzungen russischer Lyrik', *arcadia* 10/3 (1975), 273–95.

RICKERT, HEINRICH, *Der Gegenstand der Erkenntnis: Einführung in die transzendentale Philosophie*, 6th edn. (Tübingen: Mohr, 1928).

RILKE, RAINER MARIA, *Werke*, 3 vols. (Frankfurt a.M.: Insel, 1966).

ROBBINS, JILL, *Prodigal Son/Elder Brother: Interpretation and Alterity in Augustine, Petrarch, Kafka, Levinas* (Chicago and London: University of Chicago Press, 1991).

——*Altered Reading: Levinas and Literature* (Chicago and London: University of Chicago Press, 1999).

RONEN, OMRY, *An Approach to Mandel'stam* (Jerusalem: Magnes Press, 1983).

ROSENZWEIG, FRANZ, *Der Mensch und sein Werk: Gesammelte Schriften*, ed. R. Mayer *et al.*, 4 vols. (Dordrecht: Nijhoff, 1976–84).

RUSSELL, BERTRAND, *Introduction to Mathematical Philosophy* (London: Allen and Unwin, 1919).

——*Logic and Knowledge* (New York: Macmillan, 1956).

RYAN, JUDITH, 'Monologische Lyrik: Paul Celans Antwort auf Gottfried Benn', *Basis*, 2 (1971), 260–82.

SACHS, NELLY, *Fahrt ins Staublose: Gedichte* (Frankfurt a.M.: Suhrkamp, 1988).

SARTRE, JEAN-PAUL, *L'Être et le néant: essai d'ontologie phénoménologique* (Paris: Gallimard, 1993).

——*Qu'est-ce que la littérature?* (Paris: Gallimard, 1995).

SAUSSURE, FERDINAND DE, *Cours de linguistique générale*, ed. C. Bally *et al.* (Paris: Payot, 1990).

SCHELER, MAX, *Formalism in Ethics and Non-Formal Ethics of Values: A New Attempt Toward the Foundation of an Ethical Personalism*, trans. M. S. Frings and R. L. Funk (Evanston, Ill.: Northwestern University Press, 1973).

——*Wesen und Formen der Sympathie*, 6th edn. (Bern: Francke, 1973)

SCHNEEBERGER, GUIDO, *Nachlese zu Martin Heidegger: Dokumente zu seinem Leben und Denken* (Bern: n.p., 1962).

SCHOLEM, GERSHOM G., 'Kabbalah und Mythus', *Eranos-Jahrbuch*, 17 (1949), 287–34.

——'Die Schöpfung aus Nichts und die Selbstverschränkung Gottes', *Eranos-Jahrbuch*, 25 (1956), 87–120.

——*Die jüdische Mystik in ihren Hauptströmungen*, 3rd edn. (Frankfurt a.M.: Suhrkamp, 1988).

SCHULZ, GEORG-MICHAEL, '"fort aus Kannitverstan": Bemerkungen zum Zitat in der Lyrik Paul Celans', *Text + Kritik*, 53/4 (Jan. 1977), 26–41.

SCHULZE, JOACHIM, *Celan und die Mystiker: Motivtypologische und quellenkundliche Kommentare* (Bonn: Bouvier, 1976).

SCHWARZ, PETER PAUL, *Totengedächtnis und dialogische Polarität in der Lyrik Paul Celans* (Düsseldorf: Schwann, 1966).

SEARLE, JOHN R., 'The Logical Status of Fictional Discourse', *New Literary History*, 6/2 (Winter 1975), 319–32.

SHEIN, LOUIS J., 'Neo-Kantian Influences in Russian Philosophical Thought', *Germano-Slavica*, 4/4 (Fall 1983), 191–204.

SHKLOVSKII, VIKTOR, 'Voskreshenie slova/Die Auferweckung des Wortes', in W.-D. Stempel (ed.), *Texte der russischen Formalisten II: Texte zur Theorie des Verses und der poetischen Sprache* (Munich: Fink, 1972), 2–17.

—— 'Iskusstvo kak priem', in D. Kiray and A. Kovach (eds.), *Poetika: Trudy russkikh i sovetskikh poeticheskikh shkol* (Budapest: Tankönykviadó, 1982), 79–87.

SHOHAM, CHAIM, and BERND WITTE (eds.), *Datum und Zitat bei Paul Celan* (Bern: Lang, 1987).

SIDNEY, SIR PHILIP, *An Apology for Poetry or The Defence of Poesy*, ed. G. Shepherd (London: Nelson and Sons, 1965).

SILBERMANN, EDITH, *Begegnungen mit Paul Celan: Erinnerung und Interpretation* (Aachen: Rimbaud, 1993).

SOLOMON, PETRE, 'Briefwechsel mit Paul Celan 1957–1962', *Neue Literatur*, 32/11 (1981), 60–80.

SPITZER, LEO, *Stilstudien II: Stilsprachen*, 2nd edn. (Munich: Hueber, 1961).

STIEHLER, HEINRICH, '*Die Zeit der Todesfuge*: Zu den Anfängen Paul Celans', *Akzente*, 19/1 (Feb. 1972), 11–40.

STIERLE, KARLHEINZ, and RAINER WARNING (eds.), *Das Gespräch* (Munich: Fink, 1984).

STRASSER, STEPHAN, *Jenseits von Sein und Zeit: eine Einführung in Emmanuel Levinas's Philosophie* (The Hague: Nijhoff, 1978).

STRAWSON, PETER F., *Logico-Linguistic Papers* (London: Methuen, 1956).

STRELKA, JOSEPH P. (ed.), *Psalm und Hawdalah: Zum Werk Paul Celans* (Bern: Lang, 1987).

STRUVE, NIKITA, *Ossip Mandelstam* (Paris: Institut d'Études Slaves, 1982).

SZONDI, PETER, *Celan-Studien* (Frankfurt a.M.: Suhrkamp, 1972).

TANNEN, DEBORAH, *Talking Voices: Repetition, Dialogue, and Imagery in Conversational Discourse* (Cambridge: Cambridge University Press, 1989).

TARANOVSKY, KIRIL, *Essays on Mandel'stam* (Cambridge, Mass., and London: Harvard University Press, 1976).

TAYLOR, MARK C., *Altarity* (Chicago: University of Chicago Press, 1987).

TERRAS, VICTOR and KARL S. WEIMAR, 'Mandelstamm and Celan: A Postscript', *Germano-Slavica*, 2/5 (Spring 1978), 353–70.

THEUNISSEN, MICHAEL, *The Other: Studies in the Social Ontology of Husserl, Heidegger, Sartre, and Buber*, trans. C. McCann (Cambridge, Mass.: MIT Press, 1984).

TITUNIK, I. R., 'Bakhtin &/or Volosinov &/or Medvedev: Dialogue &/

or Doubletalk', in B. A. Stolz *et al.* (eds.), *Language and Literary Theory* (Ann Arbor, Mich.: Department of Slavic Languages and Literatures, 1984), 535–64.

—— 'The Baxtin Problem: Concerning Katerina Clark and Michael Holquist's *Mikhail Bakhtin*', *Slavic and East European Journal*, 30/1 (Spring 1986), 91–5.

TODOROV, TZVETAN, 'Bakhtin et l'altérité', *Poétique*, 40 (Nov. 1979), 502–13.

—— *Mikhail Bakhtin: The Dialogic Principle*, trans. Wlad Godzich (Minneapolis: University of Minnesota Press, 1984).

TURK, HORST, 'Intertextualität als Fall der Übersetzung', *Poetica*, 19/3–4 (1987), 261–77.

TIUTCHEV, FEDOR IVANOVICH, *Polnoe sobranie stikhotvorenii* (Leningrad: Sovetskii pisatel', 1957).

USPENSKII, B. A., 'Anatomiia metafory u Mandel'shtama', *Novoe Literaturnoe Obozrenie*, 7 (1994), 140–62.

VALÉRY, PAUL, *Poésies* (Paris: Gallimard, 1942).

VERLAINE, PAUL, *Gedichte (Franösisch/Deutsch)*, trans. H. Hinderberger, 4th edn. (Heidelberg: Lambert Schneider, 1979).

VOLOSHINOV, VALENTIN N., *Marxism and the Philosophy of Language*, trans. L. Matejka and I. R. Titunik (Cambridge, Mass.; London: Harvard University Press, 1973).

—— 'Discourse in Life and Discourse in Art', in *Freudianism: A Critical Sketch*, trans. I. R. Titunik (Bloomington, Ind.: Indiana University Press, 1987), 93–116.

VYGOTSKII, LEV S., *Denken und Sprechen*, trans. G. Sewekov (Frankfurt a.M.: Suhrkamp, 1986).

WEINRICH, HARALD, 'Semantik der kühnen Metapher', *Deutsche Vierteljahrsschrift für Literaturwissenschaft und Geistesgeschichte*, 37/28 (1963), 325–44.

—— 'Semantik der Metapher', *Folia Linguistica: Acta Societatis Linguisticae Europaeae*, 1 (1967), 3–17.

WEISBERG, RICHARD, *Poethics and Other Strategies of Law and Order* (New York: Columbia University Press, 1992).

WELLEK, RENÉ, 'Bakhtin's View of Dostoevsky: "Polyphony" and "Carnivalesque"', *Dostoevsky Studies*, 1 (1980), 31–9.

WERBERGER, ANNETTE, 'Paul Celan und Osip Mandel'stam oder "Pavel Tselan" und "Joseph Mandelstamm"—Wiederbegegnung in der Begegnung', *arcadia*, 32/1 (1997), 6–27.

WIEDEMANN, BARBARA, 'Grischas Apfel und bitteres Staunen. Paul Celans Übertragungen ins Rumänische', *Celan-Jahrbuch*, 5 (1993), 115–63.

WIEMER, THOMAS, *Die Passion des Sagens: Zur Deutung der Sprache bei Emmanuel Levinas und ihrer Realisierung im philosophischen Diskus* (Freiburg and Munich: Alber, 1988).

WIENOLD, GÖTZ, 'Paul Celans Hölderlin-Widerruf', *Poetica*, 2/2 (Apr. 1968), 216–28.

WILPERT, GERO VON (ed.), *Sachwörterbuch der Literatur*, 5th edn. (Stuttgart: Kröner, 1969).

WINDELBAND, WILHELM, *Präludien: Aufsätze und Reden zur Philosophie und ihrer Geschichte*, 5th edn., 2 vols. (Tübingen: Mohr, 1915).

WINKLER, MICHAEL, 'On Paul Celan's Rose Images', *Neophilologus*, 56/1 (Jan. 1972), 72–8.

WITTE, BERND, 'Der zyklische Charakter der *Niemandsrose* von Paul Celan: Vorschläge zu einer Lektüre', in A. D. Colin (ed.), *Argumentum e Silentio* (Berlin and New York: de Gruyter, 1987), 72–86.

WOLOSKY, SHIRA, 'Mystical Language and Mystical Silence in Paul Celan's "Dein Hinübersein"', in A. D. Colin (ed.), *Argumentum e Silentio* (Berlin and New York: de Gruyter, 1987), 364–74.

WORDSWORTH, WILLIAM, and SAMUEL TAYLOR COLERIDGE, 'Preface of 1800 with a Collation of the Enlarged Preface of 1802', *Lyrical Ballads* (1798), ed. W. J. B. Owen, 2nd edn. (Oxford: Oxford University Press, 1992), 153–79.

ZHIRMUNSKII, VIKTOR, *Teoriia literatury, poetika, stilistika*, ed. I. D. Levin and D. S. Likhachev (Leningrad: Nauka, 1977).

ZIAREK, KRZYSZTOF, *Inflected Language: Toward a Hermeneutics of Nearness. Heidegger, Levinas, Stevens, Celan* (Albany, NY: State University of New York Press, 1994).

Index